Final Cut Pro® 3 For Dummies®

Cheat Sheet

P9-DEH-982

File Menu Commands

Command	Keystroke Combination
New project	⌘+E
New sequence	⌘+N
New bin	⌘+B
Open	⌘+O
Save	⌘+S
Import files	⌘+I
Close window	⌘+W
Close tab	Control+W
Quit	⌘+Q

Windows Menu Commands

Command	Keystroke Combination
Viewer	⌘+1
Canvas	⌘+2
Timeline	⌘+3
Browser	⌘+4
Audio Meters	Option+4
Effects	⌘+5
Favorites bin	⌘+6
Trim edit	⌘+7
Log and Capture window	⌘+8

Edit Menu Commands

Command	Keystroke or Combination
Undo	⌘+Z
Redo	⌘+Y
Clear	Delete
Cut	⌘+X
Copy	⌘+C
Paste	⌘+V
Paste Insert	Shift+V
Find	⌘+F
Find Next	⌘+G
Item Properties	⌘+9
Select All	⌘+A
Deselect All	⌘+D

For Dummies: Bestselling Book Series for Beginners

Final Cut Pro® 3
For Dummies®

Editing Commands

Command	Keystroke or Combination
Mark in point	I
Mark out point	O
Clear in and out points	Option+X
Place marker	M
Delete marker	⌘+~
Mark clip	X
Select edit point	V
Insert edit	F9
Overwrite edit	F10
Fit to fill	Shift+F11
Superimpose	F12
Lift edit	Delete
Ripple delete	Shift Delete
Make subclip	⌘+U
Match frame	F

The Tool Palette

Group tool —
Roll tool —
Razor Blade tool —
Crop tool —

— Selection
— Track tool
— Slip tool
— Zoom tool
— Pen tool

Navigation Controls

Command	Keystroke or Combination
Play forward	Spacebar or L (repeat press)
Play backward	J (repeat press)
Forward one frame	Right arrow (→)
Back one frame	Left arrow (←)
Forward one second	Shift+→
Back one second	Shift+←
Next edit	' or down arrow (↓)
Previous edit	; or up arrow (↑)
Next marker	Shift+↓
Previous marker	Shift+↑
Beginning of sequence	Home
End of sequence	End or Shift+Home

Copyright © 2002 Wiley Publishing, Inc.
All rights reserved.

Item 1654-X.

For more information about Wiley Publishing,
call 1-800-762-2974.

Wiley, the Wiley Publishing logo, For Dummies, the Dummies Man logo, the For Dummies Bestselling Book Series logo and all related trade dress are trademarks or registered trademarks of Wiley Publishing, Inc. All other trademarks are property of their respective owners.

For Dummies: Bestselling Book Series for Beginners

3 1000 00202146 0

FEB - - 2004

TM

BESTSELLING BOOK SERIES

References for the Rest of Us!®

Are you intimidated and confused by computers? Do you find that traditional manuals are overloaded with technical details you'll never use? Do your friends and family always call you to fix simple problems on their PCs? Then the For Dummies® computer book series from Wiley Publishing, Inc. is for you.

For Dummies books are written for those frustrated computer users who know they aren't really dumb but find that PC hardware, software, and indeed the unique vocabulary of computing make them feel helpless. For Dummies books use a lighthearted approach, a down-to-earth style, and even cartoons and humorous icons to dispel computer novices' fears and build their confidence. Lighthearted but not lightweight, these books are a perfect survival guide for anyone forced to use a computer.

"I like my copy so much I told friends; now they bought copies."
— Irene C., Orwell, Ohio

"Quick, concise, nontechnical, and humorous."
— Jay A., Elburn, Illinois

"Thanks, I needed this book. Now I can sleep at night."
— Robin F., British Columbia, Canada

Already, millions of satisfied readers agree. They have made For Dummies books the #1 introductory level computer book series and have written asking for more. So, if you're looking for the most fun and easy way to learn about computers, look to For Dummies books to give you a helping hand.

Wiley Publishing, Inc.

5/09

Final Cut Pro® 3

FOR

DUMMIES®

Final Cut Pro ® 3
FOR
DUMMIES ®

by Helmut Kobler and Zed Saeed

Wiley Publishing, Inc.

BELLEVILLE PUBLIC LIBRARY

Final Cut Pro® 3 For Dummies®

Published by
Wiley Publishing, Inc.

909 Third Avenue
New York, NY 10022

www.wiley.com

Copyright © 2002 by Wiley Publishing, Inc., Indianapolis, Indiana

Published simultaneously in Canada

No part of this publication may be reproduced, stored in a retrieval system or transmitted in any form or by any means, electronic, mechanical, photocopying, recording, scanning or otherwise, except as permitted under Sections 107 or 108 of the 1976 United States Copyright Act, without either the prior written permission of the Publisher, or authorization through payment of the appropriate per-copy fee to the Copyright Clearance Center, 222 Rosewood Drive, Danvers, MA 01923, (978) 750-8400, fax (978) 750-4744. Requests to the Publisher for permission should be addressed to the Legal Department, Wiley Publishing, Inc., 10475 Crosspoint Blvd., Indianapolis, IN 46256, (317) 572-3447, fax (317) 572-4447, e-mail: permcoordinator@wiley.com.

Trademarks: Wiley, the Wiley Publishing logo, For Dummies, the Dummies Man logo, A Reference for the Rest of Us!, The Dummies Way, Dummies Daily, The Fun and Easy Way, Dummies.com and related trade dress are trademarks or registered trademarks of Wiley Publishing, Inc., in the United States and other countries, and may not be used without written permission. Final Cut Pro is a trademark or registered trademark of Apple Computer, Inc. in the United States and other countries. All other trademarks are the property of their respective owners. Wiley Publishing, Inc., is not associated with any product or vendor mentioned in this book.

LIMIT OF LIABILITY/DISCLAIMER OF WARRANTY: WHILE THE PUBLISHER AND AUTHOR HAVE USED THEIR BEST EFFORTS IN PREPARING THIS BOOK, THEY MAKE NO REPRESENTATIONS OR WARRANTIES WITH RESPECT TO THE ACCURACY OR COMPLETENESS OF THE CONTENTS OF THIS BOOK AND SPECIFICALLY DISCLAIM ANY IMPLIED WARRANTIES OF MERCHANTABILITY OR FITNESS FOR A PARTICULAR PURPOSE. NO WARRANTY MAY BE CREATED OR EXTENDED BY SALES REPRESENTATIVES OR WRITTEN SALES MATERIALS. THE ADVICE AND STRATEGIES CONTAINED HEREIN MAY NOT BE SUITABLE FOR YOUR SITUATION. YOU SHOULD CONSULT WITH A PROFESSIONAL WHERE APPROPRIATE. NEITHER THE PUBLISHER NOR AUTHOR SHALL BE LIABLE FOR ANY LOSS OF PROFIT OR ANY OTHER COMMERCIAL DAMAGES, INCLUDING BUT NOT LIMITED TO SPECIAL, INCIDENTAL, CONSEQUENTIAL, OR OTHER DAMAGES.

For general information on our other products and services or to obtain technical support, please contact our Customer Care Department within the U.S. at 800-762-2974, outside the U.S. at 317-572-3993, or fax 317-572-4002.

Wiley also publishes its books in a variety of electronic formats. Some content that appears in print may not be available in electronic books.

Library of Congress Control Number: 2002103275

ISBN: 0-7645-1654-X

3B/TR/QZ/QS/IN

Manufactured in the United States of America

10 9 8 7 6 5 4 3 2

About the Authors

Helmut Kobler is a Los Angeles-based filmmaker who's putting the finishing touches on his latest project — a sci-fi action adventure called *Radius*. (You can see scenes from *Radius* in many of this book's figures.)

Helmut used Final Cut extensively to bring *Radius* to life — all on his trusty Apple PowerBook laptop, which, as friends and family have noted, hardly ever leaves his side. He's also been a confessed Mac addict since 1987, and, in a past life, he directed and produced award-winning video games for PCs and the Sony Playstation.

If you want to know more about Helmut's film *Radius*, visit the Web site at www.radiusmovie.com.

Zed Saeed works as a digital media and film consultant with DigitalFilm Tree in Los Angeles and New York. He specializes in editing, compositing, and workflow issues. Zed served as a senior post-production consultant for Apple Computer and Oxygen Media on Final Cut Pro and digital video workflow design, and has worked with Media 100 and Adobe Systems on video-related products. He has also worked as an editor, producer, compositing artist, and broadcast designer for the Showtime Channels, Sundance Channel, and ESPN Classics. Zed has written articles on digital media technologies for magazines and has served on the faculty of New York University, Parsons School of Design, and New School University. Zed has written, produced, and edited videos that have received awards and recognition by the Academy of Television Arts and Sciences and the American Film Institute. Zed is also the author of *Final Cut Pro 2 Bible* and coauthor of *After Effects 5 Bible*.

Dedication

I would like to dedicate this book to Lois Kobler. Thanks for everything of late, Mom.

— Helmut Kobler

"Oops, it works!" — The Yak

— Zed Saeed

Authors' Acknowledgments

At Wiley, I'd like to thank acquisition editor Tiffany Franklin for bringing me into this project; project editor Linda Morris and copy editor Rebecca Huehls for helping to hone my focus and prose to *For Dummies* standards; and coauthor Zed Saeed for his contributions. Thanks, too, to Dan Brazelton, a very talented editor and Final Cut whiz, for shedding light on some of Final Cut's finer points.

I would also like to thank Andre Persidsky, Daniel Field, and especially Maura Keaney for their moral support during those long days, nights, and weekends of writing (which, combined with the job of finishing my film *Radius*, could have easily been my undoing).

Finally, I would like to thank Apple's Final Cut team for not only gracing the Mac with such a world-class, genre-defining product, but also for relentlessly improving it. I can't wait to see version 4.

— Helmut Kobler

Working on a Final Cut Pro book is always a lot of fun because I love this application so much. For me, a longtime editor, Final Cut Pro represents a big break from the old school of huge and expensive workstation-based editing. I'd like to thank the people above and beyond the Final Cut Pro team who have worked so hard over the last years to make the dream of Final Cut Pro a reality. My thanks to my teachers and my family. I am able to do these books because of all the friends who have supported me and my work over the last many years. This book is dedicated to these friends.

Special thanks to Ramy Katrib, Tim Serda, Walter "Wally Baby" Shires, and others at DigitalFilm Tree, Los Angeles.

— Zed Saeed

Publisher's Acknowledgments

We're proud of this book; please send us your comments through our online registration form located at www.dummies.com/register/.

Some of the people who helped bring this book to market include the following:

Acquisitions, Editorial, and Media Development

Project Editor: Linda Morris

Associate Acquisitions Editor: Tiffany D. Franklin

Copy Editor: Rebecca Huehls

Technical Editors: Zed Saeed, Steve Anzovin

Editorial Managers: Leah P. Cameron, Constance Carlisle

Media Development Supervisor: Richard Graves

Editorial Assistant: Amanda Foxworth

Production

Project Coordinator: Erin Smith

Layout and Graphics: Scott Bristol, Beth Brooks, Joyce Haughey, Betty Schulte, Jeremey Unger

Proofreaders: David Faust, John Greenough, Susan Moritz, Carl Pierce

Indexer: TECHBOOKS Production Services

Special Help: Diana R. Conover

Publishing and Editorial for Technology Dummies
> **Richard Swadley,** Vice President and Executive Group Publisher
> **Mary C. Corder,** Editorial Director
> **Andy Cummings,** Vice President and Publisher

Publishing for Consumer Dummies
> **Diane Graves Steele,** Vice President and Publisher
> **Joyce Pepple,** Acquisitions Director

Composition Services
> **Gerry Fahey,** Vice President of Production Services
> **Debbie Stailey,** Director of Composition Services

Contents at a Glance

Cartoons at a Glance

By Rich Tennant

Table of Contents

Introduction

Welcome to *Final Cut Pro 3 For Dummies*! Final Cut is a digital editing program that lets you capture raw video and audio (for example, dialogue, sound, and music) on your Macintosh and assemble these elements into polished productions ready for the Internet, CD-ROM, DVD, television, and even the big screen.

Thanks to Final Cut's impressive features, reasonable price, and manageable hardware requirements, it has quickly become a favorite tool among many professional editors as well as among a new breed of independent filmmakers who are making their films — from start to finish — right from their desktops.

About This Book

This book is written for two kinds of people: On one hand, it's for beginners who have no experience with Final Cut or digital video editing in general, but it's also for those who've done digital editing with another program — maybe Adobe Premiere or Avid's Media Composer — and who just need to know which button to press or menu item to choose in order to get things done.

Regardless of which camp you fall into, we think that you'll appreciate the book for its clear, down-to-earth, nontechy explanations. This book shows you the things that you're most likely to need without overwhelming you with every last nuance of every last obscure little feature. So when you turn to a chapter or a topic heading, we tell you what's most important to know about that topic right off the bat, and then we throw in some finer details to round off your grasp of it. End result? You'll be up and running with Final Cut in as little time as possible.

We admit: Final Cut can look pretty complicated and a bit intimidating at first glance. When you load it up, you're faced with lots of different windows and palettes, not to mention seemingly endless menu choices. Besides, Final Cut is a professional, somewhat pricey piece of software, so that means it *must* be complicated and hard to use, right?

Wrong! In fact, using Final Cut is like driving a car: Despite all the sophisticated gadgets and gizmos built into cars these days (environmental systems, GPS locators, night vision, and so on), all you really need in order to go anywhere is the gas, brake, and steering wheel. And so it goes with Final Cut: Despite all its features, you can honestly start editing with it very quickly by using just a few simple tools. (Twenty to thirty minutes with this book should get you to this point.) After that, you can add to your skills at your own pace.

So, don't be intimidated by this seemingly big program (or the world of digital video in general). You'll quickly see that Final Cut's bark is much worse than its bite. Here's a quick look at some of the ground we cover here. By the end of this book, you find out how to do the following:

- ✔ Equip your Macintosh so that it runs Final Cut smoothly

- ✔ Bring in (that is, *digitize* or *capture*) video, audio, and still pictures from different sources, such as videotape, music CD, or QuickTime media files

- ✔ Organize your media clips so that you can find them quickly and easily

- ✔ Arrange your video clips in time, so they tell the story you want to tell

- ✔ Add multiple audio tracks for dialogue, music, and sound effects

- ✔ Add text, such as opening titles and closing credits

- ✔ Use powerful filters to stylize the look of your video and the sound of your audio

- ✔ *Composite* different video together to create montages or special effects (for example, placing an actor filmed against a blue screen in an entirely different setting)

- ✔ Record your final movie to videotape or save it as a QuickTime file (for DVD, CD-ROM, or Internet distribution)

In other words, you'll be a movie-making machine in no time!

How to Use This Book

We don't expect you to read this book from cover to cover. For starters, you probably don't have the time to read 400+ pages, and even if you did, you'd suffer from information overload for sure!

Instead, we recommend this approach: Think about what you want to do with Final Cut, and then use this book to fill in whatever know-how you're missing. If you're completely new to digital video editing (or editing in general), you probably want to read closely, starting at Chapter 1 going until you've got your bearings. On the other hand, if you have digital editing experience, you're likely to hop and skip around, grabbing whatever you need and then moving on.

Adapt the book to your style of learning and your level of expertise. We wrote it with that kind of flexibility in mind, so you can get the most out of it with the least amount of effort or legwork.

One more thing: We recommend picking up the book every once in a while and browsing it for nothing in particular. You'd be surprised how much useful info you can pick up just by scanning headings and flipping through pages!

Foolish Assumptions

We made some (possibly foolish) assumptions about you as we wrote this book. We assume that you either don't have video editing experience, or that your experience is with a program other than Final Cut. (Maybe you've done some editing with other programs, such as Adobe Premiere or Apple's easy-does-it iMovie, but you're finally ready for the big leagues.)

We assume that you're running Final Cut under Apple's new, awe-inspiring OS X operating system. Although Final Cut also runs under the older OS 9, it truly shines on OS X. Besides, OS X is the future of the Mac, which means you'll be using OS X sooner or later . . . so why not sooner? If you feel a bit nervous about switching to OS X, we know the feeling: So were we. But trust us: OS X is easy to learn, and after a few days with it, you'll never look back. (We cringe when we see a Mac running OS 9 these days . . . yuck!) Having said all this, if you plan to run Final Cut under OS 9, you'll still be able to follow along. The software works pretty much the same way under either operating system, so you won't be lost when we're showing you what to do.

Finally, we assume that you've mastered the basics of using a Mac, given whichever operating system you're running. Your expertise should include opening and saving files in the Mac's standard dialog boxes, navigating your hard drive's files with the Mac's Finder, and so on — pretty straightforward stuff.

How This Book Is Organized

This book is organized to follow the basic workflow you'll use while editing. Part I gives you a birds-eye-view of the entire editing process, so you understand each and every step you'll take to bring your video projects to completion. Part II shows you how to import and organize the video and audio media your projects call for, while Part III shows how to edit all that media together into the story you want to tell. Part IV shows you how to add all sorts of pizzazz — such as titles, transitions, and special effects to your project — and Part V covers your options for saving your final movie to either tape or digital video files.

Let's take a closer look at each Part:

Part 1: First Things First

Part I is a quick introduction to the world of Final Cut and digital video in general. We explain how Final Cut can help you make movies, commercials, documentaries, and all sorts of other video content, as well as what's new in its latest incarnation, version 3. We also take you step-by-step through Final Cut's workflow and give you a quick tour of the Final Cut interface. We help you get up and running with Final Cut, discussing hardware and software requirements and how they affect the quality of the video you can capture and record again. We show you how to connect all your major hardware components together, give you an overview of Final Cut's numerous (and we do mean *numerous*) settings, and conclude by showing you how to create and manage Final Cut document files, which are called *projects*.

Part 11: Importing and Organizing Your Media

Part II shows you how to capture, import, and organize all the media you can use in your Final Cut projects (that is, video, dialogue, music, sound effects, still pictures, titles, and so on). We show you how to capture (that is, *digitize*) media from videotape by using a DV camera or deck that you've connected to your Mac. We also show you how to bring media into Final Cut that's from sources other than videotape — video or audio files already on your hard drive, songs from a music CD, graphics from Photoshop, and so on.

Finally, we show you how to name, annotate, and organize all these different media clips in the Final Cut Browser window (the central repository for all your media), so you can easily find 'em when you need 'em.

Part 111: Editing Your Media

Part III is where the rubber meets the road, showing you how to take all your project's media and arrange it in time so that it tells the story you want to tell. We start off with the basics of editing video and audio: how to move clips to the Final Cut Timeline window and then resize them, cut them up, or move them in time. We cover a lot of ground here, but by the time you reach the end of Chapter 6, you'll be able to edit most meat-and-potatoes projects.

Later, we round out your new skills, giving you finer control over the Final Cut Timeline, which is the heart of your editing universe, and we tackle the more-advanced editing features of Final Cut. These advanced topics are things you don't need to know to accomplish most editing tasks, but they'll ultimately give you a lot more control over your work. Finally, we cover Final Cut's Media Manager, which lets you move, copy, compress, and delete media files in a very quick, efficient way — without using the Macintosh's Finder and without breaking important links that your Final Cut projects need in order to keep track of media.

Part IV: Adding Pizzazz

Knowing how to edit media clips together is only half the fun in Final Cut. Final Cut offers tons of other tools and features that let you add real polish and pizzazz to your projects — things like slick transitions, moving titles, image and sound effects, and more. In Part IV, we show you how to use many Final Cut video transitions, which let you smoothly move from one video clip to another. We tackle how to create all sorts of titles in Final Cut: everything from standard white-on-black text to typewriter effects to the scrolling credits you see at the end of a movie, plus plenty of other options.

We also dive into all sorts of audio-related topics: how to set different volume levels for different clips, how to edit out scratches and pops in your audio, and how to use Final Cut's numerous audio filters to create effects like Echo and Reverb. We even look at the Final Cut video filters, which let you change and enhance video clips in all sorts of ways (for instance, you can adjust a clip's color balance, convert it to black and white, or apply effects filters, such as Blur, Pond Ripple, Fish Eye, and Strobe).

Two chapters are dedicated to using Final Cut's advanced effects engine to scale text, graphics, and video clips in size, change their position on-screen, change their opacity (to make them seem more transparent), and composite different images together into a single shot. We also offer strategies and tips for rendering your video and audio clips.

Part V: Outputting Your Masterpiece

After you're finished editing and adding extra pizzazz (transitions, titles, filters, effects, and so on), you're ready for Part V, which focuses on outputting your movie to its final media destination. We've got all your bases covered: We show you how to record your finished masterpiece back to videotape (for tape duplication or broadcast) and how to save your finished movie to a QuickTime digital file, which you can later burn to a DVD or CD-ROM or broadcast over the Internet.

Part VI: Part of Tens

What's a *For Dummies* book without a Part of Tens? We offer tips for managing long projects in Final Cut (by that we mean movies that overwhelm you with all the media clips you have to keep track of and that may also use more hard drive space than you've got). Finally, we serve up simple things you can do to become a more capable Final Cut editor, from honing your creative and technical know-how to upgrading your current Mac setup.

Icons Used In This Book

Tips provide extra information for a specific purpose. Tips can save you time and effort, so they're worth checking out.

Always read text marked with the Warning icon: These icons emphasize that dire consequences are ahead for the unwary.

This icon flags information and techniques that are a bit more techy than other sections of the book. The information here can be interesting and helpful, but you don't need to understand it to use the information in the book.

This icon is a sticky note of sorts, highlighting information that's worth committing to memory.

Contacting the Author

If you'd like to get in touch with Helmut Kobler to say hello, ask a question not covered here, or offer feedback (which is very much appreciated), don't hesitate to drop him an e-mail message at director@k2films.com.

Part I
First Things First

The 5th Wave   By Rich Tennant

"It's a site devoted to the 'Limp Korn Chilies' rock group. It has videos of all their performances in concert halls, hotel rooms, and airport terminals."

In this part . . .

Part I is a quick introduction to the world of Final Cut
and digital video in general. We explain how Final Cut
can help you make movies, commercials, documentaries,
and all sorts of other video content, and what's new in
Final Cut Pro 3. We take you step-by-step through Final
Cut's workflow and give you a tour of Final Cut's interface.
We discuss hardware and software requirements and how
they affect the quality of the video you can capture and
record again. We show you how to connect all your major
hardware components together, give you an overview of
Final Cut's numerous settings, and conclude by showing
you how to manage Final Cut's document files.

Chapter 1

Introducing Final Cut Pro

· ·

In This Chapter

▶ What is editing?

▶ Final Cut makes editing easy

▶ What's new in Final Cut 3

▶ Final Cut's workflow

▶ Getting to know the interface

▶ Finding help in Final Cut

· ·

*I*magine for a moment: You're a big-time director on the set of your latest movie. You've just called your last "Cut!," the A-list actors have gone back to their mansions, and the crew is dismantling the million-dollar sets. You lean back in your director's chair, close your eyes, and breath a deep sigh of relief, knowing that the film is finally finished. You can, at last, relax.

Yeah, right! In fact, this show is *far* from over. Although you may have some amazing footage, the fat lady won't be singing until you've edited it all into a polished film. Enter Final Cut Pro.

What's Editing, Anyway?

Editing film or video is a bit like writing. When you write (or when *we* write, at least), you start by putting all your ideas on paper — good or bad — so that you can see what you're working with. Then you take the *best* ideas and arrange them in a logical order so that they say what you mean, as clearly and efficiently as possible.

It works the same way when you're editing digital video. First, you scrutinize all the footage you shot on set (usually a lot). Slowly, you figure out which shots to keep and which ones to send to the cutting room floor (for any number of reasons: weak acting, technical problems, or the fact that you can see a crew member's foot in frame). Next you arrange your keeper shots, one by one, so that they begin to tell a story, and you bring in your dialogue, music, and sound effects to make the film complete.

What Does Final Cut Do?

Final Cut enables you to do all this editing work on your Mac. To be a little more specific, when you're behind the wheel with Final Cut, you can

- Capture video or audio from cameras, video decks, CDs, or existing digital files onto your Mac's hard drive.
- Organize all your media files so that you can easily find them (a project might call for hundreds of different files).
- Edit your footage together — which is almost as easy as cutting and pasting text in a word processor.
- Add audio to your movie — be it dialogue, music, or sound effects — and control the volume for each.
- Create transitions, such as fades and wipes, between shots and design titles and credits.
- Enhance video and audio with tons of custom effects filters.
- Do basic visual effects by *compositing* (that is, combining) multiple shots into one. This process is similar to the one in the popular Adobe After Effects program.
- Output your polished masterpiece to videotape or to digital files destined for DVD, CD-ROM, or the Web.

Final Cut treats your media nice

Another key Final Cut feature is that it's a *nondestructive* editor, which means that no matter what you do to your video and audio inside the program, the original media files on your hard drive are never changed or erased. Say you have a bunch of video clips on your hard drive, and you bring them into Final Cut to edit together. Although it may *seem* like you're cutting these clips into different pieces, resizing them, and even deleting them, that's not the case. When you're editing, you're really just creating and moving a bunch of digital pointers to your media. The pointers tell Final Cut what parts of the media you want to play in your final movie (in other words, play clip A to this point, and then play part of clip C, and so on). Thanks to this approach, you can work and experiment knowing that you won't end up hurting any of your precious media.

From the Stone Age to the Digital Age

You'll appreciate Final Cut even more when you consider how film and video editors worked in the days before digital.

Working in video (for instance, editing television shows and other content aimed at TV) was clunky. Video editors in the dark ages edited with two video decks. On the A deck, you played through all your raw footage until you identified the shots you wanted to use in your edited story. Then you used your B deck to record those shots to a master tape (your show-in-progress), one shot after another. The process was entirely *linear* — you'd record the first shot you wanted in your show, and then the second, the

third, fourth, and so on. And, later on, if you decided to insert or remove a shot in that sequence, you had to rewind the master tape to that point, record your change, and then *rerecord* all the shots that followed your change — UGH!

By the way, that's why Final Cut is called a *nonlinear editor.* Your footage isn't on a linear tape; it's on your hard drive and in your Mac's memory so that you can place it and rearrange it without any negative repercussions. Final Cut is to video editing what Microsoft Word is to that old Smith-Micro typewriter sitting in your garage.

Final Cut versus the competition

Plenty of other editing programs are available these days: Premiere, Avid Media Composer, Edit, SpeedRazor, and Apple's own iMovie all come to mind.

So what makes Final Cut so special? Four things:

- ✔ **It's brimming with features:** Final Cut not only delivers the big power-features that sound great on the back of the box, but also gets tons of details right — the little, thoughtful things that help you work smoothly, in a way that suits your personal style.

- ✔ **You don't need a super-computer or expensive, proprietary hardware to run Final Cut:** You can build your editing system around any fairly-modern Mac (made within the last three or so years) and everyday peripherals, such as capture cards, FireWire hard drives, and so on. Plus, although you can never have too much hardware firepower (the fastest CPUs, mondo memory, and so on), you can run Final Cut respectably on a modest iMac or iBook system. (See Chapter 2 for more about system requirements.)

- ✔ **Final Cut is affordable at $1000:** Now, admittedly, for many people, the words *affordable* and *$1000* don't usually go together, but before Final Cut came along, you had to pay several thousand dollars for software that did the same thing. So, relatively speaking, $1,000 is actually the equivalent of a K-Mart Blue Light Special (with the added bonus that you don't have to fight off angry hordes of shoppers because Apple has plenty of copies to go around).

✔ **Final Cut is hugely important to Apple Computer:** Apple thinks digital video will be the next desktop publishing (meaning it will put a huge amount of professional-level power in the hands of regular people at an affordable price), so Apple is committing big resources to make Final Cut so good that it sells Macs by the droves. Case in point: Apple did a big update to Final Cut when it released version 2 in March 2001, but it followed up with version 3 less than nine months later. Now that's commitment!

New in Final Cut 3

Speaking of improvements to Final Cut, if you have any experience with Final Cut 2, you'll be happy to see that Final Cut 3 is a significant upgrade, not just some sly ploy to collect more revenue from minor upgrade fees. Version 3 sports a ton of tweaks and optimizations, but the big-ticket additions include the following:

✔ **Works in OS X:** OS X is Apple's new, groundbreaking operating system for the Mac, but earlier versions of Final Cut wouldn't work with it. And although Final Cut 3 still works in System 9, there are good reasons to use it in X instead. For instance, Final Cut does some things faster under OS X, such as calculating the look of effects, titles, and transitions, known as *rendering*. Plus, you benefit from the fabled OS X stability (your Mac rarely, if ever, crashes).

✔ **Real-time preview:** In older versions of Final Cut, if you wanted to add effects such as transitions or superimpose titles, your Mac took a minute or two before it could play back these effects. Rendering causes this lag. But Final Cut 3 can now skip this step and play at least some of these effects for you instantly, in *real time*. (You need at least a G4 processor in your Mac to enjoy real-time rendering, and even then, you can't always avoid rendering media the old-fashioned way — see Chapter 16 for more.)

✔ **OfflineRT codec:** If you have a lot of video to capture but don't want to use so much hard drive space, you can now capture that video in a super-compressed format called OfflineRT. (Technically, it's a QuickTime codec, but this is no time for technicalities.) The end result: The video uses 1 gigabyte (GB) of disk space for every hour (as opposed to 13GB an hour for DV video). Although it doesn't look perfect, it's often good enough for editing work. When you've finished editing your project, you can easily recapture your video at a better quality, but you capture only the exact footage that your edit calls for instead of all of it.

✔ **Voice narration:** With a microphone hooked into your Mac, you can record voice narration while playing video within Final Cut. This is great if you need to narrate informational videos or news segments or if you want to record the DVD director's commentary for your latest movie.

✔ **Color Correction:** Final Cut adds new video scopes (Figure 1-1) and a set of filters to help you color correct your footage. You can adjust the blacks, midrange tones, and whites in your images, and make sure colors are *broadcast-safe*, which means they'll display properly on a television (as opposed to your computer monitor, which can display a wider variety of color).

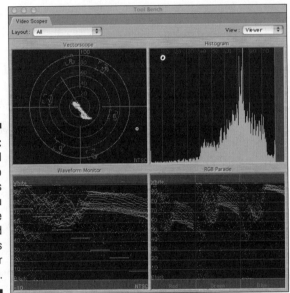

Figure 1-1: The Final Cut video scopes help you adjust the color and brightness of your video.

Going with the Final Cut Flow

Final Cut starts to make sense when you understand how you'll use it from start to finish. So we've summarized its workflow in four easy steps:

1. **Capture and import all the media — that is, video, audio, and still pictures — that you want to use in your project.**

   This media can come from a camera, video deck, or files that are already on your hard drive. The media shows up in the Final Cut Browser window, where you have easy access to it.

2. **Move your clips to Final Cut's all-important Timeline.**

   You use the Timeline to place, move, and otherwise edit clips so that they tell the story you want to tell.

3. **Add pizzazz in the form of titles, transitions (such as fades, dissolves, and wipes), and more advanced special effects.**

4. **Record your project to videotape or export it to a QuickTime file.**

   Use the QuickTime option if you're aiming for digital distribution, such as the Internet, CD-ROM, or DVD.

Final Cut may look like a sprawling behemoth of windows, dialog boxes, check boxes, and menus, but all this *seeming* complexity really boils down to four easy steps. Keep that in mind, and you'll see that this isn't rocket science.

Taking a Grand Tour of the Interface

After you've gotten a grasp on the workflow, you can expand your Final Cut expertise by taking a tour of its interface — namely its toolbar and the Browser, Viewer, Canvas, and Timeline windows, as shown in Figure 1-2. We know: Keeping track of all these elements can seem daunting. But you'll see that there's actually not much to them, and they work together in an intuitive way. *Trust us.*

Viewer window   Canvas window

Figure 1-2:
The Final
Cut
interface.

Browser window   Timeline window   The Tool palette

By the way, Final Cut's windows may be arranged differently on your screen than the way they're arranged in Figure 1-2. To get your screen to look like our screen shot, choose Window⇨Arrange⇨Standard from the menu bar at the top.

The Browser

The Browser is the central storage depot for all the media used by your Final Cut project. Just think of the Browser as a big file cabinet. When you want to work with a file (or a clip of media), you open the cabinet (or the Browser window) and grab whatever you need.

There's a lot to know about the Browser, but here are the basics: When you import a media file into your project (either from your hard drive or by capturing it from video tape), it automatically appears in the Browser, as seen in Figure 1-3. Every piece of media in the Browser is called a *clip* (a video clip, an audio clip), but the Browser also lets you create *bins*, which you can use to store groups of related media clips. (Bins work a lot like folders on your hard drive.)

Bin icons

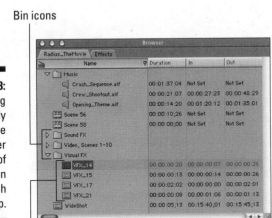

Figure 1-3: Scrolling horizontally across the Browser gives tons of information about each clip.

Clip icons

Besides clips and bins, the Browser window is also the home of any sequences you create for your movie — a *sequence* is a collection of clips — which you've edited together in Final Cut's timeline window. You use sequences to break a big project into smaller pieces; for instance, you might create each major scene in its own sequence.

The Viewer

The Viewer window lets you look and listen to your media clips before you move them to Final Cut's Timeline. You can also use the Viewer to modify your media clips by using a variety of Final Cut's effects filters, superimposed titles, and animation effects. To open a clip in the Viewer, just double-click its name or icon in the Browser window.

Playing with play controls

The Viewer sports an assortment of buttons and other gizmos, but focus for now on its play controls, shown in Figure 1-4. You can click the Play button to play your clip forward (another click pauses your clip), or use the Viewer's Jog and Shuttle controls to fast-forward and rewind, also shown in Figure 1-4. As a clip plays, you see the Viewer's playhead move across what's called the scrubber bar, frame by frame. You can click anywhere in the scrubber bar to move the playhead to that point, or click and drag the playhead anywhere.

Figure 1-4:
The Viewer lets you preview either video or audio clips (shown as a waveform) before bringing them to the Timeline.

Shuttle   The Play/Pause button   Jog

The ins and outs of ins and outs

Besides playing clips, you use the Viewer to edit clips in a very basic way by setting *in and out points*. (In fact, you also use these points in other parts of Final Cut, but they're "regulars" in the Viewer.) As shown in Figure 1-5, in and out points let you isolate only the part of a clip that you're interested in, before bringing it to the Timeline. For instance, say you have a great clip, *except* the first four seconds suffer from a shaky camera, and the last five seconds prominently feature the leg of a crew member. Because you don't want to bring the entire clip to the Timeline, you can use the Viewer to set an in point at the clip's first good frame (right after the camera shake) and an out point at the last good frame (before the leg shows up). Then, Final Cut knows to use only the frames between those points. (See Chapters 3 and 6 for more.)

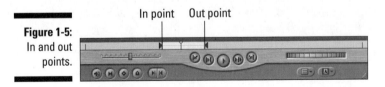

Figure 1-5:
In and out
points.

In point   Out point

The Timeline

Final Cut's Timeline window lets you arrange *when* your media clips will play in time. To better understand the Timeline, think of it as a sheet of music. Rather than place musical notes on the page, one after another, you place clips of video and sound and tell Final Cut how long to play each one; for instance, play black for two seconds, play video clip A for four seconds, then play clip B for three seconds, and so on.

So how does the Timeline work? We talk about plenty of nuances throughout the book, but check out Figure 1-6 to take in the basics. Stretching across the top of the Timeline is a bar with notches and numbers, which looks like a ruler. But those numbers aren't measurements of distance, they're measurements of time, increasing from left to right (for instance, five seconds, ten seconds, fifteen seconds, and so on). As you edit, you drag your media clips to the Timeline (a clip on the Timeline is represented by a solid-colored rectangle) and position them under a time value. That's exactly where, in time, the clips play in your story.

Figure 1-6:
Clips on the
Timeline,
playing at
0 seconds,
4 seconds,
and 8
seconds
into this
movie-in-
progress.

Video (V1) track   Clips on the Timeline   Ruler

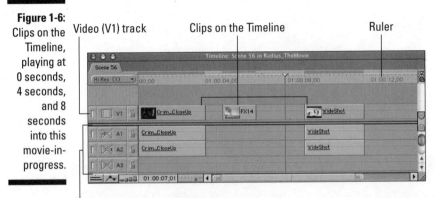

Audio tracks

You can see the video portion of a clip in the V1 row of the Timeline (each row is called a track), while its accompanying dialog goes in rows A1 and A2 below it (*A* being for audio). You can see that the clip FX14 has no audio along with it.

These are the basic building blocks of editing. You use Final Cut's tools to resize media clips on the Timeline, cut them into smaller pieces, and rearrange them until they tell your story.

The Canvas

After you've edited your video and audio clips on the Timeline and want to see (and hear) how they all play together, turn your attention to Final Cut's Canvas window. The Canvas is where you watch your movie-in-progress as you've arranged it on the Timeline. Think of the Canvas as the Timeline's right-hand man: You make an edit to your clips on the Timeline, and then you play them in the Canvas window to see how they look. Then you make another tweak on the Timeline and check it out in the Canvas window *again* — and again, and again, and again.

As shown in Figure 1-7, the Canvas looks a lot like the Viewer. You do have the same play controls, but there are some differences. (For instance, you can perform some basic edits on the Canvas instead of the Timeline.) For now, all you need to know is that the Canvas lets you play, fast-forward, pause, and rewind through your Final Cut movie. 'Nuff said.

Figure 1-7:
The Canvas
window
plays the
clips you've
arranged on
the timeline.

Play/Pause button

The tool palette

As you can see from Figure 1-8, the tool palette is your standard, garden-variety palette, sporting a handful of tool icons that you can click at will. The tool you'll find yourself using the most is the standard selection tool (the plain ol' arrow at the top of the palette), which you use for selecting and moving media clips on the Timeline. To be honest, you can edit an entire film with this tool alone, but the others make that work easier. For instance, some of the handy ones let you select huge groups of clips at once, cut clips in two, or quickly magnify your view of the Timeline so that you can see what you're doing. You'll get to know all these tools soon enough.

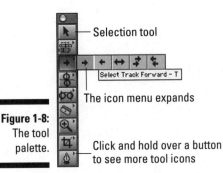

— Selection tool

Select Track Forward – T

The icon menu expands

Figure 1-8:
The tool
palette.

Click and hold over a button
to see more tool icons

If you see a little black triangle in the upper-right corner of a tool icon, more tool icons are hidden underneath it. These additional tools are all related, but do slightly different things. Just click and hold such an icon, and the hidden tools pop up for you to choose from.

Audio meters

Final Cut's Audio meters, shown in Figure 1-9, are supporting cast members, but they come in really handy when you're tweaking your audio to sound as good as possible. In a nutshell, the meters visually show you the decibel (dB) range of an audio clip (that's a fancy way of saying *loudness*). From there, you can set the volume levels of all the audio clips in your movie so that they don't overpower one another. The meters also show you when a clip of audio is too loud, which causes it to distort.

Figure 1-9:
The Audio
meters can
tell you
when your
audio is
distorting.

Mucho keyboard shortcuts

Final Cut sports tons of keyboard shortcuts to make you a faster editor. The shortcuts are extensive, letting you do everything from editing clips and navigating the Timeline to playing back video and selecting any tool in the tool palette.

We point out keyboard shortcuts as we come to them, but if you're wondering if there's a shortcut for something you're doing in the program, you can choose Help➪Keyboard Shortcuts to see a list of all of 'em, grouped by category. You can also check out the Cheat Sheet, a reference card at the beginning of this book.

Using the Help system

Like most big-budget software, Final Cut offers a built-in help system that's pretty lousy at teaching big-picture concepts, but can occasionally help in explaining a specific function.

Select any of the following three options from the Help menu:

- ✔ **Final Cut Pro Help:** This option, which takes you to the main help database, is our favorite and the one you'll probably use most often. The help system offers a table of contents for topics and also lets you search the database for keywords (such as *keyframe* or *logging*). Sometimes, you get lucky and find what you're looking for easily. Other times, Final Cut has trouble pointing you in the right direction (as in *still frame*).

- ✔ **Context Sensitive Help:** When you choose this option from the Help menu, Final Cut tries to explain the window or dialog box you're currently in.

- ✔ **Help Cursor:** When you choose this option, your mouse pointer turns into a question mark. Click anywhere within a Final Cut window, and you get help on that item — though rarely as detailed as you'd like.

Chapter 2

Getting Started

*B*efore you can get into the fun of capturing and editing your media in Final Cut, you have to get a few preliminaries out of the way. For instance, you have to figure out what hardware you need to accomplish your editing goals if you haven't already. You also have to configure Final Cut's various settings to work with your particular hardware setup. (Tons of settings are available, but the good news is Final Cut makes them easily manageable.) Finally, you have to kick off a new project, which is where the editing magic begins.

Hardware Requirements

If you've already got your Final Cut system assembled, you might want to skip to the "Getting Started in the DV Realm" section later in this chapter. But if you're still deciding what you need in order to build a workable Final Cut system, or if you have questions about how you can expand the system you already have, read on.

Realistically, a fully functional Final Cut system needs only two things:

✔ **A half-decent Mac:** Duh! For your purposes, a half-decent Mac meets these minimum requirements: a 300 MHz G3 or G4 processor, 256MB (megabytes) of RAM, and a hard drive with 40MB of free space for the Final Cut application.

✔ **A video tape deck:** You use this for capturing raw footage from video-tape, and then, when your editing work is done, recording the final movie back to tape. A camera that can pinch hit as a tape deck also works. The kind of videotape format you're working with determines the kind of video tape deck you use. The general term *digital video* includes many formats: Two of the most popular are DV and DigiBeta. The majority of Final Cut editors, however, work in the DV format because it provides excellent (although not perfect) quality and the equipment is affordable and easy to set up. Chances are that you'll use DV as well, so that's what we focus on in this chapter. If you want to find out more about other tape formats, including DigiBeta, that Final Cut can work with, see the sidebars "Working with different media formats" and "Final Cut on steroids (for high-end video formats)" later in this chapter.

So that's all you actually need to get started with Final Cut, but within these two requirements, you have plenty of different options to consider. For instance, would your ideal Mac be a laptop or desktop model, and how should it *really* be configured so that you can get your work done comfortably? (Final Cut's system requirements are bare minimums. Realistically, you'll want a faster CPU, more RAM, and a bigger, faster hard drive than Final Cut officially requires.) Also, although all you *need* is a Mac and a tape deck for editing, you might appreciate extra hardware and software components — for instance, a DVD burner to record your movies to DVDs, or a television monitor so that you can watch your movie-in-progress on a real TV instead of a smallish window on your Mac's screen.

The Skinny on DV Video

DV is a format that describes how video and audio should look and sound. All sorts of equipment can work with video in the DV format. For instance, some cameras and VCR decks are designed to record and play tapes in the DV format, and your Mac can save QuickTime video files in the DV format.

What's most noteworthy about DV video is that it's compressed. Raw video is so incredibly rich in data that recording it, playing it, and storing it with a camera or computer requires expensive, powerful hardware. But DV video is compressed five times, which means that it uses one-fifth the data that raw video needs. The compression enables you to work with video much more easily. The compressed format is also the reason you can play DV video smoothly on just about any Mac sold these days and can record it using affordable consumer video cameras. The one drawback to that compression is that DV loses some image quality — that is, its images are never quite as crisp as uncompressed video, and its colors aren't quite as true. Still, DV looks pretty darn good, and many people can't tell the difference comparing raw and DV video on regular TVs. That's why it has become such a popular format for all kinds of uses, including documentaries, news, reality TV shows, industrial and wedding videos, and even independent films.

Working with different media formats

We're assuming that you're working with video and audio in the DV format (as most Final Cut editors do), but your movies may occasionally call for media that comes in a different format, so here are a few notes regarding your options:

✔ **Other video formats:** If you need to work with video in a format different from DV (for instance, video on a high-end, high-cost tape such as DigiBeta), you can find a post-production or tape-duplication company that will transfer that media to DV tape. But remember: transferring video to DV tape compresses it by five times. (That compression is a part of the DV format, though it doesn't mean you see an appreciable loss in image and sound quality.) If you want to avoid DV compression, you have to find (most likely rent) a Final Cut system that's designed to work with those tape formats natively.

✔ **Film:** If you shot your movie on film (usually 16mm or 35mm), you need to transfer it to videotape before editing in Final Cut. Transferring film to tape is called the *telecine* process, and a film lab or post-production company can do it. When you have film footage telecined, it's typically recorded on a very high-quality tape format, such as DigiBeta or possibly HD. From there, you can have the tape transferred to DV or find a turbocharged Final Cut system that can work with those formats natively.

✔ **Audio formats:** You may wind up with audio that's recorded on a tape format, such as D88, DAT, or mag. If this is the case, you can also go to a tape-duplication or other post-production company to have those tapes transferred to data files in the .wav or .aiff format, which Final Cut can easily import.

Selecting and Configuring a Mac

Final Cut demands more hardware firepower than a word processor or Internet browser, but that doesn't mean you need a top-of-the-line Mac to run it. In fact, it runs comfortably on just about any Mac made since 1999 or 2000 (some of the older iMacs and iBooks excepted). In this section, we look at some Mac models you may want to consider, as well as what you need in terms of RAM, hard drives, monitors, and more. The different types of Macs include

✔ **PowerMacs:** These are Apple's stylish, upright towers, the crown jewels of the Mac line. They sport the fastest CPUs, the biggest hard drives, the most RAM, and also offer expansion card slots. (These enable you to add an uncompressed video capture card or high-speed SCSI controller — more on all this shortly.) If building a high-performance editing work-station is your top priority, PowerMacs are the way to go. However, that being said, a PowerMac may be overkill for your needs.

✔ **PowerBooks:** Apple's PowerBooks have become so good that they can handle tons of editing work without breaking a sweat. PowerBooks aren't as feature-packed as desktop Macs, but don't underestimate the benefits of tucking your editing system in a small shoulder bag and taking it wherever you go. You can also work around a PowerBook's limitations: You can boost memory, attach a second screen, and add more storage via FireWire hard drives. The only thing you can't upgrade is its CPU, but 'Books these days feature G4 processors, which are usually quite fast enough.

✔ **iBooks:** Although not as fast or feature-packed as PowerBooks, you can still get quite a lot done with an iBook. Limitations include the iBook's smallish screen (12 or 14 inches, which might require occasional squinting), as well as slower CPUs (G3s as of this writing), and no option to attach a second screen. But for the money, an iBook can still deliver quite a lot of editing bang for the buck.

✔ **iMacs:** You can also build a fine editing system around the iMac. Its biggest limitation is its 15-inch screen (with a resolution of 1024 x 768 pixels). Although such a screen isn't spacious, you can still work comfortably with a few adjustments. And if you get Apple's new flat-screen iMac, you also get a more-than-respectable CPU in the G4 processor.

CPU speed

How fast should your Mac's CPU be to run Final Cut comfortably? It totally depends on the kind of editing work you're doing.

If you're largely doing "cuts-only" editing, where most of your work is simply cutting up media clips and arranging them on the Timeline, with a cross fade or other transition here or there, even a G3 processor running at 400 MHz can do the job. (We don't recommend something as slow as Apple's 300 MHz requirement.) Things may certainly feel peppier on a faster machine — say, a 700 or 800 MHz G4 iMac — but the difference won't make or break your productivity.

On the other hand, if you want to do a lot of effects work in Final Cut (tons of transitions, color correction, blue/green screen work, motion graphics, and/or compositing lots of images together), your Mac's processor can make a huge difference. All those effects have to be *rendered* (precalculated and drawn) before you can play them in real time, and how fast they're rendered depends almost entirely on the brute strength of your Mac's CPU. To give you an idea of the difference a fast CPU can make, suppose that you wanted to render a movie in Final Cut. A G3 would take almost twice as long as a G4 processor, and close to three times when compared to a Mac with two G4s inside. So if you're going to be rendering a lot, we recommend splurging for the fastest Mac you can afford.

A CPU's MHz rating isn't the only major factor that determines its speed. G4 processors have special units called Altivec engines built in, which turbo-charge graphics and video work even further. So if you want to cut down your rendering times, go for a Mac with a G4 processor (even if it has the same MHz as a G3).

Memory (RAM)

We recommend you have at least 384MB of RAM in your Mac to run Final Cut under the OS X operating system. Technically, you can get away with using only 256MB of RAM in OS X, but if you try do so, the operating system ends up using your hard drive to temporarily store data that would normally go into RAM (this is called *virtual memory*). Unfortunately, your Mac tends to pause frequently as this happens, which can get downright annoying.

If you run Final Cut with 384MB of RAM, you'll still get pauses from time to time, but way less frequently. You'll also have enough room to keep a few other applications open at the same time (programs for e-mail, Web brows-ing, and sound and graphics work) so that you can switch from one program to another quickly and easily.

If you want to run Final Cut with other memory-hungry applications open at the same time (typically photo or effects programs such as Adobe Photoshop and After Effects), you'll probably want to stock your Mac with 512MB or even a gigabyte (GB) of RAM.

Disk storage for video

Video eats up a ton of hard drive space. You need 13GB for every hour of DV video stored. Unless you're doing short commercials or home videos, you probably need to add more drive space than your Mac's internal hard drive offers. One of the nice things about working with DV video is that you can use affordable hard drives to store it. (Working with video in other formats, such as uncompressed video captured from a DigiBeta tape, can require very fast and very expensive drives.) Your options come in two basic flavors:

- ✔ An internal Ultra-ATA disk drive, which can replace your main system drive (if you're using an iMac or Mac laptop) or be added to it (for PowerMacs, which can accommodate one to three extra drives in addi-tion to your main system drive).

- ✔ An external FireWire drive, which plugs into your Mac's FireWire port. (Again, most Macs made since 2000 have them. If yours doesn't, you can usually buy an add-on card that adds this port.) We tend to like external FireWire drives for a variety of reasons:

- You can easily move them around. For instance, you may need to bring footage to another Mac or PC somewhere off-site.

- They're hot-pluggable, meaning you can plug one into your Mac and use it without restarting the Mac.

- You can daisy chain (that is, connect) dozens of FireWire drives together so that you can easily add more storage when you need it.

- If you're running Final Cut on a laptop, you can buy small FireWire drives that draw power from your Mac's battery, so they don't need AC power.

Final Cut on steroids (for high-end video formats)

The most advanced Final Cut hardware set-ups are designed to work with video from high-quality tape formats such as DigiBeta or HD (for High Definition). These formats don't compress video nearly as much as the DV format, which gives images in these formats a sharper picture and richer colors. Even so, the majority of Final Cut editors are fine working in the DV world (DV video looks pretty darn good for tons of shows), but if you're curious about what it takes to build a Final Cut system that crunches Digital Beta or HD, here are the three key components:

✔ **High-end video deck:** To capture and play-back video in a high-end tape format, you need a high-end video deck that can work with those tapes. Digital Beta and HD decks run $50,000 or more, which is why most editors typically go to a post-production company to rent them.

✔ **Uncompressed capture cards:** Digital Beta and HD video is so rich and detailed that an ordinary Mac isn't powerful enough to capture or play it unless you add a special capture card. These cards, which you install in the expansion slot of a PowerMac (they don't work with iMacs or laptops), give your Mac the firepower it needs to handle video that's uncompressed. The card can capture video exactly as it's described on the DigiBeta or HD tape, so you don't lose any quality when the video goes from the tape to your Mac.

✔ **Super-fast hard drives:** Uncompressed video takes a ton of disk space (about 65GB per hour of video, compared to 13GB per hour in the DV format), so you need a speedy hard drive to record and play all that information in real time. (Slower drives cause your video to stutter.) These drives are based on the lightning-quick Ultra-SCSI interface and cost three or four times more than standard FireWire drives at the time of this writing. (Also, SCSI drives aren't as easy to set up and maintain.)

By the way, because buying a high-powered Final Cut system is financially out of the question for many people (the equipment can run well over $50,000), you can look for a post-production company that will rent you time by the hour on its own souped-up Final Cut hardware. If this sounds appealing, have your Digital Beta or HD tapes transferred to DV tape (see the "Working with different media formats" sidebar), edit the DV tape on your own Final Cut system, and then bring your Final Cut project file to the post-production company. Have them recapture only the footage your project calls for, using your original Digital Beta/HD tapes (which give you the highest-quality video). We're simplifying this process a bit, but it's entirely feasible. Talk to the folks at the post-production company for details on how to do it. They can help you understand the process and the technical pitfalls.

Not all Ultra-ATA or FireWire disk drives make the cut for video editing. Make sure your drive runs at least at 5400 RPM (Revolutions Per Minute); 7200 RPM is ideal, but if you're buying an internal drive for a laptop, 5400 RPM is the best you can get at the time of this writing. If you're choosing a FireWire external drive, make sure that it uses the Oxford 911 bridge chip set. Otherwise, the drive might not be fast enough to capture video clips in real time without skipping frames (a big no-no) or to play all of a clip's frames smoothly. Drive manufacturers don't often advertise whether their products use the Oxford chip set, so you may have to scrutinize the drive's datasheet or call the manufacturer.

In practical terms, a hard drive never has as much free space as advertised. For starters, after the drive is formatted, it loses around 7 to 8 percent of its size right off the bat. Secondly, leaving 5 to 10 percent of your drive free is good because stuffing it completely not only slows it down (which can lead to dropped frames during capture or playback) but even increases the risk of crashes. In other words, if you have a 100GB drive, it's only good for about 85GB, so factor that into your decision about how much hard drive space your video needs.

After you've been editing for a while, your hard drive can become heavily fragmented — that is, the data that make up your media files are spread haphazardly over the drive's disk, instead of being neatly and efficiently packaged together. Your hard drive runs more slowly if it's fragmented (which can lead to Final Cut skipping frames when capturing video, or playing it back). To counter this tendency, you can *defragment* your drive by using software such as Norton Utilities, available from retail stores or online at www. symantec.com.

Final Cut's official documentation recommends not capturing your media (audio and particularly video) on the same hard drive where you keep your Mac's operating system and its applications. Doing so can fragment your hard drive more quickly and lead to other minor headaches, so you may or may not want to factor this in while you decide how much hard drive space you need. For the record, we have created plenty of DV video projects using our Mac's main system drive and had no problems whatsoever.

Monitors

When running Final Cut, the most important element regarding a monitor is not its physical size, but its pixel resolution. This isn't to say a physically bigger monitor won't be easier on your eyes (it will), but the monitor's resolution determines how much information you can see on-screen at the same time. For instance, the resolution determines how many media clips you can see on the Timeline or in the Browser without scrolling.

The lowest screen resolution that works with Final Cut is 1024 x 768 pixels, which is what you get with most 15-inch monitors (like those found on older iMacs) and the LCD screens on older PowerBooks and newer iBooks. Although we wouldn't call this resolution exactly spacious, it's actually quite workable, especially if you learn to use Final Cut's keyboard commands to quickly call up overlapping windows or zoom in and out of the Timeline.

Any screen resolution higher than 1024 x 768 is gravy. If you can have your druthers, we recommend a 19-inch monitor running at 1280 x 1024 resolution, or one of Apple's Cinema Display LCD screens, which runs widescreen as high as 1920 x 1200 (and will duly impress family, friends, neighbors, and so on). Some editors, though, use two monitors at the same time (one monitor usually handles the Timeline, Viewer, and Canvas windows, while the other takes on the Browser and secondary windows, such as the Tool Bench, Favorites, or Effects). To use two monitors, you need to install two video cards in your Macintosh or use a video card that offers outputs for two simultaneous displays.

Some editors assume they can't easily use Final Cut on a PowerBook because its relatively low screen resolution (1152 x 768) doesn't offer all the space they're accustomed to. But that's not true! You can hook up a second monitor (in addition to the PowerBook's LCD), and run it at a resolution as high as 1600 x 1200 pixels.

A monitor can often work at a variety of resolutions, some of which may be better suited for Final Cut work than others. You can change your screen's resolution in OS X by choosing Apple⇨System Preferences, clicking the Displays icon (in the Hardware section), and then choosing from any of the resolutions listed.

Doing DV? You need a FireWire port

Make sure that whatever Mac you select has at least one FireWire port. FireWire is the interface used to hook your Mac to a DV camera or deck so that the devices can transfer audio and video signals back and forth. (FireWire is also used to hook up fast and affordable hard drives for storing DV video.) All new Macs made today feature one or two FireWire ports, and many models have featured FireWire since 1999 or 2000. If your Mac doesn't have FireWire, you can probably buy a third-party card that adds the capability (old iBooks and iMacs may be the exceptions, where add-on cards may not be available). However, if your Mac is old enough to not have FireWire, it may also not have the hardware muscle to play DV video anyway.

DV video tape decks and cameras

Just for the record: You don't *have* to have a DV camera or deck connected to your Mac to run Final Cut. We just assume that you need one to capture video for your project and later record it back to tape. If not (for instance, if someone else has given you an external FireWire drive with digital video files already on it), you're free to load Final Cut without any DV equipment attached.

But if you're in the market for a DV deck, the most affordable option is to use your DV video camera as a playback and recording deck because it has all the necessary functionality built right in. Option number two is to buy a dedicated DV deck, which works just like a VHS VCR, except it uses DV tapes. (If you're taking this route, check out Sony's offerings.)

Why go for a dedicated deck if your camera can fill that role anyway? Well, your camera isn't built to the same industrial-strength standards as a dedicated deck is, so if you're going to do hundreds of hours of capturing and recording, you might wear out the camera (buying an extended warranty for your camera can address this concern). Also, if you work with other people, you never know whether someone will be using your camera out in the field when you need it to pinch hit as a deck.

Either way, getting a DV camera or dedicated deck to work with your Mac is generally quick and painless. All you need is a single FireWire cable (typically a 6-pin to 4-pin connector, which costs about $15 at computer or electronics stores) to hook the camera or deck to your Mac's FireWire port. Final Cut senses that the camera or deck is connected and will know how to control it without further ado.

Other optional hardware

Although your Final Cut system doesn't have to have the following goodies, you may want to add them, depending on your needs and wants:

- ✔ **Television monitor:** Although not absolutely necessary, adding a television to your Final Cut system is a good idea. That way, you can see your media clips and edited movies on TV as you work. (If your piece is intended for TV, seeing your movie just as your audience will can be an especially big help.) Watching your footage on a TV screen is also helpful for spotting subtle things in your images, which are harder to see if you're watching video in a small window on your Mac's screen. Any TV with either RCA (also known as Composite) or S-Video input jacks will do. To learn how to set your TV up with Final Cut, see the "Connecting and preparing all your hardware" section later in this chapter.

- ✔ **DVD burner and authoring software:** One of the coolest aspects of digital media is that you can record your movies to DVDs and then play them in just about any consumer DVD player sold these days, just like a Hollywood flick. If this floats your boat (and how could it not?), you'll need a DVD-R drive. If you have a newish Mac, you might already have one built in (Apple calls its DVD-R drive a SuperDrive), along with Apple's free, award-winning iDVD software to encode your movies for DVD and to create the disc's menus and such.

If your Mac doesn't come equipped with a DVD-R drive, you can get an add-on drive from companies such as LaCie or FireWire Direct, but you may have to buy your own DVD encoding/authoring software because iDVD currently works only with SuperDrive-equipped Macs.

Because add-on DVD software gets pricey — as much as $1,000 — you should consider a SuperDrive Mac right from the start if putting your movies on DVD is something you're interested in.

✔ **Zip disk or CD-R(W):** To be safe, back up your Final Cut project files somewhere other than your hard drive (not your media, just the project files that describe what to do with that media). You can burn projects to a CD if you've got a burner, but putting them on a Zip disk is the easiest option.

✔ **Final Cut keyboard:** Post-Op sells a keyboard with Final Cut functions printed directly on their respective keys (obviously in small print). Some editors like working with these keyboards because they make it easier to invoke Final Cut's many key commands.

✔ **Turbocharged mouse:** You can buy a multibutton mouse (some with a built-in jog shuttles, track ball, or fly wheel), and program those extra buttons to perform Final Cut operations with a simple click.

✔ **Speakers or headphones:** The built-in speakers on your Mac aren't good enough to play all the nuances in your audio (and highlight any problems that should be corrected). To upgrade your Mac's audio, you have a few options. If you're hooking up a TV to your Mac, choose one with stereo speakers. Otherwise, connect a pair of speakers to your Mac or invest in a good pair of headphones.

Getting Started in the DV Realm

After you've installed the Final Cut software on your hard drive, you need to take a few steps to configure Final Cut to work with your hardware and the video format you'll be using.

Because the majority of Final Cut editors work in the DV realm, we're going to focus on setting your system to work with DV equipment and video. If your Final Cut system is based on another format (for instance, maybe you're using a third-party capture card hooked to, say, an analog Beta SP deck), check out that capture card's documentation for steps on connecting everything and establishing working settings for Final Cut.

Connecting and preparing all your hardware

Before loading Final Cut, you need to make sure that your hardware is hooked up and turned on. With DV equipment, getting everything in order is unbelievably simple: First, connect your DV deck or camera to your Mac's FireWire port (the Mac might have more than one port, but either will do) using a FireWire cable, most likely a 6-pin to 4-pin variety. Next, turn your deck or camera on!

If you want to use an external FireWire hard drive with Final Cut, turn this puppy (or puppies) on before loading Final Cut as well. Finally, if you want to add a television to your setup (so that you can watch your video on the TV screen instead of your Mac's smaller monitor), look for a Video Out jack (or jacks) on your DV camera or deck. These are probably RCA (also known as Composite) or S-Video jacks. Just connect these to the Video In jacks on your TV with RCA or S-Video cables, which you can buy at any electronics store. Doing this lets your Mac's video signal move across the FireWire cable, into your DV camera/deck, and then out again to your TV.

After you have a TV hooked up to your DV camera or deck, you have to switch the TV to one of its video channels (which show signals coming from its Video In jacks) before you can see video from Final Cut. How to do this depends on your television setup (and whether the TV is connected to a VCR, cable box, or some other device as well), but we can offer you this guidance: Look on your TV or remote control for a button that says TV/Video and press it. (Try pressing it repeatedly or press your Channel Up and Down buttons after pressing Video.) If you see a video clip that's currently displayed in Final Cut's Viewer or Canvas windows, you're in business. If not, check out your TV's manual to see how to switch to its video input channels. Also, make sure that your DV equipment and TV are connected properly.

Launching Final Cut

With your hardware set up and raring to go, use your Mac's Finder to find the Final Cut Pro application on your hard drive (wherever you installed it), and double-click it. Final Cut begins to load all sorts of files and modules it needs, but if you're running it for the first time, it prompts you for a few key settings.

The quickest way to load Final Cut is to add its icon to your Mac's Dock (only in OS X, as shown in Figure 2-1). That way, you can launch it by simply clicking its icon in the Dock. In the Finder, just drag Final Cut's application icon to the Dock to add it there. (Don't worry; you're not actually moving or affecting the original application file on your hard drive.) If you ever want to remove Final Cut from the Dock, you can also click that same icon and drag it outside the Dock again.

Figure 2-1:
The Final
Cut icon
added to the
OS X Dock.

Choosing an initial setup

When Final Cut loads for the first time, it opens a Choose Setup window, shown in Figure 2-2, which prompts for three important settings: Easy Setup, Primary Scratch Disk, and User Mode. (We detail your choices for these settings in the next few sections.)

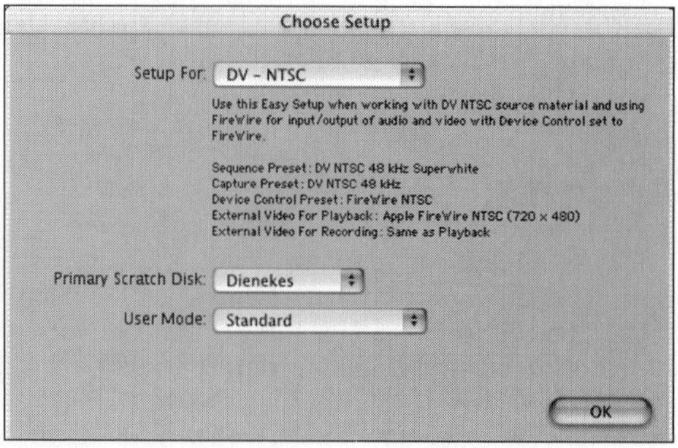

Figure 2-2:
Choose
Setup
window.

Easy Setup

Final Cut has a dizzying array of tweakable settings that tell the software how to work with your video equipment, what kind of video and audio formats you're using, and much more. You can tweak settings individually (we show you how later in this chapter), but for now, start by choosing one of four Easy Setups that Final Cut provides. Easy Setups are massive collections of related settings that you're most likely to use. Choose one of these from the Setup For drop-down list:

- ✔ **DV-NTSC:** Use this if you want to capture and edit video in the DV format, using video equipment (that is, camera, deck, and television) based on the NTSC television signal. If you're working with equipment bought in North America, this is your option.

- ✔ **DV-PAL:** Use this to capture and edit video in the DV format, using equipment based on the PAL TV signal (a European format).

- ✔ **OfflineRT-NTSC:** You still use a DV camera or deck (NTSC compatible) to capture video on a DV tape, but Final Cut *further* compresses the video using Photo JPEG technology. The result is that your compressed media takes only one tenth of the disk space of standard DV video (making the most of cramped hard drives, particularly on laptops). Although Photo JPEG's image quality won't match DV's (more compression artifacts and less frame resolution), it's often good enough for rough editing purposes. When you're ready to record your final program (you'll want to use the higher quality DV format), just switch Final Cut's Easy Setup back to DV-NTSC, recapture only the media your movie actually uses (Final Cut knows exactly where to find that media on your DV source tapes), and then record your finished movie with the better-looking DV footage.

- ✔ **OfflineRT-PAL:** This option is just like OfflineRT-NTSC, except it's for European equipment based on the PAL TV signal.

If you're using non-DV equipment (for instance, a third-party capture card, hooked to, say, an analog VHS or BetaSP deck), you need a different collection of settings. Consult your capture card's manual (or contact tech support) and see the section "Adjusting Your Project/Sequence Settings," later in this chapter.

Primary Scratch Disk

The scratch disk is the hard drive where Final Cut saves all your captured video and audio (and other files, such as rendered media). If your Mac has only one hard drive (including the internal system drive), that's automatically your scratch disk. But if you have multiple drives hooked up, you can choose which one serves as your scratch disk by choosing it from the Primary Scratch Disk drop-down list.

You can change your scratch disk at any time by choosing Final Cut Pro⇨ Preferences and then clicking the Scratch Disks tab. You can also do it from Final Cut's Log and Capture window when you're capturing media. (See Chapter 3.)

User Mode

Some editors just want to edit video and not worry about Final Cut's advanced effects features. If you fall into this camp, you can choose the Cutting Station option, which causes Final Cut to omit a lot of its effects features on its menus (giving you a more streamlined interface). But because you're here to learn this world-class program in all its glory, we recommend that you stick with the Standard option for now.

The instructions in this section apply to DV. If you have equipment that's not DV, consult the manual for your equipment and set your settings manually. (See the section "Adjusting Your Project/Sequence Settings," later in this chapter.)

When you're finished making your choices, click OK. Final Cut opens a new project for you, and you're ready to get down to business. You can easily change these settings at any time, so don't fret about making a major commitment now.

If you don't have your video deck or camera hooked up to your Mac and turned on, Final Cut gives you a message that it can't find the device. Just make sure that it's properly connected, and tell Final Cut to look for it again, or just continue on. If you continue on, Final Cut will still run fine.

Working with Final Cut Projects and Sequences

After you've established your initial setup, Final Cut automatically creates a new, untitled project, which in turn includes a new, untitled sequence (check out Figure 2-3). In other words, you're ready to get to work! Before moving forward, though, you need to know a bit about projects and how to manage them.

A project is a Final Cut document file — like a Word or Photoshop document — that you can create, save, close, and open again, like any other document on your hard drive. A project contains two different elements, which are unique to it:

- ✔ Any media files (video, audio, and still pics) you capture or import into it

- ✔ One or more Timeline *sequences*, which are collections of the project's media clips that you've edited together in Final Cut's Timeline window

Generally, you create a new project for each movie or other unique, standalone program you're working on. For instance, if you're a big-time Hollywood editor, you'd have a project for each of the films on your plate. And within those projects, you'd create multiple sequences to break your edited clips into smaller, more manageable pieces. For instance, you might create a sequence for each of the film's major scenes or acts.

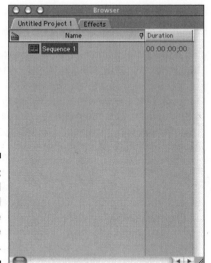

Figure 2-3:
An untitled
project and
sequence
in the
Browser.

Saving and autosaving projects

To save an untitled project (like the one Final Cut just whipped up for you),
choose File➪Save Project As. In the Save dialog box (shown in Figure 2-4), type
the project's new name in the Save As text box, navigate to a folder on your
hard drive (use the horizontal scroll bar or click the Where drop-down list for
major folders), and click the Save button. After you save a project, you see its
name appear in its tab at the top of the Browser window. From now on, to save
your project, just choose File➪Save (or press the familiar ⌘+S key combo).

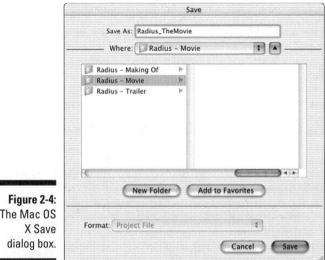

Figure 2-4:
The Mac OS
X Save
dialog box.

When you save a project, you automatically save all the sequences that are a part of that project. You can't save individual sequences, just projects.

Final Cut also includes a nice autosave feature, which automatically makes a backup copy of your project at intervals you can choose. Imagine that, after you've done a fair amount of work on your project without doing a manual ⌘+S save, your Mac suddenly crashes. (This kind of thing still happens from time to time, despite OS X's stability.) When you relaunch Final Cut, it opens the last project you manually saved but doesn't show all the latest work you did. But Final Cut *also* asks if you want to open a newer autosave version (provided you have the feature turned on, and an autosave time interval passed while you were working before the crash). If you open this backup and want to keep it, just choose File⇨Save Project, and Final Cut replaces your original project with the newer version, which now assumes the original project's name so that it's a seamless transition.

You can tweak the Autosave settings (or turn it off) by choosing Final Cut Pro⇨Preferences. Look for the Autosave Vault setting in the General Preferences tab (as shown in Figure 2-5) and make whatever adjustments you want.

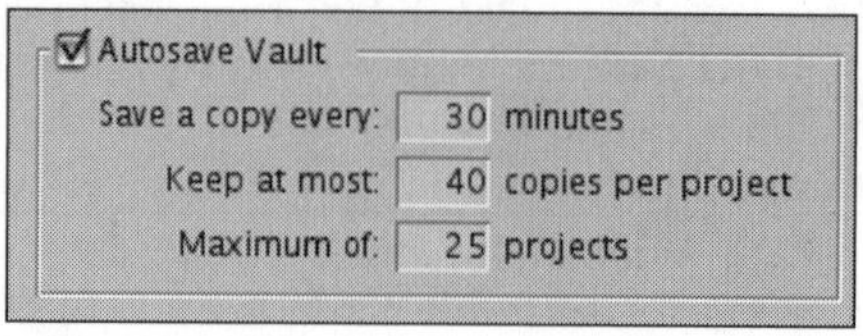

Figure 2-5:
The Autosave Vault in the General Preferences tab.

☑ Autosave Vault
Save a copy every: 30 minutes
Keep at most: 40 copies per project
Maximum of: 25 projects

Final Cut keeps your autosave backups in the same folder as your original project, in case you want to load one. These backups use the same name as your original project but append -auto at the end of the filename. By default, Final Cut keeps up to 40 successive backups per project. You can tweak the default via Preferences.

More project management: New, open, and close

If you have any experience using other applications in Mac OS X, this is pretty standard stuff:

✔ To create a new project from scratch, choose — you guessed it! — File⇨ New Project. Final Cut opens an untitled project tab in the Browser window and makes it your active project. We recommend saving the project right away.

✔ To open a project, choose File⇨Open. In the Choose a File dialog box (Figure 2-6), browse your hard drive (use the horizontal scroll bar), and double-click the project's name when you see it. Final Cut opens the project as a new tab in the Browser and makes it active.

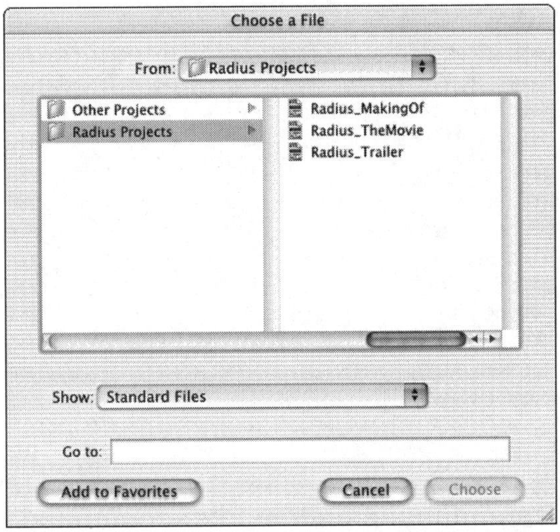

Figure 2-6: The Choose a File dialog box.

Choose a File
From: Radius Projects
Other Projects ▸   Radius_MakingOf
Radius Projects ▸   Radius_TheMovie
Radius_Trailer
Show: Standard Files
Go to:
Add to Favorites   Cancel   Choose

✔ To close a project you're no longer working on, make it active in the Browser window (click its tab at the top of the window) and choose File⇨Close Project.

You can have multiple projects open at the same time. To work with an open project, just click its tab at the top of the Browser to make it active. You'll see all its clips, bins, and sequences listed, as shown in Figure 2-7.

If you quit Final Cut with open projects (that is, without closing them first), Final Cut automatically opens those same projects the next time you load it. This is handy if you're working on the same project, day in and day out, but can be annoying if you're finished with a project and find it lurking around your workspace.

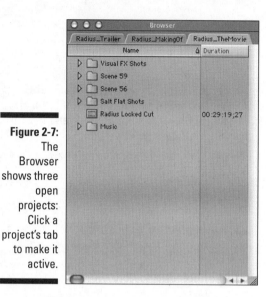

Figure 2-7:
The
Browser
shows three
open
projects:
Click a
project's tab
to make it
active.

Adjusting Your Project/Sequence Settings

After you pick an initial setup for Final Cut (as you did when you first loaded the program — see the section "Choosing an Initial Setup" earlier in this chapter), you may never need to tweak those settings again, provided your hardware setup and video and audio requirements don't change. But if they do, give us a few moments to demystify how Final Cut's settings work so that you know how to make whatever adjustments are called for.

Final Cut has three levels of settings:

- ✔ **A setting:** A setting controls a specific feature. For instance, the frame rate of a sequence, the quality of audio it's using (32 kHz, 48 kHz, and so on), or the frame size for video (640 x 480 pixels, 720 x 480 pixels, and so on).

- ✔ **A preset:** A preset is a group of related settings that you can apply quickly and easily, time and again. Final Cut has four families of presets. You can create your own presets within each family (more on how to do that in "Choosing a different presets," later in this chapter).

  - • **Sequence preset:** These settings apply to any new sequences you create in your project. (That is, when you create a new sequence, it conforms to whatever settings are defined in the current Sequence preset.) Settings include frame resolution (such as 720 x 480 pixels), frame rate and audio quality, video field dominance, and more (as shown in Figure 2-8).

- **Capture preset:** This group of settings defines how your video is captured (resolution, frame rate, compression used, and so on). If you're capturing DV video with a DV deck, you don't really have any options here, but if you happen to use a capture card, it most likely can capture video in any manner you want.

- **Device Control preset:** These settings define how your video deck or camera is controlled (which protocol is used to control the hardware, how much preroll and postroll are used, and so on).

- **External video:** These settings define whether or not Final Cut plays video to an external TV monitor you have hooked up to your system, and how it handles the video signal. (*Note:* Final Cut doesn't technically call this a preset, but it works just the same.)

✔ **An Easy Setup:** Finally, the last level of settings is the familiar Easy Setup, which is a collection of the four preset families (sequence, capture, device control, and external video). By choosing an Easy Setup, you don't have to worry about choosing individual presets. Final Cut makes four Easy Setups available to you, each featuring slightly different presets. (For instance, the sequence preset used by the DV-PAL Easy Setup calls for a video frame size of 720 x 570 pixels, whereas the sequence preset used by the DV-NTSC Easy Setup uses a frame size of 720 x 480 pixels.)

You can change Final Cut's individual presets, or you can pick an entirely different Easy Setup. When you change either a preset or an Easy Setup, any projects or sequences you create from that point on use the settings defined by your new choice. However, any existing projects or sequences keep their original settings.

Later, as you become comfortable with Final Cut, you may want to change the settings for an existing sequence. In this case, you *don't* want to change your Sequence preset because doing so only affects new sequences you create. Instead, just open the existing sequence in the Timeline window, and then choose Sequence⇨Settings. From the Settings box, you can adjust any sequence settings you want (they're the same settings you find in the Sequence preset). When you click OK, Final Cut applies your changes to that open sequence.

Changing your Easy Setup

If all you want to do is change your Easy Setup, that's easy. Just choose Final Cut Pro⇨Easy Setup, and pick a new option from the dialog box's pop-up menu.

Changing the Easy Setup doesn't affect settings for sequences you've already created — only new ones.

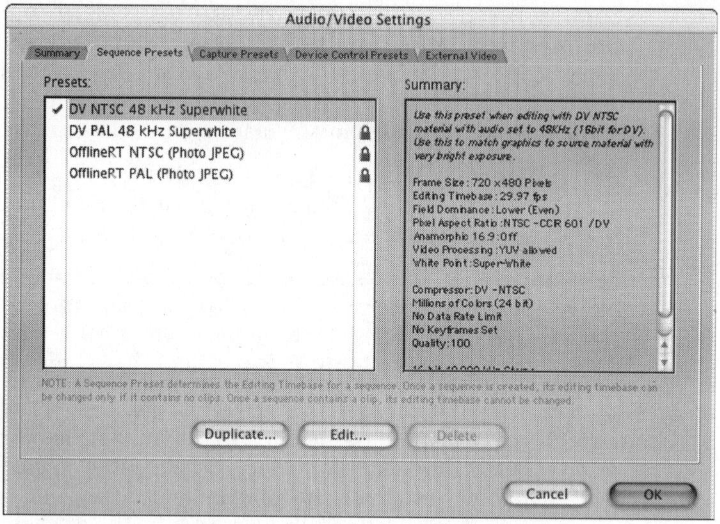

Figure 2-8:
Sequence
presets.

Choosing a different preset

If Final Cut's four Easy Setups don't offer the exact settings you need, you can change one or more of the four presets that Final Cut uses. You can choose from a number of different presets for each of the four families (in addition to any new presets you create yourself, which we show you how to do in the next section).

To choose another existing preset, try this:

1. **Choose Final Cut Pro⇨Audio/Video Settings.**

2. **In the Audio/Video Settings box (shown in Figure 2-9), make sure that the Summary tab is selected.**

   The Summary tab contains four drop-down lists, one for each type of preset (sequence, capture, device control, or external video). Below each drop-down list is explanatory text for that preset.

3. **Click the drop-down arrow for the preset you want to change and choose a preset listed in the desired preset family.**

4. **Click OK to accept the new preset.**

Creating new presets

You can also create new presets with different settings that you customize yourself:

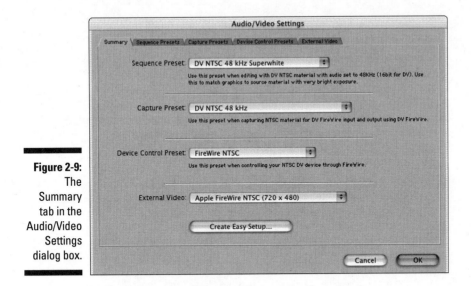

Figure 2-9:
The
Summary
tab in the
Audio/Video
Settings
dialog box.

1. **Choose Final Cut Pro⇨Audio/Video Settings.**

2. **In the Audio/Video Settings box, click the tab for the kind of preset you want to create.**

   In this example, click the Sequence Presets tab.

3. **In that tab's Presets box, click an existing preset you want to base your new preset on.**

   Figure 2-10 shows all the presets on the Sequence tab.

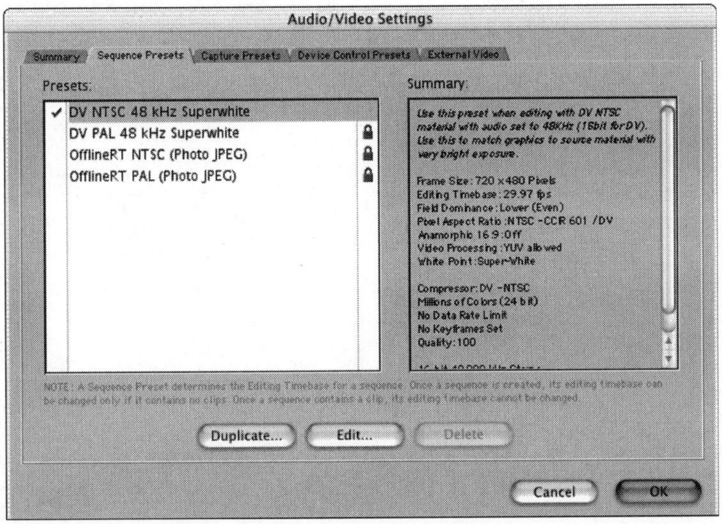

Figure 2-10:
The
Sequence
Presets tab.

When you click an existing preset, Final Cut lists all its settings in the Summary box. This helps you see which preset is most like the preset you're about to create so that you have less tweaking to do.

4. Click the Duplicate button.

Final Cut opens a Preset Editor dialog box, as shown in Figure 2-11.

5. In the Preset Editor dialog box, type a new name for your custom preset, adjust the settings as needed, and then click OK.

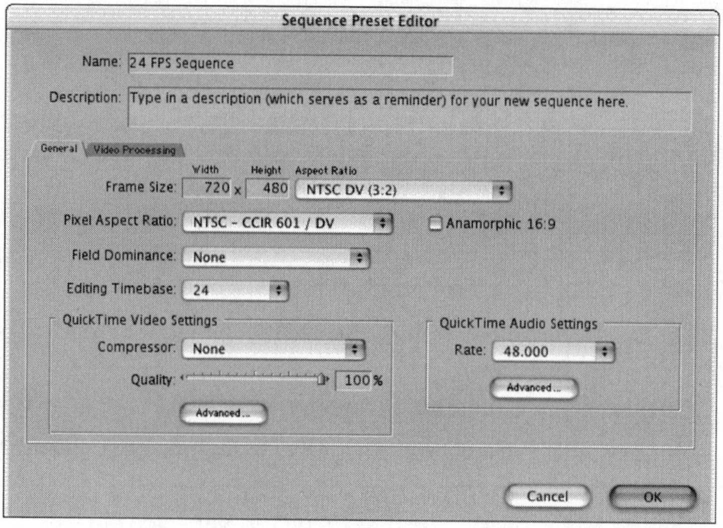

Figure 2-11:
The
Sequence
Presets
Editor.

6. In the tab's Presets box (refer to Figure 2-10), click to the left of your new preset's name to select it.

A check mark appears next to the name. Final Cut doesn't start using the preset until you've identified it as your first pick.

That's it. And if you ever want to modify your new preset again, you can select it in its tab's Presets box (refer to Figure 2-10), and click the Edit button. Or, to delete an unwanted preset, just click the Delete button.

Part II
Importing and Organizing Your Media

The 5th Wave   By Rich Tennant

"Honey—remember that pool party last summer where you showed everyone how to do the limbo in just a sombrero and a dish towel? Well look at what the MSN Daily Video Download is."

In this part . . .

Part II explains how to capture, import, and organize all the media in your Final Cut projects (video, dialogue, music, sound effects, still pictures, and so on). We show you how to capture media from video tape and how to bring media into Final Cut from other sources, such as video or audio files already on your hard drive, songs from a music CD, graphics from Photoshop, and so on.

Finally, we explain how to name, annotate, and organize all these different media clips in Final Cut's Browser window so that you can easily find 'em when you need 'em.

Chapter 3

Capturing Media from Tape

. . . .

. . . .

*B*efore you can launch into creating your long-awaited masterpiece on Final Cut, you first have to bring media into your project. With Final Cut, you can bring media into your projects in many different ways. For example, you can import QuickTime movies from stock CDs or stills that you may have made in programs such as Adobe Photoshop. However, you'll probably bring material into your projects by capturing video that you shot on your DV camera, or via a tape deck that you may have plugged into your Final Cut system, and that's what we focus on in this chapter.

You find out how to capture video from the very first step: connecting the device that you used to shoot your video to your computer. You also explore the wonderful world of timecode (those strings of numbers that tell you where you are in your video). We help you figure out how to log information about your video so that it stays organized, guide you through all the settings you need to worry about, and explain how to use a couple of Final Cut's capturing methods. And after you cover the basics, you may want to tinker with Final Cut's more advanced capturing features, which we cover here as well.

Introducing the Log and Capture Window

Capturing your clips simply means that you take your video that is on the tape and bring it into your computer as digital files. The center of your video-capturing universe is essentially the Log and Capture window in Final Cut. Shown in Figure 3-1, the Log and Capture window is where you interact with your camera or deck (which has your video tape) and capture the material into a Final Cut project so that you can edit it. In effect, you turn the shots on your tape into QuickTime movies, which are stored on your hard drive, and which you can then use in Final Cut.

Out Point timecode

Duration of selected shot   Current timecode

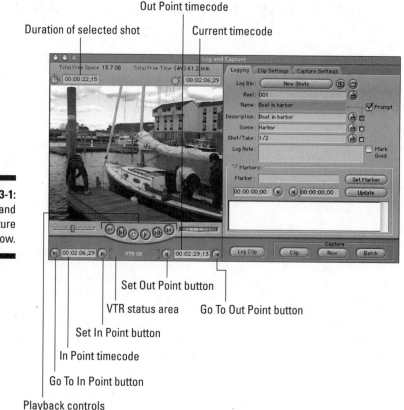

Figure 3-1:
The Log and
Capture
window.

Set Out Point button

VTR status area   Go To Out Point button

Set In Point button

In Point timecode

Go To In Point button

Playback controls

The Log and Capture window packs a lot of activity into a little on-screen box. As you move around the window, you can always see the area on the left, which shows the current frame you're working with. You use the controls and timecodes in this area to move around and see where you are in your video. On the right are three tabs:

✔ **Logging:** This is where you label clips, which can help you stay organized.

✔ **Clip Settings:** This tab contains a couple of important clip-related settings. This is also the tab you use to check your colors.

✔ **Capture Settings:** You can find device and scratch disk settings here.

You use the buttons on the bottom right to tell Final Cut how you want it to log or capture the clip and settings you specified. To find out what you need to do in each part of the Log and Capture window, read on.

Connecting Your Tape Deck or Camera

Before you can capture material from your camera or deck, you must connect it to the computer on which you're running Final Cut. If you're using a DV camera or deck, you can accomplish this by using a FireWire cable. *FireWire,* also sometimes known as IEEE-1394, is a technology that Apple invented and that enables you to move your video and audio from the camera to your computer. Most DV cameras and decks have a built-in FireWire plug, and by connecting your DV device to your computer with a FireWire cable, you can then transfer the video and audio into your drives. A common FireWire cable has a 4-pin connector on one end (for the camera) and a 6-pin connector on the other end (for the computer).

Final Cut allows you to control numerous types of tape decks or cameras with the Log and Capture window. Occasionally, you may have a compatibility issue with a model. We suggest going to Apple's Final Cut site (www.apple. com/finalcutpro) and looking up the list of devices qualified by Apple to work with Final Cut. Make sure that the camera or the deck you're using is listed on that site. Even if the site doesn't list your camera or deck as compatible, you don't have much to worry about. You can still do almost everything you need to, although you may experience glitches here and there.

If you connect a DV camera directly into the computer with the FireWire device, you must make sure that your camera is switched to the VTR setting before you attempt to capture video with Final Cut.

After you plug your camera into the computer using the FireWire cable, you can start Final Cut and choose File⇨Log and Capture.

In the bottom left of the Log and Capture window, check the VTR status area to make sure that you have good communication with your device. If you see the message VTR OK in the VTR status area, all is well, and you're ready to proceed. However, if you see the message No Communication in the status area, you either have a bad connection or the device is turned off. Try to reconnect the device again with the FireWire cable and then turn on the device to see if the message changes to VTR OK.

If you're using some other kind of setup where you have a higher quality deck, such as a Betacam SP type, you need to get a serial port adapter and use a different kind of cable, called an RS-422 cable.

Understanding Timecode

As an editor, timecode is your best friend. By understanding and working with timecode creatively, you can make your life a whole lot easier. *Timecode* is the series of numbers you see that keep changing as your tape plays. It often looks like this: 01:24:24:15 and merrily rolls along with your tape. You see timecode on tape decks and cameras and in many windows of Final Cut. Think of timecode as a ruler for measuring video time, except that the increments are in time, as opposed to distance.

Each frame of video on your tape has a timecode stamp. This timecode identifies the place on the tape where that frame is located. Timecode is measured in hours, minutes, seconds, and frames. Often, colons are used to separate the different fields. So, for example, you may say that your shot of the car leaving the driveway starts at 01:12:15:23 on your tape. What that means is that the shot is located on the tape at 1 hour, 12 minutes, 15 seconds, and 23 frames. Hours are counted in timecode format from 1 to 23, minutes and seconds from 1 to 59, and, because each second of video has 30 frames, the last counter for the frames only counts up to 29.

Sometimes you may see semicolons (;) separating timecode fields. That merely means that the timecode format is in *drop-frame* mode. Colons, on the other hand, indicate *non-drop* mode timecode. All you need to know is that if you're working with DV, you always see the colons for non-drop mode timecode. These two modes of timecode have to do with how the timecode measure *counts* the frames. Many people confuse these with actual frames of video being dropped, but that is a misunderstanding.

When you open the Log and Capture window, you see four timecode fields on the left half of the window. Here are just a few ways to work with these timecodes:

✔ **Locate your shot on tape:** When you work in the Log and Capture window, you can enter the timecode by hand if you know where on the tape your shot is located. (This comes in handy when editors and producers screen their tapes in advance, sometimes even before they get to an editing system. They take notes on where the shots are by noting down the timecode and describing the shots.) During the Log and Capture phase, you can enter these timecodes into the in and out point areas to move your tape to the point where you want to capture a shot. Simply highlight the In Point Timecode field or the Out Point Timecode field (refer to Figure 3-1) and type the numbers using the numeric keypad on your keyboard.

✔ **Go to a particular spot:** The Current Timecode field, which you can find in the top and center of the Log and Capture window, always shows the timecode of the frame that appears in the Log and Capture window. However, by entering a timecode in the Current Timecode field, you tell

Final Cut to go to that newly entered timecode location. In essence, Final Cut will control the deck and move the tape to the requested spot.

✔ **Set a duration:** By first setting an in point and then entering a duration, such as 00:00:05:00, you can tell Final Cut to capture 5 seconds of the shot. Final Cut automatically adjusts the out point per your duration. You type the new duration in the Duration Timecode field, which you can find in the upper-left corner of the Log and Capture window.

Preparing the Settings

Before you attempt to capture video in Final Cut, take a moment to think ahead. Certain settings, if set incorrectly, can have a negative impact on your project down the road. For example, you may find that for certain clips, you captured video only or audio only.

Before you move to Log and Capture in Final Cut, you first have to answer a few questions:

✔ **What do you want to capture?** In some cases, you may want to capture just the video portion of your tape or just the audio. Click the Clip Settings tab in the Log and Capture window (shown in Figure 3-2) and then choose an option from the Capture drop-down menu. You can choose Audio Only, Video Only, or Aud+Vid (audio and video).

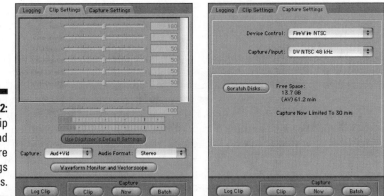

Figure 3-2: The Clip Settings and the Capture Settings tabs.

✔ **How do you want to capture the audio?** Another important setting on the Clip Settings tab is the Audio Format setting. This drop-down list enables you to keep Channel 1 or Channel 2 separate or to link them as a stereo pair. (A *channel* is simply a single track of audio on your tape.) Choose the Channel 1+Channel 2 setting if you want the audio on Channels 1 and 2 to remain separate. You might choose this option if, for example, you have

The magic of timecode

The people who designed Final Cut knew that video editors live, breathe, eat, and drink time-code. Hence, they designed some cool features that enable you to enter and work with time-code, including the following:

✔ **Skip the colons:** You don't need to type the colons between the timecodes. If you want to set the in point to 01:12:24:12, just high-light the In Point Timecode field in the lower-left corner of the Log and Capture window and type **01122412**. Final Cut knows exactly what you're trying to say.

✔ **No need to enter leading zeros:** If you want to go to the timecode 00:00:12:13, you need not enter the leading zeros. Just type **1213**.

✔ **Type a period for every two zeros:** To go to 01:12:00:00, type **0112..** in the In Point Timecode field.

✔ **Copy and Paste timecodes:** Timecode fields understand the Copy and Paste commands. By highlighting a timecode in one field, you can copy it by pressing ⌘+C (or by choos-ing Edit➪Copy) and then paste it in another highlighted field by pressing ⌘+V (or by choosing Edit➪Paste).

✔ **Move a timecode to another field:** You move any timecode from one field to another by holding down the Option key and then click-ing and dragging the timecode to the field where you want it to be (also know as Option+drag). For example, you can Option+ drag a timecode from the Browser window to the In Point Timecode field or the Out Point Timecode field in the Log and Capture window.

two separate microphones, one recording the speaker on Channel 1 and one recording the interviewer on Channel 2. Choose the Stereo setting if you have the same sound on both channels. This is the setting you'll probably use the most.

✔ **Where do you want to save the material?** If you have a few drives con-nected to your computer, you need to tell Final Cut where to store the media that it captures. Generally you save video to the fastest drive you have, which is hopefully not the main drive where the System Folder resides. (Apple encourages users not to use their main System Drive for media capture because it can interfere with System performance and slow down your work.) In the Log and Capture window, click the Capture Settings tab, and then click the Scratch Disks button. The Scratch Disks preferences panel appears, and you can assign a drive for capture by pressing the Set button and choosing a drive.

✔ **What capture settings do you want to use?** Under the Capture Settings tab (refer to Figure 3-2) in the Log and Capture window, you have two more settings that you need to check: the Device Control and the Capture/Input settings. If you're using a FireWire connection, be sure to set the Device Control setting to a FireWire NTSC setting. Make sure that a proper DV capture setting is selected in the Capture/Input drop-down list. These settings need to be FireWire NTSC, if you're working in the

United States, where the television system is NTSC. European TV uses the PAL version of DV.

For more information about setting Scratch Disks, Device Control, and Capture/Input settings, see Chapter 2.

Before logging and capturing material from your tape, you need to check another series of settings. Choose Final Cut Pro⇨Preferences, and on the General tab, check the following two settings:

✔ **Abort capture on dropped frames:** This is one setting you always want on. If Final Cut senses dropped frames during capture, it stops capturing the clip and gives you a warning. *Dropped frames* during capture are frames that Final Cut has simply missed. These missing frames manifest themselves as a stutter during playback, and you can fix them only by recapturing the clip (and by not dropping frames on the recapture, of course).

✔ **Abort capture on timecode breaks:** This setting ensures that Final Cut stops capture if it detects a timecode break on your tape. *Timecode breaks* are places on your tape where, for one reason or another, the timecode is inconsistent. Timecode breaks may have occurred because you stopped your camera in between shots and started up again or because the camera resets the timecode. Timecode breaks are undesirable if you plan to recapture your material at a later date because these breaks confuse Final Cut about the real timecode on tape once a break has occurred.

Figure 3-3 shows both these settings in the General tab of the Preferences window.

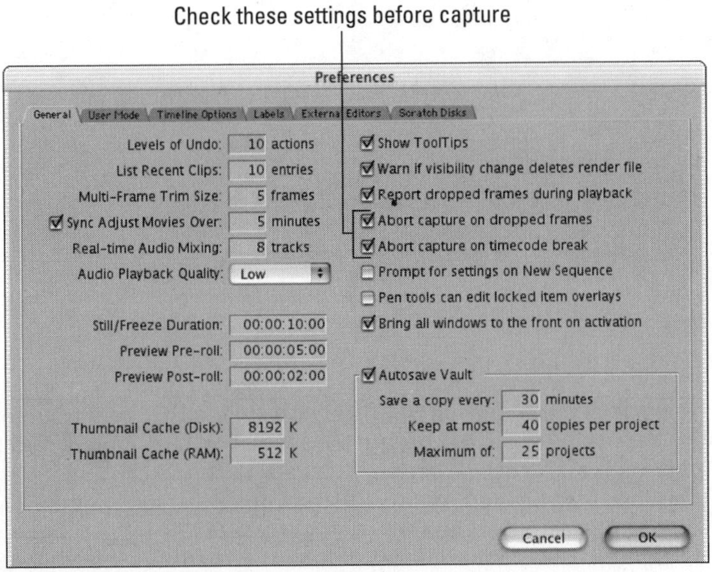

Check these settings before capture

Figure 3-3: Checking these settings aborts capture if something goes wrong.

Logging

Logging is a common practice among video editors. The process basically involves noting down the shots (or *clips* as they're called in Final Cut) and their locations (in timecodes) on the tape. Logging is helpful because it gives you a change to review and organize what you have and figure out what shots you might still need to get.

The term *logging* is from the old days of linear video editing. It was common among editors and producers to screen their videotapes before they edited them and to make note of the shots they liked. Logging was essentially a process of noting these shots and their timecode locations on a tape. In the days of digital editing, however, logging has come to mean a whole lot more.

In Final Cut, the act of logging entails using the Log and Capture window. As you scroll through your tape, you use in and out points to mark the beginning and ending timecodes for each clip, and you use the Logging tab to record information about the clip. (You can also set a number of settings on the other tabs, which we discuss later in this chapter.) When you're done tinkering with your clip, you save it. Note that you don't *capture* the clip yet; just save it in the Browser, where this *logged* but uncaptured clip appears with a red slash across it, as shown in Figure 3-4. The uncaptured clips and the information in the Browser about them serve as your log, much like the ones written by hand before the days of computer-based editing. Later, you can select this logged shot and tell Final Cut to capture it for you.

A logged or "offline" clip has a slash through it

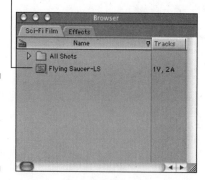

Figure 3-4:
You can later capture this logged clip.

You may be scratching your head in confusion at this point, but logging clips in this manner, without capturing, has many benefits. It allows you to screen all your reels and make selections without having to capture. Later, after you're done logging, you can decide to capture just a few of the logged reels or clips as a *batch*. (See the section "Capturing Clips by the Batch" later in this chapter.) The other shots are there for you to capture when you like.

You aren't required to log before you capture. After you log each shot, you can capture it in Final Cut. We recommend first carefully logging tapes and then capturing them later. Many editors scoff at this approach because it seems time-consuming to them, but we argue that this method saves time and energy later in the edit. If you log first, you tend to be a lot more careful about the amounts of material you capture. Editors who capture on the fly often capture a whole lot more than they need. And even at the comparatively lean data rates of DV video, you need 1 GB of hard drive space for every four and a half minutes of video.

Logging a clip

After you insert a tape into your deck or camera and connect your computer to the deck or the camera by using the FireWire cable (which we discuss in the earlier section "Connecting Your Tape Deck or Camera"), you can start logging. Before you log a clip, read the earlier section "Preparing your settings." To log clips using the Log and Capture window, follow these steps:

1. **Press ⌘+8 (or choose File⇨Log and Capture) to open the Log and Capture window.**

2. **Use the J, K, and L keys to locate your shot.**

   You can use the shuttle or the jog wheel to move around on your tape. (The shuttle control is the slider at the lower left of the window and the jog wheel is the wheel located at the bottom right of the window.) However, we find it easier to use the J, K, and L keys. Pressing the J key moves the tape backward, K pauses it, and L moves it forward. You can also press the J or the L key repeatedly to increase the speed of the forward or the backward motion. This may seem awkward at first, but you'll soon get used to it. You can see where you are on the reel by watching the preview pane on the left side of the Log and Capture window. When you pause, you can see exactly which frame you're at.

3. **When you find the beginning of your clip, press I to mark an in point.**

   The timecode for the first frame appears in the In Point Timecode field.

4. **Move through your video to find the end of your clip and then press O to mark an out point.**

   The timecode for the last frame appears in the Out Point Timecode field.

5. **On the Logging tab, enter the reel name in the Reel field.**

   Reel names are nothing more than the tape names you may have created for your videotapes. For example, "Birthday#1" and "Birthday#2" are names you would enter if these names were used on the tapes you shot for someone's birthday.

Make sure you change the reel name each time you put in a new tape. See "Managing Your Clips" later in this chapter for the details.

6. **Fill in the remaining fields to describe what happens in the clip.**

When you first name a clip, Final Cut's behavior may baffle you. If you've checked the Description, Scene, and Shot/Take boxes, Final Cut automatically makes up a name for the clip by combining the text you've entered in those three fields. If this isn't what you want, uncheck those boxes and make sure that the Prompt box next to the Name field is checked. You can then use the Name box to name your clip whatever you like.

We strongly suggest developing a naming system to keep your clips organized. We discuss this in the section "Managing Your Clips," later in this chapter.

7. **Click the Log Clip button to log the clip.**

The logged clip appears in your Browser with a red slash across it. The red line indicates that you haven't captured the clip nor saved it to your scratch disk. A small dialog box appears, asking you to name your clip.

8. **Enter a name for your clip and click OK.**

You will only need to do this if you had not checked the Description or Take boxes in the Logging tab. Otherwise, Final Cut will combine the Description and Take fields to create the name for your clip.

9. **If you have more clips to log, do so by repeating Steps 2 through 8.**
   When you're finished logging, close the Log and Capture window by clicking the small close box in the upper-left corner of the window.

As we discuss in the sidebar "The magic of timecode," you can Option+drag timecodes from one field to another. Here you can put that feature to great use. If you want to locate the spot on tape for a logged clip, Option+drag the in or the out timecode of the logged clip from the Browser to the Current Timecode field in the Log and Capture window. (Refer to Figure 3-1 if you're not sure where the field is.) Final Cut automatically cues the tape to the timecode of your choice.

Setting a Logging bin

If you just begin logging clips with no advance preparation, the logged clips by default end up in the Browser. However, if you create and select a Logging bin in Final Cut's Browser before you begin logging, Final Cut sends all logged clips to that bin. (A *bin* in Final Cut can be thought of as the same as the folders that your Mac uses to organize files.) This is handy if you have a lot of tapes to log and want each tape's logged shots to go into the bin for that reel.

Here are the steps to create a Logging bin:

1. **Create a bin that you want to assign as a Logging bin by pressing ⌘+B (or choose File⇨New⇨Bin).**

   The name of the bin is highlighted. You can rename this bin to your liking. More often than not, editors tend to name their bins by the tape names. For example, a Bin labeled "Picnic Tape#1" indicates that all shots from tape#1 are in that Bin. Others name their Bins by scene number or names of actors or subjects in the shot.

2. **Select the Bin and choose File⇨Set Logging Bin.**

   You can also Control+click the bin in the Browser and choose Set Logging Bin from the contextual menu that appears. A small slate icon appears next to the bin, as shown in Figure 3-5. The icon indicates that the bin is set as a Logging bin. All new logged or captured shots now go into this bin.

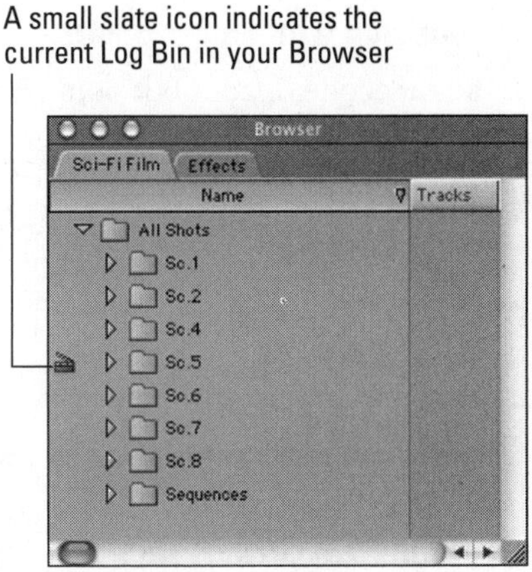

A small slate icon indicates the
current Log Bin in your Browser

Figure 3-5:
A Logging
bin.

Capturing Your First Clip

In the next series of steps, we show you how to log and capture at the same time. You find out how to quickly move around on your tape, log a shot, and capture it. To log and capture a shot from your tape, follow these steps:

1. **Press ⌘+8 (or choose File⇨Log and Capture) to open the Log and Capture window.**

2. **In the VTR status area under the playback controls, make sure that you see** VTR OK.

   If not, check your connections and make sure that your camera or deck is on and that your camera, if you're using one, is set to the VTR setting.

3. **Locate the first frame of the video you want to capture by using the J, K, and L keys.**

   Although we prefer the J-K-L method, you can also use the playback controls at the bottom of the Log and Capture window to move around on your tape and locate the shot that you want to capture. If you're not sure how the J-K-L method works, see Step 2 in the section "Logging a clip," earlier in this chapter.

4. **Press I to mark the beginning of your shot with an in point.**

   After you set the in point, the timecode of your in point appears in the In Point Timecode field, located in the bottom left of the Log and Capture window. When you're ready to capture, Final Cut begins the capture of your shot from this point.

5. **Press O to mark the end of your shot with an out point.**

   After you set the out point, the timecode of your out point appears in the Out Point Timecode field, located on the bottom right of the Log and Capture window. When you're ready to capture, Final Cut ends the capture of your shot at this point.

   At this stage, you can see the duration of your selected shot in the Duration Timecode field, located in the upper-left corner of the Log and Capture window.

6. **On the Logging tab, enter a reel and a name for your clip.**

   For details about filling in these fields, refer to the steps in the section "Logging a clip," earlier in this chapter.

7. **In the Capture area in the bottom-right corner, click the Clip button to capture your clip.**

   Final Cut cues your camera or deck to the in point and captures the clip you just selected on your tape. The clip then appears in your Browser. Be aware that this captured clip's media is also stored as a QuickTime media file on the drive you selected as your scratch disk. (See Chapter 2 for more about scratch disks.)

There you go. That's all there is to capturing media from your tape.

Capturing Clips by the Batch

Batch capturing is the process of capturing a bunch of clips in an automated fashion. If you have a lot of clips to capture, batch capturing is a real time-saver. To perform a batch capture, you must have first logged a few clips. So, in effect, the process consists of first logging a clip, which we explain how to do earlier in this chapter. After you have logged enough clips, follow these steps to do a batch capture:

1. **Select the clips that you want to capture.**

2. **Press Control+C (or choose File⇨Batch Capture).**

    Final Cut opens the Batch Capture dialog box (Figure 3-6), which has a few settings you need to review:

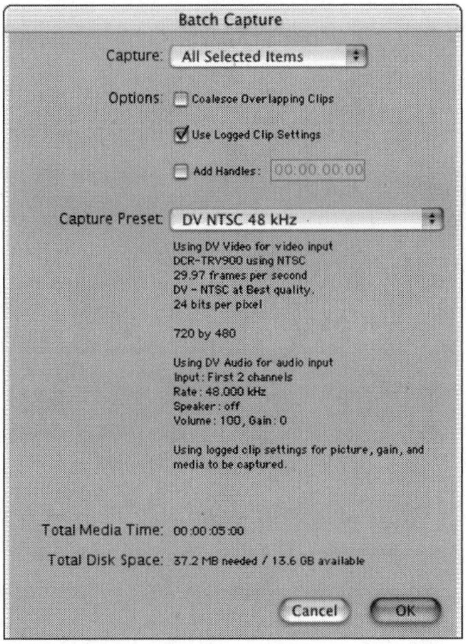

Figure 3-6: Batch Capture enables you to capture several clips at once.

- **Capture:** Make sure All Selected Items is chosen.

- **Coalesce Overlapping clips:** Leaving this option unchecked is best. Checking this option causes Final Cut to capture overlapping clips on tape as one piece of media.

- **Use Logged Clip Settings:** Check this setting if you want to capture clips with the settings they were logged in (under the Clip Settings tab). For example, if you selected Audio Only or Video Only when logging the clip, that's what is captured during the Batch process. Otherwise, Final Cut captures the tracks based on what's currently selected in the Clip Settings window. If you forget what these logged settings are, check the appropriate column in the Browser. For example, under the Tracks heading of the Browser window columns, you can note what tracks (Audio, Video, or Aud+Vid) are selected for the logged clip.

- **Add Handles:** Using this setting you can add some extra media beyond your in and out points. You may want that if your logging was *tight*, or closer to the sound bites or shots than you may have wanted.

3. **Click OK in the Batch Capture dialog box.**

   The Reel dialog box appears.

4. **Insert the reel from which you want to batch capture into your DV camera.**

5. **Click OK to continue the process.**

   Final Cut captures the clips that you selected in your Browser.

You have successfully batch captured your clips.

Managing Your Clips

Let's face it: Clips multiply like rabbits. Before you know it, you have more clips in your Browser window than you'll ever know what to do with. Organizing and managing your clips is more than just a cosmetic issue. A lack of organization can seriously hamper your work and result in serious problems. You may lose clips, confuse the links to the media, and have trouble relinking if your clips have too many similar names or lay about in an unorganized fashion. We cover this more in Chapter 5, but here are a few tips to remember:

- **Make sure that you have correct reel numbers for all clips:** When logging and capturing your shots, be sure to change the reel names every time you put in a new tape to capture shots from. This is important if you ever need to recapture or trace your shot back to a reel or need to export information from Final Cut so that you can use the information on another editing system.

- **Develop a naming scheme:** The name of the clip is the first item that appears in your Browser, and it is one you will refer to most often. Take some time to develop a naming scheme that makes sense. For example, over the years, Zed has developed a shorthand for naming clips. He uses names and also two letter shot descriptions, such as Erica-CU for Erica's close up, Bob-MS for Bob's medium shot, and House-LS for a long shot of the house. When he names his clips, he also considers the fact that Final Cut organizes the clips alphabetically by name. By naming shots of similar items with the same word, such as "Bob exits-MS" and "Bob walks away-LS," he makes sure that Final Cut groups all the clips that have Bob together.

TIP

You should devote some time to thinking about your clips because you will usually use the name of the clip to organize your project. Also bear in mind that your media files on the disk also use the same name as the clips, so your naming scheme has implications in the Browser and on the disk.

✔ **Keep names short:** Be sure to keep your clip names under 25 characters. This is important if you are going to be exporting Edit Decision Lists (EDLs). EDLs are lists of numbers you can export from Final Cut that allow other editing systems to recapture and recreate your edited movie. Names that are longer than 25 characters get shortened and edited by Final Cut in the EDL export process and are hard to read as a result.

✔ **Keep clip names significantly different:** This allows for ease of recapture because, in many locations in Final Cut, you only see the first few words of the shot name. If your shot names all have the same four or five words at the beginning, you would have trouble distinguishing between them to find the shot you want to recapture.

Let Final Cut Find Scenes for You

Final Cut has a feature that can save you loads of time from the burdens of logging and capturing: DV Start/Stop Detection. This feature detects the start and stop locations on your DV tape and marks them for easy navigation and organization.

To take advantage of the DV Start/Stop Detection feature, follow these steps:

1. **Capture the entire length of your tape (if you aren't sure how, see the earlier section "Capturing Your First Clip").**

   For example, if you have a half-hour tape, go ahead and capture it all in one go. (Just make sure that you have enough disk space for it; each 4.5 minutes of DV video takes up 1GB of disk space.)

2. **After the clip appears in your Browser, select it and choose Tools⇨ DV Start/Stop Detection.**

   Final Cut scans the clip and marks all locations where the Record/Pause button was pressed on your camera during the shooting. Small markers appear wherever you paused your camera, as shown in Figure 3-7.

You can even go further and create subclips from these markers. *Subclips* are pieces of a long clip that has been divided into smaller clips; here's how:

1. **In the Browser, drag with the mouse pointer to create a rectangle around the markers for the clip to select them.**

Select the markers and create
subclips for your scenes

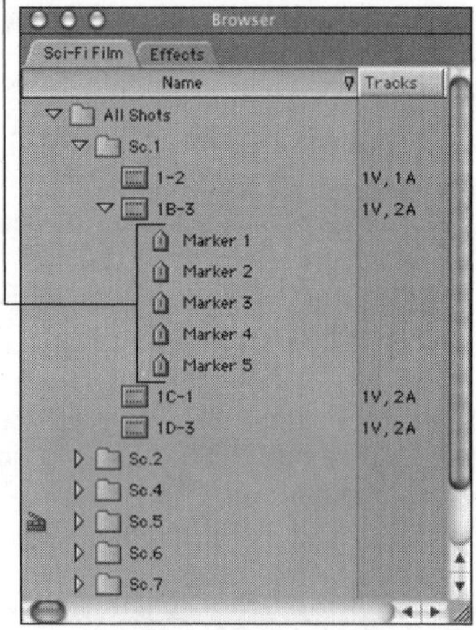

Figure 3-7:
The markers
indicate the
points when
you paused
your
camera.

2. **Choose Modify⇨Make Subclip.**

All the material between the markers appears as subclips, whose icons
look just like the clip icons in the Browser, except they have jagged
edges (as if they were ripped from a longer clip).

At this point, you may want to go ahead and rename some of your subclips to
better reflect what each of these subclips contains. You can use these subclips just like any other clip in Final Cut.

Working with Edit Decision Lists

Edit Decision Lists (EDLs) are an old and reliable method of exchanging information about edited sequences between various, otherwise incompatible,
editing systems. After you edit a program in the Timeline, also known as a
sequence in Final Cut, you can select it and export an EDL from it. This EDL
contains information in ASCII text format and enables you to re-create your
edited sequence on another edit system, such as an Avid, Media 100, or even
a online tape-to-tape system. Of course, this sequence could consist of a few
clips edited together in the timeline or an entire long-form edited show.

EDLs are nothing more than a series of numbers in a text file, but they're
powerful. With EDLs, you can do your rough cut at home on a basic Final Cut

system, export the EDL, and then enter an expensive and high-end editing environment to do the final re-creation and refining of your project.

Here's how to export an EDL from a Final Cut sequence:

1. **In the Browser, select the Sequence for which you want to export an EDL.**

2. **Choose File⇨Export⇨EDL.**

   The EDL Export Options dialog box appears. It may seem intimidating at first, but fear not: We're here to explain everything.

3. **Make the choices in the EDL Export Options dialog box, as shown in Figure 3-8.**

   "Yeah, right," you say. "Just make the choices." We explain what all the junk in this box means in the next section.

4. **Click OK.**

   A Save Dialog box appears.

5. **Give your EDL a name and save it where you like.**

   This EDL can now be transported to another edit system on a floppy (EDLs are tiny enough to fit on a floppy disk) or other removable media.

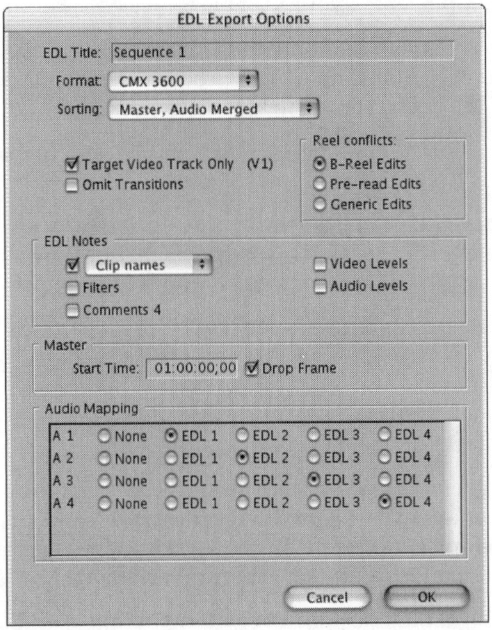

Figure 3-8:
The EDL
Export
Options
dialog box.

What is all that junk in the EDL Export Options box?

Remember that EDLs are just a text-based file. This text file contains all the information that an edit system, such as an Avid, needs to read this information and re-create a timeline of your sequence as it existed in Final Cut.

EDLs contain information about the start and end point for each clip in the sequence, the reel that the shot is from, and the track information that includes which video and audio tracks are being used and how.

Then one by one, you can recapture each shot as specified by the EDL on the new edit system. The beauty of this system is that all you need is the EDL and the proper reels or tapes from which your original material was captured to re-create the edited version.

When you first bring up the EDL Options Dialog box, you may be struck by all the settings available to you. Fortunately, they're not as scary as they look.

Here's a simplified explanation of the settings:

- **EDL Title:** Give your EDL a title. Just in case you're moving to a platform that doesn't allow spaces in filenames, use underscores in place of spaces. So for example, name your EDL file `My_First_Sequence.edl`.

- **Format:** The most common and universal format is the CMX 3600 type. Other formats, such as Sony and GVG types, are also available to you, but go with the CMX 3600 type to be safe.

- **Sorting:** Select Master, Audio Merged. This enables you to export the clips to the EDL as they appear in the sequence.

- **Target Video Track Only (V1):** Selecting this option ignores all video tracks except the main V1 track. This is the best choice because EDLs do not translate any key or superimposed tracks anyway.

- **Omit Transitions:** Selecting this choice makes your EDL cuts only, meaning that any fancy transitions or effects will not be included. You can create your transitions in the edit system that you'll use to make the final movie. The idea here is to keep your EDL as simple as possible and to perform any effects or transitions in the final edit.

- **Reel Conflicts:** Select Generic Edits if you're going to another digital editing system, such as an Avid or a Media 100. Select B-Reel Edits if you're going to a tape-to-tape edit system. In the latter case, you get a B-Reel EDL if you have transitions that occur between shots on the same reel.

- **EDL Notes:** We suggest unchecking everything here except Clip names in the drop-down menu. Checking the boxes for Filters, Comments, Video Levels, and Audio Levels may just create a messier EDL that won't translate properly.

✔ **Master:** Here you can determine whether you want a start time different from 1:00:00:00 in your EDL. Use this if the sequence you want to edit is located in the middle of a preexisting tape. In that case, find out the start timecode on the tape where the fix occurs and enter it here.

✔ **Audio Mapping:** In this box, select how the tracks in your sequence will be mapped to the tracks of your final master tape. Unless you have specific needs or an understanding of the final requirements, leave the tracks mapped as they appear.

That's all there is to EDL settings. If you want, you can edit your rough cuts in Final Cut and then export your EDL to any other system that imports EDLs. In that system, you can create your final program.

Keeping clean EDLs

Much like an apartment or a closet, keeping your EDL clean is important. However, put away any dusters that you may have whipped out. Keeping a clean EDL is a different kind of a process. By following the tips we provide in this section, you can keep a clean EDL and thus avoid headaches and a whole lot of trouble.

Here's what you need to do:

✔ **Keep clip names short:** If you're capturing material for a project and know that you're going to be exporting an EDL, keep your reel names and clip names as short as possible. EDLs limit how long a reel or a clip name can be. Limit reel names to 4 characters and clip names to 25 characters.

✔ **Limit a sequence to two video and four audio tracks:** Final Cut allows you to use 99 audio and video tracks in a sequence. However, EDLs can handle only two video and four audio tracks. Make sure that you don't have more tracks than that in your sequence.

✔ **Avoid fancy transitions and effects:** EDLs can't handle complicated effects, layering, and transitions. Only basic transitions, such as dissolves or wipes, are allowed.

Chapter 4

Importing Media Already on Your Mac

Chances are, plenty of the media you'll use in Final Cut won't have to be captured from videotape. (Capturing media from videotape means to turn it into a QuickTime file on your hard drive.) You probably already have the media in a digital form on your hard drive — for instance, an AIFF file of sound effects, an MP3 song from your favorite album, still pictures from a digital camera, or a video clip already digitized into the QuickTime format. And if the media's already on your Mac, you can bring it into Final Cut — that is, import it — with little trouble. That's what this chapter is all about: We tackle the various ways you can import media into Final Cut, and also look at some high-powered tools that help convert media from one digital format to another so that it works best with Final Cut.

And remember, the media you import into Final Cut is still completely safe. No matter how you edit your media going forward, the original media files on your hard drive aren't modified or deleted.

Your Media Is Welcome Here

What kind of media can you use with Final Cut? The good news is plenty, though we point out a couple of notable exceptions to avoid any unpleasant surprises.

For video, you can import any video files in the QuickTime file format. Because you're using a Mac, any digital video files you have on hand are probably in QuickTime anyway: It's the preferred "homegrown" format for multimedia on the Mac.

On the flip side, Final Cut doesn't work with video in other file formats, such as RealVideo or Microsoft Windows Media Format — both of which are popular on PC machines. If you have a video file in these formats (maybe you downloaded it from the Internet), you can find a small utility program to export the video's individual frames as Targa images, and then reimport those images into QuickTime.

For importing still pictures, Final Cut isn't very discerning (thankfully). You can import pictures in just about every file format known to Macs and PCs. In Table 4-1, you can see a list of some of the popular file formats that you can use in Final Cut.

Table 4-1	Popular File Formats for Still Pictures
File Format	*Description*
JPEG	A common format for photos
TIFF	Another photo favorite
TGA	Known as Targa, a biggie on the PC
SGI	Images created on SGI workstations
PNTG	The MacPaint file format
PICT	Another Macintosh format for graphics
PNG	Yet another format found mostly on the PC
QTIF	Pictures saved as QuickTime Image Files
BMP	Another popular Windows format
PSD	The format for Photoshop files

For sound and music, Final Cut welcomes all major formats: AIFF, WAV, and any other audio format that the QuickTime architecture supports. (QuickTime carries not just video but audio too.) These formats are popular on both the Mac and PC, so you can work with just about any audio you dig up.

The only sound format that Final Cut doesn't work with (well, at least) is MP3, which is a favorite in the music world because it compresses music into small files so that they can be easily stored and traded. Although you normally don't lose much sound quality with MP3 files, an MP3 file imported into Final Cut unfortunately plays with a lot of weird distortion that your audience isn't likely to appreciate (unless you want to call it "modern art," in which case you'll be hailed as a deep, brooding genius — maybe not so bad). Anyway, all is not lost. You can solve the MP3 problem with some easy steps, which we talk about later in this chapter, in the section "Convert another audio file format to AIFF with QuickTime Pro."

The rendering game

Although Final Cut can import any video or audio that's in the QuickTime format, you may have to render those clips before playing them on your timeline. Don't panic: *Rendering* isn't the end of the world — it's just a process where Final Cut takes a few moments ahead of time and converts your media to a format that it can play smoothly, in real-time. (Admittedly, it's a hassle if you have a lot of media to render.)

Final Cut makes it very clear when your media has to be rendered: When you play it on your timeline, you'll hear beeps for audio that needs to be rendered, and the Canvas window shows a title card that says "Unrendered" for any video clips (the timeline also draws a thin red horizontal bar over any clips needing rendering). But what determines why some media has to be rendered and some doesn't?

For audio clips, it's straightforward: Any audio that's been compressed (for instance, an AIFF file that's been compressed with the IMA or MACE compressor) needs to be rendered. As for video clips and still images, it all depends on the settings you've established for the Final Cut sequence you're playing your clips in. As we mention in Chapter 2, each sequence you create in Final Cut has its own settings. One of those settings tells Final Cut what kind of compression

codec your QuickTime video uses — for instance, DV, Sorenson, Animation, or even no compression are a few of your options. Any clips that use that sequence's compression codec won't have to be rendered, but any clips that don't use the same codec *will* have to the rendered. For instance, if your sequence is set to work with DV video (which is a likely scenario), you can play video clips that use DV compression without rendering them, but if you import a clip that's not in the DV format — for instance, a QuickTime movie trailer saved using Sorenson compression, or a title card you created in Photoshop — they need to be rendered. On the other hand, perhaps you're using Final Cut to assemble a slide show of still photos, in which case you probably set your sequence to work with TIFF images so that none of your photos need to be rendered. That would be a wise move, but if you tried to add a DV video clip then that would need rendering.

See Chapter 18 for more about codecs, Chapter 16 for how to render media, and the section "Converting Media Formats with QuickTime Pro" (later in this chapter) for some tips on converting media to formats that don't need any rendering at all.

Importing Your Media into Final Cut

Okay, so you've got digital media on your hard drive, and you're ready to import it into Final Cut's Browser window (you've got some editing to do, after all). You have a few options. You can import a single file (good for bringing in a random file or two after you're already in the thick of editing), or you can bring in an entire folder of files, which is the best way to get things rolling when you're working with a lot of media. You can also import those files and folders either by using a plain old vanilla dialog box in Final Cut, or by dragging files and folders from your Mac's desktop directly into Final Cut's Browser if that's easier for you.

Whatever your tactic, your end goal is the same: getting those media files into Final Cut's Browser window (Figure 4-1), which acts as the central repository for all the media in your project. When you bring a media file into the Browser, it becomes a *clip,* and it's from the Browser that you can watch or listen to your clip, make a variety of adjustments to it, and ultimately move it to the Timeline for editing. You know that your files have been imported successfully because a little clip icon appears in the Browser window, with your media's file name next to it. (Check out Chapter 5 for a full run down on the Browser.)

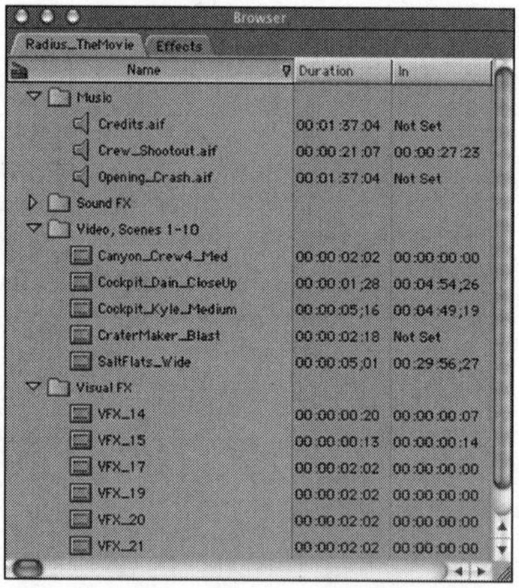

Figure 4-1:
Before you
can begin
working
with your
clips, you
must import
them
into the
Browser.

Before going on, create or open a Final Cut project (see Chapter 2), and make sure that the Browser window is visible. If you don't see the Browser, you can turn it on by choosing Window➪Browser from the menu bar, or toggle it on and off by pressing ⌘+4 as a shortcut.

Sometimes you'll want to import media that's on a CD-ROM, a DVD-RAM (which is like a super-charged CD), a puny ol' little Zip disk, or even another computer connected through a network. If this is the case, first copy that media to your Mac's own hard drive (internal or external will do) and then *import* it from the hard drive. Otherwise, you could run into two major problems:

✔ Final Cut doesn't perform well when it's working with media on slow disks or networks. Nothing compares to the speed of a hard drive.

✔ One day, you'll try to load up your Final Cut project, but you won't have the CD or other disk that your media is on. The result? A bunch of empty, glaring gaps in your project.

Better keep your media conveniently stored on your Mac's hard drive.

The following steps all apply to importing media by using Final Cut running on the Mac's new operating system, OS X. If you're using Final Cut under good ol' OS 9, you'll find that the interfaces are different — but not *that* different. (Menu names are the same, but dialog boxes have different options and look different.) If you're using the older operating system, we're confident you'll have no problem translating these steps into OS-9-ese.

Importing one file or more at a time

To import a single file or collection of files, try this:

1. **Make the Browser window active by selecting it.**

   If you have another window selected, Final Cut may not let you import files.

2. **To import your files directly to an existing bin in the Browser window, double-click that bin so that it opens in a new window.**

   Remember, a bin is Final Cut's version of a folder. If a Bin window isn't open and active, Final Cut imports your files into the Browser's top level.

3. **Choose File⇨Import⇨Files from the menu bar.**

   Or get used to pressing ⌘+I as a quick shortcut.

   This opens the Choose a File dialog box, shown in Figure 4-2.

4. **Use the Choose a File dialog box to navigate through your hard drive's folders, until you see the media file you want.**

   The dialog box is divided into columns: When you click a drive or folder name in the left column, the column to its right shows the drive's or folder's contents. Just keep clicking folders until you see the file you're looking for. If you accidentally choose the wrong folder, move the scroll bar back a bit until you see the previous levels of folders.

You can speed up your file search by telling Final Cut to show you only movies, sound clips, or still pictures. Just choose your preference from the Show drop-down list at the bottom of the dialog box.

5. **Click the media file(s) you want and then click the Choose button to add the media to the Browser window.**

To select a continuous range of files for importing, click the first and the last files of the range while holding down the Shift key (this is called Shift-clicking). Or, you can select multiple files, regardless of their order in the file box, by holding the ⌘ key while clicking them.

Either way, Final Cut adds your media files as new clips in the Browser window (refer to Figure 4-1), where you can now play with them to your heart's content. (If you can't see the Browser, choose Window⇨Browser from the menu bar, or press ⌘+4 to bring it up).

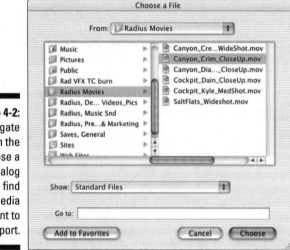

Figure 4-2:
Navigate through the Choose a File dialog box to find the media you want to import.

If you often import files from the same folder, you can make that folder a Favorite by highlighting its name in the Choose a File dialog box, and then clicking the Add to Favorites button. From now on, you can choose that folder quickly by opening the From drop-down list and looking for your folder's name under Favorite Places. No more navigating all the way through your hard drive.

Importing a folder full of files (or other folders)

If you want to import a lot of media files into Final Cut at once, go to your Mac's desktop, drag all your files in a single folder, and follow these simple steps:

1. **Make sure the Browser window is active.**

2. **Choose File⇨Import⇨Folder.**

   The Choose a Folder dialog box appears, as shown in Figure 4-3.

3. **Select the folder you want to import and click the Choose button.**

   Final Cut now adds your folder to the Browser, making it a bin. If the folder you imported contained other folders inside, you'll see that those folders have become bins within the master bin.

   Navigating this dialog box is just like navigating the Choose a File dialog box. Refer to the previous section ("Importing one file or more at a time") if you aren't sure how to navigate this dialog box.

Figure 4-3:
Importing the Scene 54 folder moves all the files and folders inside it to the Browser.

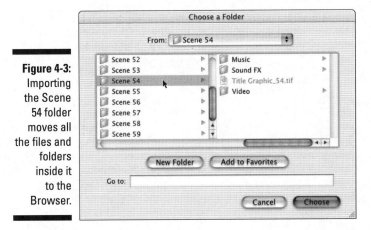

TIP

Importing whole folders instead of individual files not only saves you time, but also has a nice side effect: It encourages you to keep your media files organized into folders that make sense. For instance, maybe you keep all your video clips in a Video folder and your music in its own folder as well. The point is, you work a lot faster if you corral your media into folders, instead of leaving random files strewn all over the place.

Importing files by dragging them from the Finder

A quick way to import media files and folders is by dragging their icons directly from your Mac's Finder to Final Cut's Browser window. But why do this, when you can just use the Import File or Import Folder option within Final Cut? Because you may instinctively know how to find a file quicker by navigating to it via the Mac's Finder, rather than by using Final Cut's dialog boxes. Follow these steps to import files via the Finder:

1. **From Final Cut, click the Finder icon in the OS X Dock (Figure 4-4).**

   The Finder will become active, but if you don't have any open windows in the Finder (which will pop up automatically), the change might not be obvious because you'll continue to see Final Cut's windows visible in the background.

2. **In the Finder, find the files or folders you want to import into Final Cut.**

   If you don't currently have a Finder window open, choose New Finder Window from the File menu. Then use the window to navigate to your files or folders.

3. **Click and drag the files from the Finder window to Final Cut's Browser window.**

   You may have to move the Finder window so that it doesn't cover up Final Cut's Browser. When you drag your files to the Browser, they become clips. When you drag a folder, it becomes a bin, with the files/clips inside.

Figure 4-4:
The Finder icon and the Final Cut icon on the Dock.

Importing music tracks directly from a CD

Final Cut can also import music tracks from all your audio CDs. To import CD tracks, you must first copy the CD's tracks to your hard drive, and then import the tracks into Final Cut as you would any media file. Follow these easy steps:

1. **Place a CD in your Mac's CD-ROM drive.**

2. **From the Mac's Finder, open the CD by double-clicking its icon, so you can see its contents (as shown in Figure 4-5).**

   You can go to the Finder by clicking its icon in OS X's Dock (refer to Figure 4-4).

3. **Copy the CD track(s) you want to import to your hard drive.**

   The Finder lists the CD's tracks as files. Just click and drag the files you want to your hard drive (or preferably a folder inside your hard drive, but you can also copy the files to your desktop if that's easier). While in the Finder, you may want to give your copied tracks more descriptive names now, but you can also do this from Final Cut.

4. **Go back to Final Cut, and import the track(s) as you normally would.**

   You can jump back to Final Cut by clicking its icon in the Dock. When you import a track file, you'll see it listed in the Browser window as an audio clip.

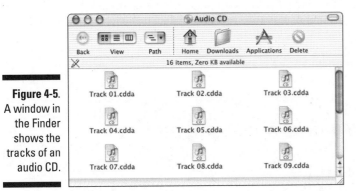

Figure 4-5. A window in the Finder shows the tracks of an audio CD.

Importing Photoshop files (layers and all)

You already know that you can import all sorts of still picture formats into Final Cut, but if you've created graphics in Photoshop that use its layers feature (for instance, a fancy title made up of overlapping images and effects), we have some good news: Final Cut can actually preserve your layers so that you can animate and otherwise manipulate them individually. We explain how it all works in this section.

When you import a Photoshop PSD file into Final Cut, it's imported not as a single image clip, but as an entire sequence. (A *sequence* is Final Cut's way of organizing a group of clips; see Chapter 6 for a full explanation.) In the sequence, each Photoshop layer is placed on its own video track. Final Cut also preserves the order of your Photoshop file's layers by assigning the background layer to the sequence's V1 track and ordering every other layer as you did in your Photoshop file. For instance, your fifth layer, including the background, would be on the V5 track.

Final Cut also interprets a lot of the settings you gave your layers in Photoshop — for instance, opacity settings, modes, and visibility. (See Chapters 13 and 15 for more on effects and compositing, respectively.) On the other hand, any layer masks you create get tossed out, and if you're using some weird compositing modes that Final Cut can't understand, it ignores those layers.

In general, though, you can successfully import some pretty sophisticated Photoshop masterpieces into Final Cut and, with a little tweaking, get them ready to take the stage in your movie.

When you import a Photoshop file with layers, Final Cut doesn't make a copy of that image; it's just referencing the original Photoshop file on your hard disk. If you go back to Photoshop and change the artwork, you see the changes reflected in your Final Cut sequence. That's pretty cool, but if your changes include adding or deleting layers in your Photoshop file, you're likely to confuse the heck out of Final Cut. So if you ever want to add or delete layers in a Photoshop file that you've already imported into Final Cut, we recommend reimporting the file rather than working with the earlier version.

A few words about still pictures

When you work with video in Final Cut, each video frame is typically sized at a resolution of 720 horizontal pixels x 480 vertical pixels (for NTSC-based DV video). But when you import a still image to Final Cut, the image probably won't match that standard video resolution. A still pic could be 640 x 480 pixels, 1280 x 960 pixels, 2560 x 1920 pixels — all depending on how the picture was taken, scanned, or otherwise edited before winding up in Final Cut. The result? When you import that image into your movie, it'll either be too small or too big to fit the video frame. A black border appears around an image that's too small, and, if the image is too big, you don't see the whole image, which makes it look cropped.

Sometimes that's a good thing. For instance, if you bring in an oversized high-resolution picture (say a high-res scan of an old map), you can use Final Cut's animation features to slowly pan or scale it through your video frame. (You'll see this used a lot in documentaries on TV.) On the other hand, sometimes you simply want your still pictures to fill the screen — nothing more, nothing less.

Fortunately, Final Cut gives you full flexibility to handle your still pictures any which way. You can bring them in with the intention of showing just parts of them, or you can resize them to fit the frame of your movie. We cover the "how-to" behind this in Chapter 14.

Converting Media Formats with QuickTime Pro

At some point in your vast Final Cut travels, you'll come to a crossroads where you have media in one format but want to convert it to another format before you import it to Final Cut. Case in point: A composer may e-mail you the latest version of your movie's musical score and format the music as an MP3 file so that you can download it quickly on the Internet. But it turns out that MP3 files play poorly in Final Cut, so you need to convert that MP3 into an AIFF or WAV format before you import it. Here's another possibility: Say you're working on a film with a lot of visual effects, and your effects artists post their test shots on the Internet so that you can download them and check them out right away. But if you want to incorporate those shots into the current edit of your film (which, for our example's sake, is set up to use video in a different codec, say DV), you'll have to render the Sorenson-compressed effects shots before you can play them with your DV shots. In fact, you might find yourself rendering the effects shots multiple times, as you move them around, cut them up, and so on.

You can avoid this rendering hassle in Final Cut by first converting the effects shots to the DV format, so Final Cut treats them like any of your other DV clips and doesn't need to render them.

The best way to convert media from one format to another is to use QuickTime Pro (Figure 4-6), which is an advanced add-on to the QuickTime 5 software that's built into every Mac. Usually, Apple charges about $30 for QuickTime Pro, but you probably already have it on your Mac because it's included with the Final Cut 3 software. QuickTime Pro has some other cool little features, by the way. You can do simple video editing by using Cut and Paste commands, and even add multiple audio tracks. But for now, we talk about how to use Pro to convert media from one format to another, focusing on three scenarios that you might find useful.

To use QuickTime Pro's features, you have to "unlock" them with a special access code. You probably did this when you installed Final Cut itself, but if you're unsure, you can check to see whether QuickTime Pro is activated on your Mac by opening the QuickTime Player application. (Look for an icon in the OS X Dock or check your Applications folder.) After you open the application, chose QuickTime Player➪Preferences➪Registration, and see whether the QuickTime Key setting says `Pro Player Edition`. If you see it, you're all set.

If you don't see Pro Player Edition, you haven't activated QuickTime Pro yet, but don't panic. First, in the materials that came in your Final Cut box, look for a sheet of paper that lists the special *key code* for unlocking the Pro edition, and then follow the written steps for doing so. If you can't find the code, get on the Internet, and surf over to www.apple.com/quicktime. Choose the Get QuickTime Pro option, and get your credit card warmed up in the bullpen.

Figure 4-6: QuickTime Pro is actually a collection of advanced features built into the QuickTime 5 player software.

Radius_TheMovie.mov

In and Out selection markers

Convert another audio file format to AIFF with QuickTime Pro

So say you have an MP3 file (maybe some hot song you want to use as background music in your movie — provided you're not violating any copyright laws!) and need to get it into a format that Final Cut prefers — AIFF is the best choice. Here's how to do it (and remember, these steps work for converting *any* audio file format over to AIFF — be it MP3, Sorenson, PureVoice, or whatever else):

1. **Open the QuickTime Player application.**

   An icon for the QuickTime Player is probably already in the OS X Dock. Click the icon, or you can also find the program in your OS X Applications folder.

2. **Choose File⇨Import.**

3. **In the Open dialog box (shown in Figure 4-7), navigate through your hard drive until you find the MP3 or other audio file that you want to convert.**

   Click a folder in the dialog box, and you see its contents in the column to its immediate right. Keep opening folders until you find your file.

4. **Select the file you want and click the Open button.**

   The QuickTime Player opens your MP3 file in a new window with QuickTime's familiar Play, Rewind, and Fast Forward controls at the bottom of the window. Make sure to keep this window active. Don't click or open any other windows before the next step.

5. **Choose File⇨Export.**

   This opens up the Save Exported File dialog box, where you can name your newly converted file, set other options, and ultimately save it.

6. **From the Export drop-down menu at the bottom of the dialog box, choose Sound to AIFF, as shown in Figure 4-8.**

   This drop-down menu lets you choose the format for your new sound file. Although you have other options, such as Sound to WAV, AIFF files are more popular on Macs, so stick with that.

7. **Click the Options button.**

   This brings up yet another dialog box, as shown in Figure 4-9, with a handful of techie-looking settings.

8. **In the Sound Settings box, choose the settings that define the quality of your new AIFF file and then click the OK button.**

   These different settings affect your new AIFF file's size. Smaller sizes are easier to handle on crowded hard drives and can be sent over the Internet more quickly, but smaller sizes also compromise your sound's quality. It's all up to you, but we recommend sticking with the highest settings.

   1. Set the Compressor to None. This means that QuickTime won't compress your sound.

   2. Choose 44.1 as your Rate, which guarantees nice sound fidelity. Choosing lower rates squeezes your music into a smaller file size but leads to lower quality.

   3. For Size, choose 16 bit.

   4. Choose Stereo (if your original audio file is in stereo, that is). Just so you know, choosing Mono cuts your file size roughly in half because there's no longer separate sound data for two stereo speakers (left and right).

9. **From the Save Exported File As box, name your new AIFF file, navigate to the folder you want to save it to, and click Save.**

   Congratulations. QuickTime leaves your original MP3 or other audio file untouched. But you now have a copy of it in a file format that Final Cut can import without a hitch.

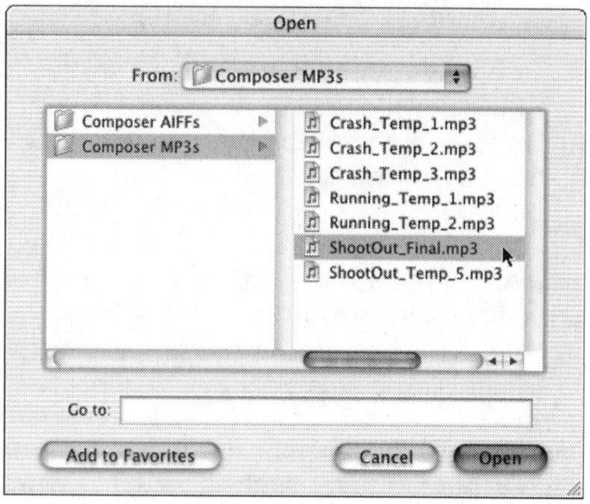

Figure 4-7:
The Open
dialog box.

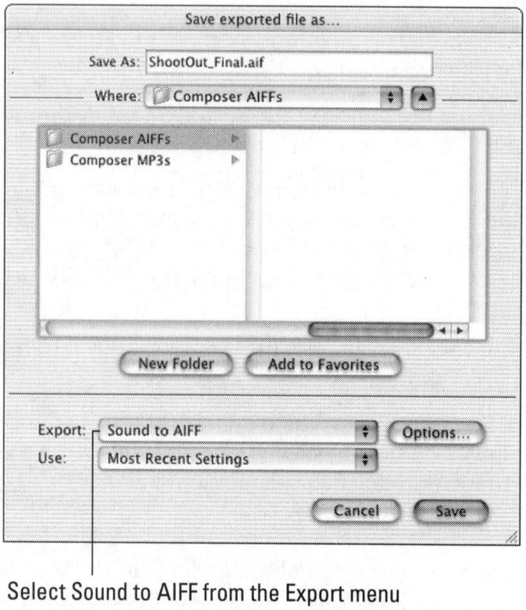

Figure 4-8:
The Save
Exported
File As box,
with Sound
to AIFF
selected.

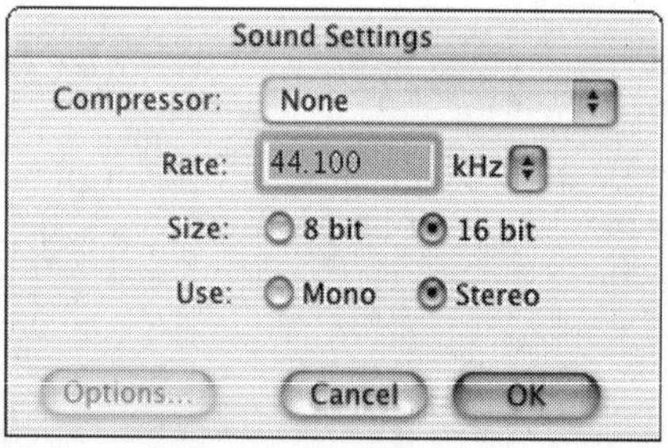

Select Sound to AIFF from the Export menu

Figure 4-9:
The Sound
Settings
dialog box.

When you export an MP3 file (or audio compressed with other technologies, such as IMA or MACE) to the AIFF format, the AIFF version doesn't improve on the MP3's sound quality, even if you kept your AIFF sound settings as high as possible. Why not? Well, the MP3 source is already compressed so that its file size is smaller, which is MP3's strength, and the AIFF file it spawns can't magically recover data that's been lost during the MP3's original compression (again, the same goes for other compressed audio). You might say, "Fine by me. The MP3 source sounded great anyway." But here's the catch: Although MP3 sound holds up on your Mac's built-in speakers or an average television or headphone set, if you were to compare it to the same sound when originally uncompressed (especially on a good sound system), you'd know that the MP3 rendition wasn't quite up to snuff. We say this only to warn you about converting MP3 sound to an AIFF format, and then using it in your *finished* Final Cut movies. MP3-based sound is great placeholder material, but when you're finally ready to wrap up your movie, you'll want to use sound that was never compressed for best results.

How to convert video to DV with QuickTime Pro

Depending on the kind of editing you're doing, you may run into an instance where you have QuickTime video clips that have been compressed in a codec other than DV video, or are otherwise formatted in a way you want to change.

For instance, the sci-fi film *Radius* called for a lot of visual effects shots. The film's effects artists posted placeholder versions of these shots on the Internet, so Helmut, the movie's producer, could quickly download each one and offer comments. Naturally, Helmut wanted to see how the shots looked when edited into the film, but he experienced two hitches:

- ✔ The effects artists typically compressed their QuickTime shots with the Sorenson Video codec, not the DV codec, which meant he would've had to render the shots when he tried to combine them with the DV footage of our film in Final Cut. (When you do a lot of rendering, you tend to look for ways to avoid it.)

- ✔ The artists typically sized their test shots at 480 x 320 pixels, which kept each shot's file size small for quick compression and downloading, but also made the shots too small to fill the entire TV screen when edited into the film. (A frame of TV video is about 720 x 480 pixels.)

To solve both the rendering hassle and this size limitation, he used QuickTime Pro to convert each effects shot to a DV stream, which would automatically size them to DV's native frame rate (29.97) and frame size

(720 x 480) and compression, and also allow us to combine the effects shots seamlessly with our existing DV footage from the film — no rendering or any other hassles.

Granted, you may never, ever need to do this sort of thing, but this exercise illustrates QuickTime Pro's flexibility for reformatting media in all sorts of ways.

To convert QuickTime video saved in any compression format to a DV stream, follow these steps:

1. **Use the QuickTime Player application to open the video file you want to convert.**

   Double-clicking the QuickTime video file opens it in the QuickTime Player. You see the video in a new player window with the familiar play, fast-forward, and rewind controls.

   Make sure this window stays active. In other words, don't click another Player window, if others are open.

2. **Choose File⇨Export.**

   This opens the Save Exported File As dialog box, where you can name your soon-to-be converted movie, set other options, and then save it.

3. **From the Export drop-down list shown in Figure 4-10, choose Movie to DV Stream.**

   You're telling QuickTime Pro that the new movie you're about to make will still be in the QuickTime format but using DV compression and DV's frame rate and frame size. You can also save this new file as an AVI movie, a popular PC format, along with other options too.

4. **Click the Options button.**

   This brings up the DV Export Settings dialog box, shown in Figure 4-11.

5. **In the DV Export Settings box (Figure 4-11), choose between NTSC and PAL. (NTSC is the American standard, PAL is for Europe.)**

6. **Set the quality level for your audio and then click OK.**

   You can format this video's accompanying audio (if there is any) at 32 kHz, 41 kHz, or 48 kHz — click the Rate pop-up button and select the option you prefer.

7. **In the Save Exported File As dialog box, name your new movie, navigate to the folder you want to save it to, and click Save.**

   QuickTime saves your new, exported file while leaving the original QuickTime video file that it's based on untouched. Try opening your new movie (now recompressed and resized in DV) in the QuickTime Player to see how it looks.

When you convert movies from one format to another, you're going to lose picture quality. For instance, if you convert a video clip that was compressed in Sorenson video to DV video (or vice versa), the new file is, in effect, compressed twice, and shows some compression artifacts. (Artifacts are imperfections in the video — they look like little splotches and oversized pixels.) Even worse, if the video's pixel resolution was scaled up by a large amount during the conversion, you may see a *lot* of artifacts in the converted video. Still, while double-compressed or scaled-up video won't look ready for primetime broadcast, it can still suit other purposes. If your movie's final destination is the Internet, however, an audience watching your video in a typically small viewing window (at a low frame rate) might not notice.

When you convert a movie from one format to another using QuickTime Pro, you don't have to convert the entire movie if you want only a part of it. To select a smaller sample of a bigger movie for conversion, open the movie in the QuickTime Player and drag QuickTime's In and Out selection markers to set the in and out points of the sample you're interested in (see Figure 4-6, way back). Now, choose Edit⇨Copy, open a new movie window by choosing File⇨New Player, and then choose Edit⇨Paste to copy your movie selection into the new player window. Now, just export this smaller movie as you normally would.

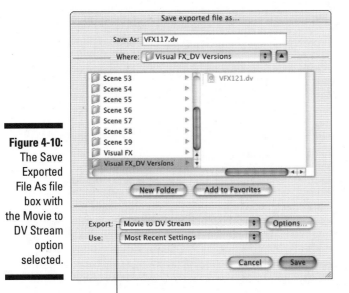

Figure 4-10:
The Save Exported File As file box with the Movie to DV Stream option selected.

Select Movie to DV Stream

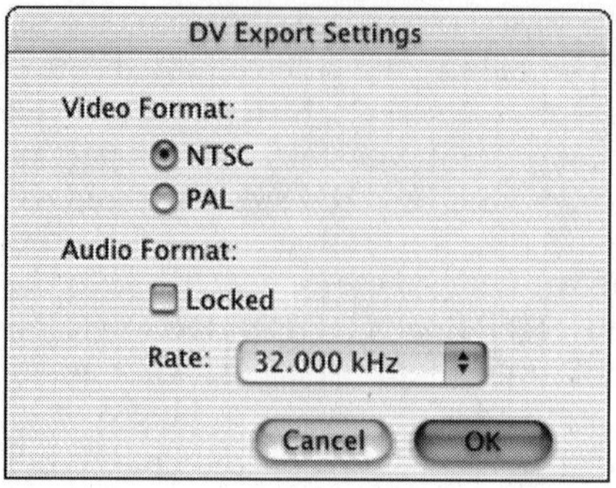

Figure 4-11:
The DV
Export
Settings
dialog box.

Chapter 5

Organizing Your Media Clips

*E*verything you capture or import ends up in your Browser window in a Final Cut project. Your Browser works much like your hard drive: A hard drive has many folders, with many files inside each folder. Similarly, the Browser has *bins,* which look suspiciously like (you guessed it) folders. Inside these bins, you can store your clips, sequences, and any old captures or imported files you may want to bring into your Final Cut project.

The Browser is a versatile and feature-laden holding area. You can name bins, store bins within bins, color-code your clips, and view loads of information about your clips and media. And the Browser helps you stay organized, too: It is a powerful tool in your fight against clip chaos. Chapter 3, by the way, also offers some key suggestions for organizing your elements. We suggest reading that chapter before embarking on any project of great length.

The Browser, shown in Figure 5-1, can also be a very good way to troubleshoot your clips. There may be an occasion you may find that a clip is misbehaving in the timeline; it may not be playing correctly by skipping, or some such problem. By comparing the columns for this clip with the other clips (that are playing well), you can often find out what the problem is. In some cases, you may notice that the data rate of the miscreant clip may be too high, or that it may be the wrong frame size. Hence, the Browser can also be an extremely useful troubleshooting tool.

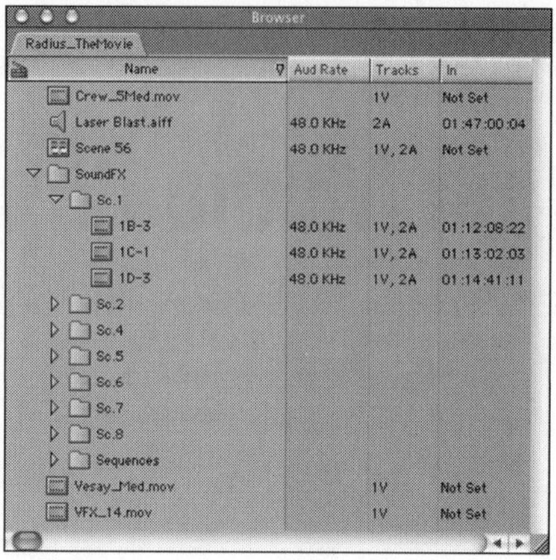

Figure 5-1:
The
Browser
window.

Everything Goes into the Browser

It's about as simple as that: Your captured media, imported files, music tracks from CD, as well as any sequences you create, all go into the Browser.

With Final Cut, you technically can drag and drop clips and other items directly from the Finder level (your Mac Desktop) to your sequence. However, we discourage you from doing so. Always bring your media into the Browser first: It's a good organizational habit that may save you trouble when you are trying to find the original clip for a project. If you're not sure how to import media into the Browser, check out Chapter 4. For information on capturing media from tapes, see Chapter 3.

In the Browser window, you can have more than one project open at a time. Each project has its own tab, indicating the name of the project. You can bring a project forward by clicking the tab. You can also freely copy and paste clips, move bins, and sequences between projects.

To open a project into a separate window, drag its tab away from the main window. To close a project, Control+click its tab (hold down Control as you click) and choose Close Tab from the pop-up menu.

Figuring out icons

Each type of item in the Browser has its own icon. Table 5-1 shows the icons in the Browser window and what they stand for. In some cases, you can turn to the designated chapter to find out more.

Table 5-1	Icons of the Browser Window	
Icon	*Item*	*To find out more, see...*
	Bin	Chapter 1
	Open bin	
	Locked bin	
	Marker	Chapter 3
	Video/Audio Clip	Chapters 8 and 12
	Subclip	Chapter 3
	Audio Clip	Chapter 12
	Offline Clip	Chapter 3
	Sequence	Chapter 2
	Graphic/Still	Chapter 4
	Video Filter	Chapter 13
	Video Transition	Chapter 10

(continued)

Table 5-1 *(continued)*

Icon	Item	To find out more, see...
	Audio Filter	Chapter 12
	Audio Transition	Chapter 10
	Generator	Chapter 11

Bins are like folders

The Browser works much like the hard drive of your computer. On your hard drive, you have numerous folders that contain files and subfolders. You can name and rename these folders and move files between them. Similarly, in the Browser window, you can create new bins (which are like folders) and store clips and other bins within them. Here are some functions you can perform with bins:

- **Making New Bins:** To make a new bin in your Browser, choose File⇨New⇨Bin (⌘+B). You see a new bin appear in your Browser with its name highlighted for renaming. Click in the name field of the bin and give it a new name.

- **Adding Items to Bins:** Adding items to bins is like adding files to your folders in the Mac OS. Simply drag any item into your bin to add to the item to that bin. You can also drag a bin into another bin.

- **Opening Bins:** Each bin has a small triangle next to it. (Apple calls it the *disclosure triangle*. Whoopee-doo — How impressive!) To open your bin, you can click the triangle so that it points down and reveals the contents of your bin. You can also double-click a bin to open it in its own Browser-like window.

Working with Browser Columns

The Browser, at a glance, enables you to see lots of facts about your media clips and items, such as duration, scene and shot information, and timecode.

Being able to see information about your clips is the first step in getting organized. For example, you can check the Reel column and store all the clips from a certain reel into a separate folder. (Editors commonly organize their clips by storing them in Bins that are named after reels.)

You can choose between two column views, which enable you to see information about your clips in two different ways:

✔ **Standard Columns:** The Standard Columns is the default view in the Browser window.

✔ **Logging Columns:** The logging view eliminates information that is not relevant to logging, such as Reverse Alpha or Composite.

Both views of the columns have a vast array of headings. In this section, we cover some of the more important ones.

To switch between these views, Control+click any column heading and choose Standard Columns or Logging Columns from the pop-up menu that appears, as shown in Figure 5-2.

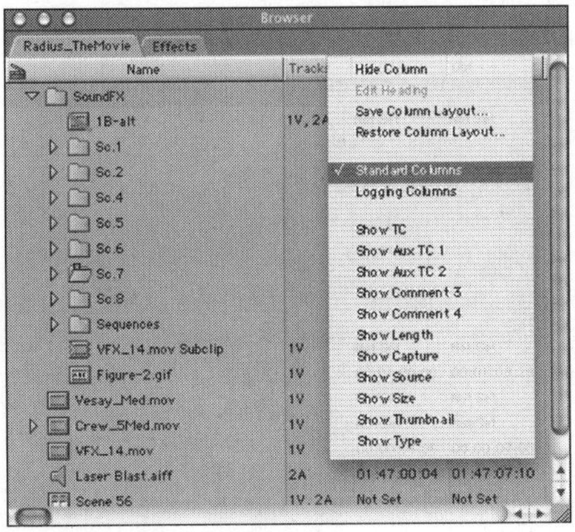

Figure 5-2:
Selecting
Logging or
Standard
Column
view.

Understanding the column headings

The Browser boasts over 41 different column headings that you can display or hide. You may not need a whole lot of them in your project, but, as long-time editors, we've learned that you can never have enough information about your media in the Browser.

These are some of the column headings you will probably use the most:

- ✔ **Name:** The name column is the first column of your Browser, and nothing you do will change that. (It's a stubborn column and likes to be first.) The name of your clip is the name you entered in the Log and Capture window. You can also rename the clip in the Browser by double-clicking the name of the clip. Be aware, though, that the actual media file (which also uses the name of the clip) maintains the old name.

- ✔ **Reel:** This column shows the reel name as you entered it in the Log and Capture window.

- ✔ **Capture:** You can see the current capture status of your clip in this column. The indicators that appear in this column are Not Yet, OK (which means the clip has been captured), Aborted, and Queued. Another indicator that appears in this column is Error, indicating that your clip dropped frames during the capture process.

- ✔ **Data Rate:** Indicates the data rate of your captured clip. For DV clips, it always hover around 3.6 MB/sec. (megabytes per second). However, when using third-party capture cards, the rate may be different, so use this column to see at what data rate your clips are being captured.

- ✔ **Size:** This column shows the size of your clip in megabytes (MB) as it exists on the drive. Using this column, you can identify unnecessary clips that take up large amounts of hard-drive space.

- ✔ **Source:** Each clip you capture is stored as a media file on a drive. This column enables you to see the path of the media file. In short, if you want to find out exactly where you stored a clip's file on your drive, look in this column.

- ✔ **Media Start:** This column indicates the timecode of the first frame of your clip. This is not the in point of your clip, but the starting timecode of your entire captured clip.

- ✔ **Media End:** Here, you can see the timecode of the last frame of a clip. This is not the out point of your clip, but the end timecode of your entire captured clip.

- ✔ **In:** This indicates the timecode of a clip's in point. This may not necessarily be the very start of your clip. If you move the in point, the timecode changes here to reflect that move.

- ✔ **Out:** This column shows the timecode of a clip's out point. This is not necessarily the very end of your clip.

Working with column headings

With so many different column headings, you need to manage them and organize them in some logical fashion. You can add or delete columns, rearrange their locations, and change their widths to match your needs. Here are a few simple things you can do to keep the columns looking just the way you like:

- ✔ **Adding columns:** To add a new column heading that is not visible, Control+click any column heading and choose a heading from the pop-up menu that appears.

- ✔ **Hiding columns:** To hide any column, Control+click the column heading you want to hide and choose Hide Column.

- ✔ **Rearranging columns:** To rearrange the order of the columns, you can click and drag any column heading to move it to the left or right.

- ✔ **Changing column width:** Many times, you may find the width of the columns to be too narrow. For example, your clip names may get hidden behind other columns. You can click between two column headers and drag left or right to change the width of the columns.

- ✔ **Saving Column layout:** After you've created a column layout, you can save it for later use. This is especially helpful if several people are using the same Final Cut Pro workstation. To save a layout, Control+click any column heading and choose Save Column Layout from the pop-up menu that appears. Name and save your layout.

- ✔ **Restoring Column Layout:** To restore a Column layout, Control+click any column heading and choose Restore Column Layout from the pop-up menu that appears. Choose the column layout you named and saved.

Modifying settings in a column

All the columns in the Browser show you information about the clips or the sequences in the Browser. You can change many of these column settings by using one of the following on-screen elements:

- ✔ **Browser item names:** You can rename any bin, clip, subclip, sequence, or marker in the Browser by clicking its name and typing in a new one.

- ✔ **Check marks:** Some fields in the columns show check marks. By changing the check marks, you can change the settings they indicate. For example, in the Good column, you can change the Good status by simply clicking the check mark that appears in the field. (Originally, the Good setting is a carryover from the Log and Capture window that indicates a clip you felt was good for use during the log and capture phase.)

- ✔ **Fields in the Browser:** You can modify fields in the Browser (such as Reel, Log Notes, Scene, and Take) by clicking in them and entering the new information, such as a new Reel name. Depending on the fields, you may need to single-click or double-click.

✔ **Pop-up menus:** You can change other fields, such as Reel Name, by Control+clicking them. A common example is when you've used multiple reels for a project and later realize that, for one of the clips, you've forgotten to change the name of the Reel during the Log and Capture phase. Control+clicking the Reel name field in the Browser opens a pop-up menu with the names of all the reels you've been using. You can then choose a reel from this pop-up menu to reflect the correct reel name.

Sorting clips by column

The sort feature is one of the more helpful features in the Browser window. To sort by name, simply click the top part of the name column. You see a small green arrow pointing downwards (indicating a sort), and your clips sort themselves in alphabetical order. Similarly, you can click the Duration column, and your clips are sorted by how long they are.

To reverse sort, simply click the column heading again so that the small green arrow points upwards. This indicator means that your column has been reverse sorted. In a reverse sorted name column, for example, clips whose names start with a Z are at the top, and the ones whose names start with an A are at the bottom.

Viewing Clips in Different Ways

In the Browser, you can see the clips in a few different views, as shown in Figure 5-3. To select the different methods of viewing, choose View➪Browser Items and choose from one of the four views in the submenu:

✔ **List:** The List view is the most efficient and shows the most information. The only drawback is that you don't see an icon for the image of your clip. You can however, Control+click any column heading and choose Show Thumbnail to bring up small thumbnails for each clip. (*Thumbnails* are small postage-sized views of the video contained in your clip.)

✔ **Small Icons:** The Small Icon view displays small icons for clips and items in the Browser. We find that this view isn't helpful because the icons are too small to be seen clearly.

✔ **Medium Icons:** Medium Icon view displays a slightly larger view of the icons. The thumbnails are fairly large and easy to view.

✔ **Large Icons:** The Large Icon view shows the largest icons of any of the views. This view is helpful for looking for a shot if you can recall the first video frame, which is the frame shown in each clip icon.

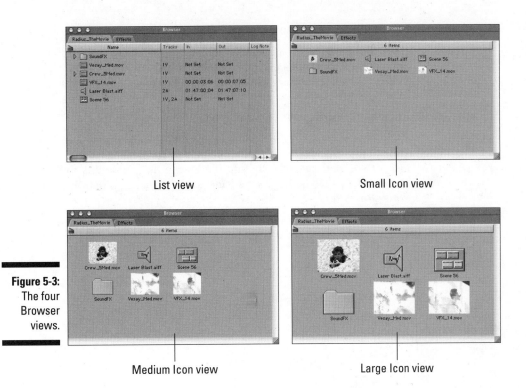

List view

Small Icon view

Figure 5-3:
The four
Browser
views.

Medium Icon view

Large Icon view

The Large Icon view (choose View➪Browser Items➪As Large Icons) has a few features that we find very useful when editing a project. The first feature is that it shows a frame of the clip, called a *poster* frame. (By default, you see the very first frame.) In the following steps, we explain how to use this view along with the Scrub tool to scroll quickly through your clips, as well as how to change which image is used as the poster frame. The Scrub tool allows your clip to play through in the small thumbnail view.

Many times, editors and producers like to utilize the Large Icon view to locate and organize their shots. These next few steps can get you started organizing your material and viewing your clips in a more efficient manner:

1. **Make sure that your Browser is selected and choose View➪Browser Items➪As Large Icons.**

   Your Browser window switches to the Large Icon view.

2. **Clean up your Browser by choosing View➪Arrange.**

   This step is necessary because, whenever you switch to the Large Icon view, you may find that your clips become disorganized like a messy drawer full of socks.

3. **Select the Scrub Video tool from the tool palette.**

   If the tool palette isn't visible, choose Window⇨Tools to bring it up. The Scrub Video tool looks like a hand with two small arrows and is part of the flyout menu of the Zoom tool, which looks like a magnifying glass (see Figure 5-4).

4. **Click and drag any video clip with the Scrub Video tool.**

   With the Scrub Video tool, you can quickly scroll through your video clips to find the shot you may be searching for. This is often a whole lot faster than loading each clip into the Viewer and searching through it. Drag to the left to go backwards and to the right to go forwards in your clip.

5. **While clicking the image with the Scrub Video tool, press the Control key if you want to set a new Poster frame for your Large Icon view.**

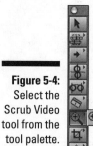

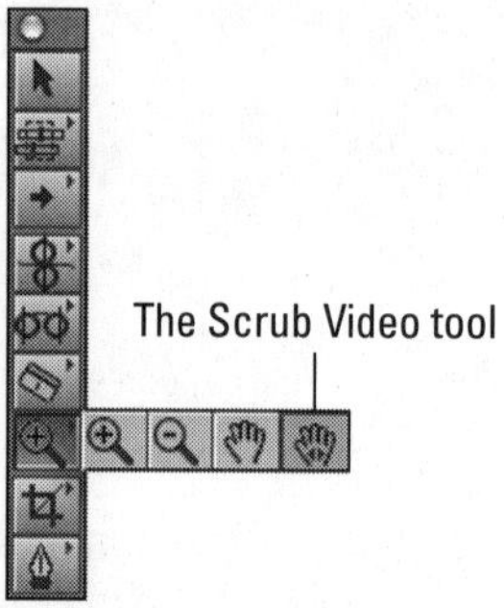

Figure 5-4:
Select the
Scrub Video
tool from the
tool palette.

The Scrub Video tool

TIP

If, during scrubbing, you need to move a clip around in the Browser window, turn off scrubbing by pressing the ⌘ key to get your pointer back. Then click and drag the clip to its new location.

Adding Transitions and Effects to the Favorites Bin

Every Browser window comes with a default Effects tab. Under this tab, you can find all the effects that Final Cut provides, such as Dissolves and Wipes. (By the way, you can also find the same effects under the Effects menu. For more on transitions and effects, see Chapters 10 and 14.) Under the Effects tab window is a Favorites bin, where you can store transitions and effects that you may have modified for your use and want to reuse again. You can rename these effects and transitions as well. For example, you may find that you're using a Dissolve of 10 frames in your timeline again and again. You can drag this Dissolve from the Timeline and into the Favorites bin in the Browser window and reuse it as many times as you like.

1. **Select the Transition or effect you want to add to the Favorites bin.**

   To select a transition or an effect, click the Effects tab in the Browser. (If one is not visible, choose Window⇨Effects to bring it up.) Then open the category folders and select a transition you like.

2. **Choose Modify⇨Make Favorite Effect.**

   The transition of your choice is copied to the Favorites bin. You can rename this transition by double-clicking its name in the Browser and typing in a new name.

   From now on, you can drag this transition or effect from the Favorites bin (instead of having to burrow like a rabbit through all those folders full of effects and transitions) and add it to your clips.

These effects in the Favorites bin are also available to you if you choose Effects⇨Favorites.

Editors use the Favorites bin to store modified effects and transitions. For example, you can double-click any transition in the Browser to open it in the Viewer window and change its duration. Then you can drag the transition into the Favorites bin and rename it as you like. This way, you can have various modified effects and transitions available to you in your Favorites bin.

I Know I Left That Clip Somewhere

On a large project of any scope, the Browser can quickly become a rabbit hole, full of cluttered bins within bins and shots stored willy-nilly. Of course, we hope you never allow this disorganized state to occur. But then, we'd be less than candid if we didn't admit that our own Browsers are often a disorganized mess.

Mercifully, the Final Cut designers have included an awesome search function in this application. Using this search function, you can search for an item and have Final Cut retrieve it for you. The following sections explain how to do different types of searches.

Searching by clip name or comments

The most basic search is looking for a clip by name. (Of course, you have to remember the name of the clip you're looking for.) You can also search by comments you may have added to the missing clip. For more on the different types of criteria, flip ahead to "Searching by an endless array of other criteria."

Here's how to do a basic name search in Final Cut:

1. **Choose Edit⇨Find (⌘+F).**

2. **In the Find window that appears (as shown in Figure 5-5), select the name of your project under the Search drop-down menu.**

3. **In the For drop-down menu, choose All Media.**

4. **In the two drop-down menus at the bottom, choose Name in the left one and choose Contains in the right one.**

5. **Type the name for the clip you want to search for in the lower-right field of the Find window and then click the Find Next button.**

   You can type part or all of the name in the Name field.

6. **The Find window closes and the first clip in the Browser matching the name is highlighted.**

7. **Choose Edit⇨Find Next (⌘+G) to find the next clip based on the name you entered.**

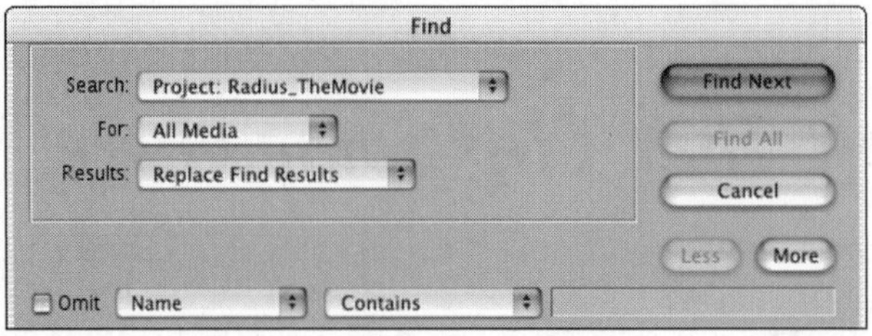

Figure 5-5:
The Find
window.

You can also click Find All so that the search function will find all the clips with the text in their names. Find All brings up a Find Results window containing all the clips Final Cut found.

Each time you use ⌘+G, the next clip that has the same name you were searching for is highlighted for you.

Searching by an endless array of other criteria

The Find window is a versatile search tool. You can search by an almost endless array of criteria, such as Name, Type, Length, and any one of the four Comment fields where you may have entered a comment for a clip.

You can also create more than one criterion for a search by clicking the More button and adding to the list of your criteria.

A creative mixing and matching of the options available in the Find window will narrow down just about any item you may go searching for.

If your results produce more than one clip, the results will be presented to you in the Find Results window. In this window, you can select an item and click the Show in Browser button to locate the selected item in the Browser.

Defining the scope of your search

The top part of the Find window allows you to define the scope of the search you are about to begin.

- ✔ **Search:** Select an option from the pop-up menu to determine which open projects or folders you want to search. The choices are All Open Projects, Effects, or Current Open Project.

- ✔ **For:** Here, you can indicate which type of media you want to restrict the search to: All Media, Unused Media, or Used Media. This is an important setting because you may not want to search through media you have not used in the sequences.

- ✔ **Results:** Under this choice, you tell Final Cut what to do with the results after the search feature presents them. The choices here are

  - • **Replace Find Results:** Selecting this option replaces the results of a previous search.

  - • **Add to Find Results:** Choosing this option adds the results of the current search to any previous search you may have done.

Defining the criteria of your search

You can add or eliminate search criteria by using the More and Less options. The More and Less option buttons are located in the lower-left section of the Search window.

- ✔ **More:** Clicking the More button gives you additional criteria that you can use for your search. For example, you may want to search for a name and also a log note.

✔ **Less:** This button reduces the next level of criteria. This button is available only when some of the More options are enabled.

✔ **Omit:** Check this box in the lower-left corner if you want to omit certain criteria, rather than add it. For example, you may want to omit any clip with the name *car* from your criteria of search.

✔ **Any Column:** In this drop-down list, which is next to the Omit check box, you can specify any column you may want to search. Using this setting, you can search any and all columns in the Browser.

✔ **Contains:** This drop-down list, which is to the left of the Column drop-down list, allows you to narrow your search.

The choices here are Starts With, Contains, Equals, Ends With, Less Than, or Greater Than. At first glance, these choices may seem confusing, but after you experiment with them, you realize they are quite powerful.

For example, you may have some clips that end in the word *cars,* while others begin with the word *cars.* To search only for the clips that end in *cars,* choose Ends With.

✔ **Text field:** Type the text you want to search for in the text field in the lower-right corner.

✔ **Find Next and Find All:** These buttons are in the top-right corner of the Find window, and you use them to start your search. The Find Next button highlights the next item in the Browser that matches your search criteria. From here you can then press ⌘+G to locate the next item that matches the search. The Find All button tells Final Cut to locate all the items that meet your search criteria and gather them in the Find Results window, which is shown in Figure 5-6.

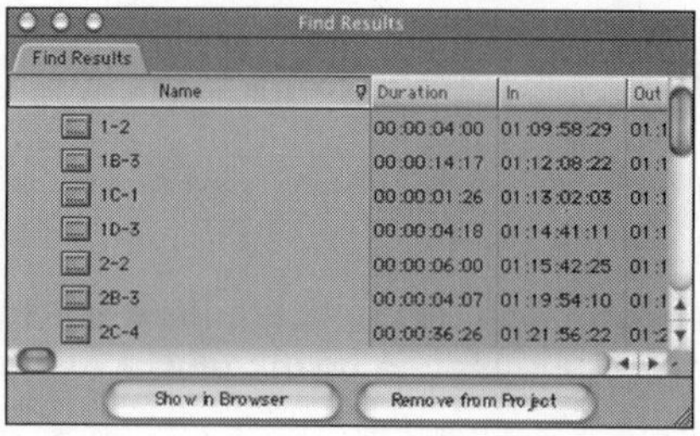

Figure 5-6:
The Find
Results
window.

Part III
Editing Your Media

The 5th Wave   By Rich Tennant

TROUBLE ON THE SET

©RICHTENNANT

All the software in the world won't make this a great film. Only you can, Rusty. Only you and the guts and determination to be the finest Frisbee catching dog in this dirty little town. Now come on Rusty—it's magic time.

We're losing the light, Dad.

In this part . . .

We start off Part III with the basics of editing video and audio: how to move clips to Final Cut's Timeline window and then how to resize them, cut them up, or move them in time. We round out your new skills, giving you finer control over Final Cut's Timeline. We also tackle Final Cut's advanced editing features. Finally, we cover Final Cut's Media Manager, which lets you move, copy, compress, and delete media files in an efficient way.

Chapter 6

Editing Basics

· ·

In This Chapter

▶ Working with the windows

▶ Moving clips to the Timeline

▶ Resizing clips

▶ Cutting clips in two

▶ Deleting clips

· ·

*E*diting is a unique form of magic. You begin the process with hordes of raw, rambling video, audio, and still pictures that, taken on their own, mean nothing. But through editing, you weave all those disparate parts into a new whole — something with its own identity, something with the power to entertain, inform, provoke, gall — take your pick, as long as it's not "put to sleep."

On the other hand, while the process of editing may seem complex and mysterious to the uninitiated (again, like magic), that's just an illusion. In fact, once you begin to explore editing's tools and methods (cutting, moving, and deleting), you'll realize that they're all very straightforward, even — dare we say — *simple*. So let's dive right in and start demystifying them.

Final Cut is stuffed with keyboard shortcuts, and the more shortcuts you use, the faster you edit. Of course, keyboard shortcuts may not be as intuitive as other methods, but we think you'll benefit in the long run if you start getting used to them! We point out all the handy shortcuts as we go, but you can also look them up by choosing Help➪Keyboard Shortcuts from the menu bar. For a quick reference to Final Cut's most frequently used shortcut commands, check out the Cheat Sheet inside this book's front cover.

Final Cut is a nondestructive editor

If you're new to editing, you may be seized with the fear that you'll accidentally change or even destroy your precious video or audio media — for good. And to this we say, "Get a grip. It just ain't gonna happen!" The defense presents

✔ **Exhibit A:** If you move media clips to the Timeline and then cut off some frames, you can retrieve those lost frames with a simple click and drag of your mouse.

✔ **Exhibit B:** If you delete clips you've imported into the Browser, Final Cut *does not* erase them from your hard drive. To retrieve them, you just have to reimport them.

✔ **Exhibit C:** You can always undo up to your last 99 actions. So even if you cut, trimmed, moved, or deleted a clip 30 minutes ago, you can probably take it back.

In other words, you're invincible! Nothing can hurt your project, so fear not. Dive in, experiment, and feel free to brew up endless combinations of clips with the knowledge that a big fat safety net is just below you.

Note: Okay, maybe there's one exception to our claim that *nothing* can hurt your project. In Chapter 9, we cover the Media Manager, a great tool for organizing your media that truly *can* delete or overwrite media on your hard drive (but you really have to make an effort to do that). If you just can't wait, flip to Chapter 9 for details on the Media Manager. Otherwise, just remember that the Media Manager is the one exception to the nondestructive rule.

Understanding the Process: Final Cut's Windows

At the center of all your editing work is Final Cut's Timeline window, where you visually arrange all your video clips, audio clips, and still pics in time. But Final Cut's other major windows play a big part in editing, too:

✔ **The Browser:** As shown in Figure 6-1, the Browser is where you store and organize all the media clips you've imported into your project before you move them to the Timeline.

✔ **The Viewer:** The Viewer window is where you watch (or listen to) clips before you move them from the Browser to the Timeline (double-clicking a clip in the Browser opens it in the Viewer).

✔ **The Canvas:** The Canvas window plays whatever clips you've arranged in the timeline window. In other words, it's the window you'll use to preview your movie-in-progress.

✔ **The Tool Palette:** Although it's not technically a window, the Tool Palette contains the editing tools that you'll use for cutting, moving, and resizing clips, among other things.

Viewer   Canvas

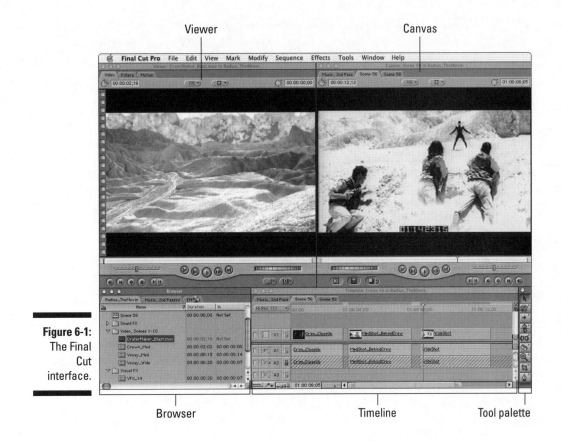

Figure 6-1:
The Final
Cut
interface.

Browser   Timeline   Tool palette

As you edit, you'll constantly move back and forth between Final Cut's windows. The overall process goes something like this:

1. Find clips in the Browser.

2. Preview them in the Viewer.

3. Arrange them in the Timeline.

4. Watch them in the Canvas.

5. Resize, split, or rearrange them back on the Timeline (by using the appropriate tool from the Tool palette).

6. Check out your edited clips *again* in the Canvas window, to see how they play.

7. Move on to the next scene and do it all over again.

If this sounds a bit daunting, forget about it. Editing in Final Cut Pro is like learning to drive a car with a stick shift: You wonder how you can possibly steer the wheel, hit the gas or brake, *and* shift gears at the same time (not to mention tune the radio, chat on the phone, and decipher those directions you scrawled on a napkin). But sure enough, before you know it, it's all second nature. So it goes with Final Cut.

You'll work more quickly if you learn to switch between Final Cut's windows via keyboard shortcuts. ⌘+1 activates the Viewer window, ⌘+2 the Canvas, ⌘+3 the Timeline, and ⌘+4 the Browser. Go ahead and try 'em out.

A nice thing about editing in Final Cut is that there's never just one way to do something. For instance, if you want to trim frames from a clip, you can do it by using the Viewer window, clicking and dragging the clips' edges on the Timeline, or doing a cut and then a lift edit or ripple delete. We explain what all this means in due time, of course, but the point is that you have lots of flexibility to develop your own style of working.

Getting to know the Timeline

Final Cut's Timeline lets you arrange all your video and audio clips so that they tell the story you want to tell. To understand how the Timeline works, think of it as a page of sheet music, but instead of placing musical notes of different lengths (quarter notes, half notes, whole notes), one after another, you're placing video and audio clips of different lengths, one after another. And when you want to see how your clips play together, you can watch your movie-in-progress in Final Cut's Canvas window.

A couple things worth noting on the Timeline, right off the bat (check out Figure 6-2):

Sequence tabs   Playhead   Timeline ruler

Figure 6-2:
The
Timeline.

Audio tracks   Tracks on the Timeline

Video tracks

✔ **Timeline ruler:** This ruler stretches across the top of the Timeline and looks like a conventional ruler (see Figure 6-2), except it marks increments in time (4 seconds, 8 seconds, and so on), not distance. So, when you place a media clip on the Timeline, it plays at the point in time where you've placed it on the Timeline's ruler. For instance, if the clip starts at the 4 second mark on the ruler, the clip plays 4 seconds into your movie.

The ruler's markers show hours, minutes, seconds, and finally frames of video (this is known as *timecode*). So a measurement that reads 01:02:40:04 means you're in the first hour, second minute, fortieth second, and fourth frame of your story.

✔ **The playhead:** The playhead (refer to Figure 6-2) is like a record needle on an old LP record player: The music plays wherever the needle is, and your movie plays wherever the playhead is on your Timeline. In the Timeline's ruler area, click the spot where you want the playhead to start playing. The playhead automatically jumps to that point in time, and you see whatever video frame happens to be under the playhead in the Canvas video. To begin viewing your movie from that point, click the play button in the Canvas window.

✔ **Timeline tracks:** The Timeline is divided into horizontal rows called *tracks.* You use tracks to play two or more clips at the same time, by placing the clips on different tracks, stacked on top of each other (refer to good ol' Figure 6-2). For instance, if you want your movie to feature dialogue and background music playing together, just put the dialogue clip on one track and the music directly below it on a different track.

Timeline tracks come in two flavors — video and audio — so you put your video clips on video tracks and your audio clips on audio tracks. You can have up to 99 tracks of each, but for most purposes, you need only a handful of them. Video tracks are numbered V1, V2, and so on, while A1, A2, and so on are for audio tracks.

Final Cut gives you lots of control over tracks, which comes in handy if your movies need a fair number of them. For instance, you can lock tracks in case you don't want the clips on them to be affected by other editing you're doing, and you can turn tracks off, so they don't play (for instance, if you just want to hear the dialog track, not the music tracks). See Chapter 7 for more details.

✔ **Sequence tabs:** If you recall, a sequence is a collection of clips you've organized on the Timeline (you'll typically use sequences to break a movie down into smaller, more manageable parts — for instance, you might create each of your movie's scenes in its own sequence). Every currently open sequence in your project is represented by a tab in the upper-left corner of the Timeline window, and you can work with each sequence simply by clicking its tab. (See Chapters 5 and 7 for more about how to create and manage sequences.)

Playing back video: The Viewer and Canvas windows

Before you get into the thick of editing, let's talk a moment about the one thing you'll do in Final Cut more than anything else, which is play back video using either Final Cut's Viewer or Canvas windows.

The Viewer window plays a single media clip so that you can check it out, see what you like about it, and possibly make edits to it (which we'll get to later in this chapter). You open a clip in the Viewer by double-clicking the clip either from the Browser window or from the Timeline, if you've already moved the clip there.

Although the Viewer lets you play a single clip, the Canvas window plays the sequence of clips you've assembled in the Timeline window — in other words, it's what you'll watch to see your movie-in-progress, so you can judge how all your edited clips work together.

The Viewer and Canvas windows do two very different things, but luckily, they work very much alike in that they both offer essentially the same playback options: You can play video forward and in reverse at normal speeds, you can zoom through it with a super fast-forward and rewind, move slowly, or jump to any point with a single mouse click. Here's a look at some of the controls that work in both the Viewer and the Canvas (as shown in Figure 6-3):

- **Play button:** Click it to play and click it again to pause.

- **Scrubber bar and playhead:** The scrubber runs horizontally across the Viewer and Canvas windows, right under your video. The length of the scrubber bar represents the length of your clip (Viewer) or movie (Canvas), and you can position the scrubber's playhead anywhere on the bar by clicking your mouse there. The window shows whatever frame of video is at the playhead position. By the way, notice that the Canvas and Timeline's playheads mirror each other: When you position the playhead in the Canvas's scrubber, the playhead in the Timeline jumps to the same position.

- **Jog control:** Click and drag the shuttle to the left or right to slowly roll the Viewer or Canvas's playhead forward or back, as little as a frame at a time (you can also move the playhead frame by frame with the arrow keys).

- **Shuttle control:** Click and drag to the left or right to rewind or fast-forward. The further you drag the shuttle head from its middle point, the faster your playback is.

Timecode duration Zoom   Current timecode

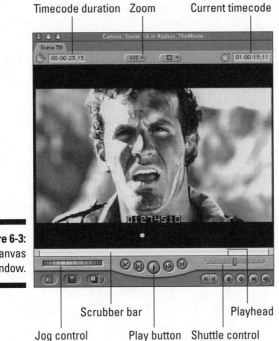

Figure 6-3:
The Canvas
window.

Scrubber bar   Playhead

Jog control   Play button Shuttle control

As intuitive as these play controls are, they do have a downside. As you
play your clips over and over again, scrutinizing each little frame or edit, you
start to tire of constantly moving and clicking your mouse around the Viewer
or Canvas. So instead, put your fingers on the keyboard and try out these
three keys:

  ✔ **J:** Play backward (in reverse, like a rewind)

  ✔ **K:** Stop

  ✔ **L:** Play forward

Keeping your fingers on these keys gives you lightning-quick control over
video playback. Plus, you can use the same keys to quickly go into fast-
forward or fast-rewind modes, rather than use the shuttle control. For
instance, to fast-forward, just press L twice. Press the L key a third or fourth
time for a faster rewind.

You can also use the space bar to play and stop video in the Canvas or
Viewer, instead of using the L and K keys.

If the Viewer or Canvas windows don't play your video smoothly, click the Zoom icon at the top of either window (see Figure 6-3), and choose Fit to Window from the Zoom pop-up menu. This scales your video to match the size of your window, and allows it to play without any jerkiness.

Timecode Information in the Canvas and Viewer

Both the Canvas and Viewer windows give you handy timecode information about the clip or timeline sequence you're working.

The Timecode Duration field (see Figure 6-3) tells you how long your clip or your entire timeline sequence is. (The Viewer window reports the clip's length, and the Canvas reports the sequence's length, measured at the last frame of the last clip of your timeline sequence.)

The Current Timecode field tells you the timecode of whatever frame the Viewer or Canvas's playhead happens to be on. See for yourself — click inside either window's scrubber bar to move the playhead from place to place, and watch the Current Timecode value change.

Timecode measures hours, minutes, seconds, and frames. So the timecode value 01:04:40:26 means 1 hour, 4 minutes, 40 seconds, and 26 frames. However, when you read the current timecode for a sequence in the Canvas window (this doesn't apply to timecode for clips in the Viewer window), it's traditional to start any sequence at 1 hour, not zero hours. So if a sequence's current timecode says "01:04:40:26", that means the sequence is 4 minutes, 40 seconds and 26 frames long, NOT 1 hour, 4 minutes, 40 seconds and 26 frames long.

Moving Clips to the Timeline

When you're editing, you'll spend a lot of time moving media clips from Final Cut's Browser window to the Timeline as you weave them into your story. Final Cut gives you a few options for accomplishing this; we start with the easiest, most intuitive approach and end with the quickest, most flexible.

To insert or overwrite? That is the question

When you add a clip to a track on the Timeline, you're making what's called an *edit*. And the two edits you're most likely to make in Final Cut are *insert* edits or *overwrite* edits. The difference between these two edits is simple:

With an insert edit, Final Cut creates new room on the Timeline track for your clip, so it doesn't copy over other clips that are already there (in other words, this edit works and plays well with others). When you do an overwrite edit, Final Cut adds your clip to the Timeline, but if the new clip is long enough to run into other clips already on that track, the new clip erases the existing ones (a decidedly selfish kind of edit). Figure 6-4 shows the original arrangement of clips A, B, and C and then what happens when clip D is added after clip A with both an insert and overwrite edit.

Figure 6-4: The effects of an insert edit and an overwrite edit.

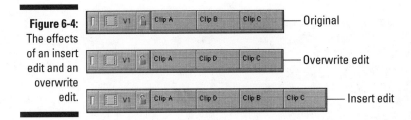

So, which type of edit should you use? It depends on what you're trying to do. If you want to add a clip to a bunch of other clips, use an insert edit. But if you don't like how a certain clip is working on the Timeline, and want to see how a new one does in its place, an overwrite edit might be better. The important thing is that you don't think too much about any of this. You'll develop a natural feel for it all soon enough. In any case, here's the easiest, most intuitive way to do either edit:

1. **Position the Timeline playhead wherever in time you want to add your new clip.**

   Final Cut will place your clip wherever the playhead is on the Timeline. So click your mouse in the Timeline's ruler to position the playhead at that point in time. (To fine-tune the playhead's position, you can move it frame by frame with the arrow keys.) The Canvas window shows the current frame the playhead is on (if a frame is there, as opposed to empty space).

   Although you can position the playhead anywhere, you usually position the playhead at the edge of existing clips (at the first or last frame of a clip). If this is the case, make sure that Final Cut's Snapping feature is turned on (check under the View menu). This feature makes positioning the playhead at a clip's edge easy work. (See the section "Speeding Up Editing with Snapping" later in this chapter.)

2. **Drag your clip from the Browser window to the Canvas window.**

   Yes, drag it to the Canvas, not the Timeline. As you drag, a number of buttons pop up over the Canvas window, giving you several choices for the kind of edit you want to make, as shown in Figure 6-5. Don't release the mouse button yet!

3. Move the mouse over either Insert or Overwrite, and then let go of the mouse button.

Final Cut now either inserts or overwrites your clip to the Timeline. If your clip includes both video and audio in it, the video portion appears on the timeline's video track, while its audio goes on one or two audio tracks (one track for mono audio and two tracks audio captured in stereo — see Chapter 12 for more on audio).

How simple was that?

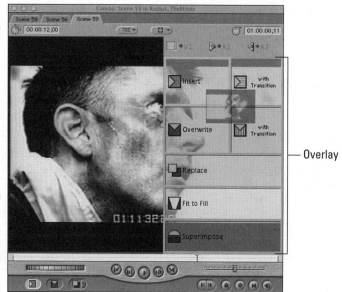

Overlay

Figure 6-5:
The Canvas window's pop-up edit window.

Some clips, when moved to the timeline, will have to be rendered before playing properly. (*Rendering* is when Final Cut figures out ahead of time how to play a clip.) You'll know a clip has to be rendered because Final Cut will draw a thin red horizontal line above it in the Timeline window, and the Canvas window will say "Unrendered" when you try to play the clip. To render it, select it on the Timeline, and choose Render Selection from the Sequence menu (or just press ⌘+R).

Moving clips to the right track on the Timeline

If your Timeline has a lot of tracks, you need a way to tell Final Cut which track a clip should go to. For instance, if you have multiple audio tracks for stereo dialogue, sound effects, and music, you don't want to insert a clip of music on dialogue track. What to do? Well, this section can help you stay on track.

Look at the left side of the Timeline, where the tracks begin. As shown in Figure 6-6, to the left of each track name is a little icon called a target track control — a filmstrip for video tracks and left/right speakers for audio tracks. (Audio tracks show a 1 in the left speaker if they're designated stereo left audio and a 2 if they're designated for right audio — see Chapter 12 for more about stereo audio.) Go ahead and click these icons to turn them on and off. Note that an icon turns yellow when it's on, and that only one track can be turned on at once. So when a track's icon is turned on, it's your designated track — that is, it's the track where all your clips go when you do an edit.

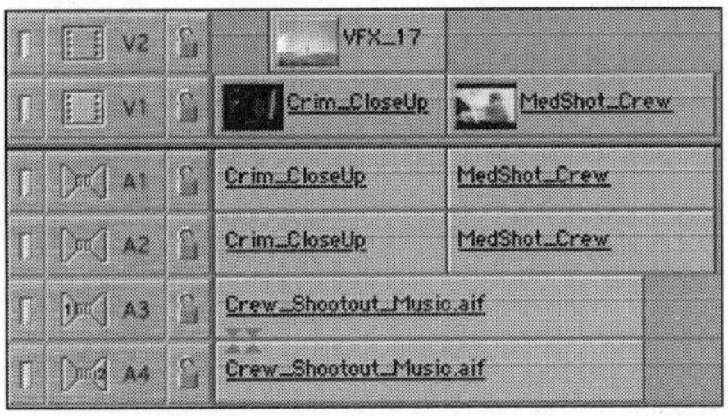

Figure 6-6:
Click a
track's icon
to turn it on
or off.

Just for the record, you don't have to designate a track each time you make an edit — just when you want to change the currently designated track to a new one.

Turbocharge your insert and overwrite edits

When you become comfortable doing insert and overwrite edits by dragging clips to the Canvas (and designating your target tracks on the timeline), you may want to try out this more direct approach:

Click a clip's icon or name in the Browser window, and simply drag it to any point in time on the timeline (regardless of the playhead's position), and any track on the timeline (regardless of your target tracks). As you drag your clip to its track (video or audio), notice that the upper third of the track has a horizontal line running through it (see Figure 6-7, it's easy to miss). If you drag your clip *above* this line, Final Cut will insert your clip on the timeline (your mouse pointer becomes an arrow pointing to the right, signaling an insert). But if you drag your clip *below* this line, Final Cut overwrites your clip on the timeline (your mouse pointer becomes an arrow pointing down when you're in overwrite mode).

Figure 6-7:
Moving
clips to
tracks on
the Timeline.

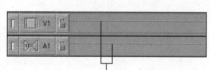

Drag a clip above these lines for an Insert;
drag below for an Overwrite

Setting in and out points to move parts of clips to the Timeline

When you're moving clips to the Timeline, you can move either the entire clip or just a part of it. At first, you may feel more comfortable dragging entire clips to the Timeline and then trimming them down after they're there. But in many cases, it's better to look at the clip ahead of time, identify only the part you're interested in by setting in and out points, and *then* move the abbreviated clip to the Timeline. This method keeps the Timeline less cluttered. Here's how to set in and out points:

1. **Find the clip in the Browser and double-click it to open it in the Viewer.**

2. **Within the clip, find the first frame you want to move to the Timeline.**

   To find the frame, click your mouse in the Viewer's scrubber bar (refer to Figure 6-8) to move the playhead until the playhead is on the frame you want. The frame in the Viewer window corresponds to the frame that the playhead is on.

3. **To set an in point, click the Mark In button in the Viewer or simply press I (see Figure 6-8).**

   You'll see an in point symbol (it's a triangle pointing to the right) appear at the Viewer's playhead and also in the top-left corner of the frame you've marked (this makes it easy to find marked frames).

4. **Mark an out point at the last frame you want to move to the Timeline.**

   Same routine as Steps 2 and 3, but click the Mark Out button in the Viewer window (or just press O).

Congratulations: You've now marked a range of frames within a larger clip. When you move this clip to the Timeline (using any of the steps we just covered), Final Cut moves *only* the frames that fall within your in and out points.

If you set an in point on a clip, but no out point, Final Cut assumes the out point is the last frame of the clip. And if you set an out point, but no in point, Final Cut assumes the in point is the first frame of the clip.

Figure 6-8:
The Viewer
with in and
out points.

Scrubber bar   In and Out points

To move an in or out point, just click and drag the in/out arrow in the Viewer's scrubber bar to a new location. You can clear in and out points by choosing the option from the Mark menu, or by pressing Option+X.

Recycling a clip by setting different in and out points

In the thick of editing, you might want to use the same clip over again, but in each instance, you may want to set different in and out points. For example, you have a clip whose early frames would be great at the beginning of your movie, but its later frames would also be useful towards the end of the story. When you want to use different parts of the same clip, you open it in the Viewer, set in and out points for the first part of the clip, and move those frames to the Timeline. Now go back to the Browser, open the same clip in the Viewer window again, set different in and out points, and move the clip *again* to the Timeline. Voilà: You now have two entirely different clips on the Timeline, each one taken from the same master clip.

Selecting Clips on the Timeline

After you get your clips to the Timeline, you have to select them before you can edit them in various ways (for instance, move or delete them). Doing so isn't rocket science: You select a clip on the Timeline by using the selection tool, which is the arrow-shaped tool on the tool palette. To select a single clip on the Timeline, just make sure that you're using the selection tool and click the clip.

Sometimes, you'll want to select a number of clips at once, or a range of frames within one or a group of clips. Table 6-1 runs down some of the handy tools that Final Cut offers for selecting multiple clips.

Table 6-1	Tools for Selecting Clips on the Timeline	
	Tool	*What It Does*
	Selection tool	To select multiple, continuous clips, click the first clip, then hold the Shift key while clicking the last clip, and Final Cut selects all clips in between. To select multiple but noncontinuous clips (those that aren't one after another), hold down the ⌘ key while clicking each clip.
	Group selection tool	Select a range of whole clips by dragging a selection marquee across any clips you want. You can also hold shift to select multiple groups of clips with this tool. If your clips are linked (like the way audio clips are usually linked to their corresponding video), this tool will select those linked clips too.
	Track forward tool	This handy tool selects whatever clip you click *and* every clip on that track that follows it (that is, to the right of the clip you click). This is a godsend when you trim or delete one clip amid a long continuous sequence so that there's an unwanted empty gap among the clips. The solution is to select all the clips *after* that gap, and then move them over to close the gap in one fell swoop.

Tool		What It Does
	**All tracks forward tool**	Works just like the track forward tool, but when you click a clip, you'll select both it and *every* clip that follows it — on not one but all tracks. It's a great option if you want to select not only clips on your video track, for instance, but also your audio tracks at the same time (when you want to move or delete them all together.)

TIP After you select clips with any of the tools in Table 6-1, you can quickly move the entire group by clicking one of the highlighted clips and then dragging your mouse.

TIP If you select a clip or clips but then decide not to do anything with it, deselect it. To deselect a clip, click your mouse away from the clip (provided you don't have a track selection tool active), or press ⌘+D with your free hand (for Deselect All) to save you from mouse-moving overload.

Moving a Clip That's Already on the Timeline

After a clip is on the Timeline, you can click and drag it anywhere else in time or to another track. (For instance, you can move an audio clip from track A1 to A2, no problem.) But here's something new: When you drag a clip elsewhere on the Timeline, you can *overwrite* it to its new location, or do what's called a *swap edit*.

Overwrites are straightforward. When you move your clip, it fills as much space on the Timeline as it needs, erases any clips that are already there, and leaves an empty gap on the Timeline where it once was (as shown in Figure 6-9). To do an overwrite edit, you simply click and drag your selection to the point on the Timeline where you want it. As you'll see from practice, this usually isn't the most helpful of edits, partly because you usually don't want to leave an empty gap between edits.

When you do a swap edit (shown in Figure 6-10), Final Cut inserts the selection (meaning it creates new space on the Timeline so that it doesn't overwrite any existing clips) *and* closes the gap left behind. For instance, let's say you've arranged clips A, B, C, and D on the Timeline one after another, but decide that clip C should actually come *before* B. Simply drag C in front of B, as shown in Figure 6-10, and you have a seamless sequence of clips: A, C, B, D, and no empty space where C once was. To do a swap edit, hold down the Option key while you drag your selection.

TIP

You can overwrite or swap a clip or clips directly *into* another clip, not just to its border. For instance, you can drag clip B to the 5th frame of clip A, not just to the beginning or end of clip A.

REMEMBER

You can move not only single clips by clicking and dragging, but large groups of clips too (or just a range of frames within a clip). To select those clips, use one of the many selection tools in the Tool palette. See Table 6-1 for a rundown of these tools.

TIP

You can also move clips by using the time-honored, no frills cut, copy, and paste commands. Select a clip or clips, and choose either Cut or Copy from Final Cut's Edit menu (or press ⌘-X or ⌘-C respectively). Position the time-line's playhead where you want to paste the clips, and then choose Paste from the Edit menu to overwrite the clips at that point, or Paste Insert to insert them. Final Cut pastes the clips to whatever track you've designated as your target track.

Figure 6-9:
An overwrite edit, as clip C moves into B's position.

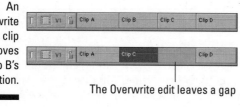

The Overwrite edit leaves a gap

Figure 6-10:
A swap edit, as clip C moves into B's position.

Linking and unlinking clips

If a clip on the timeline includes both video and audio, Final Cut normally keeps those related elements linked: If you try to select, move, resize, cut, or delete a linked clip on the Timeline's video track, Final Cut does the same to its related clips on the audio tracks as well (and vice versa). At times, however, you may want to unlink related clips or link unrelated clips together.

To unlink video from audio (and vice versa), select the linked clip on the timeline, and choose Modify⇨Link to toggle linking off. Be warned: If you unlink video and audio and then move one without the other, they'll become out-of-synch;

for instance, an actor's dialogue will no longer match his lip movement. Final Cut makes it easy to spot such cases by displaying a red tag on each timeline clip that's out of synch, along with a time value telling you how much the clip is off.

To link video and audio clips back together (whether they were originally linked, or are totally unrelated), just select the clips on the timeline, and choose Modify⇨Link to toggle linking back on. A little underline appears beneath the clip names to indicate that they're now linked.

Speeding Up Editing with Snapping

Snapping makes aligning media clips on the Timeline easy because it makes clips magnetically stick to each other or to other elements on the Timeline (such as the Timeline's playhead, In and Out points set on the Timeline, or markers you've placed). Go ahead and try out this feature: When you move a couple of clips to the Timeline, drag one towards the other — when the clips get close, they'll automatically snap together.

You can turn snapping on or off in Final Cut, but you'll want it on for most editing work. It's on by default, but you can verify that by making sure that Snapping is checked on the View menu. On rare occasions, you'll want to make precise edits that snapping interferes with. In this case, just turn off Snapping by choosing View⇨Snapping.

Resizing Clips Already on the Timeline

After you place your clips on the Timeline, most of your editing energy is devoted to resizing those clips — that is, trimming frames from one clip or adding frames to another. You can do these edits one of two ways:

✔ Drag a clip's edges in or out on the Timeline.

✔ Open the clip in the Viewer window and set new in and out points for it, which automatically resize the clip on the Timeline.

Which tack should you take? When you open a clip in the Viewer, you can play through the entire clip, back and forth, until you've found the right frame to extend or trim it to. It's the easiest way to gauge the clip you're working with, but you can't beat the speed of resizing clips directly on the Timeline. In the end, give both methods a try, and you'll develop a natural feel for when each is best.

Resizing clips directly on the Timeline

If you want to resize clips as quickly as possible, do it directly on the Timeline:

1. **Choose the selection tool from the tool palette.**

   It may already be selected, but you can also press A just in case.

2. **Move your mouse pointer to the edge of a clip on the Timeline.**

   When the mouse is over either the clip's left or right edge, your mouse pointer becomes a resize symbol, as shown in Figure 6-11.

3. **Drag the clip's edges in or out to resize it to a new frame.**

   Dragging inwards trims the clip, and dragging outwards extends it (if there are unseen frames to extend to). Keep an eye on the Canvas window: As you drag, it shows which frame is at the clip's edge. Also, on the Timeline, a pop-up number shows you how many frames you're trimming or extending the clip to.

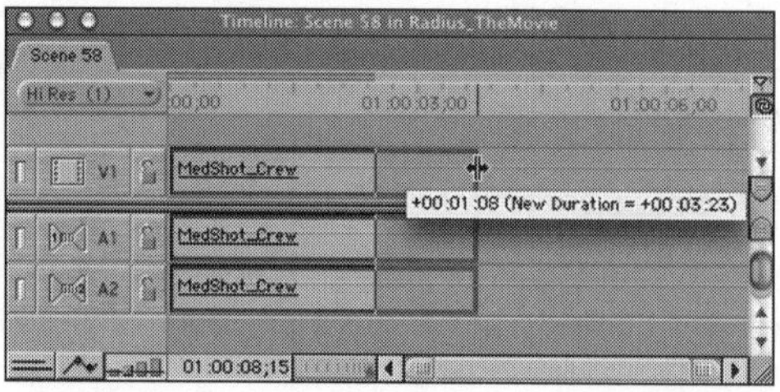

Figure 6-11: A drag of a clip on the Timeline.

If you're trimming a clip on the Timeline, you can use Final Cut's Snapping feature to easily drag the clip's edge to whatever new frame you're trimming to. Just follow these steps:

1. **Make sure Snapping is turned on.**

   On the View menu, Snapping is checked if it's on.

2. **Position the Timeline's playhead at the frame you want to trim your clip to.**

   You might want to play the clip a couple of times to look for the best place to trim it to. To position the playhead precisely on that frame, move it frame by frame with your keyboard arrow keys.

3. **Now drag either the start or end edge of the clip towards the playhead.**

   Final Cut quickly snaps that edge to that point (and therefore the frame you're trimming to).

When you resize a clip by dragging its edges, you may find that you can't move the clip's edge to the exact frame you want — even if you drag the mouse an insy-tinsy bit, the edge can jump several frames at a time. To fix this, zoom in on the Timeline for more precision. You can zoom by pressing ⌘++ (the ⌘ key and the plus key) or by using the Zoom In tool on the tool palette, shown in Figure 6-12. With the Zoom tool selected, click the Timeline anywhere. To zoom in even further, keep pressing ⌘++ or keep clicking the Timeline with the Zoom tool. To zoom out, press ⌘+− (⌘ and the minus key) or use the zoom out in the tool palette.

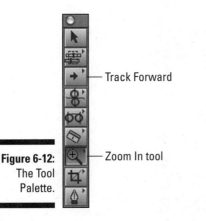

Track Forward

Zoom In tool

Figure 6-12: The Tool Palette.

Resizing clips in the Viewer window

The Viewer window method isn't as quick as the preceding one, but it's the way to go when you want to do a precise edit. Here's how:

1. **Make sure the selection tool in the tool palette is active.**

2. **On the Timeline, double-click the clip you want to resize.**

   Final Cut opens the clip in the Viewer window (check out Figure 6-13). You can see the entire clip, even if you originally moved only part of it to the Timeline. But if you've already trimmed the clip (maybe you set in and out points when you first moved it to the Timeline), you see the clip's current in and out points on the Viewer's scrubber bar.

3. **Mark a new in and/or out point(s) to trim or extend the clip.**

   If you want to adjust the clip's first frame, you set an in point at the frame where you want the clip to start. If you want to adjust the clip's last frame, you set an out point at the frame where you want the clip to end.

   As you mark a new in or out point, Final Cut automatically adjusts the size of your clip on the Timeline (making it longer or shorter — with a few exceptions, which we cover in a moment).

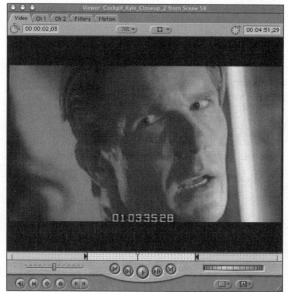

Figure 6-13: Set in and out points in the Viewer window to resize a clip precisely.

Limitations of resizing clips

Just when you think you've mastered the fine art of resizing clips, we've got a bit of bad news: The steps we just outlined have some annoying limitations. Here are the two biggest culprits:

✔ Final Cut won't let you extend a clip if another clip is next to the edge you're extending. In other words, if you have clips A, B, and C arranged side by side and want to extend either edge of clip B, you can't do it. Clips A and C effectively block it, refusing to move over on the Timeline to make room for B's extended frames.

✔ What's more, if you trim a clip that's next to other clips, your trim creates a gap in the Timeline. In other words, if you have clips A, B, C, and D next to each other and decide to trim frames off the end of clip B, then clips C and D don't automatically move over to fill the space left by B's trim. Your Timeline looks like this: clip A, trimmed B, empty space, and then clips C and D.

But now for the good news! You can use some of Final Cut's other tools to solve these two headaches. One handy option is the Track Forward or All Tracks Forward tool (check out Figure 6-12 again), which enable you to quickly select a group of clips on one or all tracks, and move them either forward or back on the Timeline in one fell swoop. By doing this, you can quickly create room for a clip you want to extend, or close gaps left by a clip you just trimmed.

The most quick and efficient way to deal with resizing clips is to use Final Cut's advanced editing tools from the Tool palette — things like Roll Edit, Ripple Edit, Slip Item, and Slide Item — which let you extend and trim clips in all sorts of ways, while Final Cut seamlessly adjusts all the other clips in the Timeline, sparing you from worrying about them.

So, by now, you're probably wondering: "Why didn't these guys mention these tools in the first place?" They can be a bit overwhelming to new editors, and are harder to appreciate if you haven't worked without them. So try resizing your clips by using the steps that we explain here, but when you think you're ready, head on over to Chapter 8, where we tackle Final Cut's advanced tools in all their glory.

Cutting a Clip into Two

After you've dragged a clip to the Timeline, you'll sometimes find the need to cut it into smaller pieces. For instance, you might want to cut a clip in two

✔ To use its early frames at the beginning of your sequence and its later frames in another place

✔ To trim off an extra frame you don't need

✔ To insert a third clip between the two, freshly cut parts

Final Cut lets you cut clips in two different ways: You can cut a single clip on *one* track of the Timeline, or your cut can carry through *all* tracks on the Timeline, simultaneously splitting any clips carried on those tracks (see Figure 6-14).

The type of cut you do depends on what's going on in your movie. For instance, say you're working on a sequence that uses three tracks on the Timeline: one video track, one audio track for dialogue, and another audio track for background music. Suppose your video track features a stock analyst talking about stocks and bonds, but while the analyst is talking, you decide to quickly cut from the analyst to new video of the New York Stock Exchange — all the while, the analyst's dialogue and the background music continue to play over this new shot, uninterrupted. To insert the clip of the Stock Exchange, you have to make a cut in the video clip featuring your analyst, but should you cut through just the clip on the video track, or through the clips on the dialogue and music tracks as well? In this case, you want to cut only the analyst clip on the video track and leave the clips on the audio tracks untouched because you don't want the change in the video to interrupt the audio.

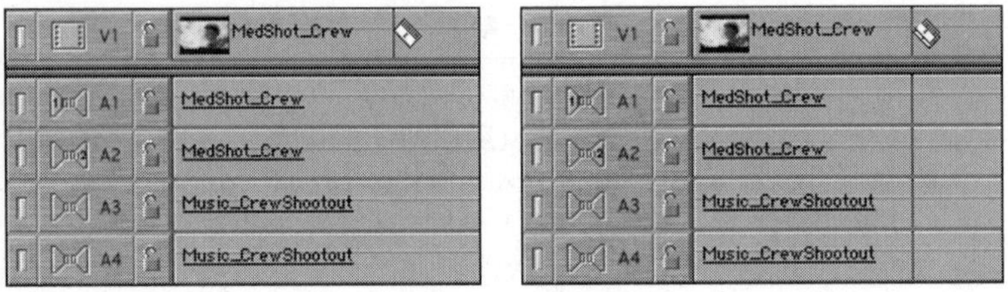

Figure 6-14:
Clicking the Razor Blade tool in the video track cuts only the clip in that track, whereas the Razor Blade All tool also cuts through all the tracks.

On the flip side, suppose that in the middle of your stock analyst interview, you decide that Mr. Analyst is getting a little dry, so you want to cut away to an entirely different scene, perhaps an establishing shot of some glistening corporate campus, with a new voice over in your dialogue track and new background music, too. To cut from the stock analyst segment to this new scene, you want to cut the stock analyst clips on *all* your tracks because you want them all to end at the same point, which is also the point where you begin your new scene.

Here's how to cut clips on one or multiple tracks:

1. **Move the Timeline's playhead to the frame where you want to make a cut.**

   Click in the Timeline's ruler to move the playhead to that point, or use your keyboard's arrow keys to move frame by frame for extra precision. Keep an eye on the Canvas window — it shows whatever frame the playhead is on.

2. **Choose the Razor Blade tool or the Razor Blade All tool.**

   If you want to cut a clip on only one Timeline track, press B for blade or choose the Razor Blade tool from the tool palette, as shown in Figure 6-15.

   If you want to cut clips on *all* the Timeline tracks, use the Razor Blade All tool. You can just press B twice on your keyboard, or you can choose the tool from the tool palette. (It's hidden beneath the Razor Blade. Just click and hold your mouse over the razor blade icon, and the Razor Blade All tool pops out as well.)

3. **Click the clip you want to cut.**

   Line up the blade with the Timeline's playhead so that you cut the frame you picked in Step 1. If you have the Snapping feature turned on, Final Cut automatically snaps the blade to the playhead, so you can line up the two very quickly. (Turn snapping on and off from the View menu, or press N.)

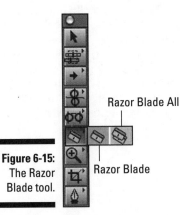

Razor Blade All

Figure 6-15: The Razor Blade tool.

Razor Blade

TIP

What happens if your Timeline sports many tracks, and you want to make a cut through *some* of those tracks, but not all of them? It's easy: Use the Razor Blade All tool, but before cutting, lock any tracks you don't want your cut to affect. To lock a track, click the little lock icon to the left of each track. By locking a track, you protect any clips on it from being cut, moved, or otherwise changed.

When you cut a clip in two, each new clip "remembers" all the media (video or audio) the original, larger clip had. You can recover these frames by clicking and dragging out the edges of each of the cut clips.

You may be tempted to use the Razor Blade to cut a clip in two, so that you can insert a third clip in between (for instance, to show actor A, cut to actor B, and then cut back to your original shot of actor A). However, you can use an even easier alternative that doesn't involve the Razor Blade at all. See "Moving a Clip That's Already on the Timeline" earlier in this chapter for the technique to use when you want to insert one clip into another (effectively splitting the first clip).

Deleting Clips from the Timeline

When you have no more use for a clip on the Timeline, you delete it so that it doesn't play in your movie or clutter up the Timeline. (**Remember:** Even when you delete a clip from the Timeline, it stays put in the Browser window, so you can use it again.) There are two different ways to delete a clip in Final Cut: the first way is called a *lift edit*, and the second is a *ripple delete*.

Doing a simple lift edit or a ripple delete

A lift edit is your no-frills, garden-variety delete. You select a clip and then delete it, leaving an empty gap in your Timeline (which plays as black void in your movie). This may be fine by you, but if the deleted clip is followed by other clips on the Timeline, you probably want to move all those clips to the left so that they fill in the empty gap. And that's where the ripple delete comes in: It deletes your clip and automatically "ripples" all the following clips to the left so that there's no empty gap, as shown in Figure 6-16. (But there are occasional side effects; see the sidebar "The unforeseen dangers of the ripple delete," elsewhere in this chapter.)

Figure 6-16:
This sequence of clips changes when clip B is Lifted or Ripple Deleted.

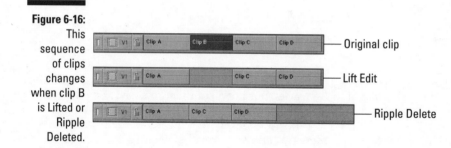

You'll probably use the ripple delete most in your work, but here's how to do either one:

1. **Select the clip or clips you want to delete on the Timeline.**

   You can select a single clip by clicking it with the Selection tool, or select a group of continuous clips by clicking each one while holding down the Shift key.

   You can also use Final Cut's other tools to select groups of clips, entire Timeline tracks, or just parts of tracks. See "Selecting Clips on the Timeline" for more about selecting clips.

   In some cases, you may have placed a video clip on your Timeline that comes linked with its own audio clips (this is especially true with DV video). When video and audio clips are linked, deleting the video clip also cuts the linked audio clips (or vice versa). If you don't want to do this, you can always unlink the video and audio clips by selecting the clips and then choosing Modify⇨Link so that the Link command is unchecked.

2. **Press the Delete key to do a lift edit or press Shift+Delete to do a ripple delete.**

Cutting and pasting clips on the Timeline

You can cut clips from one place in the Timeline and paste them somewhere else, which is a pretty handy trick. Here's how:

1. **Select the clip or clips you want to cut.**

   See "Selecting Clips on the Timeline" for more about selecting clips and all the wonderful selection tools on the Tool Palette.

2. **Cut the clip using either a lift edit (press ⌘+X) or a ripple delete (press Shift+X).**

   If you choose Edit⇨Cut from the menu bar, you do a lift edit. See the preceding section if you don't know what a lift edit or a ripple delete is.

3. **Position your playhead elsewhere on the Timeline.**

4. **To paste the selection you cut, choose Paste (press ⌘+V) or Paste Insert (press Shift+V) from the Edit menu.**

When you paste a selection, it's overwritten on the timeline, while Paste Insert inserts it. See the section "To insert or overwrite? That is the question" earlier in this chapter.

The unforeseen dangers of the ripple delete

Sometimes a ripple delete can change how clips in different tracks synch up together, leading to problems. For instance, say you're editing a music video and just spent endless hours timing your video cuts to beats in the music track. But suppose you decide you don't like a video shot in the middle of your sequence, and ripple delete it. All the video clips to the right of your deleted clip now shift over (to close the gap on the Timeline) and, unfortunately, fall out of synch with your music because you didn't delete anything from the music track. To dodge this headache, skip using a ripple delete altogether. Instead do a lift edit and find a new video clip to fill in the gap left by the deleted one.

Deleting parts of clips on multiple tracks

You can also delete just a portion of a clip (or a range of clips) by setting in and out points on the Timeline and then deleting any video and audio that fall within those points. As you become comfortable with Final Cut, you'll probably favor this tactic — it's so direct; see Figure 6-17.

1. **Move the Timeline's playhead to the first frame of the range you want to delete.**

   The Canvas window shows whatever frame is currently under the playhead. Make sure you haven't accidentally selected another clip in the Timeline before setting your in and out points — otherwise, Final Cut will delete the selected clip, not what you designate now. You can quickly deselect any clips on the Timeline by pressing ⌘+D.

2. **Mark your in point by pressing I for in or by clicking the Mark In button in the Canvas window (Figure 6-17).**

   An in point (a triangle pointing to the right) appears in the Timeline and in the Canvas window's scrubber (both display in and out points that you've set in your movie).

3. **Move the Timeline's playhead to the last frame of the range you want to delete and mark an out point.**

   You can click the Mark Out button in the Canvas window (Figure 6-17), choose it from the Mark menu, or just press O for Out. Train yourself to use the keyboard shortcut if you can.

4. **Do a lift edit or ripple delete by pressing the Delete key or Shift+Delete respectively.**

   Final Cut now cuts out all the frames that fall within your in and out points on all tracks of the Timeline.

In and Out points   Canvas

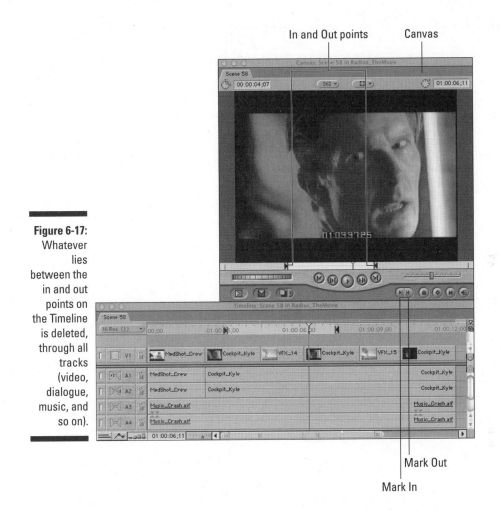

Figure 6-17:
Whatever
lies
between the
in and out
points on
the Timeline
is deleted,
through all
tracks
(video,
dialogue,
music, and
so on).

Mark Out

Mark In

When you delete media by using in and out points, Final Cut makes your cuts through *all* the tracks on your Timeline (video and audio). This might be fine by you, but if not (for instance, if you want to cut out frames from a video track, but leave dialogue and music tracks untouched), you can protect those tracks by locking them. Click the lock icon to the left of each track you want to preserve before making a cut.

Chapter 7

Getting to Know the Timeline

*I*f you read Chapter 6, you bit off and chewed quite a bit: all the skills you need to edit an entire film from start to finish. In this chapter, you nibble on smaller fare — the kind of things that can help you work more smoothly with Final Cut's Timeline (which is where most of your blood, sweat, and tears are spilled while editing).

All About Timeline Tracks

One of the most important things you can do with the Timeline is to take control of your tracks. (You remember Timeline tracks, don't you? For a refresher, see Chapter 6, and check out Figure 7-1 here.) For instance, sometimes you want to turn off certain tracks so that Final Cut won't play any of the clips on them — turning off your music tracks to better hear dialogue, perhaps. Or you may want to lock a track, so any clips on it can't be accidentally resized or moved. Or you want to ensure that when you move new clips from the Browser to the Timeline, they go to exactly the tracks you want. The Timeline enables you to do all of this and more.

Locking tracks so they can't be changed

When you lock a track on the Timeline, you're preventing any clips on that track from being resized, moved, deleted, or changed in any other way. Why would you want to freeze a track like this in the course of your editing? For any number of reasons, all of which involve your wanting to make changes to clips that are on *some* of the tracks in your film, but not on *all* of them. For example, suppose that your movie sports a number of tracks (a video track and audio tracks for dialogue, sound effects, and music) and you want to cut out a scene's video, dialogue, and sound effects but leave the music tracks completely untouched (see Figure 7-2).

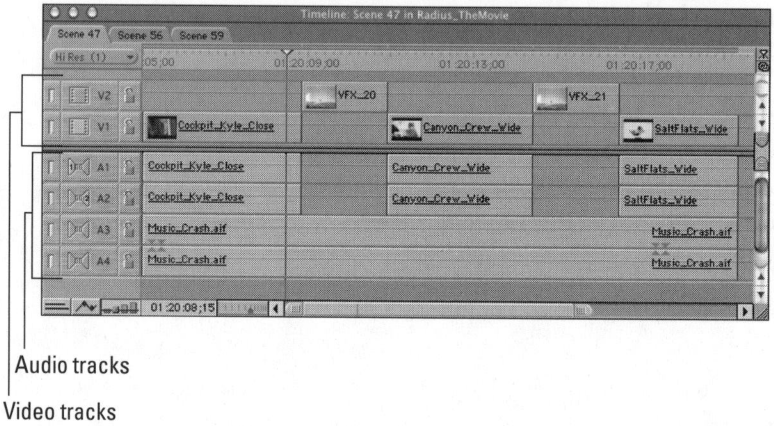

Figure 7-1:
Using tracks helps you organize different kinds of clips on the Timeline.

Audio tracks

Video tracks

In this case, you'd first lock the music track and then make your cut to the rest of the Timeline tracks. (See Chapter 6 for options on the best way to make the cuts.) End result? Final Cut cuts through the clips on all your tracks *except* the music tracks because they're locked!

To lock a track, just click the Lock Track control for that particular track. (The Lock Track control is a little padlock icon to the left of each track — see Figure 7-3.) Final Cut draws diagonal lines through the entire length of the track to let you know that that track is now off-limits.

To unlock a track, just click the Lock Track icon again, and your locked track becomes fully editable again.

TIP

One other reason to lock your tracks is when you know that you're finished tinkering with them. If you've labored over a group of clips and honed them to picture-perfect perfection, just lock the tracks that carry those clips so you don't accidentally change them while working on other parts of your film.

Hiding and soloing tracks

If your movie uses a lot of tracks, you may sometimes want to play only *some* of the tracks but not others — for instance, maybe you want to watch your movie while carefully listening to its dialogue track, but without hearing the tracks that carry your sound effects and music. In this case, you can hide those distracting tracks. On the other hand, if you have a single track that you want to see or hear all by itself, you can easily tell Final Cut to play this track only and ignore all the others; this technique is called *soloing* a track.

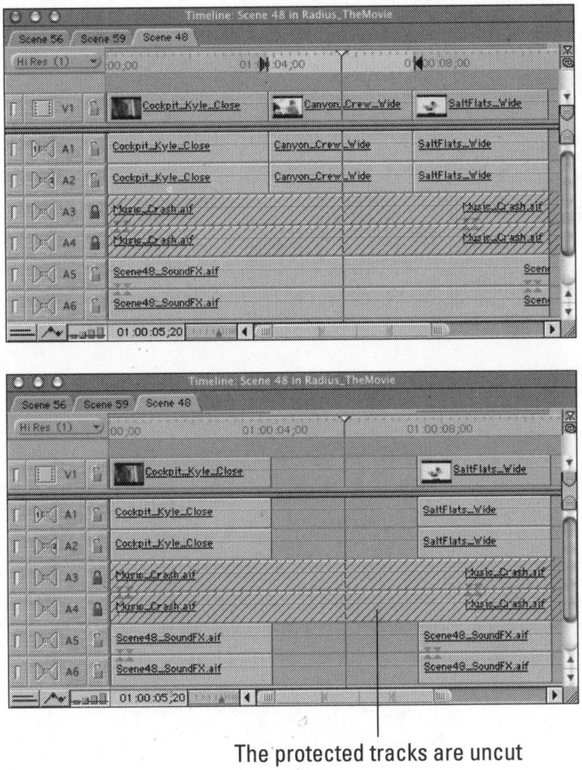

Figure 7-2:
Before and after cutting: All tracks except the protected ones are cut.

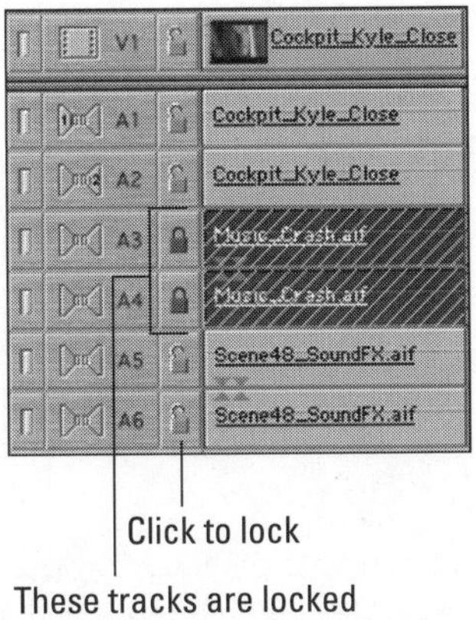

The protected tracks are uncut

Figure 7-3:
The Lock Track control icons, both locked and unlocked.

Click to lock

These tracks are locked

To hide a track so that its clips don't play in your sequence, just click the Track Visibility control (the little rectangular icon at the far left side of that track), as shown in Figure 7-4. When you're ready to bring the track back to normal, just click that icon again.

Figure 7-4:
The Track
Visibility
Control,
showing
some tracks
turned
on and
some not.

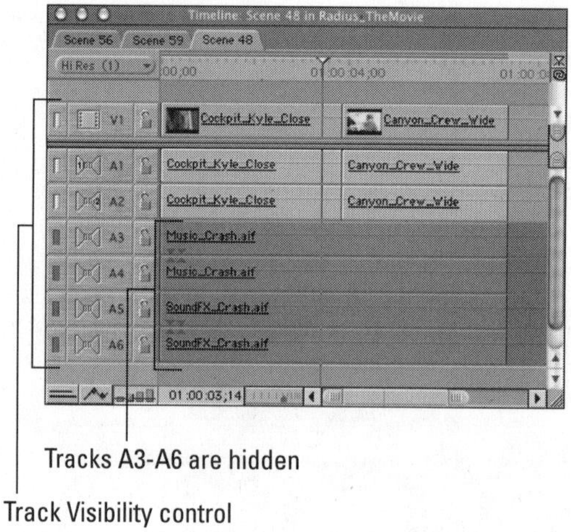

Tracks A3-A6 are hidden

Track Visibility control

To solo a single track so that it's the only one that Final Cut plays, just hold the Option key down while clicking the Track Visibility control for that track.

In one instance, hiding tracks on the Timeline has an unwanted effect: If you rendered some of your video or audio clips before Final Cut could play them, you lose those renders when you hide the track that they're on. Don't panic too much. Losing the renders doesn't hurt your original clips; it just means that you'll have to re-render them. You really have no good reason to throw out rendered clips, but in the meantime, you can recover those renders by choosing Edit⇨Undo. (See Chapter 16 for more about rendering.)

Designating your target tracks

Final Cut lets you designate one of your video tracks and two of your audio tracks (for left and right stereo channels) as so-called *target tracks*. By doing this, you're telling Final Cut that these target tracks are the main ones you're focusing on, and that various edits you make should affect those tracks instead of any others on your Timeline.

Here are a few instances when Final Cut works with the target tracks you've selected:

✔ When you move video and audio clips from the Viewer or Browser to the Timeline (other than by dragging them), they go to whatever tracks you've targeted.

✔ When you copy and paste clips on the Timeline, the pasted clips appear on whatever tracks you've targeted.

✔ When you use the Match Frame feature (good for synching video to audio — see Chapter 8), Final Cut matches to the clip the playhead is on — but if your playhead is on multiple clips, Final Cut picks the one on your target track.

✔ When you want to mark clips, or add keyframes to them, Final Cut works with clips on your target tracks.

Targeting a video track

To turn any video track into your video target track, just click the track's Target Track control, as shown in Figure 7-5. Clicking the control again turns off targeting for that track. (The control turns yellow for on and gray for off.)

Targeting two audio tracks

You can target *two* audio tracks because most of the audio you work with uses two tracks to carry the audio's left and right stereo channels (refer to Figure 7-5).

Click to target a video track

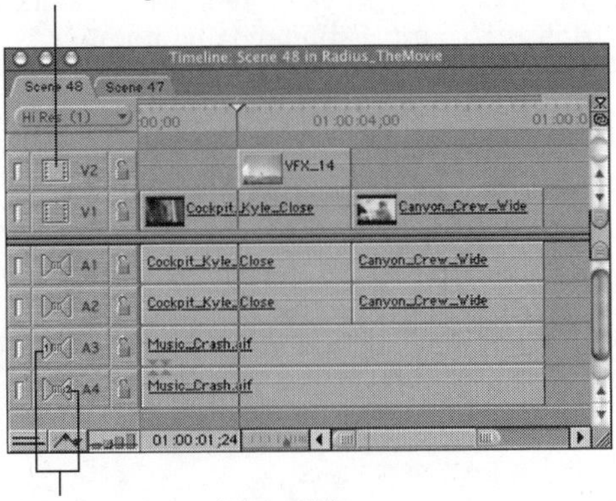

Figure 7-5:
The Target Track control buttons for video and audio tracks.

You can target a left or right stereo audio track by clicking the Target Track control buttons.

To make an audio track your left channel target track, click the Left speaker icon on the audio track's Target Track control. A little numeral 1 appears in the icon, showing that it's now your channel 1 (that is, the target track). To target a track as your right channel target track, just click the Right speaker icon on the track's Target Track control; a little numeral 2 appears in the icon. You can click these icons again to turn off targeting for the tracks as well.

Turning off your target tracks

Editing with your video and audio tracks targeted is usually best, but sometimes you may want to turn off that targeting when you don't want to affect those tracks with an edit you're about to make. For instance, suppose you want to add a clip of video to the Timeline, but that clip also has two channels of audio built in (typical of DV video). To move the clip's video without the audio, just turn off your targeted audio tracks, and Final Cut moves only the clip's video to the Timeline. To move only the clip's audio to the Timeline, make sure that no video tracks are targeted when you do the move.

Adding and deleting tracks from the Timeline

Adding and deleting tracks as you build sequences of clips on the Timeline is natural. For example, you may want to add a video track to carry visual effects or titles for your movie or add a slew of audio tracks to hold different versions of your composer's musical score. (Having each version on the Timeline lets you easily compare one revision with another.) At the same time, as you add tracks while you edit your movie, you may find reasons to toss out other tracks — maybe you decide not to use the clips on a track or two. Or you find that you have so many tracks that you can't keep them straight, so you decide to consolidate their clips to a more manageable number.

You probably want a lot of audio tracks in your sequence to carry things like simultaneous dialogue clips, sound effects, music, and so on. But while Final Cut lets you add up to 99 audio tracks to the Timeline, it can't actually play all 99 tracks *at the same time*. Playing a clip of audio is no easy feat for your Macintosh; and if you ask it to play more than, say, eight at once, it'll crack under the pressure. (Actually, it will play a repeating BEEP in place of the lush audio you expect.) The good news is that you can *still* play all those audio tracks together, but you have to *render* their clips first.

Adding a single track

If you want to add a track to the Timeline quickly, you have two options:

✔ Simply drag any clip (that is, a clip that's either already on the Timeline or that's currently in the Browser window) to the unused area above the last video track on the Timeline (for video clips) or below the last audio track (for audio clips).

When you let go of the mouse button, Final Cut creates a new track on the Timeline and puts your dragged clip right in it (see Figure 7-6).

✔ Hold the Control key and click your mouse anywhere in the track header, as shown in Figure 7-7. Then choose Add Track from the pop-up menu that appears. Final Cut adds a track directly below the track on which you clicked the header.

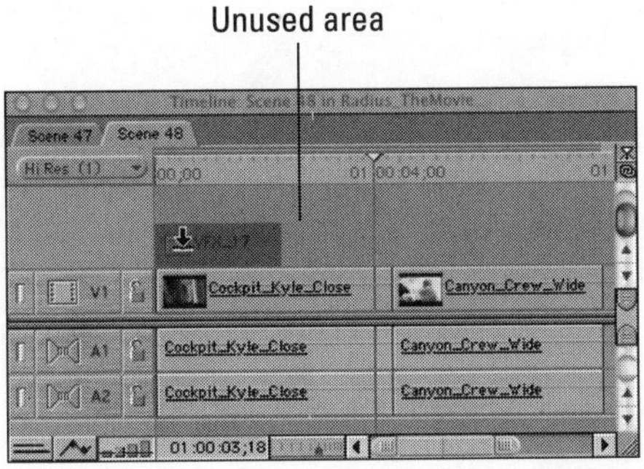

Figure 7-6: To add a video track, drag the clip to the unused area of the Timeline above the last video track.

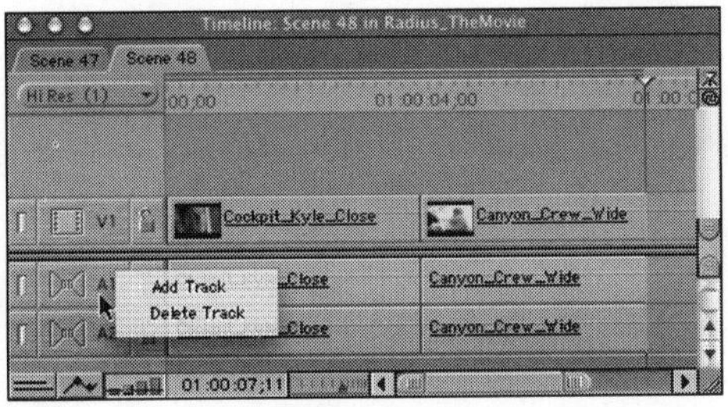

Figure 7-7: The pop-up add/delete menu for tracks.

Adding multiple tracks

To add multiple tracks to the Timeline in one fell swoop, make sure that the Timeline window is active and follow these steps:

1. **Choose Sequence⇨Insert Tracks.**

2. **In the Insert Tracks dialog box (Figure 7-8), type the number of video or audio tracks to add.**

   If you want to add video tracks but not audio tracks (or vice versa), you can uncheck the box next to either option to avoid adding any tracks (or just leave the number of tracks to add at zero).

3. **Choose where on the Timeline to insert them.**

   You have three options:

   • **Before Base Track:** This option inserts your new track(s) *before* the first video or audio track (that's your *base* track) and renumbers any existing tracks to make room. Say you already have two audio tracks (A1 and A2) on the Timeline, and you add another two before the base. Your two new tracks become A1 and A2, and the original audio tracks become A3 and A4.

- **After Target Track:** Final Cut inserts your new track(s) immediately *after* whatever track you've currently designated as a target track. See "Designating your target tracks," earlier in this chapter, for more about target tracks.

- **After Last Track:** Pretty straightforward: Final Cut slips your new tracks behind the very last video or audio track on the Timeline.

5. **Click OK to insert the tracks.**

Figure 7-8:
The Insert
Tracks
dialog box.

Deleting a single track

Here's the quickest, easiest way to delete a single track: Hold down the Control key and click your mouse anywhere in that track's header (refer to Figure 7-7); then choose Delete Track from the pop-up menu that appears. Final Cut tosses out that track (along with any clips on it) and renumbers all the following tracks.

Deleting multiple tracks

To give a group of tracks the old heave-ho, make sure that the Timeline window is active and follow these steps:

1. **Choose Sequence⊏⇨Delete Tracks.**

2. **In the Delete Tracks dialog box, shown in Figure 7-9, click the Video Tracks and/or Audio Tracks check boxes, depending on what kind of tracks you want to delete.**

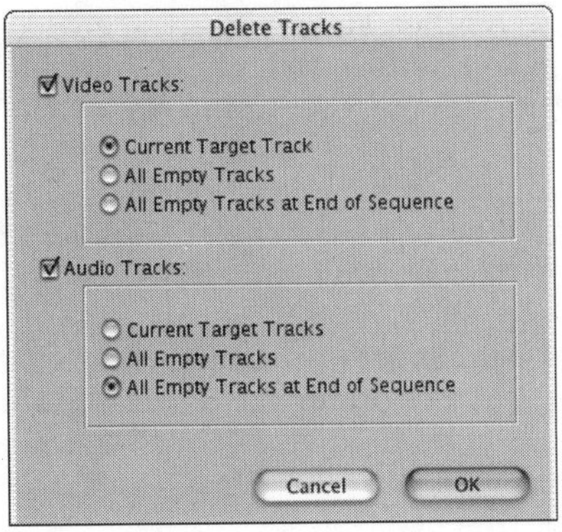

Figure 7-9:
The Delete
Tracks
dialog box.

3. **Under Audio Tracks and Video Tracks, choose from these options:**

   - **Current Target Track(s):** Final Cut deletes whatever track (or two tracks, for audio) you've currently designated as a target track. See "Designating your target tracks," earlier in this chapter, for more about target tracks.

   - **All Empty Tracks:** This deletes all tracks that have no clips on them. (Perhaps you used these tracks as temporary staging areas to assemble clips before moving them to your main tracks, and you no longer need these tracks.)

   - **All Empty Tracks at End of Sequence:** This one's a bit more obscure: It deletes any empty video tracks that are *above* and any audio tracks that are *below* the outermost tracks that have clips on them. Say what? For example, suppose that you have six audio tracks, and tracks A3, A5, and A6 are empty. Choosing this option would delete tracks A5 and A6, but not A3 because it's followed by track A4, which has clips on it.

4. **Click OK to complete the deletion.**

Customizing Your View of the Timeline

You can customize your view of the Timeline so that it shows tracks and clips in whatever way suits your work style. For example, if you're editing on a small monitor or laptop screen, you may want to show your Timeline tracks in Reduced view so that more of them fit on-screen at one time. (This action saves you the time you would have used scrolling up and down your tracks.) Or suppose you're mixing all your movie's audio together (that is, setting each clip's volume levels relative to each other, so they're all nicely balanced); to make this a lot easier, the Timeline can show each clip's volume level visually and even let you raise or lower the volume level with a simple click and drag.

When you customize your view of the Timeline, you can do it either for only your currently open sequence (so you can have different settings for different sequences) or for all new sequences that you create from that point on.

To customize the Timeline for all sequences you create, choose Final Cut⇨ Preferences and then click the Timeline Options tab. To customize only your current sequence's Timeline, make sure that the sequence is active. (You'll know it's active if you see its contents on the Timeline.) Then choose Sequence⇨Settings and click the Timeline Options tab.

Whichever way you chose to arrive at the Timeline Options tab, the tab gives you the same choices as are shown in Figure 7-10. (This view is from the Settings dialog box.) Here are your options:

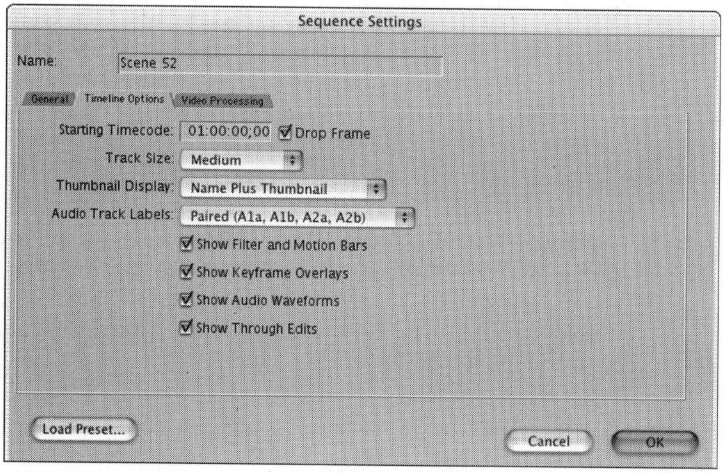

Figure 7-10:
The Timeline Options as they appear in the Settings dialog box.

✔ **Starting Timecode:** This situation is rare, but you may want to change the Starting Timecode value for your sequence so that instead of starting at 01:00:00:00, the sequence starts at, say, 03:24:43:00. (Perhaps you're planning on merging the sequence into an existing recorded tape and want to get the sequence's timecode in synch with the tape's.) Anyway, just type the new value into this box, and you see that value reflected on the Timeline's ruler.

✔ **Track Size:** You can set your tracks to be taller or shorter. If you're peering into a big monitor and the tracks are hard to see, make them larger here. If your screen real estate is cramped, consider going to Reduced view, which can fit a lot of tracks on even a modest iBook's screen (see Figure 7-11).

✔ **Thumbnail Display:** This option lets you decide how video clips are shown on their tracks (see Figure 7-12). You can choose from the following modes:

- **Name:** Just a clip's no-frills name

- **Name Plus Thumbnail:** Shows a clip's name and a thumbnail image of its first frame

- **Filmstrip:** Shows thumbnails for as many frames as fit in the Timeline's current zoom level

Personally, we like Name Plus Thumbnail the best. (Seeing the first frame of a clip helps keep us oriented.) Filmstrip mode makes our heads spin.

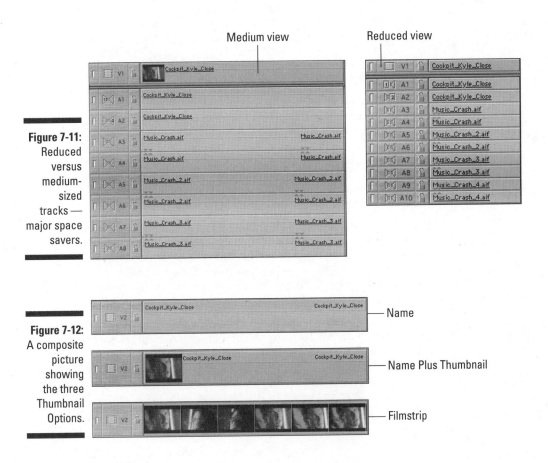

Medium view   Reduced view

Figure 7-11:
Reduced
versus
medium-
sized
tracks —
major space
savers.

Figure 7-12:
A composite
picture
showing
the three
Thumbnail
Options.

Name

Name Plus Thumbnail

Filmstrip

✔ **Audio Track Labels:** When you capture audio, you usually capture it in stereo — that is, each clip you capture actually consists of *two* clips: one for the audio's stereo left channel, and one for the audio's stereo right channel. Normally, when you move stereo audio to the Timeline, Final Cut places each clip on its own track, and the tracks are numbered sequentially (for instance, *A1, A2,* and so on). But by setting your Audio Track labels as Paired, Final Cut labels each audio track to reflect the fact that two are related (that is, they are stereo pairs). So instead of numbering the tracks for an audio clip's left and right channels as *A1* and *A2,* Final Cut labels the two tracks *A1a* and *A1b,* as shown in Figure 7-13. This system makes it easier to keep track of which audio tracks are related stereo pairs.

✔ **Show Filter and Motion Bars:** Check this box, and the Timeline shows thin horizontal bars below each clip that uses either a filter or a motion setting. (Green bars show clips with filters, and blue bars show clips with motion settings.) With just a quick glance at the Timeline, you can see what settings you've applied to your clips (refer to Figure 7-13). Even better: If you've set keyframes in your filters or motion settings, those keyframes show up in the bars as well. (You can even click and drag them to new places within your clips, right on the Timeline.) See Chapters 12 and 13 to learn more about audio and video filters, respectively, and Chapter 14 for more about motion effects.

✔ **Show Keyframe Overlays:** This option draws a horizontal line through any clips on your Timeline. This horizontal line represents opacity levels for video clips and volume levels for audio clips. What's great about this option is that you can click and drag these lines up and down to adjust your levels right on the Timeline without having to open another settings window. You can also set keyframes right here: Simply press the Option key and click your mouse anywhere on the levels line. (You can remove keyframes by option-clicking them as well.)

✔ **Show Audio Waveforms:** Check this box, and any audio clips on your Timeline will show their waveforms (see Figure 7-13). This option can be handy for synching your video clips to events in dialogue, sound effects, or music (the waveforms visually show the events), but be warned: Calculating all those waveforms on the fly can slow your Mac considerably.

✔ **Show Through Edits:** Final Cut normally uses two red triangles to show through edits on the Timeline. A *through edit* takes place when the adjacent frames of two clips are actually continuous frames, as if they were part of the same clip. For example, if you had one clip and used the Razor Blade tool to cut it into two parts, that cut would be a through edit because the *first* frame of the *second* clip is just a continuation of the *last* frame of the *first* clip. If these markers bug you for any reason, you can turn them off right here.

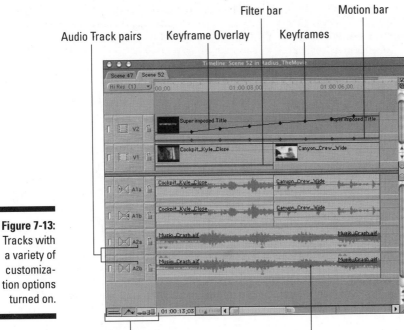

Figure 7-13: Tracks with a variety of customization options turned on.

Click these buttons to set track size, show Filter and Motion bars, or show Keyframe Overlays.

Audio Waveforms

The best number of tracks?

Final Cut lets you create up to 99 video tracks and 99 audio tracks in a sequence — in other words, *a whole lotta tracks*. But how many should you use? Can you gain anything by using more or fewer tracks?

Here's our best answer: When you're building a sequence of clips, think about the "theme" of your clips and try to give each theme its own track. We know that sounds a tad abstract, so try this example on for size: Helmut's film *Radius* sports over 150 visual effects shots (plus a ton of conventionally filmed clips). As he edited *Radius,* he decided to keep the effects by themselves on a separate track. Why? He was constantly swapping in newer, more-polished

versions of each effect (as the artists went from prototypes to finished shots), and finding and replacing effects on a crowded Timeline was a lot easier when the effects were on their own track.

The moral of this story isn't "use fewer tracks" or "use more tracks;" it's "use the *right* number of tracks." Before you build your sequence, just stop and think about how you can effectively use tracks to organize your clips by theme (again, consider visual effects, music, dialogue for different characters, sound effects, title graphics, and whatever else) with an eye for how you might edit those themes down the road.

By the way, you can customize many aspects of the Timeline without visiting the Timeline Options tab at all. You can click buttons directly on the Timeline to set your track size, show filter and motion bars, or show keyframe overlays (refer to Figure 7-13).

Navigating the Timeline

When you're editing, you'll find yourself constantly moving the Timeline's playhead from one place to another (think of the playhead as a record needle on your video — see Chapter 6 for more). Sometimes, you may move the playhead through a clip in search of the perfect frame to trim the clip to or make a cut on. Or you'll move the playhead to some edit point on the Timeline (where a clip ends or begins, or where two clips come together) so that you can adjust the edit in some way.

Final Cut offers a bunch of useful tricks that you can use to move the Timeline's playhead wherever you want. We touch on some of these in Chapter 6, but laying them all out together (so that you can see all your options) is a good idea.

For many of these options to work, either the Canvas window or the Timeline has to be selected. (Remember that these two windows mirror each other.) Sure, you may be saying "Duh!" but we just had to be official-like and say it.

Moving the playhead anywhere on the Timeline

Here's how to move the playhead instantly to any spot on the Timeline:

- **Timeline ruler:** As shown in Figure 7-14, you can click your mouse anywhere in the Timeline ruler to move the playhead to that point in time on the Timeline.

- **Go to timecode:** You can also move the playhead directly to any timecode value on the Timeline (refer to Figure 7-14). Just type the value into the Current Timecode box, which you can find in either the Canvas window or the Timeline window. (Make sure that you don't have a clip currently selected, or Final Cut moves that clip instead of the playhead.)

Timecode values are described in terms of hours, minutes, seconds, and frames. (You can see them listed in the Timeline's ruler.) So typing in the value **01:20:15;29** would move the playhead to the first hour, 20th minute, 15th second, and 29th frame of your Timeline sequence.

Markers   Timeline Ruler

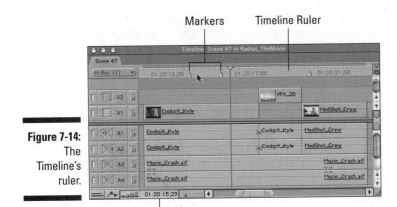

Figure 7-14:
The
Timeline's
ruler.

Current Timecode box

Moving the playhead linearly through the Timeline

In Chapter 6, we show you the easiest way to move the playhead linearly through the Timeline. But here are our recommendations for moving the playhead in a few different ways (see Figure 7-15):

- **Shuttle control:** To move the playhead forward and back at a variety of preset speeds, try using the Canvas window's Shuttle control. You can click and drag this control all the way to the left or right for quick rewinds/fast-forwards, or you can set the control closer to its middle point to move the playhead slowly through your clips.

- **Keyboard shortcuts:** We find the quickest, most convenient way to move the playhead is by pressing J-K-L on our keyboard. Press J to move the playhead backward, K to stop it, and L to move it forward.

- **Click and drag:** If you really want to move the playhead along the Timeline in a hurry (often, while scrolling a long sequence through the Timeline), just click your mouse in the Timeline's ruler and drag it left or right.

- **Hand tool:** Select the Hand tool (Figure 7-17) from the tool palette, click anywhere on a Timeline track, and drag left or right to scroll your view of the Timeline (or up and down to see tracks out of view).

- **Frame by frame:** You have two options to move the playhead frame by frame when you want to be very precise:

  - **The Jog control:** Use the Canvas window's Jog control, which lets you slowly drag your mouse back and forth across the control, moving the playhead frame by frame.

- **Arrow keys:** Pressing your keyboard's left-arrow key moves the playhead backwards in time by one frame, while the right-arrow key moves it forward by one frame.

✔ **Edit by edit:** Instead of moving the playhead to the next *frame*, you can move it to the next *edit point* (the start or end of a clip, as well as any in and out points you've set on the Timeline). To do so, click its Next Edit or Previous Edit buttons in the Canvas, respectively.

✔ **Marker by marker:** If you have set markers, you can move your playhead forward to the next marker by pressing Shift and the up-arrow key, or back to the previous marker by pressing Shift and the down-arrow key. More on markers in Chapter 8.

Figure 7-15:
These Canvas controls move the playhead in different ways.

Jog control   Previous edit   Next edit   Shuttle control

Zooming In and Out of the Timeline

Final Cut lets you zoom in on your Timeline, which shows you a smaller sample of time in your sequence and makes your clips bigger so that you can resize, move, cut, or otherwise edit them with frame-by-frame precision (just like in Photoshop, where you can zoom in on a small portion of a photo to tweak individual pixels). You can also zoom out of the Timeline as well, making clips appear smaller and letting you get a bird's-eye view of your entire sequence (see Figure 7-16).

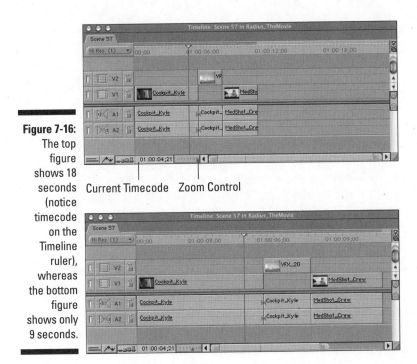

Figure 7-16:
The top figure shows 18 seconds (notice timecode on the Timeline ruler), whereas the bottom figure shows only 9 seconds.

Current Timecode   Zoom Control

In Chapter 6, we touch on the easiest way to zoom the Timeline, which is by using the Zoom In and Zoom Out tools in the tool palette, as shown in Figure 7-17. After you've selected either tool, just click it repeatedly on the Timeline to zoom in or out. (Holding the Option key also toggles each tool's zoom between in and out.)

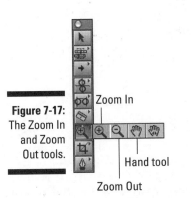

Figure 7-17:
The Zoom In and Zoom Out tools.

Zoom In

Hand tool

Zoom Out

But when you're in the thick of editing, choosing a separate tool just to zoom the Timeline is often a hassle. Instead, you want to do this seamlessly, and Final Cut offers a couple of different ways to take care of this matter:

✓ **The Zoom Control:** The Zoom Control is very straightforward. Click to the left of the control to zoom in and see more detail on the Timeline. (Whatever clips you see on the Timeline stay centered as you zoom in.) Click to the right, and you zoom out, seeing less detail but more clips in your sequence. You can also click and drag the control if that suits you.

✓ **Keyboard shortcuts:** To zoom in one level, press ⌘++ (you can press it repeatedly to keep zooming in). To zoom out, try ⌘+− (minus). When you zoom by using your keyboard, Final Cut keeps any clip you've selected centered on the Timeline; if none are selected, it keeps the playhead centered. (Try it both ways, and you'll see the difference.)

By now, you know more about Final Cut's Timeline than you ever *wanted* to know. But having come this far, we may as well show you a few last icons and buttons that may come in handy (check out Figure 7-18 to follow along):

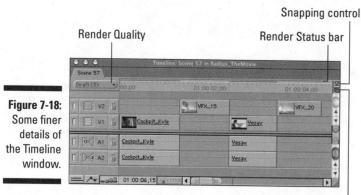

Figure 7-18:
Some finer
details of
the Timeline
window.

✓ **Render status bar:** This bar shows the render status of any clips on the Timeline. (See Chapter 16 for more on rendering.) If a clip's on the Timeline, but it needs to be rendered before playing, you see a red line in this status bar, drawn right over the needy clip. And if you've already rendered a clip, the render status bar replaces the red line with a blue one. Notice that the render bar is actually divided into two parts — the top line shows status for video clips, and the bottom line for audio.

✔ **Render quality button:** You can set different quality levels for renders you do (high res, low res, draft res — the better the quality, the longer the render takes, and the more space it takes on your hard drive). If you want to quickly change the default quality setting that Final Cut uses for renders, just click here and choose your new setting from the pop-up menu that appears.

✔ **Snapping control:** By clicking this icon, you can quickly turn snapping on and off. For more about snapping, see Chapter 6.

✔ **Linking control:** Normally, when you select a video clip that has audio clips linked to it (or vice versa) on the Timeline, Final Cut automatically selects all the linked clips together. (See Chapter 6 for more about linking.) But clicking this icon turns this linking off, so you can select just the clip you click without all of its "dependents."

Chapter 8

Editing Wizardry

You already know enough about Final Cut to cruise through most editing projects on autopilot, but if you want to turbocharge your work, this chapter's got what you need. In fact, this chapter is very likely to have *more* than what you need. One editor may find some material helpful, but another won't have a use for it: It all depends on the kind of work you're doing. That's why our advice is to read a few topics that are likely to apply to just about everybody — our coverage of advanced editing tools, for instance — and then skim through the rest of the chapter's headings and see what else jumps out at you.

Beyond Insert and Overwrite Edits

In Chapter 6, we show you two different ways to edit a clip to the Timeline: You can either insert it (Final Cut scoots over any clips on the Timeline to make room for your new clip), or you can overwrite it (Final Cut brutally erases any clips or segments of clips that stand in the new clip's way). But Final Cut offers a few other options — such as replace edits, fit to fill edits, and superimpose edits — that can come in quite handy, depending on the situation.

Replace edits

A *replace edit* works like an overwrite edit, but it replaces a single clip on your Timeline with a range of frames from a clip that you've opened in the Viewer window. (That range equals the number of frames used by the original clip on the Timeline, so the length of your movie doesn't change when you replace a shot.)

When you do a replace edit, Final Cut pays particular attention to where you've placed the playhead in your source clip (that is, the clip in the Viewer), and where you've placed the playhead on the Timeline (you'll see why in a moment). Here's a quick and easy way to do a replace edit:

1. **Place the clip you want to replace on the Timeline.**

   See Chapter 6 if you need a refresher on this skill.

2. **Position the Timeline's playhead on the in point of the clip you want to replace.**

   Make sure that the Timeline track your clip is on is a target track — see Chapter 7 for more about setting target tracks.

3. **Open your source clip in the Viewer and position the Viewer's playhead on the frame that should be the first frame of the clip when it's added to the Timeline.**

4. **Click and drag the clip to the Canvas window and choose Replace from the Overlay that appears, as shown in Figure 8-1.**

   Final Cut replaces the clip on the Timeline with the source clip in the Viewer. The new clip's first frame will be whatever frame you positioned the Viewer's playhead on in step 2. The remaining frames to the right of the Viewer's playhead are placed on the Timeline until they fill the same number of frames occupied by the original clip you're replacing.

   Any excess frames from the Viewer will be left off the Timeline — for instance, if the Timeline clip was 50 frames, only 50 frames from the Viewer are added, even if the Viewer clip contained 70 frames.

When doing a replace edit, you don't *have* to position the Timeline's playhead at the first frame of the clip you want to replace, but we suggest doing that because it's easier to see how replace edits work. In fact, you can position the Timeline's playhead on any frame within a clip. When you do the replace edit, Final Cut centers the frame at the Viewer's playhead to the frame at the Timeline's playhead, and fills in the Timeline clip with frames from both the left and right side of the Viewer's playhead (sounds a bit complicated, but it becomes clear once you see this phenomenon in action).

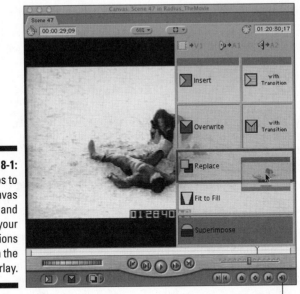

Figure 8-1:
Drag clips to
the Canvas
window and
pick your
edit options
from the
Overlay.

Match Frame button

If you get an Insufficient Content for Edit error message while replacing a clip, it means that the source clip in your Viewer doesn't have enough frames to replace all the Timeline clip's frames. (The source clip needs the same or greater number of frames on *each* side of the Viewer's playhead as the Timeline clip has on each side of the Timeline's playhead.) If you run into this annoyance, try resizing the Timeline clip so that it's smaller (and, therefore, has fewer frames to fill up) and then try your edit again. If the replace edit works this time, just resize the new Timeline clip back to its original length.

Synch audio and video with a replace edit and match frame feature

You can use Final Cut's replace edit with its Match Frame feature to quickly synch up an event in a video clip with an event in an audio clip (for example, to synch a dancer's exaggerated step to a beat of music in a music video). Try these steps:

1. **On the Timeline, position your video and audio clip so they're stacked together within the same time frame.**

   Don't try to synch the video and audio events yet — just make sure that the clips are stacked on top of one another so they share the same time slot.

2. **Position the Timeline's playhead at the point where your audio event takes place.**

   For greater precision, you may want to display your Timeline clips bigger and set them to show audio waveforms. (To do this, choose Sequence⇨Settings and then select the Timeline Options tab. Under the Track Size drop-down box, select the size you prefer.)

3. **Turn off targeting for all your audio tracks by clicking the speaker icons next to each of your audio tracks.**

   After turning the audio tracks off, you should *not* see a little *1* or *2* in any of the icons.

4. **Without moving the playhead, do a match frame by pressing F. Alternatively, you can click the Match Frame button in the Canvas window (refer to Figure 8-1).**

   In the Viewer window, Final Cut opens the source clip that your *video* came from, placing the Viewer's playhead at exactly the same frame where the Timeline's playhead is positioned. (In other words, the Viewer and Canvas windows should now show exactly the same frame because each window's playhead is on the same frame.) This, by the way, is how Final Cut's Match Frame feature works — it looks at whatever frame you've positioned the Timeline's playhead on and opens that frame's source clip in the Viewer window.

5. **In the Viewer window, move the playhead to the frame you want to synch with your audio event.**

   Remember that you positioned the Timeline's playhead on that audio event in Step 2. You're now about to synch up the Viewer's video frame with that audio event on the Timeline.

6. **Do a replace edit: Drag the match frame clip from the Viewer to the Canvas window and choose Replace from the Overlay that appears.**

   Final Cut now replaces the current video clip on the Timeline with the match frame version in the Viewer (lining up the Viewer's playhead frame with the playhead on the Timeline, which happens to mark your audio event). Your video and audio should now be synched!

Fit to fill edit

Fit to fill is aptly named because that's exactly what this edit does: It literally forces a clip to fit any space you set for it on the Timeline. It does this by speeding the clip up or slowing it down.

For example, suppose you've finished editing your movie, but are waiting for a fancy animated opening title from a motion graphics artist. You've reserved a five-second slot in your movie for the title, but when you finally get it, it's only four-seconds long! You can't edit the title into your Timeline as is, so you fit to fill the title into the gap you reserved for it. The result? Final Cut figures out how to play the four-second clip slower, so it actually fills its five-second slot.

Here's how to do a fit to fill edit:

1. **On the Timeline, choose the range of frames you'll fit to fill your clip to.**

   You can select an empty Timeline gap or existing clip by clicking it, or by setting in and out points on the Timeline to define a range of frames.

2. **Open the clip you want to fit to fill in the Viewer window and set its in and out points.**

   You don't have to set in and out points if you'd like to fit to fill the whole clip.

3. **Drag your clip from the Viewer to the Canvas window.**

   When you drag the clip over the Canvas, you'll see the Overlay appear, listing your different editing options.

4. **Choose Fit to Fill from the Overlay (shown in Figure 8-1).**

   Final Cut adds your clip to the Timeline, setting it to play at the appropriate speed. Now you have to render the clip by selecting it and choosing Sequence⇨Render Selection. If the clip needs to play faster than normal (to fit a smaller space than it was designed for), Final Cut renders it so that it skips frames while playing. If the clip needs to play slower than normal, Final Cut renders it with some duplicated frames.

Superimpose edit

When you superimpose a clip, Final Cut moves it to the Timeline but places it on the next available track *after* your current target track. If you need to stack multiple clips on top of each other (for instance, if you're about to composite lots of different images together into one shot or add all sorts of audio clips that will play simultaneously), this is a great way to get those clips on separate Timeline tracks quickly.

You perform a superimpose edit the usual way — that is, by opening a clip in the Viewer window, dragging it to the Canvas, and choosing Superimpose from the Overlay that appears. But a superimpose edit is unique in one important way: Normally, when you edit a clip to the Timeline, Final Cut places it where the Timeline's playhead happens to be — but not this time!

Instead, Final Cut looks at the position of the Timeline's playhead, and if a clip is already at that point in time on your targeted track, that clip's in and out points on the Timeline become the in and out points for your super-imposed edit (as you can see in Figure 8-2).

For instance, suppose you're superimposing a five-second video clip on the Timeline but place the Timeline's playhead where you already have a two-second clip on your V1 target track. When you superimpose your five-second clip — surprise! — only two seconds actually make it to track V2 on the Timeline.

Figure 8-2:
Three clips super-imposed with the V1 track clip, matching its in and out points on the Timeline.

This strange functionality might seem like an annoying bug, but when you're in the superimposing mood, you usually want superimposed clips to match each other's durations, so this unique twist works in your favor. And if it doesn't, you can set your own in and out points on the Timeline before superimposing a clip — in this case, Final Cut ignores the length of any clip on your target track and edits your new clip into the edit points that you set.

You can superimpose a group of clips together, each going to its own Timeline track, by selecting the group in the Browser window and dragging them to the Canvas window, where you can choose the Superimpose option from the Canvas' Overlay (shown in Figure 8-1).

Splitting Video and Audio Edits

Usually, when you edit your clips (either by setting in and out points in Final Cut's Viewer window or by adjusting those points after the clips are on the Timeline), you're affecting both the video and audio segments of clips at the same exact point — in other words, when a video clip begins or ends, its audio does so too (or vice versa).

But by doing a split edit, you can actually set different in and out points for a clip's video and audio. For instance, you can end a clip's video while letting its audio continue on (as you can see in Figure 8-3), or you can begin a clip's audio first and then bring in its video a moment later.

For instance, pretend that you're editing a new-millennium take on *Romeo and Juliet*. We see Juliet standing on her balcony, calling out, "Romeo, hey Romeo. Where are you, man? Your cell phone goes straight to voicemail, and your pager's off, too!" But as Juliet calls out, we cut to Romeo, in the darkness below, to see his reaction as she continues to speak. (Translation: We've cut away from the video portion of Juliet's clip but let her audio keep playing.) That's a split edit in action, and you see 'em used all the time in movies, television, and so on.

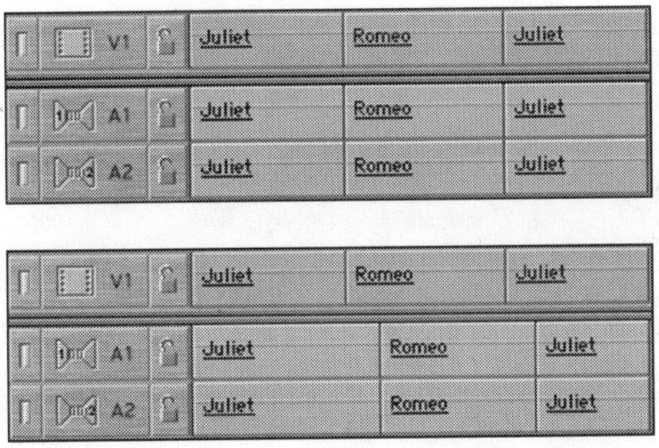

Figure 8-3:
Before and after a split edit on the Timeline.

Splitting edits from the Viewer

You can set up a clip's split edit points in the Viewer. Doing so is almost as easy as marking simple in and out points, but you can mark up to four points — in and out points for video and in and out points for audio.

1. **Open a clip in the Viewer window.**

2. **Position the Viewer's playhead on the frame where you'd like your video to begin and set a video in point by choosing Mark↪ Mark Split↪Video In.**

   You can also press ⌘+Option+I to mark your video in point.

3. **Repeat Step 2, but mark your Video Out, Audio In, and Audio Out frames by choosing those options from the Mark Split submenu (see Figure 8-4 to see all video and audio in/out points set).**

   You can skip setting an out frame for either your video or audio — if you don't, Final Cut just makes the clip's last frame your out point. (The same works in reverse if you set out points, but not in points, for video and audio.)

Also, if you want your video and audio to either start or end on the same frame (in many cases, you want to split either the beginning of a clip but not the end or vice versa), just place a simple in or out point on that particular frame.

4. Move your clip to the Timeline.

You can drag your clip directly to the Timeline or drag it to the Canvas window. After moving your clip to the Timeline, notice that the clip's video and audio points are set differently, reflecting how you split them in the Viewer.

TIP

When you've moved your split-edited clip to the Timeline, you can still adjust the clip's video and audio in/out points by clicking and dragging them on the Timeline.

Figure 8-4:
Split video
and audio
edits in the
Viewer.

Video in point   Video out point

Audio in point   Audio out point

TIP

To clear a clip's split-edit points, open the clip from the Browser window and choose Mark➪Clear Split. The Clear Split submenu lets you clear each in and out point or all audio or all video points together.

Splitting edits on the Timeline

You can also create split edits after your clips are on the Timeline. Personally, we prefer this approach because you can see not only the clip whose audio and video you're splitting, but also the clips that you'll eventually integrate it with. But the decision to use the Timeline or the Viewer is up to you.

The easiest way to split a clip on the Timeline is to simply drag its video and audio to different points. Just hold down the Option key and drag either your video or audio to a new point — it's that easy.

You'll naturally use split edits to carry over one clip's audio so that it overlaps onto another clip. (For instance, remember our example — earlier in this chapter — of Juliet's dialogue continuing on, even though we've cut to the next video clip of Romeo in the bushes below her balcony.) When you're overlapping one clip's audio to another clip, putting each clip's audio on a different audio track so you can hear each playing is not unusual. For instance, when we carry Juliet's dialogue over Romeo's video, we still want to hear the audio for Romeo's clip — his breathing, the rustling of the bushes around him, and so on. And we do that by keeping Juliet's audio and Romeo's audio on two different tracks, as shown in Figure 8-5.

Figure 8-5:
Splitting
audio and
video on
overlapping
tracks.

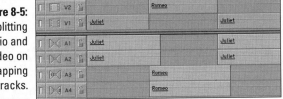

Power Editing Tools

After you've moved your media clips to the Timeline, most of your editing sweat goes towards tweaking those clips so they cut smoothly from one to another. In Chapter 6, we introduce you to all the basic tools and techniques to do just that, but don't stop there! In fact, Final Cut sports a range of advanced tools — things like roll and ripple edits, or slips and slides — that let you do certain edits in one simple step instead of two, three, or four steps (as can be the case when you're working the old-fashioned way).

Most of these tools are designed to be used towards the end of your editing work, when you've already laid out your material and want to tweak a few clips (add a few frames here, cut a few frames there) without changing the length of your movie (or sequence). Why is preserving length so important? Because, in the late stages of your work, you may have already laid down sound effects, music, and so on — things that are carefully synched up with your film. Or maybe your film just has to fit within an allotted time, like a TV commercial does. At any rate, these tools, with the exception of the Ripple Edit tool, are all designed to let you make tweaks to clips but minimize the effects those changes have on other clips and your sequence in general.

You can do these advanced edits in many ways, but we think the quickest and most intuitive approach is to simply select a new tool from Final Cut's tool palette, and apply it directly to clips you've already placed on the Timeline. Still, some of these tools and techniques can seem a bit confusing when you're reading about them the first time around. So don't get frustrated if you stop and say "Huh?" — just take the time to study the figures we show you and make sure to try out some of this stuff on your own clips.

Editing clips often means making small, precise changes to them; but if you have Final Cut's Snapping feature turned on, you may find it hard to be as precise as you want because your mouse pointer will keep snapping to the edges of nearby clips, instead of the frame you want to be on. If this is the case, just press N on your keyboard to turn off Snapping. (You can even toggle snapping while dragging a clip or its edges.)

Resizing clips with roll and ripple edits

Roll and ripple edits let you resize clips on your Timeline without having to separately move adjacent clips forward or back to accommodate your changes. (For instance, you won't have to create a gap on the Timeline before extending a clip into that gap, and you won't have to close an unwanted gap after trimming a clip so it's shorter.)

Both of these edits affect how two adjacent clips (that is, side-by-side clips) join together on your Timeline. When you perform either a roll or ripple, you're either adding or taking away frames from your first clip (known as the *Outgoing clip,* the one that's earlier in time) or your second clip (known as the *Incoming clip*), but you're maintaining their edit point — that is, the two clips stay connected, never leaving a gap in between.

Rolling your edits in the Trim Edit window

A *roll edit* lets you simultaneously move the edit point between two clips, making one clip longer and the other shorter, all in one fell swoop. Let's say you have clips A, B, C, and D on the Timeline, side by side, and want to do a roll edit between clips A and B. Check out Figure 8-6. The top image shows clip A and B at the same size, before the roll edit. The next image shows a roll edit extending clip B at the expense of A. The bottom image is another roll edit in the opposite direction: extending clip A at the expense of B. No matter which way you move the roll edit pointer, clips C and D say the same.

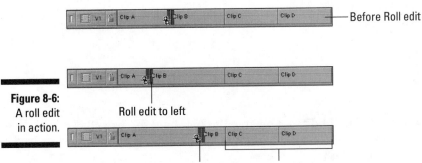

Figure 8-6:
A roll edit
in action.

When you do your roll edit, you're changing the out point of clip A and the in point of clip B, but you're not changing the combined length of the two clips; therefore, you're not shifting any following clips (C and D) either forward or backward along the Timeline.

So why would you want to do a roll edit, besides to show off your Final Cut acumen to family and friends? A roll edit is a great tool to use when you're trying to match the same action, as you cut from one clip to another. For instance, suppose you have the dubious distinction of editing *Rocky XXXIV,* and you want to cut from a medium shot of Rocky throwing his knockout blow to a close-up of his glove landing squarely on the jaw of his hapless challenger. In this case, you'd put these two clips side-by-side, trying to match the actions as close as possible, and then use the roll edit to fine-tune the edit point — looking for the perfect frame to exit out of the first clip and enter into the second clip.

Roll edits are easy to do right on the Timeline:

1. **Choose the Roll Edit tool from the Final Cut tool palette (as shown in Figure 8-7) or just press R (for "roll") on your keyboard.**

   Your mouse pointer becomes a Roll Edit symbol.

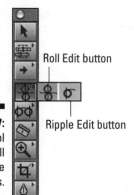

Roll Edit button

Figure 8-7:
The Tool
palette's roll
and ripple
tools.

Ripple Edit button

2. **Click the Roll Edit tool on an edit point between two clips on the Timeline and drag the edit point either right or left (forward or backwards in time).**

   As you drag, keep your eye on the Canvas window: As shown in Figure 8-8, it goes into a two-up clip display — the frame on the left shows the last frame, or out point, of your Outgoing clip (again, the clip to the left of the edit point), while the frame on the right shows the first frame, or in point, of your Incoming clip. When you release the mouse, your roll edit takes affect on the Timeline.

Figure 8-8:
The Canvas
window
becomes a
two-up clip
display.

And again, when you extend a clip by a certain number of frames, you're also shortening the adjacent clip by the same number of frames, so the two clips continue to share the same edit point. In other words, what you give to one clip, you take from the other (and vice versa).

When you can't drag (that is, roll) your edit point any further along the Timeline, you've reached the last frame of either your outgoing or Incoming clip. Because no more frames are available for either clip to give, that's the limit of your roll edit.

Ripplin' with ripple edits

A *ripple edit* lets you resize a clip by moving its in or out point on the Timeline — sounds simple enough, eh? But what makes ripple edits so cool — and probably the most handy editing tool you'll ever have — is that when you resize a clip, Final Cut automatically "ripples" that change through the rest of your Timeline sequence, moving clips forward or back in time (to make room for a clip you've extended or to close the gap left by a clip you've trimmed).

For instance, imagine that you've placed clips A, B, C, and D on the Timeline side-by-side, but you decide to trim a few frames off the end of clip B (the out point) while *also* moving clips C and D to the left so they fill the empty gap left by B's trimmed frames, as shown in Figure 8-9. The top image shows the Timeline before a ripple edit. In the middle image, the ripple edit shortens clip B and moves clip C over to fill in the gap. In the bottom image, the ripple extends clip B and moves clip C out to make room. Normally, by using the steps that we describe in Chapter 6, you'd trim clip B and then have to manually move clips C and D over to fill the gap — probably by using the Select Track Forward tool. But the Ripple Tool does it in one easy step — ain't progress nifty?

Figure 8-9:
Move the
ripple edit
tool to the
left or right
on the
Timeline.

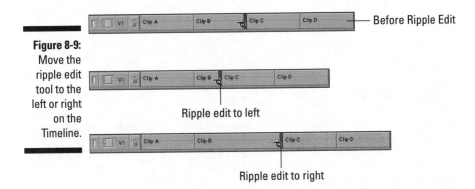

Before Ripple Edit

Ripple edit to left

Ripple edit to right

Like the Roll Edit tool, the Ripple Edit tool is specifically designed to work with two clips — one on either side of an edit point. You can move either the Outgoing clip's (that is, the first clip's) out point or the Incoming clip's in point. Here's how to Ripple clips on the Timeline:

1. **Choose the Ripple Edit tool from the Final Cut tool palette (refer to Figure 8-7).**

   Alternatively, just press R *twice* on your keyboard. Your mouse pointer becomes a Ripple Edit symbol.

2. **Click to the immediate left of an edit point with the Ripple Edit tool to select the Outgoing clip, or to the immediate right to select the Incoming clip.**

   You're letting Final Cut know which of the two clips at the edit point you want to affect. Final Cut responds by highlighting a thin slice of the clip next to the edit point. (Figure 8-9 shows clip B selected in this way.)

3. **Click and drag the selected side of the edit point either forward or backwards in time to extend or trim it.**

   As you drag, keep your eye on the Canvas window: It goes into its two-up clip display — the frame on the left shows the last frame, or out point, of your Outgoing clip (again, the clip to the left of the edit point), while the frame on the right shows the first frame, or in point, of your Incoming clip.

   When you release the mouse, Final Cut ripples the effects of your edit through all the following clips in your Timeline sequence. Seeing those clips shift in time can sometimes be disorienting (especially if you've extended or trimmed the edit point's incoming clip), but go ahead and play your new edit in the Canvas window and you should see that all's well (if not, just choose Edit⇨Undo and try again).

   If you can't extend a clip's in or out point any further along the Timeline, then you've reached its last frame, so no more frames are available to extend it to.

Slip-slidin' clips

Slip edits and slide edits are two other specialized tools in your editing arsenal. While you probably won't use them day in, day out (as you would the Ripple Edit tool), they definitely save you a few steps in certain scenarios.

Like roll and ripple edits, slips and slides are easiest when done directly on the Timeline, so that's what we focus on.

Give a clip the slip

A *slip edit* changes a single clip's in and out points, but *not* its duration *or* its position on the Timeline.

This sounds pretty abstract, so try this example on for size: Suppose you open a clip in the Viewer, and it's 90 frames long, but you decide to edit only its middle 30 frames (31–60) to the Timeline. After those frames are on the Timeline, you can use the slip tool to change the 30 frames that clip shows — for instance, frames 1–30 or 15–45, and so on (as shown in Figure 8-10).

So now you're thinking: "Hmmm, pretty clever, but why on earth would I ever do that?!?" You can turn to the Slip Item tool when you've carefully edited a group of clips and need to change one clip in the sequence but don't want to affect any others. For instance, maybe you've meticulously synched some video to music beats or other sound events, but then you realize that one clip isn't working as smoothly as you'd like with the clips around it. If you don't want to extend or trim that clip (because that would change the duration of your sequence and throw off the synch with your audio), you can do a slip edit and try to find a better range of frames within the problem clip — without changing its position or length in your sequence.

But enough theory, here's how to slip a clip in the real world:

1. **Choose the Slip Item tool in the tool palette (as shown in Figure 8-11) or just press S (for "slip") on your keyboard.**

   Either way, your mouse pointer becomes a slip edit symbol.

2. **Click a clip on the Timeline and drag your mouse either left or right to slip its frames.**

   When you click the clip, Final Cut shows a rectangle frame that represents the total frames available to your clip. Drag left to move the clip's latter frames into position or right to see its earlier frames.

   Also, keep your eye on the Canvas window — as you drag, it shows a two-up display of the new in and out frames for your clip (as shown in Figure 8-8). Release the mouse when you're happy with those new in and out points.

3. **Play your slipped clip from the Timeline to see how it looks.**

Sliding a clip

The Slide Item tool is an unusual beast in that it moves an entire clip either forward or back on the Timeline, while *also moving* the edit points on either side of the clip. Translation: As you move a clip with the Slide Item tool, you are at the same time trimming or extending the clips to either side of it to accommodate the clip in its new location while keeping its edit points intact.

Rectangle frame shows all frames available

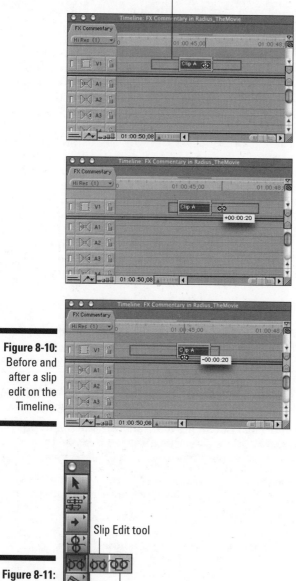

Figure 8-10: Before and after a slip edit on the Timeline.

Slip Edit tool

Figure 8-11: The tool palette's Slip and Slide tools.

Slide Edit tool

Say you've arranged clips A, B, and C side by side on the Timeline (as shown in Figure 8-12), and each clip is 30 frames long. If you *slide* clip B forward in time by 15 frames, you'll also be trimming clip A's out point by 15 frames and extending clip C's in point by 15 frames. The result? Clip A is now only 15 frames long, clip B keeps its original 30-frame length but will now be in a new position on the Timeline, and clip C is 45 frames long (provided it had extra frames to extend out to, of course).

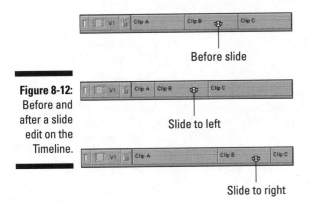

Before slide

Figure 8-12:
Before and
after a slide
edit on the
Timeline.

Slide to left

Slide to right

While we admit you're not likely to use the Slide Item tool regularly, it can be helpful to move an important clip (usually to match a beat of music or some audio event) without changing the edit points of any other clips in your sequence. Here's how:

1. **Choose the Slide Edit tool in the Final Cut Tool palette (refer to Figure 8-11), or just press S twice on your keyboard.**

   Your mouse pointer becomes a slide edit symbol.

2. **Click a clip on the Timeline and drag your mouse either left or right to slide it forward or back in time.**

   The Canvas window switches to a two-up display (see Figure 8-8), showing the new out-point frame of the clip to the left and the new in-point frame of the clip to the right.

3. **Release the mouse when you think that you've moved your middle clip to a good spot.**

4. **Play your edited clips from the Timeline to see how they look.**

Use Markers to Highlight Important Moments

Markers are little signposts that you can place anywhere in a media clip or Timeline sequence to identify (or "mark") frames that are important to you. In the next few sections, we show you how to master 'em.

Setting markers

You can set markers inside an individual clip or within a sequence on the Timeline. Set them in clips to flag important moments within that clip, and set them in a sequence to flag important moments in your edited story (for instance, a frame where you might want to insert additional clips, or possibly trim or extend a clip to, and so on). You can set as many markers as you want — Final Cut just numbers them sequentially (Marker 1, Marker 2, and so on) until you rename them. (We show you how to rename markers in the section "Renaming and deleting markers" later in this chapter.)

Within a clip

To set a marker within a clip (see Figure 8-13), try this:

1. **Open your clip in the Viewer window.**

2. **Position the Viewer's playhead on the frame you want to mark and press M (for "mark") on your keyboard.**

   You can also click the Add Marker button in the Viewer window — refer to Figure 8-13.

Keep doing this to set as many markers as you'd like. And when you add the clip to the Timeline, you'll see those markers within the clip (flip ahead to Figure 8-15).

You can use markers to break up a clip into smaller subclips, which is a great way to quickly divide a long, unwieldy clip into smaller, bite-sized morsels. To take advantage of this cool little feature, open a clip by double-clicking it from the Browser window. In the Viewer window, set markers at each frame where you'd like a new subclip to begin. From now on, Final Cut's Browser will identify that marked-up clip with a little triangle next to its name — just click the triangle, and the Browser lists each and every marker you set in that clip (see Figure 8-14). In fact, the Browser now treats each marker as if it's an individual clip (where each new clip starts at the first frame you marked in the original clip and ends at the frame *before* the *next* marker you set). All the usual things you can do to clips apply to these subclips — you can rename them, open them in the Viewer window, set In and Out points for them, and move them to the Timeline. Cool, eh?

Current Timecode

Figure 8-13:
Markers set
for a clip in
the Viewer
window.

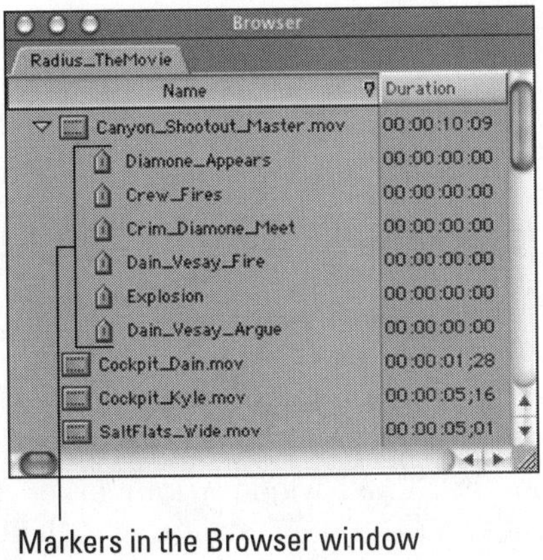

Click to add a marker

A marker comment

Individual markers

Figure 8-14:
A clip
shows its
markers in
the Browser
window.

Markers in the Browser window

You can actually set markers *while* a clip is playing in the Viewer (as opposed to stopping playback to set the marker). Just start playing your clip, and press M or click the Add Marker button anytime you want to place a marker on the fly. Granted, this method isn't highly precise (unless you've got incredible hand-eye coordination), but it's the best way to lay down a lot of markers in a hurry.

Within a sequence

Setting a marker on the Timeline (that is, a marker that highlights a point in time, not a frame in a particular clip) isn't much different, as shown in Figure 8-15:

1. **Make sure that you haven't currently selected any clips on the Timeline.**

   To be safe, you can press ⌘+D to deselect any clips, or choose Edit⇨Deselect All.

2. **Position the Timeline's playhead on the frame to mark and, you guessed it, press M to place the marker.**

Markers on Timeline

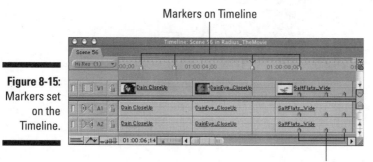

Figure 8-15: Markers set on the Timeline.

Markers on clips

Even if you're working in the Timeline, you can still set markers within a particular clip (as you would if you opened the clip in the Viewer). Just select the clip on the Timeline, position the Timeline's playhead within that clip, and press M for marker. Your marker appears within the clip itself (refer to Figure 8-15), not above it on the Timeline.

Renaming and deleting markers

You can edit markers either from the Viewer window (for markers inside clips) or from the Timeline (for markers on the Timeline). Just follow these steps:

1. **In the Viewer or Timeline, position your playhead directly on a marker.**

   If you're looking at a long clip or Timeline sequence, it may *look* as if you've positioned your playhead directly on a marked frame, but you may still be off by a frame or two. If you are indeed on a marker, you'll see it change color. For guaranteed results, you can also jump the playhead to the previous and next markers by pressing Shift+↑ or Shift+↓ on your keyboard.

2. **Choose Mark⇨Markers⇨Edit or just press M on your keyboard.**

   Either way, Final Cut opens the Edit Marker dialog box.

3. **In the Edit Marker dialog box (Figure 8-16), make your edits and click OK.**

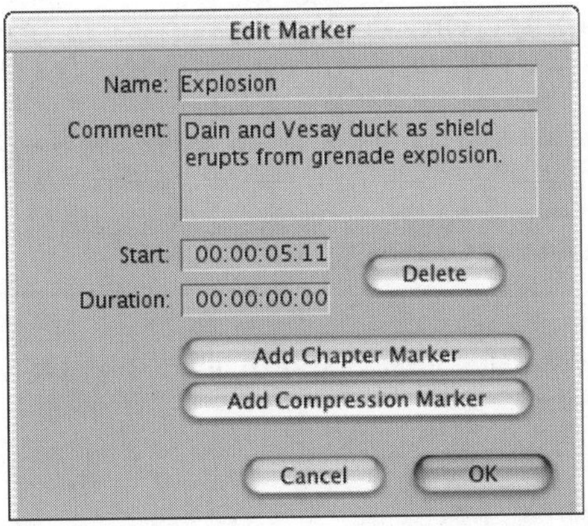

Figure 8-16:
The Edit
Marker box.

4. **Type in a new name for your marker; for instance, Jack Runs.**

   Naming your markers something meaningful is helpful if you ever need to search for a marker by name (which we cover in the following section).

   You can also type in a comment for your marker (a habit that is helpful when, a few weeks down the road, you can't remember why you placed the marker in the first place).

5. **Click the OK button to close the Edit Marker box.**

   Or, to delete the marker, click the Delete button.

Searching for markers

You can quickly search for markers you've set in either your clips or your Timeline sequence. A word of advice, though: To get the most out of these searches, we recommend renaming your markers so they're more descriptive than the default names Final Cut gives 'em (Marker 1, Marker 2, and so on). See the preceding section for more about naming markers.

To search for Timeline markers, follow these steps:

1. **Press the Control key and click the timecode box in the Timeline (refer to Figure 8-15).**

2. **Choose your marker from the timecode pop-up menu, and Final Cut moves the Timeline's playhead to that marker.**

To search for markers within a clip, follow these steps:

1. **Open the clip in the Viewer.**

2. **Now, press the Control key, click the Viewer's timecode box (refer to Figure 8-13), and choose your marker from the timecode pop-up menu.**

You can also search your Timeline sequence for markers by using Final Cut's Find command:

1. **First, make the Timeline or Canvas window active.**

2. **Choose Edit⇨Find.**

   This brings up the Find dialog box, as shown in Figure 8-17.

Figure 8-17:
The Find
dialog box.

Find in Scene 52	
Find: Explosion	Find
Search: Names/Markers	Find All
Where: All Tracks	Cancel

3. **Select Names/Markers from the Search drop-down box and type part or all of your marker's name into the Find box.**

4. **Click the Find button.**

   Final Cut moves the Timeline's playhead to the first clip or sequence marker that fits your description. (Clips have to be on the Timeline for their markers to be recognized in a search.)

5. **To move to the next marker that fits your description, choose Edit⇨Find Again.**

From the Viewer, Canvas, or Timeline windows, you can quickly jump the playhead to the next or previous marker: press Shift+↓ on your keyboard for Next and Shift+↑ for Previous.

Final Cut slow-mo versus the real thing

You may notice that your slow-motion effects never look quite as smooth as the slow-mo shots you see in big Hollywood films. Why not? Hollywood films ordinarily shoot their footage at 24 frames per second, but when they want to capture slow motion, they crank their camera's frame rate higher, to maybe 50 frames per second or 75 frames per second. This approach uses a lot of frames to capture an action, and when those frames are played back on a movie projector at regular speed (for example, 24 frames per second), the result is a silky smooth slow-mo effect, where each frame is different from the last and captures a small bit of time and motion.

Now consider Final Cut, which usually duplicates frames to create a slow-motion effect. Because you're seeing the same frames two, three, or more times, instead of unique frames, the slow-mo effect seems a lot choppier. Even when you use the Final Cut Frame Blending option, the software has no way to invent new frames that look as good as a genuine frame shot by your camera.

Changing a Clip's Speed

Slowing down and speeding up video clips are great ways to add drama and suspense or frenetic action to your movie. When you slow down a clip, Final Cut is actually adding frames to the clip, so it takes more time for the clip to play. Likewise, when you speed up a clip, Final Cut just tosses frames out, making the action seem to go quicker. Here's how to add either effect:

1. **On the Timeline, select a clip you want to play slower or faster.**

   If you want to change the speed of only part of an existing clip, you have to cut that part of the clip from the rest (try the Razor Blade tool) so that it's separate.

2. **Choose Modify⇨Speed.**

3. **In the Speed dialog box (as shown in Figure 8-18), type in either a new percentage of speed *or* a new time duration for your clip.**

   When you change the clip's speed, you're also changing its duration. (A clip that plays twice as fast as usual only lasts half as long as usual, right?) Final Cut lets you set the clip's speed either way, depending on your needs. For instance, if you're trying to fit your clip into a fixed amount of time, type in a new duration value, down to the last frame. Or if you're just going by gut instinct, try using a percentage. (A percent lower than 100 percent makes the clip play in slow motion, and a higher value speeds it up.)

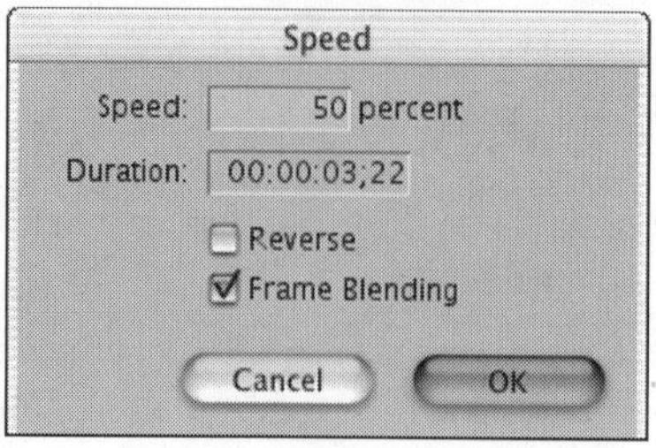

Figure 8-18:
The Speed
dialog box.

WARNING!

When you enter a new percentage for your clip's speed, try to stick to
whole, even numbers, which result in the smoothest looking video.

4. **Check Frame Blending on or off.**

This option is handy for slow-motion clips. Ordinarily, Final Cut creates
a slow-mo effect by taking your original clip and duplicating frames. But
repeating the same frames over and over again can create a stuttering
effect; so when the Frame Blending option is turned on, Final Cut tries to
create entirely new frames that are blends of the original frames in your
movie. For instance, instead of playing frame 1 twice, Final Cut would
play frame 1 once and then draw a new frame that is halfway between
frame 1 and frame 2 (and so on). The result is smoother slow-mo effect.

5. **Click OK and render your clip.**

When you click OK, you see that your clip has gotten either longer or
shorter on the Timeline (as shown in Figure 8-19). And because you've
basically created a new kind of clip, you have to render it before seeing
your speed effect in action (just select the clip, and choose Sequence⇨
Render Selection).

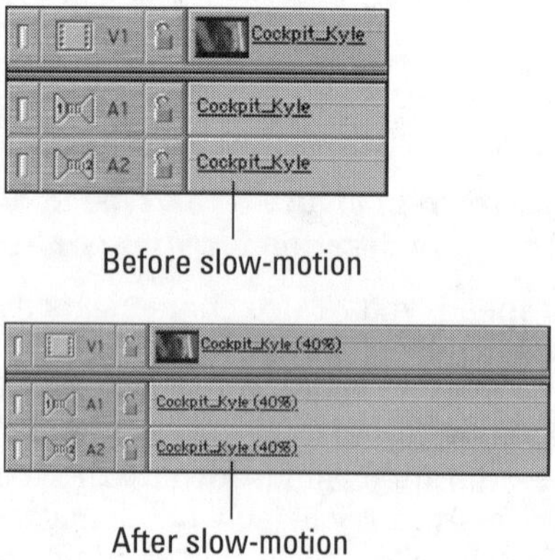

Figure 8-19:
A clip
before and
after a slow-
motion
effect.

Before slow-motion

After slow-motion

Playing a Clip Backward

Occasionally, you may find it handy to play a clip backward instead of forward. For instance, in the film *Radius,* Helmut needed footage of a timer counting down to zero, but the timer prop could only count up, not down. No problem: The cameraman just filmed the timer counting up and then Helmut reversed the footage after it was on the Timeline, so it seemed to be counting down. To reverse a clip, perform the following steps:

1. **On the Timeline, select the clip you want to reverse.**

   If you also want to keep a version of the clip that plays forward on the Timeline, duplicate the clip with the Final Cut Copy and Paste commands and choose one of the copies to reverse.

2. **Choose Modify⇨Speed.**

3. **In the Speed dialog box (refer to Figure 8-18), check the Reverse box, click OK, and render your clip.**

   Notice on the Timeline, that your clip's name is now followed by a "-100%" in parenthesis. This tells you that your clip is playing at 100 percent speed, but in reverse. Because you've created a new kind of clip, you have to render it before seeing your reverse in action.

Stopping Action with a Freeze Frame

In the course of your movie, you may want to suddenly freeze the action on a single frame of video and hold it for a moment. (This stylistic touch was hot in the 1970s and is coming on strong again these days.) Final Cut lets you do this easily by turning any frame in an existing clip into a still picture that lasts as long as you want. To freeze a frame, perform the following steps:

1. **In the Viewer, open the video clip you want to freeze.**

2. **Move the Viewer's playhead to the frame you want to freeze.**

3. **Choose Modify⇨Make Freeze Frame.**

   Final Cut opens that frame in the Viewer, treating it as a new clip of video. The frozen frame has a duration of ten seconds by default.

4. **In the Viewer, move your frozen frame's in or out points to change its duration (as shown in Figure 8-20).**

Figure 8-20:
A freeze
frame in the
Viewer.

You can see the frame's current duration in the Viewer's Clip Duration box (in the upper-left corner of the Viewer). You can also, of course, trim or extend the freeze frame clip after it's on the Timeline.

5. **Move your freeze frame clip from the Viewer to either the Timeline or the Browser by clicking anywhere in the Viewer's image area and dragging the freeze frame to its destination.**

   When you create the freeze frame in the Viewer, the freeze frame is not added to the Browser as a clip (as if you'd just imported a movie or still picture into Final Cut). You don't have to add it to the Browser, but we recommend moving it there anyway, just so the freeze frame becomes a permanent clip in your project, which you can quickly reuse if you need it again. Otherwise, move it right to the Timeline and edit it into your sequence like any other video clip.

   After your freeze frame is on the Timeline, you have to render it because you're essentially creating a new video clip from what was once just a single frame (select the freeze frame clip, and choose Sequence⇨Render Selection).

To save a bit of time, you can actually freeze a frame directly from the Timeline. Just position the Timeline's playhead on a frame of video and choose Modify⇨Make Freeze Frame. You see that frame appear in the Viewer window, ready to be moved to the Browser or back again to the Timeline.

Nesting a Sequence into Another Sequence

Final Cut lets you assemble a group of clips into a sequence, but you can *also* assemble a group of sequences into *yet another* sequence (as shown in Figure 8-21). This process is called *nesting* sequences, and it's particularly handy because it lets you break down bigger projects into more manageable morsels. For instance, you can edit each of your movie's scenes (or acts, or any other division you want to make) in its own sequence, and then edit those finished sequences together to assemble your full-fledged project.

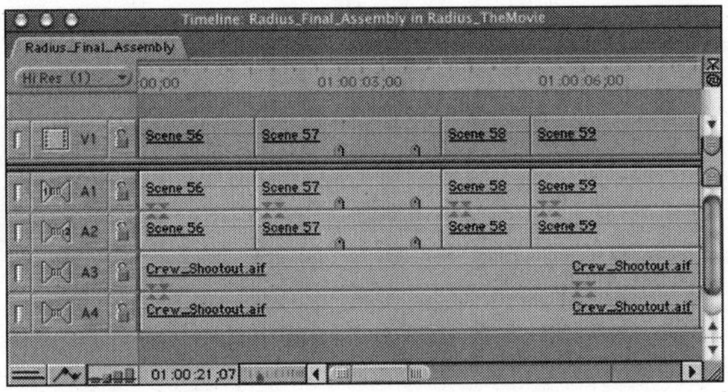

Figure 8-21:
Nested
sequences
on the
Timeline.

In any event, here's how to nest one sequence into another (take a deep breath first; this is pretty tough):

1. **Double-click a sequence's icon in the Browser to open it on the Timeline.**

   This will be the sequence that receives any other sequences you're nesting.

2. **Click and drag another sequence from the Browser window to the Timeline.**

   That's it. You've now added (sorry, *nested*) the second sequence into the first, as if it were a single media clip — except it probably contains lots of clips, already pre-edited.

That's it!

After you've nested another sequence into your Timeline, Final Cut treats that nested sequence like any old media clip. You can apply the same effects to a nested sequence as you would to individual clips — add audio and video filters, set volumes and opacity levels, and even animate them with motion settings. When you do so, the effects apply to all the video and audio in your nested sequence. As far as Final Cut is concerned, the sequence is a single clip of media.

If you've nested sequence A into sequence B but then decide to edit sequence A again (for instance, to get access to trimmed video and audio in your original media clips), you can quickly open sequence A just by double-clicking it on the Timeline. This action opens the sequence on the Timeline, where you can edit its clips one-by-one (you can get back to the earlier sequence by clicking its tab at the top of the Timeline window). Added bonus: Any changes you make in sequence A automatically appear in its nested version in sequence B. Pretty cool, eh?

Customizing the Final Cut Interface

As you get comfortable working in Final Cut, you'll probably want to customize the layout of the program's major windows and palettes to suit your work style. For example, if you're working on a Powerbook or iBook, you may want to shrink the Viewer and Canvas windows so that you can work with a larger Timeline and Browser or vice versa, as shown in Figure 8-22. Or if you have two monitors hooked up to your Mac (you lucky dog), you can put the Browser window on that second monitor, so you can spread it out and see all your available clips.

Final Cut already comes preprogrammed with a handful of different window layouts. To use these existing layouts, just choose Window⇨Arrange and then pick one of the layout options in the Arrange submenu. Go ahead and check 'em out — some, like Wide, give you an extra wide Timeline.

And if those stock layouts don't cut it for you, you can create two custom layouts that will always be available to you directly from the Windows menu. To do your own thing, try this:

1. **Drag Final Cut's major windows and palettes into a layout that works for you.**

   You can position the Browser, Viewer, Canvas, Timeline, and Tool Bench, as well as the Tool palette and Audio Meters. Final Cut won't save alternate arrangements of other windows, such as Effects or Favorites.

2. **Hold down the Option key, choose Window⇨Arrange; from the submenu that appears, choose Set Custom Layout 1 or Set Custom Layout 2.**

   You're assigning your window layout to one of Final Cut's two custom layout slots. Now, whenever you launch Final Cut, it will open into whatever layout you set last. And you can always choose a different layout by choosing from the submenu under Window⇨Arrange.

Figure 8-22:
An
alternative
window
layout.

As you scientifically contemplate the most precise, optimized layout for your windows, consider this: Not all of those windows need to be visible at once! If you have limited screen space (for instance, if you're running Final Cut on an iMac or laptop), you may want to overlap your Timeline, Viewer, Canvas, and Browser, so each window can be bigger when you're actually using it, but disappear under another when you're not. The key to making this work is using the keyboard shortcuts to call up the window you want to work with quickly — use Command-1 for the Viewer, Command-2 for the Canvas, Command-3 for the Timeline, and Command-4 for the Browser. With some practice, you can get quite good working this way.

Adding a Voice Over to Your Sequence

One of the cool new features you find in Final Cut 3 is the Voice Over tool, which lets you connect a microphone to your Mac and record your voice (or an actor's) as Final Cut plays through a Timeline sequence. The Voice Over tool provides a quick and easy way to add voice narration to any movie — maybe you're editing a documentary or training program (or just going hog wild with those vacation videos from Fiji).

You can also use the Voice Over tool to record a rough cut of your film, adding commentary for sound and visual-effects designers at key points. Or if you really want to push the envelope, you could even record *ADR* dialogue in your movie. (*ADR* stands for Automatic Dialogue Replacement, where an actor has to lip synch lines they recorded on set, but that aren't useable because the original recordings are too noisy or distorted.)

Having recorded your voice, Final Cut turns it into an audio clip and adds it to the Timeline on its own audio track. You can record your voice-over through your entire Timeline sequence or through just a part of it. You can also set the fidelity of the sound you record and the volume level for your headphones. (By wearing headphones, you can listen to your voice recording as your Mac "hears" it.) Here's how to do it:

1. **Connect your microphone to your Mac.**

   Any microphone that's compatible with OS X will do. You may have to install specific drivers for the mike, but hopefully not, because OS X is designed to work with many devices right out of the box.

2. **On the Timeline, position your playhead where you plan to begin recording your voice-over.**

   You can also set in and out points on the Timeline if you just want to record a segment of your sequence.

3. **Choose Tools⇨Voice Over.**

   Final Cut opens the Voice Over dialog box, which is actually a tab in Final Cut's overall Tool Bench window. Figure 8-23 shows this dialog box.

4. **In the Voice Over dialog box's Name box, type in a name for the voice-over audio clip you plan to record.**

5. **Choose the settings for this voice-over.**

   1. Click the Source pop-up menu to choose either Built In Audio Controller (use this for internal and external mikes) or DV Audio (in case you have a DV camera hooked up and are recording live through its microphone).

   2. Click the Input pop-up menu to select the microphone you'll be recording from. Choose Internal Microphone if you're using the mike built into your Mac, or the External/Line In option if you're using a plug-in mike.

   3. Click the Rate pop-up menu to set the sample rate (that is, the quality) for your voice recording. Choose the rate that matches your current Timeline sequence's settings (you can see what that is by choosing Sequence⇨Settings and noting the rate listed under

the QuickTime Audio Settings heading in the dialog box). If you can't match your sequence's exact rate, choose the option from the Rate pop-up menu that is closest to your Sequence's rate.

4. Correct for any delays (known as *latency*) that occur between the time when your microphone picks up an audio signal and when the device capturing that signal actually records it by using the Offset pop-up menu. Most USB capture devices suffer from a one-frame latency, so choose an offset of one frame to counteract that. If you're capturing audio from a DV camcorder, try an offset of three frames.

5. To set the volume level for your recording, move the Gain slider to the left or right.

6. Set the volume level for your headphones by moving the Volume slider left or right

   Your range is from 0–60 decibels; keep volume low but still loud enough to hear your voice through the headphones.

7. If you check the Sound Cues box, Final Cut plays a series of beeps a few seconds before recording begins and a few seconds before it ends.

   These beeps aren't recorded in the actual voice-over audio; they just help the person recording the voice-over gauge when to start speaking and when to stop.

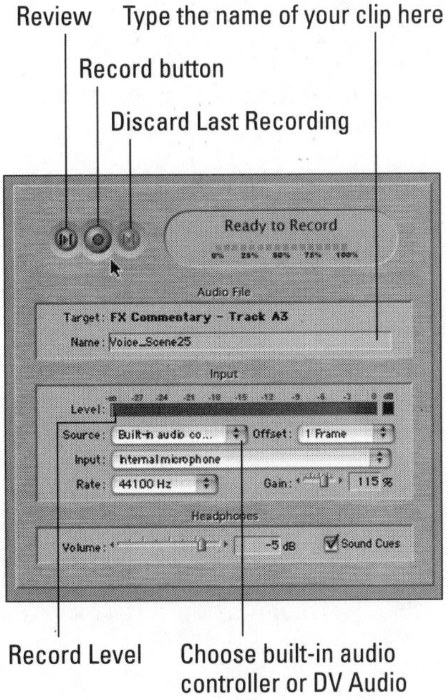

Review   Type the name of your clip here

Record button

Discard Last Recording

Figure 8-23: The Voice Over comes in handy for documentaries, training videos, and director's commentaries.

Record Level   Choose built-in audio controller or DV Audio

6. **In the Voice Over dialog box, click the Record button to start recording.**

   Don't start speaking immediately: Final Cut first does a 5-second count-down before recording. (You can see the countdown in the Recording Status box.) After recording does get under way, Final Cut starts playing your sequence at whatever point you specified and starts another count-down in the Recording Status box. This countdown tells you how many seconds until it stops recording (that is, until it reaches the end of your sequence or an out point you set on the Timeline).

   As you record, keep an eye on the Voice Over tool's Level meter and make sure that your recording levels aren't going into the red on the far right of the meter. (If so, you can reduce your gain by moving the Gain slider to the left and try again.)

7. **Click the Stop button (this button toggles between Record and Stop) to stop recording at any point or continue recording until the Timeline playhead reaches an out point or the end of the sequence.**

   Final Cut places a new audio clip containing your voice narration on a new audio track on the Timeline.

8. **Review your work and decide whether to keep it or give it the ol' heave-ho.**

   Click the Voice Over tool's Review button to play your sequence with its new voice narration. Click the Discard Last Recording button if you want to erase that narration clip from your Timeline.

If you're trying to record a long voice narration, don't try to do it in one fell swoop if you can avoid it. Instead, record narration for a small segment of your sequence, get it right, and then move on to the next.

When you finish a voice narration, Final Cut adds the new audio clip to the Timeline but not to your Browser window. This situation means that you won't have a permanent copy of the narration clip — if you delete the narra-tion clip from the Timeline, it's gone for good. So we'd recommend dragging any narration clips you want to keep to the Browser window, where they'll become an official audio clip in your project.

Chapter 9

Managing Your Media While Editing

· ·

· ·

*I*n this chapter, we look at how to manage your media files as you edit your project. Whether you're a novice or a pro, the single greatest challenge you face in movie-making, apart from the creative process itself, is media management. Managing media files presents two challenges: maintaining adequate hard drive space for your project and keeping your media files organized so that Final Cut can keep the files connected or "online" to that project. And how do we mere mortals deal with these challenges? The Media Manager. It meets these challenges and more.

Video is data-intensive. A small amount of video can take up a lot of disk space, and video projects can include many files stored in many places. Having as many as 200 files (video clips, stills, music clips, voiceover clips, titles from draw or image manipulation applications, and so on) for a 5-minute tutorial or promo isn't unusual. Often, a given clip contains only a sliver of data that you plan to actually use in your project. Thus, even with a large hard drive or disk array, space quickly becomes an issue. Media Manager helps you keep tabs on how much space your media requires.

To improve your video, conserve space, and keep yourself organized, you may find yourself moving or otherwise altering video all over the place. For example, to conserve hard drive space, you might decide to alter a set of titles to a different file format or cut footage in a clip you never plan to use. These kinds of actions, however, can have nasty consequences: Your project may lose connection with the files, which is called going offline. (*Offline* means files still exist and are on your drives or media some place, but Final Cut doesn't know where.) Sometimes, files just seem to disappear as a consequence of some action you didn't notice or intend, like accidentally renaming a bin. Media Manager can prevent or recover from these situations by gathering your media for you and placing it all in a common location, and by making a backup of all that same media to a place and in a way that is easy and convenient.

Editing Media with the Media Manager

Media Manager is a tool within Final Cut that gives you control over numerous features of your media files (Figure 9-1). With the Media Manager, you can

- ✔ Delete any unwanted or unused media from a project quickly and globally.
- ✔ Move parts or all of a project from one location to another without breaking any links. (Breaking links takes files *offline*.)

Media area

Summary area

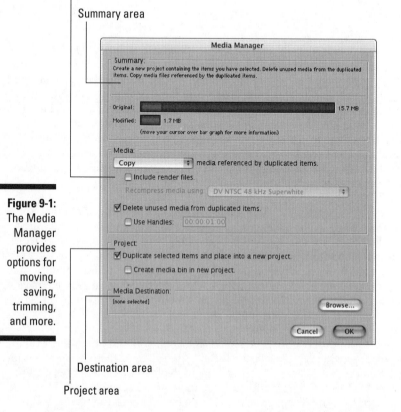

Figure 9-1:
The Media
Manager
provides
options for
moving,
saving,
trimming,
and more.

Destination area

Project area

✔ Single out items related to a sequence so that they can be saved separately.

✔ Compress part or all of a sequence.

✔ Trim your media.

✔ Use it as a simple and effective way to back up your project.

Accessing the Media Manager

To open and use the Media Manager, remember two things:

✔ Before you can open the Media Manager, a project with media assigned to it must actually be in the Browser window. That's easy to keep in mind: no media to manage, no Media Manager.

✔ In the Browser, you must select the media you want to manage.

To open the Media Manager window, select a sequence or clip(s) in the Browser, and either choose File⇨Media Manager or Control+click one of the selected items in the Browser, and then choose Media Manager from the pop-up menu that appears.

Using Media Manager: Important and Useful Tasks

In Media Manager, big tasks are reduced to small, manageable ones. But Media Manager is a powerful tool, and like any tool, you must take proper precautions when handling it. The most important precaution is understanding what's happening to your data during the process you initiate. In this section, we help you both understand and perform key tasks.

Deleting unwanted media

Imagine that, for all practical purposes, your latest project is done. You have put away your source tapes and now you want to free up hard drive space and get on with a new project while leaving the old one around until the boss confirms it. How can you quickly consolidate the files for your project and also remove any unused items? If you want to delete all the material outside your in and out points, follow these steps:

1. **Select a sequence in the Browser that you want to consolidate and open Media Manager by choosing File⇨Media Manager.**

2. **Choose Use Existing from the Media drop-down menu in the upper-left corner of the Media area, as shown in Figure 9-2.**

   Note that the Include Render Files option is selected automatically.

3. **Check the Delete Unused Media From Selected Items box.**

4. **If you want to leave a little extra room around the in and out points, check the Use Handles option and enter a value in the box.**

   To enter this value, select the Use Handles check box and type in the number of seconds you want your handles to last. For example, in Figure 9-2, we've entered 00:00:02:00 to create a 2-second handle for the media, which is more than enough for any future trimming operations.

5. **Review the information in the Summary area to confirm you made the correct selections and then click OK.**

6. **A Confirm Media Modifications box opens and warns you that you cannot undo this action.**

   At this stage, you can choose either to Abort or to Continue.

7. **Click Continue to finish the process.**

   This function of Media Manager deletes material from your source files. Make sure deletion is what you want to do before you hit the Continue button.

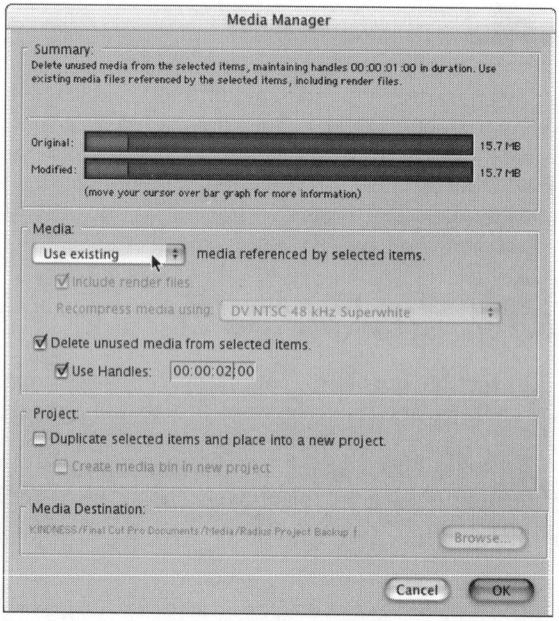

Figure 9-2:
Deleting media you no longer need.

Media Manager

Summary:
Delete unused media from the selected items, maintaining handles 00:00:01:00 in duration. Use existing media files referenced by the selected items, including render files.

Original: 15.7 MB
Modified: 15.7 MB
(move your cursor over bar graph for more information)

Media:
Use existing media referenced by selected items.
☑ Include render files
Recompress media using DV NTSC 48 kHz Superwhite
☑ Delete unused media from selected items.
☑ Use Handles: 00:00:02:00

Project:
☐ Duplicate selected items and place into a new project.
☐ Create media bin in new project

Media Destination:
KINDNESS/Final Cut Pro Documents/Media/Radius Project Backup (Browse...

Cancel   OK

Part of the genius of Final Cut is in its ability to let you retain an entire clip of virtually anything (sound effects, music, video, and so on) while allowing you to pick and choose the portions you want for your movie. It doesn't delete the parts of a clip that you don't plan to use: That's why it's a *nondestructive* editor. If you change your mind about which portion of a clip you want to use, your entire clip is still there. Talk about having your cake and eating it, too! Ah, but if you use Media Manager to get rid of those parts of clips you decided not to use, say goodbye because that extra material will be erased from your hard drive.

But because you're clever enough to be using Final Cut in the first place, you'll do two things to save your bacon in case of a problem or premature deletion using Media Manager:

✔ You'll remember to keep a copy of the original media on tape, CD, or DVD.

✔ You'll adequately label your media with a system that corresponds to the clips in your project.

The sweetest words to a project manager's ears: "Don't worry, I kept the originals as a backup, and I know right where they are."

Safely moving projects to new locations

Why is moving media *safely* such a big deal? The captured media exist as files on the hard drive you designated as your scratch disk. (See Chapter 2 for more on scratch disks.) The icons representing clips in the Browser window are merely pointers (a kind of alias) to the actual media files. If you arbitrarily move a media file in the Browser, you break the link between the clip representations in the Browser and the actual media file itself. These clip icons (aliases) have no way of finding and maintaining that link without your help. If you move or rename a bin of clips in the Browser, you break every link in that project. With Media Manager, you can move part or all of a project to a new bin or disk and *not lose the links between the clips and their respective media files*.

Say you just bought yourself a new FireWire hard drive, and you want to move your current project to a new bin on that drive. Here are the steps:

1. **In the Browser, select all the items in your project that you want to move and open Media Manager by choosing File⇨Media Manager.**

2. **In the Media Manager window, choose Move from the Media drop-down menu in the upper-left corner of the Media area, as shown in Figure 9-3.**

   Make sure the Delete Unused Media from Selected Items and Use Handles options are unchecked.

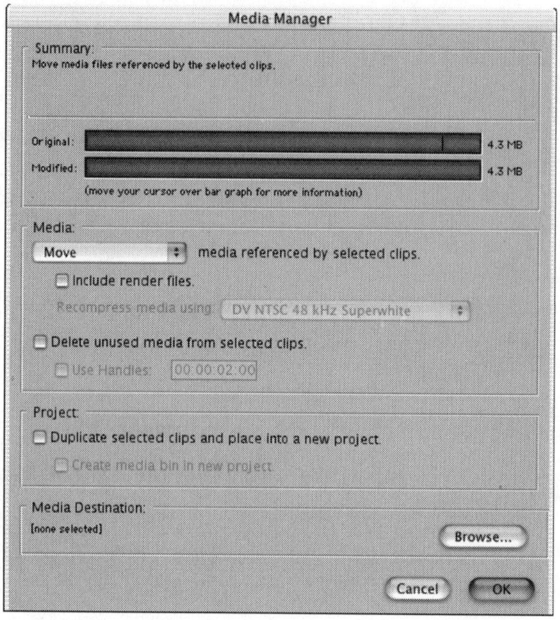

Figure 9-3:
Moving files
to new
locations.

3. **Check the Include Render Files option to save render files linked to your sequence.**

   Of course, if you don't want to save your render files, leave this box unchecked. Why would you not want to save your render files? Well, for one, you can always get them back by rendering. And avoiding moving the render files may save you space on your destination disk.

4. **Click the Browse button to select a new drive or location.**

   You'll be presented with the Choose a Folder dialog box. Navigate to the drive where you want to save your media.

5. **Create a new folder to hold the sequence and its media.**

   In the Choose a Folder window, you can click the New Folder button to create a new folder. This is the folder that will contain your final media and project.

6. **Check the Summary areas to confirm that you made the correct selections and that you have adequate disk space, and then click OK in Media Manager.**

   In the Summary area, Final Cut indicates whether you have adequate disk space to move these files.

7. **The Confirm Media Modifications box opens and warns you that you cannot undo this action.**

   If you're sure this is what you want to do, click Continue and the operation is complete.

Duplicating and saving sequences for future use

Suppose that you've been working for some time on a sequence that is the generic opening background for a series of tutorials you're doing for a class. You have sweated over them for days. You know you'll use that sequence again. They look perfect, and you don't want to run the risk of corrupting or deleting them. So you decide to make a copy and tuck it away for safekeeping, say on a backup disk or on a temporary partition that you plan to burn to a CD-ROM later. Here's how:

1. **Select a sequence in the Browser you want to duplicate and open Media Manager by choosing File⇨Media Manager.**

2. **In the Project area, check the Duplicate Selected Items and Place into a New Project box.**

3. **If you want only the media from the sequence itself, check the Delete Unused Media from Selected Items option.**

   Of course, deleting unused media will make your final media size smaller. Leaving this option unchecked will move even the unused media in the sequence and create larger file sizes.

4. **Next, choose Copy from the drop-down menu in the upper-left corner of the Media area to create new copies of your media (see Figure 9-4).**

   Alternatively, you could make other choices, such as Create Offline, which results in an Offline Sequence with no media linked to it. You could use this offline sequence to recapture your media at a later time.

5. **Check Include Render Files to save render files linked to your sequence.**

6. **Click the Browse button to select a drive where you want to move your media.**

   Create a bin to hold the sequence and its media.

7. **Check the Summary area to confirm you made the correct selections and that you have adequate disk space, and then click OK in Media Manager.**

8. **In the Save dialog box that opens, name your project, confirm the location for the save, and click Save.**

   A little sideways bar graph appears indicating the data is being saved.

A new tab appears in the Browser window, confirming that your sequence is now a separate collection of media in a new location.

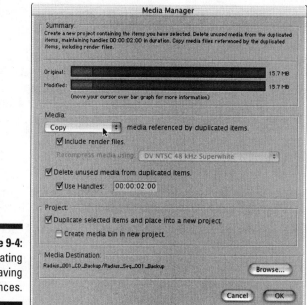

Figure 9-4:
Duplicating
and saving
sequences.

Trimming media

Imagine you're down to the end of your project, and you have figured out what material you really need. Space on your drive is at a premium and now you need to just get rid of the unused portions of the source files. You need to think carefully here: What source files am I using? What can I afford to trim? How many times do I use material from the same file but different pieces, the same, or overlapping? If you have sorted out all that and know you have a long media file that could be trimmed significantly, this section is for you. Follow these steps:

1. **In the Browser, select just the sequence you want to trim and open Media Manager by choosing File⇨Media Manager.**

2. **Check the Delete Unused Media from Duplicated Items box.**

3. **In the Media area, choose Use Existing from the drop-down menu in the upper-left corner (see Figure 9-5).**

   Note that the Include Render Files box is checked automatically.

4. **If you want to leave a little extra room around the in and out points, check the Use Handles option and enter the length of the handle.**

   To enter this value, select the Use Handles field and type in the numbers. For example, in the example shown in Figure 9-5, we have entered 00:00:02:00 for a 2-second handle.

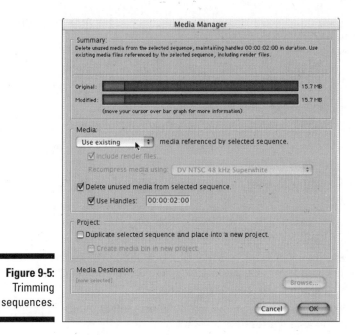

Media Manager

Summary:
Delete unused media from the selected sequence, maintaining handles 00:00:02:00 in duration. Use existing media files referenced by the selected sequence, including render files.

Original: 15.7 MB
Modified: 15.7 MB
(move your cursor over bar graph for more information)

Media:
Use existing ▼   media referenced by selected sequence.
☑ Include render files.
☐ Recompress media using: DV NTSC 48 kHz Superwhite ▼

☑ Delete unused media from selected sequence.
☑ Use Handles: 00:00:02:00

Project:
☐ Duplicate selected sequence and place into a new project.
☐ Create media bin in new project.

Media Destination:
[none selected]   Browse...

Cancel   OK

Figure 9-5:
Trimming
sequences.

5. **Review the Summary area to confirm you made the correct selections, and then click OK in Media Manager.**

6. **A Confirm Media Modifications box appears, warning you that you cannot undo this action.**

   You can choose either to Abort or to Continue in the Media Modifications dialog box.

7. **Click Continue to finish the process.**

We offer this caution: This action deletes material from your source files. Make sure this is what you want to do before you click the Continue button.

Performing simple backups

Want to put the whole project in the vault on your new FireWire external drive? Want to just burn all the sequences and the corresponding media to a DVD? Or back them up to a third hard drive in your tower? Media Manager helps you quickly and easily copy your entire project to a backup drive or partition. If your computer is networked, you can place the backup on the server.

1. **In the Browser, select all the material you want to back up and open Media Manager by choosing File⇨Media Manager.**

2. **In the Media area, choose Copy from the drop-down menu in the upper-left corner if you want to leave your original source media files alone and create new copies (see Figure 9-6).**

3. Check the Include Render Files option to save render files linked to your sequence.

Bear in mind that because all render files can be re-created by re-rendering, many users choose not to save their render files in a backup. Depending on how many renders you have in your timeline, this can result in a significant space savings.

4. Click the Browse button to select a new drive or location.

The Choose a Folder dialog box appears. Navigate to the drive where you want to save your media.

5. Create a new folder to hold the sequence and its media.

Still in the Choose a Folder window, you can click the New Folder button to create a new folder. This is the folder that will contain your final media.

6. Check the Summary area to confirm that you made the correct selections and that you have adequate disk space on the target disk or media, and then click OK in Media Manager.

7. In the Save dialog box that opens, name your project, confirm the location for the save, and click Save.

A little sideways bar graph comes up, indicating the data is being saved.

This is a backup, so none of the deletion or replace options are selected.

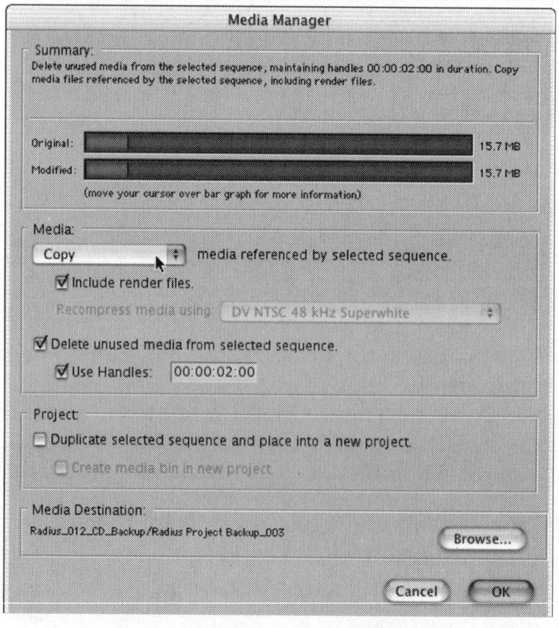

Figure 9-6:
Backing up
a project.

Using Media Manager with OfflineRT Compression

With Final Cut 3, Apple introduces OfflineRT, a compression scheme that creates compressed, nimble files of timecode-accurate video. Designed with the mobile editor in mind, OfflineRT can be used on a Powerbook (check with Apple at `www.apple.com/finalcutpro` to see if yours is fast enough). OfflineRT enables you to edit to your heart's content and to view many effects and transitions in real time (that's where the RT in OfflineRT comes from).

Now here is the best part: Media Manager lets you create OfflineRT files for a draft edit with the greatest of ease and then convert them back again. In the steps in this section, you can use Media Manager to export a sequence to your Powerbook by using OfflineRT so that you can edit your sequence on the go. When you get back to your desktop computer, you can then export the sequence back to your desktop, but this time, you set the sequence to DV NTSC in Media Manager.

Although OfflineRT is basically designed for creating a rough draft of your sequence, the quality is good enough to do serious edits. This is possible because your Mac is doing a lot less work: The file format is a PhotoJPEG codec at 320 x 240 and 35 percent compression. That works out to a compression rate of approximately two hours of video for every gigabyte of hard drive space, meaning you can pack most if not all of the video for an average-sized feature film on a typical Powerbook 20 GB internal drive.

1. **In the Browser window, select the sequence that you want to save in the OfflineRT format.**

2. **Control+click the selected sequence and choose Media Manager from the contextual menu that appears.**

   Alternatively, you can also select the sequence in the Browser and select File⇨Media Manager.

3. **In the Media drop-down menu, choose Recompress, as shown in Figure 9-7.**

   The Recompress option allows you to export your selected media by recompressing it with a sequence preset other than the one you used for your media.

4. **From the Recompress Media Using drop-down menu, choose OfflineRT NTSC (Photo JPEG) preset.**

5. **Click the Browse button to select a drive or location.**

   The Choose a Folder dialog box appears. Navigate to the drive where you want to save your media.

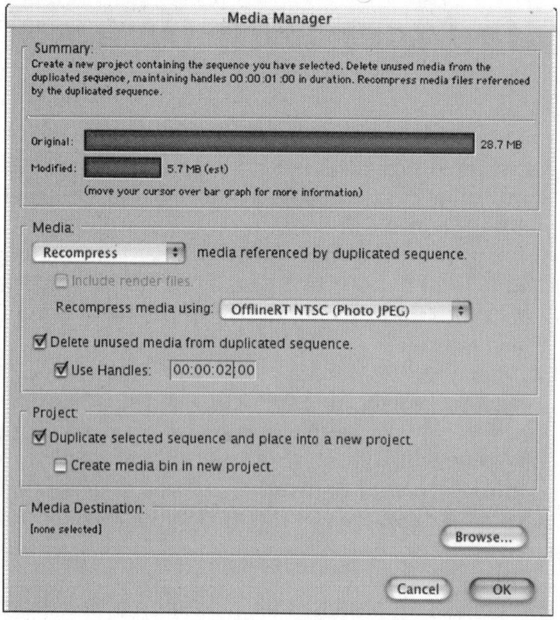

Figure 9-7:
Media
Manager
settings for
creating an
OfflineRT
version of
your
sequence
and media.

6. **Create a new folder to hold the sequence and its OfflineRT media.**

   In the Choose a Folder window, you can click the New Folder button to create a new folder. This is the folder that will contain your final media and project. Later, you may move this entire folder to a Powerbook or another computer to edit in the OfflineRT format.

7. **Check the Summary areas to confirm that you made the correct selections and that you have adequate disk space, and then click OK in Media Manager.**

   In the Summary area, Final Cut indicates whether you have adequate disk space to move these files.

   The Confirm Media Modifications box opens and warns you that you cannot undo this action.

8. **If you're sure this is what you want to do, click Continue and the operation is completed.**

   Now that your media is saved in the OfflineRT format, you can move it to your Powerbook for mobile editing, or to another computer. The OfflineRT format allows for real-time effects and speedy renderings.

Who says you can't hang out at the beach and still make movies?

Auto-Relinking Media Files

Your clips in the Final Cut Browser window are linked to their respective media files (stored on your drives) by location. If by any chance you move the media files around on your drives, Final Cut will be unable to link back to them. These unlinked files are also known as *offline* files: Offline clips have a red slash across them in the Browser.

However, Final Cut sports a very handy auto-relink feature that you can use to relink back to the media files you just moved. Note that Final Cut automatically presents this relinking option when you have moved some media files around. We also outline a method for manually relinking files in the following section.

To auto-relink files in Final Cut:

1. **Open a Final Cut project that has broken links between clips and their media files.**

   Note that the links may have been broken because you knowingly or unknowingly moved the media files on the drives to another folder.

   If the project contains broken links, the Offline Files box is automatically presented to you, as shown in Figure 9-8. The main section of this dialog box lists the names of the unlinked files.

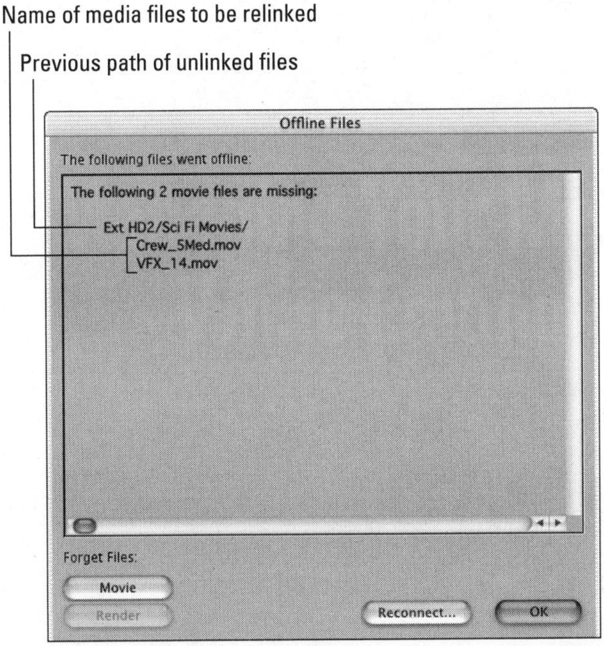

Name of media files to be relinked

Previous path of unlinked files

Figure 9-8: The Offline File dialog box warns you about unlinked files.

Offline Files

The following files went offline:

The following 2 movie files are missing:

Ext HD2/Sci Fi Movies/
Crew_5Med.mov
VFX_14.mov

Forget Files:
Movie
Render
Reconnect...
OK

2. Click the Reconnect button to relink the media files in the list.

The Reconnect Options box appears, as shown in Figure 9-9. Choose the kind of files you want to reconnect and then click OK. In this dialog box, you may choose to relink just the files that are Offline, or relink Online files to other Media files, or choose to relink render files as well.

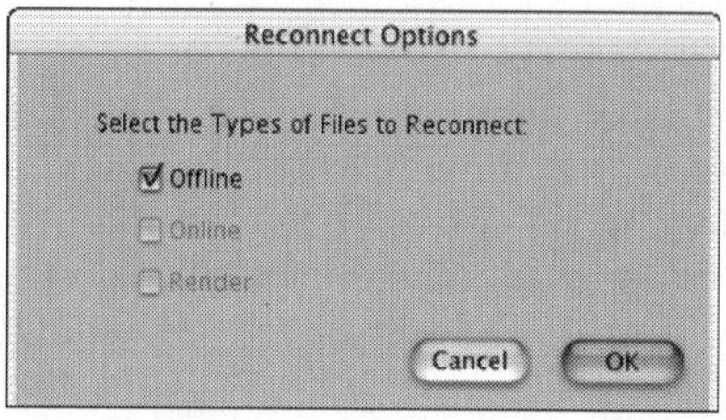

Figure 9-9:
Select
which type
of files you
want to
reconnect.

3. Click OK when you've made your choices in the Reconnect Options dialog box.

Final Cut searches for the offline files by name and brings up the Reconnect dialog box (shown in Figure 9-10) for you to identify the files. If Final Cut finds the file, it highlights it in the Reconnect dialog box.

4. Select the correct file and then click Choose.

Final Cut Pro will relink the file and continue through the list of other unlinked files.

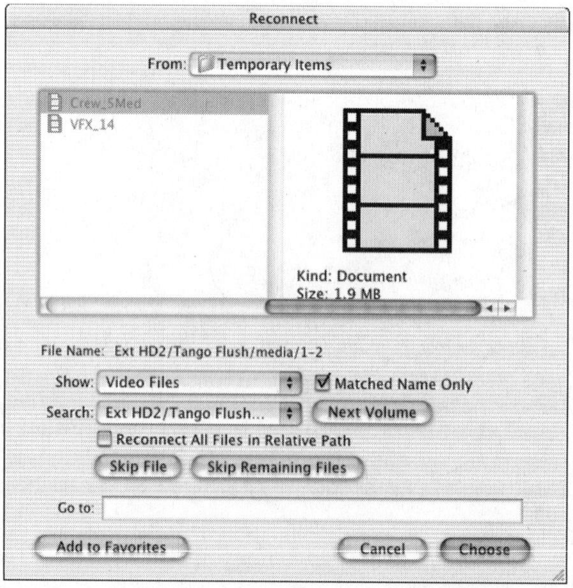

Figure 9-10:
The
Reconnect
dialog box
allows you
to select
media files
for relinking.

A handy option in the Reconnect dialog box is the Reconnect All Files in Relative Path check box. That means that if you find one media file in a folder where all your other media files are located, checking this option will relink all other files as well.

Manually Relinking Files

When you open a project, Final Cut automatically checks links between the clips in your Browser and media files on your drives. If any of the media files have been moved, deleted, or renamed, Final Cut warns you with the Offline Files dialog box.

When Final Cut presents you with the Offline Files dialog box, you have the choice of auto-relinking (which we discuss in the previous section), or bypassing the relinking phase by clicking OK. You may want to skip relinking for now for any number of reasons. For example, you may want to finish up another task and then return to relinking later.

If you choose to manually relink your files, perform the following steps:

1. **In your Project's Browser window, select an offline clip or clips (indicated by a red slash) and choose File⇨Reconnect Media.**

   Alternatively, you can also Control+click an offline clip and choose Reconnect Media from the contextual menu.

   The Reconnect Options box appears.

2. **Select the type of files you'd like to reconnect and click OK.**

   In the Reconnect Options dialog box, select Offline because you're trying to relink files that are offline. Note that you'll also have the choice of relinking online files, which means that you can relink online files to media files that don't originally belong to the clips.

   Final Cut searches for the media files by name and presents them in a dialog box.

3. **Highlight the appropriate file and click Choose to reconnect the files.**

When you select an offline clip in the Browser and reconnect the media file via the contextual menu's Reconnect Media option, only that clip is relinked to the media file. If that same offline clip was used in a sequence, the clip in the sequence will not be relinked. In order to reconnect an offline clip both in the Browser and its use in a sequence, you must select the clip in the Browser and highlight the sequence before you select the Reconnect Media command.

Part IV
Adding Pizzazz

The 5th Wave   By Rich Tennant

©RICHTENNANT

THE LEVINES EDIT THEIR AFRICAN SAFARI VIDEO

"Do you think the 'Hidden Rhino' clip should come before or after the 'Waving Hello' video clip?"

In this part . . .

In Part IV, we explain how to use Final Cut's many video transitions, which let you smoothly transition from one video clip to another. We also dive into all sorts of audio-related topics: how to set different volume levels for different clips, how to edit out scratches and pops in your audio, and how to use Final Cut's numerous audio filters to create effects. We even look at Final Cut's video filters, which let you change and enhance video clips in all sorts of ways.

This part explains how to use Final Cut's advanced effects engine to scale text, graphics, and video clips in size; change their positions on-screen; change their opacity; and composite different images together into a single shot. We also offer strategies and tips for rendering your video and audio clips.

Chapter 10

Transitions

A transition is the visual magic that takes your eyes (and then your mind) to the next clip in a movie. Leonard Bernstein once defined music as "one note after another." When you get down to it, a movie is like that too: one frame, one clip after another. The difference between a good movie and one that is hard to watch often depends on which clip comes next and how the editor made it appear.

Most of the video we see on TV and in the movies is edited by people with an enormous array of expensive tools to make transitions from one clip to another. You may have watched with awe and envy at how they did it — until now. With Final Cut Pro in *your* hot little hands, you can go from clip to clip like a pro, minus the studio full of expensive equipment.

Power to create should breed success, right? Whoa! Some really baaaad movies and documentaries (full of horrible transitions) are made in expensive studios. You can avoid such mistakes if you follow a few simple rules. In this chapter, we demystify transitions and, just as importantly, help you use transitions effectively.

One more note: Transitions are as much about the creative process as anything else in Final Cut. Learning how to use them involves thinking about your movie's theme, texture, and look. While you take in this chapter, try to avoid just looking at the details: Keep the "big picture" — the look and feel of your movie — in mind.

Okay, so what is this chapter *really* about? All about using transitions in Final Cut: You will learn to apply, modify, save, and work with transitions of all kinds. Off we go!

Transition Types in Final Cut

Here are some of the important transition types provided in Final Cut and what they do:

- ✔ **3D Simulations:** As the name implies, these six transitions imitate an action in three dimensions. You can use them to zoom in and out and create spins, cube spins, and swings. They have an action, high-tech feel and are often used in commercials and news shorts.

  The transitions under the 3D simulations are Cross Zoom, Cube Spin, Spin 3D, Spinback 3D, Swing, and Zoom.

- ✔ **Dissolves:** A *dissolve*, the most common transition, is an equal fade out of a clip, over an equal fade in of another. These transitions morph the image into something else by gradually erasing what was there previously.

  The dissolves available to you are Additive dissolve, Cross dissolve, Dither dissolve, Fade In, Fade Out, Non-Additive dissolve, and Ripple dissolve.

- ✔ **Iris:** Like looking through a telescope, an iris puts the focus on the center of the frame, and the edges change toward that center. You can manipulate an iris transition in dozens of ways.

  Iris transitions include Cross, Diamond, Oval, Point, Rectangle, and Star.

- ✔ **Map:** By selecting or inverting specific channels, dramatic solarizing effects can be created during the transition. Solarizing appears to burn out the edges of images and reminds one of psychedelic effects from the '60s.

  The Map transitions are Channel map and Luminance map.

- ✔ **Page Peel:** The first clip peels away to reveal the second. You can make lots of adjustments to this effect. Add some extra frame handles on this one because they are particularly important. Also, think about the relationship between the two images as one is peeled away. If you peel slowly top to bottom while talking heads are on each screen, you may find your audience laughing at what looks like Mr. Potatohead.

- ✔ **QuickTime:** QuickTime has its own category in the Effects menu of Final Cut's transitions. You can find the QuickTime transitions (like all the other transitions) under the Video Transitions folder on the Effects tab of your Browser. This array of transitions includes some that are similar to transitions already in Final Cut as well as interesting ones, such as Radial, where the first clip swings out in an arch like the hands of a clock to reveal the second.

  The 13 QuickTime transitions are Alpha Compositor, Chroma Key, Cross Fade, Explode, Gradient wipe, Implode, Iris, Matrix wipe, Push, Radial, Slide, Wipe, and Zoom.

✔ **Slide:** Your uncle's old slide projector could never push slides out of the way like this collection. Top, bottom, split — you name it, frames can be made to do just about anything.

The Slide transitions in Final Cut are Band slide, Box slide, Center Split slide, Multi-Spin slide, Push slide, Spin slide, Split slide, and Swap slide.

✔ **Stretch (and Squeeze):** The clips are distorted in ways that makes objects look like they visited with Stretch Armstrong. Be careful: You can make people look weird with this tool.

This set of transitions includes Cross Stretch, Squeeze, Squeeze and Stretch, and just Stretch, for those mellow days!

✔ **Wipe:** Wipes differ from dissolves in that they don't blend. They move one thing out of the way with another, but wipes give you more options than slides. Wipes are fun. Zed loves the Jaws wipe. It's a great way to amuse your friends when showing that fishing trip.

The 14 wipes available to you are Band wipe, Center wipe, Checker wipe, Checkerboard wipe, Clock wipe, Edge wipe, Gradient wipe, Inset wipe, Jaws wipe, Random Edge wipe, V wipe, Venetian Blind wipe, Wrap wipe, and Zigzag wipe.

Applying Your First Transition

You will probably be tempted to jump in and apply transitions as you edit, and, especially if you're a perfectionist, you may tempted to fiddle with your project and never make your deadline. We suggest getting the story down first: That's the important thing. Let the transitions be your icing on the proverbial cake.

Transitions are special effects that take you from one clip to the next. You've probably seen examples of the basic transitions. The simplest is a cut to the next clip. Final Cut does this automatically when you lay a clip on the Timeline next to another clip. Play the sequence and watch the last frame of one clip disappear and the first frame of the next clip appear in its place. Another common transition is Fade-to-Black, which gradually and evenly dims the lights in your clip until there is nothing but inky darkness. A Cross-dissolve fades the images in the first clip (as if bleached) until there is no image while brightening the faded images in the next clip until they are completely visible. Wipes, as the name implies, wipe away one clip using another. The simplest form is much like your uncle's slide shows on his old Argus projector: one slide, or frame, just pushes the other out of the way.

However, because something like 95 percent of the time you'll be working with simple dissolves, you'll want to master a dissolve first. To do so, follow these steps:

1. **Place two trimmed clips side by side in the Timeline.**

   To trim your clips, load them one by one into the Viewer by double-clicking them in the Browser. For each clip, mark an in point about 1 second into the clip and then mark an out point 1 second before the end of the clip. The trimming is important because untrimmed clips don't have any unused frames that can be used during a transition. When you trim your clips, unused frames can be used for the duration of the transition. Place these trimmed clips next to each other, just like you would when making a cut from one to another.

2. **Click the cut point (where the two clips meet) so that it is selected.**

3. **Choose Effects⇨Video Transitions⇨Dissolve⇨Cross Dissolve.**

   The Video Transitions submenu is a galore of transitions. Subcategories include dissolves, iris, wipes, and lots more, but for now stick with the basic Cross Dissolve.

4. **To render your Cross Dissolve, select the transition in the Timeline by clicking it and then choose Sequence⇨Render Selection.**

   Now you can play your transition by placing your playhead before the transition and pressing the spacebar to play it in the Timeline.

   Figure 10-1 shows two clips with an edit between them, then the selected edit, and finally, a Cross-dissolve transition added between the two clips.

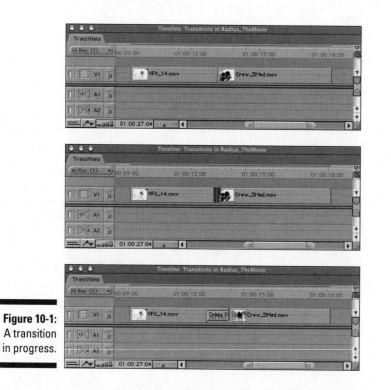

Figure 10-1:
A transition
in progress.

Understanding unused frames

Every transition has one thing in common: handles. Handles are the extra frames (outside the in and out points of your selected clip) that you need at the end of one clip and the beginning of the next to use for a transition. In short, the clips need to have unused frames that overlap past the edit point between them.

A transition takes a specific amount of time to unfold before the audience. (The Final Cut default for all transitions is 1 second or 30 frames.) If one clip is disappearing over the course of one second while another appears during that same one second, the transition take

up a total of 60 frames — 30 from one clip and 30 from the other. In the case where you have a transition of half a second, you need the same amount of time present at the ends of both clips as extra frames for the transition.

The way to handle handles is to *always* leave enough extra footage (frames around after your in and out points) so you have a handle. Of course, the simplest way to leave handles on your clips is to mark the in point a bit into playing the clip (as opposed to the very first frame of the clip) and then to mark the out point a few seconds earlier than the end of the clip.

The Many Ways to Apply a Transition

Final Cut often offers more than one way to accomplish a task. The reason for this flexibility is that editors edit in many different ways. Some prefer keyboard shortcuts, while others love dragging items. In the following list, we discuss a few of the methods you can use to apply transitions in Final Cut:

- **Drag the transition from the Browser to the cut point:** In the Browser, click the Effects tab to display the effects. The effects are grouped by category into bins. Click the little triangle next to Dissolve, for example, to see all the types of dissolve effects, as shown in Figure 10-2. Now drag the desired transition to the cut point, where the two clips meet in the Timeline.

  If you hate to dig through all those folders to find your usual transitions each time, drag them to the Favorites bin. A copy is made in this new location, leaving the original where it belongs, so you won't have to go scurrying like a mouse down the nested items each time you need a transition.

- **Drag from Browser to Canvas:** Select the edit point between two clips in the Timeline, clicking the area where the two clips join. Next, drag the transition from the Effects tab in the Browser window to anywhere in the Canvas window. This process is just like editing a shot into the Timeline, except that this time you're adding a transition. We did say Final Cut had many ways of accomplishing the same task!

- **Create and use a default transition:** To create a default transition, Control+click any transition in the Browser window and choose Set

Default Transition from the pop-up menu that appears, as shown in Figure 10-3. To use a default transition, Control+click the edit point and choose Add Transition from the pop-up menu that appears. When you see how easy this is, you'll want to set defaults for all your favorite transitions.

✔ **Use the keyboard shortcut:** Selecting the edit point where you want to add a transition and then press ⌘+T (T for transitions, of course). This method adds the default transition, which you can specify if you like.

✔ **Copy and paste a transition:** Copy and paste a transition from one edit point to your previously prepared new edit point. (Make sure you have handles at your new edit point!) This is handy if you have a custom transition at your 2nd edit point and want to apply it at the 20th edit point in your sequence. Alternately, you can Option+drag-and-drop your transition from one edit point to another to make an exact copy of your transition in the new location.

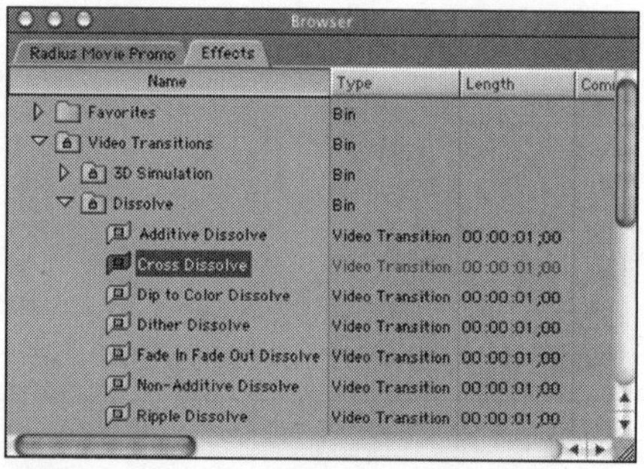

Figure 10-2:
The Effects tab in the Browser window tab stores all transitions.

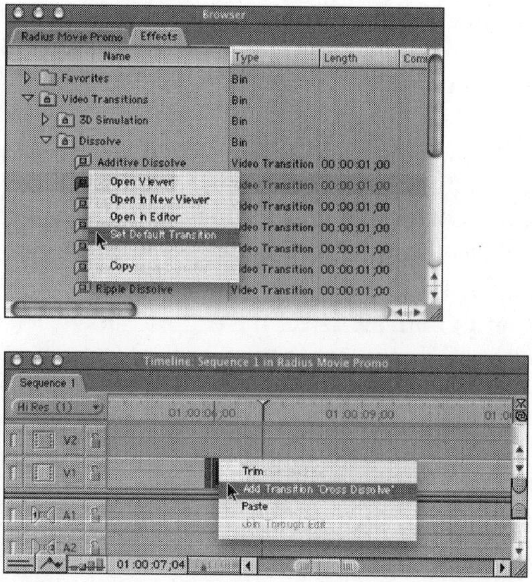

Figure 10-3:
Setting and using a default transition.

Editing with Transitions

Doing an overwrite and insert edit with a transition is an edit you'll use a lot after you have mastered it. Final Cut, beyond the basic insert and overwrite edits, also offers the insert and overwrite with transition edits. These save you a lot of time that would be otherwise wasted dragging items and applying transitions. Here's how to edit two clips together and, in the process, perform an insert edit with a transition:

1. **Double-click the first clip into the Viewer and set an in and an out point on it by pressing the I and O keys.**

   Make sure there are enough extra frames past the out point to accommodate the transition's time.

2. **Add this clip into the Timeline by dragging it into the Canvas window.**

   Note that you can also drag the clip directly into the Timeline.

3. **Place the playhead at the insertion point in the Timeline where you want the next clip to begin.**

4. **Load the second clip into the Viewer by double-clicking it in the Browser and, again, set an in and an out point on it.**

5. **Drag the clip from the Viewer to the right side of the media area in the Canvas window.**

   This reveals the set of options, as shown in Figure 10-4.

6. **Drop the clip into the Insert . . . with Transition section in the Canvas window.**

And like magic, your clip is right where you intended with no tweaking required.

Figure 10-4: Dragging a clip to the right side of the media area in the Canvas reveals Overwrite and Insert options.

Rendering Transitions

After you've placed a transition, the single most annoying part of desktop editing awaits you: waiting for the render. Rendering is the process that Final Cut must go through to combine your transitions with your clips and turn them into viewable frames. Any time you see a red line at the top of the Timeline window, you know you're in for a wait before you can see your masterpiece. The following sections explain some of the ways to render your transitions. For more on rendering, including timesaving tips, see Chapter 16.

Rendering a single transition

To render a single transition in your Timeline:

1. **Select the transition in the Timeline.**

2. **Choose Sequence⇨Render Selection.**

   Alternatively, you can press ⌘+R.

   The rendering process begins, and a render status bar shows the progress. Click Cancel in the status bar to cancel the rendering or press Esc to accomplish the same goal.

Rendering multiple transitions

You can also choose to render more than one transition in the Timeline.

1. **Select the transitions in the Timeline.**

   Select the first one by clicking it and then hold down the ⌘ key and click to select multiple transitions in the Timeline.

2. **Choose Sequence⇨Render Selection.**

   Alternatively, you can press ⌘+R.

   The rendering process begins, and a render status bar shows the progress. You can cancel anytime by clicking the Cancel button in the status window.

Rendering all transitions in a range

If you have a lot of transitions to apply, you may want to just apply them all in the Timeline without rendering them one by one. Using the method outlined here, you can render everything in your Timeline in one go after you're finished applying transitions.

1. **Select or open a sequence in the Timeline window.**

2. **Choose Sequence⇨Render All.**

   You can also use the Option+R shortcut to begin rendering everything in the Timeline.

Modifying Your Transitions

More often than not, after you have applied, rendered, and played a transition, you're not immediately satisfied. You want to modify it. Final Cut allows you to modify your transitions in numerous ways. You can change the duration of your transitions, change their alignments in respect to the edit point, or simply move them around.

Changing the duration of a transition

There are a few ways to modify the duration of your transition. Here's one of the most common:

1. **Control+click the transition in the Timeline.**

2. **Choose Duration from the pop-up menu that appears, as shown in Figure 10-5.**

3. **In the Duration dialog box, type a new duration and click OK.**

Another method to change the duration of your transition is simply to drag the ends of the transition to change the overall duration:

1. **Click and drag either end of the transition.**

   A timecode pop-up tip appears, as shown in Figure 10-6.

2. **Drag the edge of the transition and watch the timecode change.**

   With a little practice, you'll be able to change the duration of your fades on the fly. What's really cool is that the impact of your customization is displayed in the Canvas window as you drag.

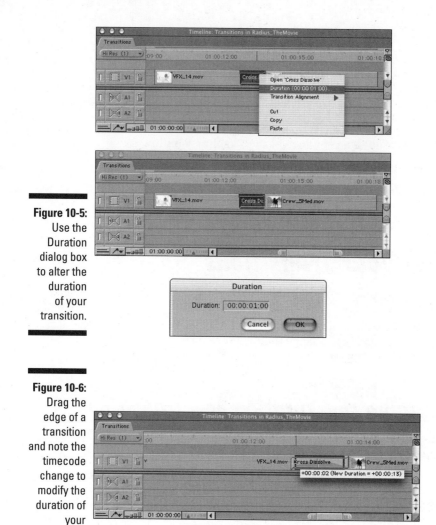

Figure 10-5:
Use the Duration dialog box to alter the duration of your transition.

Figure 10-6:
Drag the edge of a transition and note the timecode change to modify the duration of your transition.

Changing the alignment of a transition

By default, transitions center on a cut. That is, they "saddle" the cut equally on both sides — half of the transition on the outgoing clip and the other half on the incoming side.

You can change the alignment of the transition by Control+clicking a transition and choosing Transition Alignment from the pop-up menu that appears. Choose to either start, center, or end the transition on edit from the submenu that appears. Figure 10-7 shows the method of transition alignment selection and their results.

If you find yourself changing the alignments of your transitions frequently, you may want to use the keyboard shortcuts to perform this function. Select a transition and press Option+1 to start the transition at the cut point. Pressing Option+2 centers the transition on the edit point, and pressing Option+3 ends the transition at the cut point.

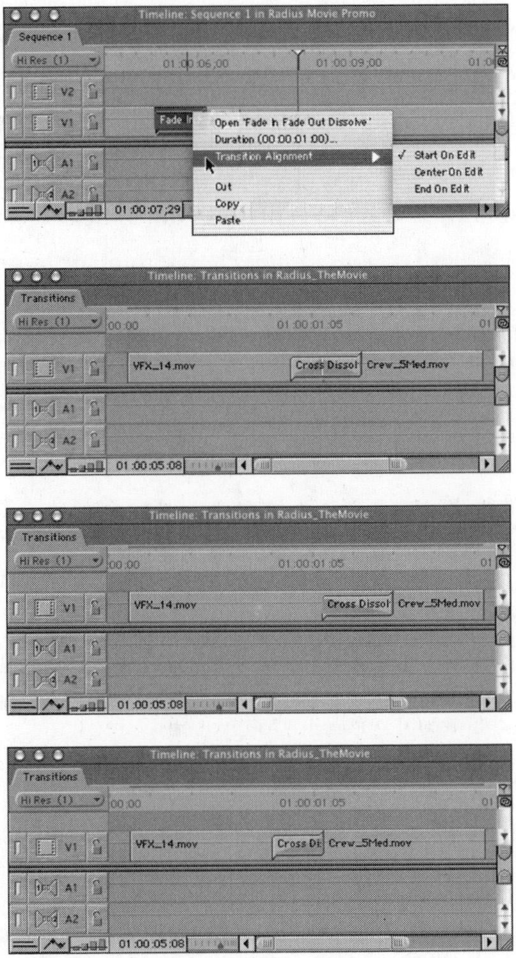

Figure 10-7:
Control+ click a Transition and select from the Transition Alignment choices.

Moving transitions

In Final Cut, you can move a transition from one edit point to another. This process will remove the transition from the first edit point and locate it to the new one. If by any chance, you happen to have a transition at the next edit point, it will be replaced. To move a transition, drag a transition from its current location to the new edit point.

Note that you can even align the transition to center, end, or start on the edit point. As you drag the transition to the new edit point, you'll feel the transition snap to the edit point (center, beginning, or end).

Replacing transitions

Many times, you may be unhappy with your choice of the transition you just used. In that case, you can easily replace the transition with another one. Final Cut keeps the duration of the previous transition as well as the alignment to the edit point and simply applies a different type of transition. To replace a transition:

1. **Select the transition you want to replace in the Timeline.**

2. **Choose Effects⇨Video Transitions and choose another transition from the submenu options.**

   The new choice replaces the older transition. Unhappy with this one too? Well, keep replacing it until you get the feeling you're searching for, my friend.

Creating Fade Ins and Fade Outs

Creating a fade in or a fade out in Final Cut couldn't be easier. You can use a transition at the one end of your clip, and you automatically get a fade in or a fade out. The transition most commonly used for this purpose is a Cross-dissolve, but you can choose any transition to create a fade.

To create a fade in and fade out on a clip, follow these steps:

1. **Trim and edit a clip into the Timeline.**

   You can load a clip into the Viewer by double-clicking it in the Browser and then trim it by marking an in point a second into the clip and an out point a second before the very end of the clip.

   Make sure that there is no clip located to the left or the right of this clip, except for the empty space in the Timeline.

2. **Drag a Cross-dissolve transition from the Effects tab in the Browser window and drop it at the beginning of the clip.**

   This step gives you a fade in from black into your clip.

3. **Drag a Cross-dissolve transition from the Effects tab in the Browser to the end of the clip.**

   This step gives you a fade out to black from your clip.

4. **Select the first transition and then ⌘+click to select the second one as well.**

5. **Render by choosing Sequence⇨Render Selection.**

   You have just created a fade in and fade out for your clip. (See Figure 10-8.)

TIP

When dragging a Cross-dissolve from the Effects tab to the end of a clip to create a fade out, hold down the ⌘ key. This allows you to add the transition only at the start or at the end of an edit point.

Figure 10-8:
A fade in and a fade out on a clip in the Timeline.

Saving and Organizing Your Custom Transitions

You will soon find, as most editors do, that you use certain transitions more than others. What's more, often these transitions have different durations than the 1-second default that Final Cut offers.

Using the following steps, you can save your transitions and rename them as you see fit. These steps assume that you have a few transitions applied in the Timeline and have modified them to your preferred duration.

1. **Drag the Effects tab out of the Browser window so that it is a separate window.**

2. **Create a new bin in the Browser window by pressing ⌘+B.**

3. **Name this bin something intuitive (Custom Fades, for example).**

4. **Drag and drop the new bin into the Favorites bin in the now separate Effects window.**

5. **Drag a transition from the Timeline where you applied it and into the new bin that you just created.**

   This step saves the name of the transition as well as its duration.

6. **Rename the transition according to its purpose so that you'll remember what it does.**

   To rename the effect, double-click its name and type in a new name for it. Editors commonly rename transitions to indicate their duration as well. For example, *Cross Diss10fr* means a Cross-dissolve with a 10-frame duration.

These steps apply to any item in the Effects window. Just drag any item from any of the Effects subfolders into the Favorites bin and rename it. You can create an infinite variety of effects variations. Just try to keep them organized and appropriately named so that you can find them later.

Customizing a Transition with Transition Editor

The Transition Editor window provides a number of tools and options for a more precise control over your transitions. These customizing features increase in number depending on the complexity of the transition you're using. The advantage is obvious: You can set up a special transition for repeated use (maybe a 3D cube spin for a short commercial or a very precise type of Cross-dissolve for your movie project) and then save it for repeated use.

You can load a transition into the Transition Editor window (see Figure 10-9) one of two ways: either by double-clicking a transition in the Timeline or by double-clicking a transition on the Effects tab of the Browser window. Each method allows you to change and modify your transitions. However, if you double-click a transition from the Timeline, you modify only that existing transition on that particular sequence. You don't modify all transitions of that type.

Here are some of the tasks you can accomplish in the Transition Editor window:

✔ **Change the duration of your Transition:** Enter a new duration in the timecode field in the upper-left side of the window (refer to Figure 10-9) to change the duration of your transition.

✔ **Drag your transition:** Using the Drag Hand icon, you can either drag the transition into the Timeline to apply to a cut point, or drag it back to the Browser into the Favorites bin, which is on the Effects tab.

✔ **Reverse your transition:** Click the Reverse button to reverse the direction of your transition.

✔ **Change the start and end percentage:** Use the Start and End sliders to change the starting and ending percentages of your transition. This is especially useful during some wipes where you may want the transition to start out at 50 percent (half-way through the transition) for any reason.

✔ **Changing the edit point around the transition:** Another neat task you can accomplish in the Transition Editor window is to change the edit point under the transition. For example, you can drag at the ends of the two clips shown in the window and change the location between the clips where the edit occurs. The transition automatically moves with the edit point.

Duration Timecode

Clip handle

Alignment buttons

Playhead

Recent Clips menu

Drag Hand

Figure 10-9:
You can use the Transition Editor window to accomplish some precise tweaking of your transitions.

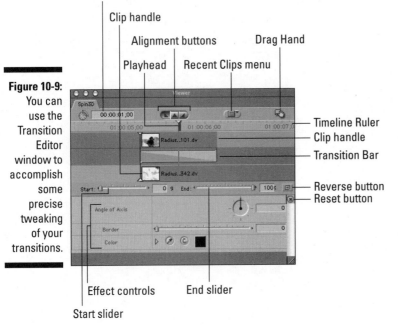

Timeline Ruler

Clip handle

Transition Bar

Reverse button
Reset button

Effect controls

Start slider

End slider

Chapter 11

Adding Text to Your Videos

• •

In This Chapter

▶ Choosing the right font

▶ Creating a title with a generator

▶ Superimposing titles and text over video

▶ Customizing text on the Controls tab

▶ Understanding how text generators are used in video

▶ Building your collection of custom titles

▶ Placing titles and text created outside Final Cut

• •

*T*itles and text on video and TV? At one time, that was an oxymoron, like jumbo shrimp. But the digital age has changed all that. The crude and ugly text of yesteryear is gone and a whole new era is here. That realization came to many of us when we saw the opening text in *Star Wars* roll out in front of us and into infinite space: "In a galaxy far, far away . . ." The galaxy of text and title effects is right here — right on your desktop. The 21st century of text effects means high definition and high efficiency.

You can pick any font. You can choose any color. You can fade it in, blow it up, scroll it, click it by like a typewriter, or create your own effect. But there are practical limitations because you have to live with the old and the new. (And let's not even get into the artistic limitations that should prevent you from picking *any* font, adding *any* color, and blowing it up.)What looks grand on the desktop does not always look so good on the TV. It doesn't take much imagination to envision your dad looking at your clever production and yelling, "Ma, pass me the binoculars so I can read the credits . . ." And then there's that scrawl at the bottom of the window at the Fox news channel that seems to be swimming half underwater most of the time.

Take this chapter seriously and you won't stumble with text. You'll be able to impress while still making sense. Final Cut has many ways of creating text, and we cover some of these in this chapter. You find out how to create crawls and scrolls as well as other ways of moving text. We also explain how to save and reuse the text effects that you create.

Video Text Basics

The first step in building effective titles in your movie is to understand the basics about text, text effects, and how they work in the video environment.

Computer video and conventional TV video (identified by the abbreviation NTSC in North America; the PAL variety is the standard in Europe) is made up of lines of images that are drawn on the TV tube at a very high rate of speed. These lines create a frame on the screen about every 30th of a second.

Computer monitor video is displayed at 30 frames per second. But the NTSC picture is actually created at 60 fields per second. There are two fields to a frame, with each field appearing for one 60th of a second. All the odd-numbered lines (Field 1) appear in a frame for a 60th of a second, and then the even lines (Field 2) appear for a 60th of a second. Your eyes say, "Hmmm. Looks like one frame to us!" and your mind accepts the illusion.

The problem is, these two *interlaced* frames don't really match up perfectly. The brightness and position of the lines vary slightly, which isn't a problem when the screen displays a large object. A thin line, however, especially a light vertical line on a dark background, vibrates or *buzzes*. It looks like a tiny sparkler from the Fourth of July, with light bouncing here and there. The problem is worse if the text is moving across the screen, and much worse if you're watching a thin line on a poor quality TV. If you have a DVD handy with a wide-screen version of your favorite flick, screen the credits at the end on your old home set. In particular, check out the smallest print up close, and bring some aspirin with you.

Bottom line: What looks good on your computer monitor may not look good on a TV screen. Test and preview everything before you finalize your project. The way to test and preview is to try and buy the best television monitor you can afford and not rely entirely on the computer monitor for the final output look of your text.

Here's another quick tip that can help you to avoid flickering artwork on your final video output: Avoid using artwork with lines thinner than 1 pixel in your final video. If you're using Photoshop or Adobe Illustrator files, be sure to make the lines in your artwork about 2 to 3 pixels thick.

In the following sections, we look at some things you can do to make your text as crisp and legible as possible, given the limitations that we just described in the making of a television image.

Select the right font size

Tiny print doesn't cut it in video. Small print, whether used for credits on a roll or newsprint in someone's hand in a still shot, may work on your desktop, but won't on a TV. So how do you know what *will* work? This is as much art as science: We can't give you any hard and fast rules. Fonts vary in size between faces to such a degree that saying eight points is the smallest you should consider isn't necessarily true for all font faces. You may get by with six points on some faces. (We find that 36 points is a good place to start.) Bottom line: Test before you commit. And test it on a decent television monitor. Don't use the computer monitor for your testing or the old black-and-white TV you bought back in college.

Avoid thick and thin

We're not talking about crash diets here, in case you were wondering. We're talking about avoiding fonts with thick and thin parts to each letter. For example, take a closer look at Times — the font face you're reading right now. Notice the contrast between the thicker lines, such as the vertical part of the uppercase C, and the thin lines, such as the horizontal line in the lowercase letter t. In addition, Times has little turns, or *serifs*, such as the ends of the top of the capital T. Fonts with these little curlies at their ends are called by their family name, *serif fonts*. The narrow lines of the serifs on these fonts can *buzz*, (also called *flickering*) or disappear altogether in some situations. For example, the e may look like a *c* or an *o*. *Sans serif* fonts, such as Arial, Helvetica, and Futura, don't have serifs or any curlies, which makes these fonts easier to read on a TV. For easy readability, stick to this sans serif family of fonts. In fact, a proverbial "Cult of Helvetica" exists in the television business. This cult is made up of people who use nothing but endless variations on the Helvetica font. Hey, it works!

Use unique textures and colors sparingly

Some third-party, text-effect applications, such as TypeStyler, can do amazing things with a font face, such as contorting them or creating bizarre shapes out of text. You may choose to apply a special texture to your font face, but you may run into the same buzzing and legibility problems that occur with a serif font. For example, a dark color on a title that crawls across the screen may disappear over a night sky. The key is to view your final output on a TV monitor.

Use only TrueType fonts

Final Cut Pro uses only TrueType fonts, which are the Apple standard for fonts. Note that Final Cut simply uses the TrueType fonts that are installed in your Mac OS System folder. If you have a bunch of TypeOne or Postscript fonts (and most people do), you can't use them in Final Cut. That's the bad news. The good news is that you can find satisfactory TrueType versions of almost every font you would want to use in Final Cut. You can get these fonts by downloading them from the Web. A good place to start is at www. microsoft.com/typography/fontpack/default.htm, or begin your search at www.Macfonts.com.

Also, inexpensive utilities for converting TypeOne or Postscript fonts to TrueType are available over the Internet. One useful TrueType converter is Chris Reed's TTConverter1.5, which is a shareware available for only $10. To obtain it, email Chris Reed at chrisreed@aol.com.

After you've considered all the technical stuff, you can move on to building some great-looking titles. In the next sections, we show you how.

Choosing a Text Generator

Before you begin building a title, you need to select a text generator for your text clip. In Final Cut, a *text generator* is the main tool for creating text. A generator is just like any effect, except that unlike an effect, which can only be applied to a clip, the generator can itself be added like a clip to the Timeline.

You can select a text generator in one of two ways. You can select a text generator from the generator pop-up menu located in the lower-right corner of the Viewer window. (See Figure 11-1.) When a selection is made, this text generator loads into the Viewer where you can then edit the text.

Alternately, you can locate the text generators on the Effects tab of your Browser. Click the Video Generators bin to open it and, in the Text bin, locate the text generators. You can drag a text generator from the Effects tab window directly into the Viewer for further editing.

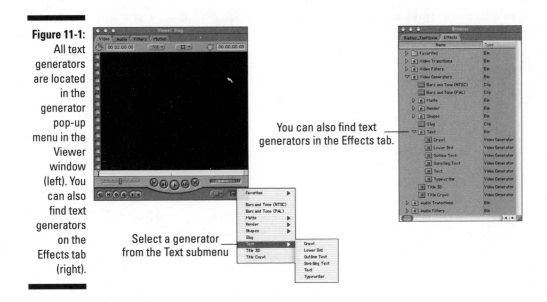

Figure 11-1:
All text generators are located in the generator pop-up menu in the Viewer window (left). You can also find text generators on the Effects tab (right).

You can also find text generators in the Effects tab.

Select a generator from the Text submenu

Creating Text

The initial releases of Final Cut had limited titling capability. Lots of people griped, so Apple has since added some great tools to generate pleasing screen text with almost every effect you could want in a desktop editing package. With lots of options, unfortunately, comes lots of complexity. Your first experience with the tools that we discuss in the following sections may be a bit intimidating, like the first time you looked inside a computer. However, that initial feeling passes quickly because making text is all pretty logical and organized. And the best part is that you don't have to know everything first. Experimenting won't break a thing. If you make a mess, you can always undo with the ⌘+Z shortcut.

We start by explaining all the things you need to do to create a text generator and insert it into your video. Then we zoom in on the Controls tab, which contains a number of different settings that you can tweak to make your text look just right. And finally, we discuss what each text generator does and how you can put Final Cut's text generators (Scrolling Text, Crawl, and so on) to use in a video.

Creating and adding text to a video

Whether you need to add the video's title to the beginning of your video, use a scroll to create the credits at the end, or add text somewhere in between, you can start with this section. Follow these steps to create text in Final Cut:

1. **Open the Viewer window by choosing Window➪Viewer.**

   You can also use the ⌘+1 shortcut to open the Viewer.

2. **In the Browser, on the Effects tab, twirl down the small triangle next to the Video Generators bin and then open the Text sub-bin, which contains the text generators.**

3. **Click and drag a text generator, which looks like a small clip with some color bars on it, from the Effects tab to the Viewer.**

   For example, if you want to add credits to the end of your video, click and drag the Scrolling Text generator. To find out what the generators do, see "Touring the text generators" later in this chapter.

   After you drag the generator to the Viewer window, you can see white text that says SAMPLE TEXT on the Video tab, and the Viewer window also sports a new tab called Controls.

   To view a generator at its default settings, click the Play button in the Viewer.

4. **Click the Controls tab to modify the default settings for the text generator.**

   On the Controls tab, you can find all the settings that you can change for your text. Figure 11-2 shows the Controls tab details for the Text generator. The tab for the text generator you choose may be a bit different, depending on what the generator does.

   For a better working layout, you may also want to click and drag the Controls tab into a separate window by itself. Then, as you make changes to your text on the Controls tab, you can see how the changes look by checking the SAMPLE TEXT shown on the Video tab in the Viewer window.

5. **Replace the SAMPLE TEXT and make changes to your text.**

   To do so, highlight SAMPLE TEXT in the Text field on the Controls tab and replace it with your own text. For example, you may want to type **The End**.

6. **Tweak the other settings on the Controls tab if you want.**

   The other settings in the Text Generator's Control tab work much like a basic word processor. For example, by using the Font drop-down menu, you can change the font to your liking. See the following section ("Understanding the options on the Controls tab") for details on modifying these settings.

7. **Change the duration of your text generator.**

   All text generators come at a default time of 10 seconds in length. To change this setting, highlight the timecode in the Duration field (located in the upper-left side of the Viewer window) and type a new duration, such as **5:00** for a duration of 5 seconds. A scroll for the final credits may require a longer duration so that the audience can actually read them. For example, a scroll duration of 15 seconds means that, from the top to the bottom of the screen, the text takes 15 seconds to scroll by.

8. **Move your text generator to the Timeline by dragging it from the Viewer to the Timeline or to the Canvas.**

   At this stage, you can simply click and drag the text in the Viewer window and move it directly to the Timeline, or you can drag it to the Canvas window and select from any of the edit Overlays that will appear, such as Insert, Superimpose, and so on.

   If you want to superimpose the generator clip over a video clip, first move the video clip into the Timeline, making sure that the playhead is located anywhere over the edited clip in the Timeline. Next, drag your text generator from the Viewer to the Canvas window and select the Superimpose option from the Edit Overlays. The Superimpose edit places the text in a new video track, above your current video track for the clip. What's more, the duration of the text generator is automatically adjusted to that of the underlying clip. Figure 11-3 shows the Text generator clip superimposed in the Timeline over a video clip.

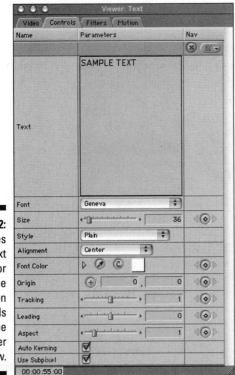

Figure 11-2:
Attributes for the Text generator can be changed on the Controls tab of the Viewer window.

Superimposed Text generator clip on V2 track

Video clip on the V1 track

Figure 11-3:
A Text
generator
clip can
be super-
imposed
over a
video clip.

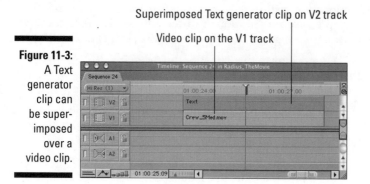

If you want to scroll text over a black background, however, you can drag the text from the Video tab of the Viewer window down to a video track in the Timeline.

9. **Render and play your text.**

Select the text generator clip in the Timeline and choose Sequence⇨Render Selection. After the rendering is complete, place your playhead just before the text in the Timeline and press the spacebar to play through your text.

After altering any of the text generators, you can drag the text from the Viewer window back to the Browser and rename it like any old clip. Later, you can drag this text as many times as you like into the Timeline. This tip can be handy if you need to reuse the same title more than once.

Understanding the text options on the Control tab

After you open any text generator in the Viewer window, the Controls tab appears in the Viewer window as well. On the Controls tab, you can find the various options that you can control for that text generator.

Discussing each setting for every text generator would take up more space that what we have in this chapter. So in the following list, we discuss some of the most common settings you'll see when using the text generators:

✔ **Text:** The Text pane in all text generators contains the text SAMPLE TEXT by default. To add your own text, you have to highlight the default text and then type the new text that you require. Some text generators, such as the Lower Third one, will have two separate areas for text entry, one for the top line and one for the bottom.

✔ **Font:** Select the font from the drop-down list. Final Cut uses all the TrueType fonts that are loaded in your system. After you select a font from this menu, the Text pane updates the font to show you what the font looks like.

✔ **Size:** To select the font size, click in the Size box and then type the size (in points). A good point size to start with is 36, but as with all other settings, you should experiment to find what works best for your project. By the way, you can also use the slider to change the font size.

✔ **Style:** Use the drop-down list to select the style that works for your project. Options here include Plain, Bold, Italic, and Bold/Italic. Italicizing a font is generally not a good idea for video because it can create flickering on your screen.

✔ **Color:** This is really a cool feature, as you can see in the detail of the color options shown in 11-4. (Refer to Figure 11-2 to see where the Color pane is on the Controls tab.)

Click triangle to reveal HSB sliders

Eyedropper for color selection

Hue direction

Color swatch

Figure 11-4:
The Color
pane of the
Controls tab.

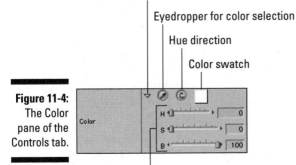

HSB sliders for text color

You have three ways to select the color of your text:

• **Eyedropper:** The Eyedropper button is right next to the little drop-down triangle. Clicking the Eyedropper button changes the cursor to an eyedropper. Click anywhere in the Canvas window with this eyedropper tool to pick any color you like out of your video. Presto! Your color selection is now in the color swatch to the right of the Eyedropper button, back on the Controls tab. And this selection is applied to the text.

• **Color Picker:** Click the small, square color swatch located to the right of the Eyedropper tool, and the Color Picker wheel opens. The Color Picker displays many small squares of various colors. You can click any color to select it. The Color Picker also displays the RGB values for the selected color. (*RGB values* are numeric descriptions of color relating to the amounts of red, green, and blue in that color.) You can modify any of the preset colors by fiddling with their values. Or, if you happen to know exactly what the values are for the color you want, enter them in the Color Picker. When you're finished in the Color Picker, click OK to close it.

- **Hue, Saturation, Brightness:** Not enough options for you yet? Click the little triangle text to the Eyedropper tool and down drops a menu with the HSB sliders. The H stands for Hue (or tint), S for Saturation (the intensity of your color), and B for brightness. Changing these sliders changes the color of the small color swatch and gives you direct feedback about your color choices. Close the menu by clicking the triangle.

The small circle with the arrow, located between the Eyedropper and the color swatch, is the Hue Direction control. Clicking this button reverses the hue selection that you've made.

✔ **Spacing:** Spacing refers to the space between the letters. If you drag the slider to the right, the spacing between the letters in a word increases. Be careful, however, because you don't have to move the slider far before your audience can no longer make sense of the words crawling across the screen. Note that, for tight spacing, you can type negative numbers in the text box to the right of the slider. Some headline fonts bunch up if you use negative values.

✔ **Leading:** Leading controls the space between lines of text. You enter a percentage or use the slider to affect this setting. The higher the percentage, the bigger the space between lines of text.

✔ **Location:** You can choose where you want the text to appear on-screen. The higher the number, the lower the text is on the screen.

✔ **Direction:** In the case of a Crawl generator, select either Left or Right from the drop-down list. Left means your crawl heads for the left side of the screen, which is almost always the best option. A crawl that heads right will make your audience go nuts. In the case of a Scroll, you will see the choices in the Direction menu as Up or Down, which indicate whether your text scrolls up or down.

✔ **Auto Kerning:** Kinda sounds like the name of a World War I field general, doesn't it? When you turn on Auto Kerning by clicking this check box, the general lines up the characters in an automatic and precise way so that they're all nice and tidy. Some fonts don't respond well to his commands, so sometimes you may just want to send him packing.

Note that the Auto Kerning setting affects the Spacing setting as well. If the Auto Kerning setting is checked on, you can use the Spacing slider. Turning off the Auto Kerning setting causes the font to use its default spacing, and the Spacing slider has no effect.

You can animate attributes for text generators (such as size, color, origin, tracking, and so on) by using keyframes. Basically, if a text attribute on the Controls tab has a little diamond-shaped keyframe button, then you can use keyframes with it. To find out how to animate items in Final Cut by using keyframes, see Chapter 14.

Touring the text generators

Each text generator in Final Cut has different characteristics, purposes, and features to appreciate, and each one has hazards to watch out for as well. Following we describe all the text generators available to you in Final Cut and what their features and benefits are.

Crawl

The Crawl generator in Final Cut produces a line of text that moves across the screen. It emerges like a ticker tape from the side of the screen. In this generator, you also select the font, size, style, spacing, color, and vertical location of the text.

- **Typical use:** The text crawl is a common device on TV news that is used to warn of breaking news. This consists of just a single line of text crawling across the bottom of the screen from right to left.

- **Feature notes:** You can do virtually anything with the Crawl text generator, including all the usual text variations. You can also use it with the myriad of filters, such as drop shadow and blur. With keyframes, you can change the crawl in midstream and for as many different locations and directions as you might imagine.

Lower 3rd

As the name of this text generator suggests, it enables you to draw two lines of text in the lower-third portion of your screen. As in most other text generators, you can select all aspects of the type, including the font, style, size, tracking, and color.

- **Typical use:** Displaying text that identifies the name and organization of a news feature personality or interviewees in a documentary. This is a common device during news shows where an interviewee is being identified.

- **Feature notes:** It helps to use a bit of a drop shadow when using this text effect to make your text stand out from the background image.

Outline Text

The Outline Text generator in Final Cut creates an outline around the letters; for example, you can create black text with a white outline or vice versa. It dresses the text for greater on-screen visibility.

✔ **Typical use:** Making text easier to read over a busy background.

✔ **Feature notes:** The Outline Text generator has the basic features of text editing software, such as the ability to change the font, the size, and so on. These features make Final Cut a tool of choice for creating outlined text. Final Cut's sliders and other tools enable you to create an outline text clip quickly. Best of all, clip controls for text and line graphics enable you to fill either the text or the outline with an image of a clip you apply, not just a solid color.

Scrolling Text

The Scrolling Text generator creates titles that run bottom to top as if on a scroll. You can also flip-flop them to run from the top down.

✔ **Typical use:** Commonly used for displaying credits at the end of a film.

✔ **Feature notes:** The length of the clip to which you apply this text effect determines how fast the text goes by. If you have long text credits applied to a short clip, the text will flash by. If you have a few text credits applied to a lengthy clip, the pace of the credits can be agonizingly slow. There is an unstated rule for the rate on these scrolls, a rate that feels right to the general audience, who wants to read the credits but doesn't want to work too hard at it. You have to experiment with the amount of text and the length of your clip before you find what works in your project. Layout, spacing, type style, font, and even the color influence the effectiveness and legibility of the scroll. You have control over all these and more in this Final Cut text generator.

Text

The Text generator, for starters, creates static text in the center of the screen. (You can move it later to anywhere else in the screen.) Like a full-featured word processor or a good draw program, this text generator enables you to control virtually everything about the text, such as the font, size, and color of your text.

✔ **Typical use:** Creating text on-screen between scenes, as in those reruns of *Law & Order* or *X-Files*.

✔ **Feature notes:** You can get beautiful, detailed text using the Subpixel feature (refer to Figure 11-2). The Subpixel feature in this text generator calculates the text drawing down to a very minute and refined (hence *subpixel*) level. This type of calculation is important if the text needs a polished, refined look. The text takes longer to render when the subpixel feature is enabled, but it's worth it. Don't miss the Use Subpixel check box, which is at the bottom of the Controls tab and easy to overlook. The default view leaves the check box hidden at the bottom of the Controls tab.

Practicing safe text

Home televisions use a cathode ray tube to display the images of your video. Many of these tubes have a slight "overscan," where certain items closer to the edges can be cropped off. The overscan on televisions varies from TV to TV. Over the years, engineers have come up with a safety area grid that allows editors to ensure that their text isn't cropped off on some TVs.

The safe area grids are called Title Safe and Action Safe, as shown in the following figure, and they're available to you via the Final Cut overlays. To select an overlay, click the Video tab in the Viewer. Next choose View⇨Overlays. You see two aqua colored rectangles in the Viewer window. The inner rectangle is the Title Safe grid; no text should be laid out outside the edge of this inner rectangle. The outer grid is the Action Safe grid; no action of importance should be placed outside the outer rectangle. In short, when shooting your video, don't place the most critical element outside the Action Safe grid; otherwise, many home viewers may never see your critical element.

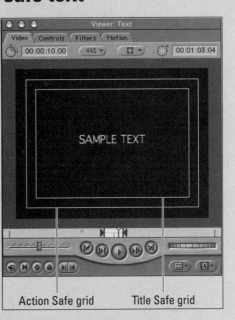

Action Safe grid   Title Safe grid

When laying out any titles in Final Cut, be sure to have these overlays turned on and make sure that no text is laid outside the Title Safe grid.

Typewriter

Although typewriters have become boat anchors and doorstops for most people, they're still the perfect metaphor for words presented one letter at a time. That's what this little generator does; it creates one letter at a time, any way you want.

- ✔ **Typical use:** Mimicking an old Teletype by displaying a tape and a letter at a time on the screen or splattering letters and words in a wave. Maybe you're doing a *film noir* detective film set in 1939 Los Angeles, and you want to indicate the time and place in a style evocative of the time period. You can do it with Typewriter. Keep in mind that getting carried away with this generator can kill readability.

- ✔ **Feature notes:** When used, the Typewriter text generator defaults to a timing of 10 seconds. Whatever text you enter in the text generator takes 10 seconds to type onto the screen. Be aware that when you first apply this generator, you don't see any text. You have to play the effect to see the text type. Press the spacebar to play the Typewriter generator in the Viewer window.

Building Your Collection of Custom Titles

Working with the great variety of titling choices in Final Cut reminds us of our friend from Nigeria's first visit to Home Depot: "How does one use all this? I didn't even know it existed until today!" But with Final Cut, it won't be long before you're looking for more. Here are some guidelines to building and using your own collection of specialized titles:

- ✔ **Create your own visual library.** Build an effect in each title generator and throw in some extra filters and effects (after you have worked through Chapters 13 and 14). Then drop them on top of a plain color slide. This little mini-movie of titles can remind you of options you might forget if you don't do movies every day.

- ✔ **Save your old special titles.** Why go to all that work again? Keep them in well-labeled bins and copy and paste them into other projects. If you're doing a series that uses the same general format, keeping a collection that moves from episode to episode just makes sense. Use Media Manager (Chapter 9) to create and manage your effects archive.

- ✔ **Trade ideas and titles with other Final Cut users.** User groups provide the perfect environment for sharing ideas and techniques. As a whole, this community is an unselfish lot. (See Chapter 20 for suggestions on finding these groups.) Final Cut user group Web sites are full of tips and hints. If someone gives you a great idea, we recommend creating a sample that uses the idea instead of relying on your memory. The sample title takes up little room on a disk, and you don't need to spend a lot of time on it either. Just get the sample in a form so that you can save it. For little money, you can burn a CD with whole collections of things you heard about, re-created, and saved.

Placing Titles and Text Created Outside Final Cut

You can create titles and text in other programs and import that text into Final Cut. However, overlays of text, where the video will be seen behind the text, create special circumstances and needs. A lot of software out there promises to help you do this. An entire library of books has been written on creating and manipulating images in these various programs.

However, one product, Adobe Photoshop, is recognized as the leader in this field. It is especially useful for creating images to be used in Final Cut. It has features that make it easy and fast to create such images. The details of working in Photoshop are outside the scope of this book. Refer to *Photoshop 7 For Dummies*, by Deke McClelland and Barbara Obermeier (published by Wiley), for an excellent guide for learning the many features in Photoshop.

Working with Photoshop and Final Cut

Although Photoshop and Final Cut work well together, they're still different applications, and as you move between the two, you may experience some bumps along the way. Remember these important points about creating files in Photoshop and bringing them into Final Cut:

- ✔ DV uses rectangular *pixels* (colored squares of light that make up an image) whereas computer programs, such as Adobe Photoshop, use square pixels. This means that, after you create an image on a computer, it has to be resized to look right in a video presentation. Left untouched, it looks distorted. You find out how to compensate for this difference and prevent distortion in the final image in the example later in this chapter.

- ✔ DV doesn't work well with certain colors that can be created in desktop software. DV renders some colors in a way that makes them appear too bright or washed out. Applications such as Adobe Photoshop will display a yellow exclamation icon (!) in their color pickers when the color you selected exceeds the video spectrum. When selecting colors in Photoshop, avoid this warning by toning down your colors.

- ✔ Text and images imported into Final Cut from another program can't be changed in Final Cut. To edit them, you must open the original files in the applications that you used to create them, edit, and reimport into Final Cut.

Preparing Photoshop text for Final Cut

In this section, we explain how to prepare text files created in Adobe Photoshop for use in DV video. As you go through these steps, bear in mind that the frame size for DV is 720 x 480 pixels. However, in Adobe Photoshop, you need to start out working with a size of 720 x 534 pixels. This odd size is needed because, later in these steps, you squeeze down the file size to 720 x 480. The distortion that you see from this squeeze will automatically correct itself when the Photoshop file is imported into Final Cut.

The following provides you with steps and tips for bringing text created in Photoshop into Final Cut:

1. **Create your text as an image in Photoshop (refer to *Photoshop 7 For Dummies* if you need help).**

   Your image should have the following dimensions: a width of 720 pixels, a height of 534 pixels, and a resolution of 72 pixels per inch.

2. **When you're finished with your creation, save the file.**

3. **Make a copy with the same name as the original, but add "version 2" or "import" to the filename.**

4. **Open the copy in Photoshop (close the original file — it is now your backup).**

You're about to edit this image for importing into Final Cut.

5. **Choose Image⇨Image Size.**

The Image Size dialog box opens.

6. **Uncheck the Constrain Proportions box.**

7. **In the Pixel Dimensions area, change the height from 534 pixels to 480.**

Remember these numbers as you may need them every time you need to prepare a text file in Adobe Photoshop, for use in Final Cut, when working with DV based video.

Figure 11-5 shows the Photoshop file before and after the height change. The Os appear distorted, but importing them into Final Cut will correct the distortion automatically.

Before the size change, the Os are okay.   After the size change, the Os look distorted.

Figure 11-5:
Before and after shots show that text prepared for Final Cut looks distorted.

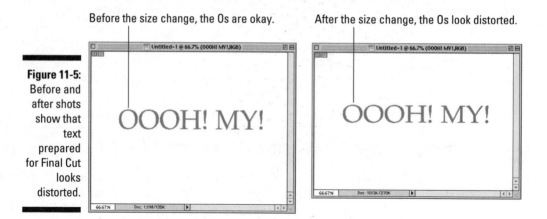

8. **Be sure to check Resample Image.**

Whoa! Someone flattened my image! That's just the way it should look to look good in Final Cut.

9. **To make sure the colors in your image will look good in video, choose Filter⇨Video⇨NTSC.**

10. **Save the file and make sure it has the Photoshop extension (.psd).**

11. **Start up Final Cut or open a Final Cut project you may have created earlier.**

12. **In Final Cut, choose File⇨Import⇨Files and locate your Photoshop file.**

13. **Select the file and click Choose.**

    Your Photoshop file is imported into Final Cut's Browser. Use this Photoshop still as a clip anywhere in the Timeline. The distortion that you created in the text is automatically compensated for, and your text appears correctly proportioned.

Chapter 12

Audio Excellence

· ·

· ·

*A*udio is one of the most underappreciated and underestimated aspects of filmmaking. It's easy to see why: Video/film is a visual medium, and it's easy to get excited about great shots and sequences, whereas recording and editing good audio isn't nearly as "sexy." And yet audio contributes a ton to your movie's ultimate impact — mediocre audio (like uneven volume levels or distortion and hiss) is the quickest way to make a film seem amateurish.

Fortunately, Final Cut gives you plenty of latitude for designing a quality audio experience. You can set the volume levels for an entire track of audio, just a clip, just a part of a clip, or even a part *of a frame* of a clip. By selectively setting volume, you can mix all the audio elements of your movie — that is, multiple dialogue tracks, music, and sound effects — so they all blend smoothly together (so no one element overpowers the other, unless you want it to). And by setting a clip's volume with super-precision (by increments as small as 1/100 of a frame), you can edit out minor distortions, such as the occasional pop of a microphone, or bigger audio annoyances, such as actors breathing excessively or someone's cell phone ringing on set while the camera's rolling.

You can also use audio transitions to smooth cuts from one audio clip to another (just as you'd use a cross-dissolve video transition to gracefully blend one video clip into another).

You can even use audio filters to add special effects to your audio (like echoes or walkie-talkie-like distortion) to enhance the dynamic range of your audio; or you can use audio filters to cut out unwanted noise, such as the hum of a noisy camera on set or the dull murmur of traffic on the street outside.

Filling Some Gaps in Your Audio Expertise

We touch on a variety of audio issues throughout the previous chapters of this book. Because we don't want to repeat stuff you already know, here we focus on some important gaps that we don't cover elsewhere. If you want to revisit some key audio topics, try these:

- ✔ Establishing your sequence's audio settings — Chapter 2
- ✔ Capturing audio from a camera or tape deck — Chapter 3
- ✔ Importing different audio files (and converting audio into formats that work best with Final Cut) — Chapter 4
- ✔ Opening and editing audio in the Viewer and Timeline windows — Chapter 6
- ✔ Getting audio out of and back into synch — Chapter 6
- ✔ Creating, managing, and deleting audio tracks on the Timeline — Chapter 7
- ✔ Using split edits to edit audio separately from its associated video clip — Chapter 8

Now, onto some new stuff!

Stereo versus mono audio

Final Cut can work with mono or stereo audio clips, but what's the difference between the two? Mono audio came of age in the early days, when radios, record players, and televisions used just a single speaker. But in the stereo world, audio plays through *two* speakers (a left speaker and a right), where elements of the overall audio play differently on either one (louder on one speaker, softer on the other). The result is that stereo audio sounds a lot fuller and richer than mono because it has more of a 3-D spatial quality.

Final Cut can work with audio clips that are recorded in mono or stereo. You import mono audio as a single clip (said to be *one channel*), while stereo audio is actually made up of two clips — one for the left stereo speaker and one for the right (*two channels*). You don't have to tell Final Cut specifically whether you're working with mono clips or stereo clips — it can figure that out for itself. If you import mono audio, you see that it occupies only one audio track on the Timeline, whereas stereo audio clips take up two tracks on the Timeline (with one clip track per stereo channel), as shown in Figure 12-1.

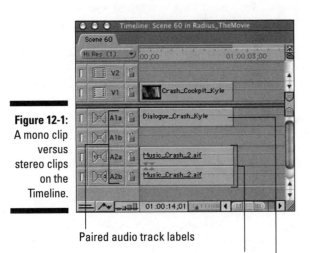

Figure 12-1:
A mono clip
versus
stereo clips
on the
Timeline.

Paired audio track labels

A stereo clip takes up two tracks.

A mono clip takes up one track on the Timeline.

When you import stereo audio to the Timeline, the two clips that make up your audio are called *stereo audio pairs*. These two paired clips are linked together and essentially act as one — that is, moving, resizing, or cutting one has the same effect on the other. But if you ever want to break the link these paired clips share (for instance, you may want to pan a mono clip from the stereo pair — more on this in the section "Changing Pan and Spread," later in this chapter), just select them on the Timeline and choose Modify⇨ Stereo Pair.

When you move stereo audio to the Timeline, Final Cut puts each clip representing the audio's two stereo channels on its own track. By default, Final Cut numbers these tracks sequentially (A1, A2, A3, and so on), but if you have a lot of stereo clips on the Timeline, telling which clips are paired to each other gets hard. To help identify stereo pairs, choose Sequence⇨Settings, click the Timeline Options tab, and then choose the Paired option from the Audio Track Labels pop-up menu. Final Cut now displays your audio tracks as pairs (A1a, A1b; A2a, A2b); refer to Figure 12-1.

Strategies for high-quality audio

Here are a few tips for starting off with high-quality audio and keeping it that way:

✔ **Find a good microphone.** If you're working in a pro or semipro realm, you already know how important a high-quality microphone can be. If you're shooting audio with a DV camera, we seriously, seriously suggest buying or renting a separate microphone for the camera. Even buying a consumer add-on model (typically $50–$100), which sits directly on your camera, improves on the poor audio you get from most cameras' internal mikes.

✔ **Get a good pair of headphones.** If you can't design and mix your audio in a studio (which typically offer high-grade speaker systems and good room acoustics), a great, relatively inexpensive alternative is to buy a good pair of headphones. You can find them for about $100, and they make a big difference.

✔ **Always work with high-quality audio.** Whether you're capturing audio from CDs or video tapes or getting digital files from a composer or sound designer, keep your audio in a high-quality format. 48 kHz, 16-bit stereo is as good as you can get, but 44.1 kHz, 16-bit will do fine as well. Fortunately, DV cameras and decks, as well as dedicated audio gear, can deliver one of these formats or the other, but just make sure that you've set them to record or capture at these levels (and that your Timeline sequence is set to accommodate these levels as well — see Chapter 2 for more on sequence settings).

If you've set a Timeline sequence to work with 48 kHz audio, the sequence can also accept clips at 44.1 kHz (or vice versa). But if you bring in audio that's significantly different from your sequence settings (for instance, if you import a 32 kHz audio clip into a 48 kHz sequence), Final Cut may play those clips with distortion.

Rendering audio

You may run into a few instances (or many, depending on your project) where Final Cut won't be able to play your audio until it's been rendered. Rendering is necessary when Final Cut doesn't have the processing power to play an audio clip in real time, so you have to let Final Cut calculate how the clip should sound ahead of time, before actually playing it. (See Chapter 16 for more about rendering.) Here are a few instances where you may have to render your audio:

✔ If you've imported audio that's been compressed by an audio codec, you have to render it first. Of course, you want to work with uncompressed sound any time you can because it sounds better, but from time to time, you may have to settle for audio that, for one reason or another, has been compressed with an audio codec such as IMA or MACE.

✔ If you add an audio filter to a clip, you have to render the clip before hearing the filter's effects.

✔ If your sequence tries to play a lot of audio clips *at the same time,* your Mac may not have the processing power to keep up, so you'll have to render the clips first.

When Final Cut plays a series of beeps instead of whatever you're expecting to hear. (You also see a red horizontal line drawn over the clip in the Timeline's render bar, as shown in Figure 12-2.) To render that audio, just select it on the Timeline and choose Sequence⇨Render Selection (⌘+R).

A red line indicates that
a clip needs rendering

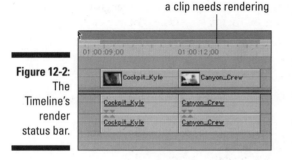

Figure 12-2:
The
Timeline's
render
status bar.

Using Keyframes for More Audio Control

Before we get into the thick of audio editing, take a look at the one tool you're likely to use no matter what kind of audio work you're doing: keyframes. *Keyframes* are like little markers you can place at different points in time within a clip, where each keyframe gives you the opportunity to change some value that affects the clip. What's more, Final Cut automatically figures out how to transition smoothly from one keyframe's value to the next, leaving you with little work to do (as shown in Figure 12-3)!

If this sounds pretty abstract, consider this example: Imagine that you have a clip of music that's set to play at 0 decibels. (0 decibels doesn't mean silent, by the way. It simply means the volume level that the clip was originally recorded at.) You want to slowly fade out so the clip ends in complete silence, which is a decibel level of -60. With the audio clip open in Final Cut's Viewer window, just set a keyframe where you'd like to start your fade (for example, 15 seconds before the clip ends) and then place a second keyframe at the very end of the clip, setting the volume for that keyframe to -60 decibels. That's it:

When Final Cut plays your clip, it evenly fades volume over the clip's last 15 seconds (from 0 decibels at the first keyframe to -60 decibels at the next keyframe, 15 seconds later).

What's more, you can easily move keyframes or change their values after you've placed them. For instance, to make your audio fade out even faster, you can move its first keyframe forward in time by, say, 5 seconds, so the transition between your first and second keyframes lasts only 10 seconds instead of 15. And you can set as many keyframes throughout a clip as you want, giving you a phenomenal degree of audio control.

Pretty cool, eh? Better yet, keyframes are handy for more than just setting a clip's volume levels. You can use them to change the effects of audio transitions and filters as well. (They're also a major player in visual effects work you do within Final Cut, as you can see in Chapters 13 through 15.) We show you how to work with keyframes as we go, on a case-by-case basis.

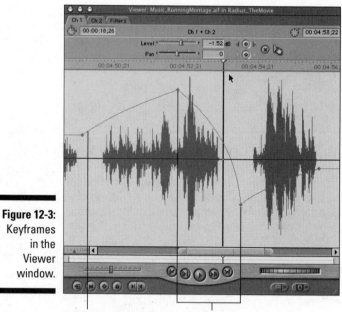

Figure 12-3:
Keyframes
in the
Viewer
window.

Volume Level overlay   Keyframes

Setting Volume Levels

When you import an audio clip, Final Cut sets its volume at 0 decibels, but you can change that level to as high as 12 decibels (louder) and as low as -60 decibels (silence). You can make these changes either in the Viewer window or directly on the Timeline. So which route should you take? It's a matter of preference, but in general, we find that the Viewer is easier for fine-tuning audio (for instance, if you're setting lots of precise keyframes), whereas using the Timeline is quick and lets you see a clip's volume relative to any other clips on the Timeline.

When you're setting a clip's decibel level in Final Cut, you should know that the decibel values you use are all relative from clip to clip — that is, just because two clips are set at the same decibel level *doesn't* mean that they actually play at the same volume. That's because a clip's volume actually depends on *two* factors:

- ✔ The volume level the clip was originally recorded at (by a microphone, or a composer's or editor's mixing computer, and so on)
- ✔ The volume you set for it after it's in Final Cut

It may seem strange that Final Cut sets a clip at 0 decibels of volume when you first import it (zero, it seems, should mean silence), but that actually means Final Cut plays the clip at the volume level it was originally *recorded* at, without adding or taking away any decibels. But if two clips were recorded at different levels in the first place, you can see how giving the clips the same level in Final Cut doesn't make them play at equal volumes.

Changing a clip's volume in the Viewer

When you're adjusting an audio clip's volume in the Viewer, you can set a new level for the entire clip or for just a part of it, thanks to keyframes.

Changing the volume for an entire clip

To change an entire clip's volume, try this:

1. **Open your audio clip in the Viewer window.**

   You can double-click the audio clip from the Browser window or from the Timeline if you've already placed the clip there.

   Either way, the Viewer displays your clip as an audio waveform.

2. **Change the clip's volume one of three ways (as shown in Figure 12-4):**

   - • Drag the Level slider left or right.
   - • Type in a new decibel value in the Viewer's Level box (anywhere between -60 and 12 will do) and press Return.
   - • Click and drag the Level overlay line up or down.

Level Overlay

Level slider Level box

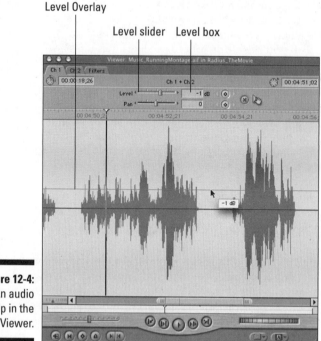

Figure 12-4:
An audio
clip in the
Viewer.

The highs and lows of dynamic range

When you set the volume levels for audio clips (dialogue, music, effects, and so on), you're establishing the *dynamic range* of your soundtrack — that is, the range between the softest and loudest volumes used in your movie.

Dynamic ranges vary widely, depending on your content: For instance, a couple arguing and then making up could go from yells to whispers — that's a wide dynamic range. On the other hand, your garden-variety heavy metal rock anthem probably has a more narrow range because it's likely to blare from start to finish.

Make sure that your dynamic range gives your content the room it needs, but without getting too extreme. A good test for range is to play your soundtrack on whatever TV or computer sound system you expect most of your audience

has. (Chances are, you want to aim for modest equipment instead of sexy top-of-the-line hardware that few people can afford. Also, if you intend to compress your soundtrack — for instance, to allow your movie to be played over the Internet or on CD-ROM — then apply whatever compression codec you expect to use to the soundtrack before testing its dynamic range.) If your audio sounds clear and you don't need to adjust volume during the movie (turning up soft parts or turning down the loud ones), you're in good shape. But if you hear sound distortions (usually a sign of things getting too loud) or can't hear things in some parts, you need to narrow your range by finding the troublesome audio and adjusting its volume. (You can also apply some audio filters for greater control — see this chapter's "Audio Filters" section.)

Changing the volume for part of a clip

You can use keyframes to change the volume in only part of a clip instead of the whole enchilada (for instance, to fade a music clip gently in or out). You do that by setting a keyframe in the clip, giving that keyframe a volume level, and then setting another keyframe elsewhere in the clip and giving that keyframe a *different* volume. End result? Final Cut either increases or fades the clip's volume across the range of keyframes you set. Try this out:

1. **Open your audio clip in the Viewer.**

2. **Position the Viewer's playhead on the frame where you want your volume change to begin.**

   You're often likely to set keyframes on or near noticeable events in your audio (like a beat of music, a pop of a microphone, or an unusually quiet moment). You can pinpoint these events by studying your clip's wave-form (spikes in the waveform indicate loudness and dips indicate quiet moments). Then, set the Viewer to show the waveform in greater detail so that you can place your keyframe on the "perfect" frame. To increase the waveform's detail (effectively stretching it out across the Viewer window), just drag the Zoom control to the left (check out Figure 12-5). On the other hand, you can shrink your view of the waveform (to see more of it at once in the Viewer) by dragging the slider to the right.

3. **Place a keyframe by clicking the Insert/Delete Keyframe button in the Viewer, as shown in Figure 12-5.**

   You can also press Control+K (for keyframe) on your keyboard. Either way, Final Cut places a volume keyframe at that frame of audio, setting that keyframe's volume to the clip's current volume level.

4. **Move the Viewer's playhead to the last frame where your volume change should end.**

   For instance, if you wanted to smoothly dip your volume from 0 decibels to -30 decibels across 90 frames, you'd move the Viewer's playhead 90 frames ahead, to the frame where the volume should finally reach -30 decibels, and therefore stop dipping.

5. **Set a keyframe at that point and then set its volume level.**

   You can set the keyframe's volume level one of three ways: drag the level slider left or right, type in a new decibel value in the Level box, or drag the level overlay line up or down.

   In the Viewer, you can see the level overlay rise or fall from the first to the second keyframe you set.

6. **Play the clip to listen to your volume change.**

   You can listen to the clip right in the Viewer, of course. But you may want to go back to the Timeline and play the clip from there, so you can listen to it while watching whatever video it's working with.

If you want to fine-tune your work, you can go back to the Viewer and set more keyframes or adjust the ones you already set.

Insert/Delete Keyframe

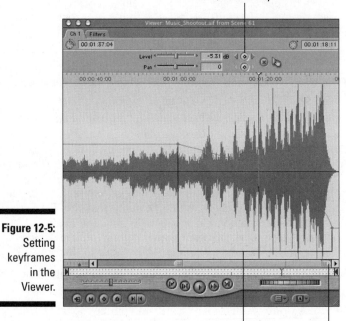

Figure 12-5:
Setting
keyframes
in the
Viewer.

Keyframes   Zoom Slider

Moving, changing and deleting keyframes

Final Cut makes it easy to change keyframes you've already placed. With your keyframed audio clip open in the Viewer, try the following:

- ✔ **To change a keyframe's level value (making it louder or softer):** Click and drag the keyframe's icon (the little diamond symbol on the clip's Level overlay) either up or down to increase or decrease its value, respectively. As you drag, watch the keyframe's value change in the Viewer's Level box (refer to Figure 12-5).

- ✔ **To set a new volume levels for two adjacent keyframes:** Click and drag the level overlay line between the two keyframes up or down.

- ✔ **To move a keyframe forward or back in time so that it affects volume earlier or later in the clip:** Click and drag the keyframe's icon to the left or right.

- ✔ **To delete a keyframe altogether:** Option+click (hold down the Option key and click) an existing keyframe icon. (Your mouse pointer changes to a Pen symbol.)

Clean up audio distortion with audio meters

When you're setting a clip's volume, you want to make sure that it never gets loud enough to distort. (Not only does distortion sound bad, it can damage your speakers.) Contrary to your first instincts, the best way to measure volume levels is *not* to listen to your audio on nice speakers or headphones because, while your audio may sound great on *your* own equipment, it can easily distort on someone else's hardware (computer, television, headphones, what have you). The best way to gauge a clip's or movie's volume is to use Final Cut's audio meters. Audio meters help keep audio levels from peaking into the red, which indicates that your audio is distorting. Choose Window⇨Audio Meters if your meters aren't already on-screen.

Using those meters is easy. Just play a clip from the Viewer, or play your movie from the Timeline and watch the meter's left and right vertical bars jump up and down as your audio plays. The bars represent the decibel level of the left and right channels of stereo audio, and if either bar goes into red (that is, reaches about the -3 decibel mark), you know that your audio is distorting. (Again, you may not *hear* it, but it's happening nonetheless!) And if you want to check your levels frame by frame, you can just position the playhead on a given frame and check the meter's reading.

So, what to do if your volume creeps into the red zone? Simple: Lower your volume by moving the clip or movie to a lower decibel level or by using keyframes or audio filters (like the compressor/limiter filter — see "Audio Filters") to lower only the spots that peak on your meters. Each approach has consequences: By lowering your entire clip/movie volume, you could make already-soft areas *too* soft. On the other hand, if you just lower the volume for the loud parts, you may find that the difference between your audio's soft areas and loud areas isn't great enough anymore. (This is a case of shortening your dynamic range — see the nearby sidebar called "The highs and lows of dynamic range.") Which route you ultimately choose is up to you, depending on your priorities.

Subframe editing in the Viewer

You can set keyframes even more precisely within an audio clip — instead of setting keyframes frame-by-frame in the Viewer, you can set them every 1/100 of a frame! This kind of precision is helpful if you want to edit out little pops you may hear every once in a while. (Such sounds often occur at a clip's in or out points as you cut from one clip to another.) You can correct these little hiccups by setting keyframes around them and dropping the volume level for those keyframes:

1. **With your clip open in the Viewer, magnify your view of the audio waveform as much as Final Cut allows.**

   You can use the Viewer's Zoom slider, Zoom Control, or the shortcut ⌘++ (⌘ and the plus key) to magnify your view.

   When you've zoomed in all the way, you see that the Viewer's playhead highlights a single frame at a time. A single frame is indicated by the dark shadow of the playhead (as shown in Figure 12-6).

2. **To move the playhead by fractions of a frame, instead of a frame at a time, hold down the Shift key and slowly drag the playhead to the part of the clip's waveform that indicates a pop.**

3. **Just set a few keyframes around the pop and lower their volume levels to silence the pop.**

Follow the steps that we outline earlier in "Changing the volume for part of a clip." Four keyframes usually work best, as shown in Figure 12-6.

Subframe keyframe

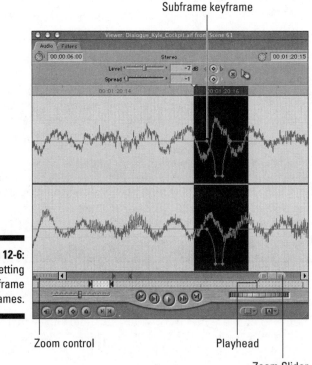

Figure 12-6:
Setting
subframe
keyframes.

Zoom control   Playhead

Zoom Slider

Adjusting a clip's volume on the Timeline

Sometimes, changing a clip's volume directly on the Timeline is easier than using the Viewer window (provided you've moved your clip to the Timeline already). Although using the Timeline isn't as precise as using the Viewer, it's quick and lets you more easily match your volume changes to your movie's video.

1. **Click the Clip Overlay button in the Timeline (see Figure 12-7).**

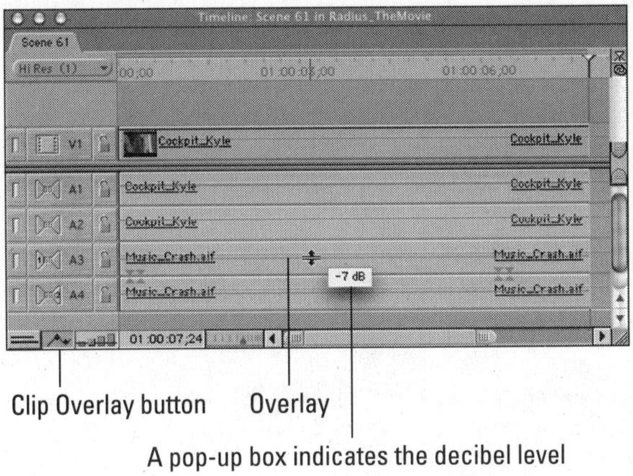

Figure 12-7:
The Clip
Overlay
button helps
you see an
audio clip's
volume.

Clip Overlay button   Overlay

A pop-up box indicates the decibel level

Final Cut shows a thin horizontal line (called an *overlay*) through each audio clip on the Timeline. This overlay represents each clip's volume — the higher the line is within the clip, the louder the clip plays.

2. **Use the Selection tool to raise or lower the volume for the entire clip or just part of it.**

To change the volume for the entire audio clip: Click and drag its overlay line up or down to raise or lower volume, respectively.

To adjust the volume for only part of the audio clip: Set different keyframes on the clip's overlay line (see "Using Keyframes for More Audio Control" earlier in this chapter).

• To set a keyframe, first make sure Final Cut's Selection tool is active. Now Option+click the audio clip's volume overlay, and your mouse pointer becomes a pen symbol. Final Cut adds a keyframe icon, which looks like a diamond, at that point on the overlay.

• To adjust a keyframe, click and drag the keyframe icon on the audio clip's overlay to the left or right in order to change the keyframe's location in time or up and down in order to adjust the keyframe's volume.

• You can click the overlay line between two keyframes and move it up or down to adjust the volume for both keyframes at once.

• To delete an unwanted keyframe, Option+click the keyframe. A little minus sign appears next to the pen pointer as it hovers over the keyframe.

Final Cut can show a clip's audio waveforms directly on the Timeline, which helps you set keyframes more precisely (as shown in Figure 12-8). The quickest way to toggle waveforms on and off is to simply press ⌘+Option+W. And if you want to see those waveforms as big and clear as possible, choose the biggest track size by clicking one of the taller bars within the Track Size button on the Timeline (again, as shown in Figure 12-8).

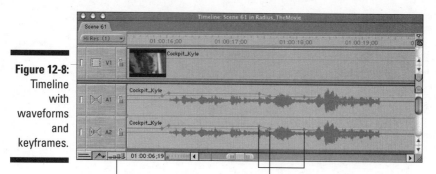

Figure 12-8:
Timeline
with
waveforms
and
keyframes.

Track Height button   Drag keyframes on the Timeline to adjust volume

Changing Pan and Spread

Unless you've worked with audio before, you've probably never heard of *pan* and *spread*. Nonetheless, setting and changing these elements lets you design a more sophisticated stereo audio experience. Both pan and spread are used to move your movie's audio from one speaker to another. For example, imagine editing a scene where a character is speaking off-screen. To make it feel like the character's voice is coming from the right or left (instead of front-and-center), you could pan the voice clip so it only plays on one speaker or the other. Or imagine your characters caught in a fierce storm, where you can use spread to move howling stereo wind from one speaker to another, heightening the sense of movement.

Spreading that audio around

If your audio clip is divided into stereo pairs (left and right channels), you can adjust the clip's *spread*. (If your clip is mono, you can't spread it, but you can pan it. See the upcoming section, "Panning left and right," for more.) Adjusting the spread lets you swap the channels — and therefore the speakers — your stereo pairs are played through. For instance, if you want a clip that's playing through your left stereo channel/speaker to play through the right channel/speaker, you adjust its spread.

Changing a clip's spread is easy: Open it in the Viewer and use the Spread slider or Spread box to enter a value between the following three ranges, as shown in Figure 12-9:

- ✔ -1 plays your clip's left channel through the left speaker and your right channel through the right speaker. (This is Final Cut's default setting.)

- ✔ 0 plays the left and right channels equally on each speaker. (You're essentially playing your stereo pairs in a mono format because each plays at the same volume on each speaker.)

✔ 1 swaps your channels, so the left channel plays on the right speaker and vice versa.

From time to time, you may import a stereo audio clip, only to notice that it's playing through only one of your two stereo speakers. This situation usually means that, although the clip is in stereo, no audio data appears in one of its stereo channels. (Maybe it was originally recorded in mono and then converted to stereo, or a technical glitch occurred during recording and only one channel was captured.) To fix this, just set the clip's spread to 0. Final Cut now plays its single working channel on both speakers, making it essentially mono.

Spread slider   Spread box

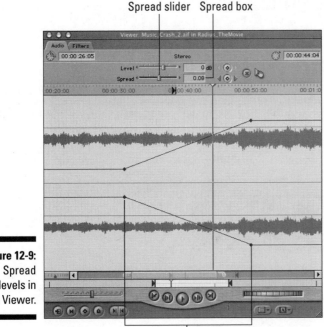

Figure 12-9:
Spread
levels in
the Viewer.

Keyframes

Panning left and right

If you're working with a stereo audio clip, you can adjust its spread. But if you're working with a mono clip, you can adjust its *pan* — that is, you can play the mono clip equally on both stereo speakers or play louder on one speaker and softer on the other.

To control a clip's pan, just open a mono clip in the Viewer and adjust the Pan slider or enter a value in the Viewer's Pan box. (Note that a stereo clip automatically features a spread slider when opened in the Viewer, but a mono clip automatically features a pan slider.)

✔ 0 plays your mono clip equally between your left and right speakers (that is, with no pan).

✔ -1 plays your clip only on your left speaker.

✔ 1 plays your clip only on the right speaker.

Picking a value between 0 and 1 or 0 and -1 favors one speaker without playing completely silent on the other.

Remember, you can pan only a mono audio clip, not a stereo paired clip. If you want to pan a stereo clip, break it into two mono clips by selecting it on the Timeline and choosing Modify➪Stereo Pair. You're breaking the pair into two separate clips and can now pan either one to your heart's content.

Creating Audio Transitions

You can use the Final Cut cross-fade transitions to smooth over awkward or obvious cuts in your audio (that is, when one audio clip ends and the next begins). You have two cross fades to choose from — each one essentially fades out the volume for your outgoing clip while fading the incoming clip in (as you can see in Figure 12-10), but they do it a little differently.

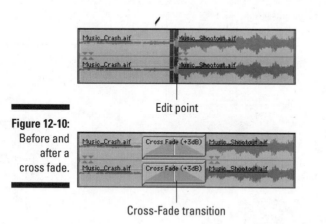

Edit point

Figure 12-10:
Before and
after a
cross fade.

Cross-Fade transition

Applying an audio transition is easy:

1. **Select an edit point between two adjacent audio clips.**

2. **Choose Effects➪Audio Transitions.**

3. **Then choose either Cross Fade (0 dB) or Cross Fade (+3 dB) from the Audio Transitions submenu.**

What's the difference between the two choices? It's subtle, but Cross Fade (0 dB) briefly dips volume as your first clips fades out and the second fades in, while Cross Fade (+3 dB) keeps volume steady through the whole transition. But don't fret much over which cross fade to use: Give each a try, and simply pick the one that sounds best. You can easily replace one transition for another by selecting the transition on the Timeline and then choosing a new Transition from the Audio Transitions submenu. Or you can press Delete to simply toss the selected transition.

If you get an error message saying `Insufficient content for edit` while trying to apply a cross fade, consider this: To do a fade between two audio clips, each clip needs to have additional frames available to it beyond its Timeline edit points. The default cross fade lasts 1 second. Therefore, your first clip (the outgoing clip) needs an additional 15 frames beyond its out point, and the second clip (the incoming clip) needs an additional 15 frames available before its in point (assuming that you're working in a 30-frame-per-second sequence of course — if you're working in a 24-frame-per-second project, then each clip would need 12 extra frames). The cross fade uses these extra frames to make a smooth transition between your two clips.

After you've applied a cross fade, you can customize it to play over more or fewer frames on the Timeline — just click and drag its edges to stretch or shrink it. And having resized a cross fade, you can now save it as a Favorite in case you ever want to apply a transition that size somewhere else. Saving a cross fade as a Favorite is simple:

1. **Open Final Cut's Effects window (see Figure 12-11); either choose Windows➪Effects or click the Effects tab in the Browser window.**

2. **Click and drag your customized transition from the Timeline to the Favorites bin in the Effects window to add it there.**

   We recommend that you rename the transition now (as you would any clip in the Browser window — see Chapter 5), so that you can recognize it later. After you name it, you're free to use that exact transition any time you like; just choose Effects➪Audio Transitions➪Favorites.

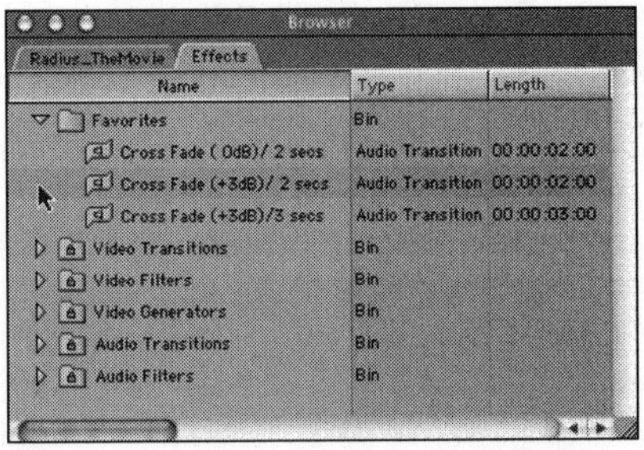

Figure 12-11:
The Favorites bin in the Effects menu.

Audio Filters

After you bring audio into Final Cut, you may want to change its sound in some way — for instance, to add a little reverb to a big sound effect, to add an echo on a character's voice, or to tone down the hum of some electrical equipment your microphones picked up on set. Good news: You can do it all, thanks to Final Cut's library of 16 audio filters, which you can apply to clips on the Timeline and tweak to your heart's content.

Granted, if you're new to audio tweaking, figuring out the Final Cut audio filters can be a little daunting. For starters, most of them use not-so-warm-or-user-friendly names like DC Notch, High Shelf Filter, and Parametric Equalizer, leaving the uninitiated with *absolutely no idea* as to what each does. Secondly, most of the Final Cut filters give you a number of technical parameters you can adjust within that filter — things like Frequency, Threshold, Ratio, and Attack Time — making them even more daunting.

But don't fret! After you get past that initial bewilderment, getting a grip on Final Cut's audio filters isn't so hard. You just need to take a little time to understand what the filter's purpose is — and what controls you can use to fine-tune it.

Describing each filter in detail is beyond the scope of this book, but later in this chapter, we describe the major categories that Final Cut's 16 filters fall into, and tell you how they basically work. This understanding gives you a good foundation to build on. In the meantime, we tackle the ways you can apply and work with audio filters. If you already know how to apply filters, flip ahead to "Equalization filters" to get a rundown of the major types of filters and what they do for your audio.

Applying and rendering an audio filter

You can apply a filter to an audio clip in a variety of ways, but the easiest, most straightforward approach is to follow these steps:

1. **Select the audio clip on the Timeline, choose Effects⇨Audio Filters, and pick a filter from the Audio Filters submenu.**

   You now see a red horizontal line drawn over your filtered clip in the Timeline's render bar, meaning that you have to render the clip before hearing how it sounds.

2. **To render the clip, first make sure that the clip is selected; then choose Sequence⇨Render Selection (or use ⌘+R).**

You can also apply a filter to an audio clip on the Timeline by dragging filters from the Effects window.

1. **Open Final Cut's Effects window (as shown in Figure 12-12), and then click the Effects tab in the Browser or choose Windows⇨Effects.**

2. **In the Effects window, drag any filter in the Audio Filters bin to an audio clip on the Timeline.**

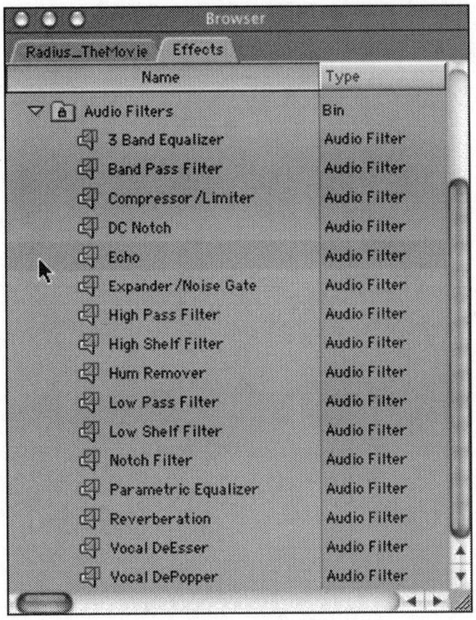

Figure 12-12: Audio filters in the Effects tab.

Tweaking a filter's parameters

After you've applied a filter to a clip, you probably want to tweak whatever parameters it offers. (A handful of filters don't have parameters, but most do.)

1. **Open the filtered audio clip in the Viewer and click the Viewer's Filters tab (as shown in Figure 12-13).**

   You can now see any filters you've applied to that clip as well as any sliders or other controls you can use to tweak the parameter's values.

2. **Tweak away by moving the sliders for each parameter.**

   As you change a parameter's values, you see the level line for that parameter move up or down.

3. **After you're done tweaking, make sure the filtered clip is still selected on the Timeline and then render the clip.**

   Choose Sequence⇨Render Selection to render it. Now play the clip on the Timeline and listen to the filter's effects on it.

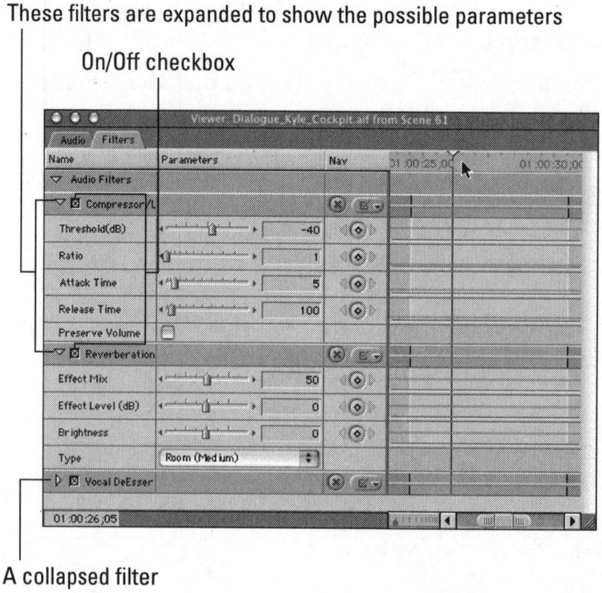

These filters are expanded to show the possible parameters

On/Off checkbox

Figure 12-13:
Three filters
applied to a
clip, seen
from the
Viewer's
Filters tab.

A collapsed filter

If you've applied more than one filter to a clip, you see them stacked in the filter tab (again, check out Figure 12-13); the top filter will be the first one you applied, followed by the second, and so on. This order is important to keep in mind when you render all the filters together — Final Cut renders your audio with the first filter, and then renders the *rendered* clip with the second filter, and then renders *that* rendered clip with the third filter, and so on. In other words, the order in which you apply your filters can seriously affect how a clip sounds when all the rendering is finally done. With that in mind, you can rearrange the order of your filters within the Filters tab by clicking and dragging them up and down.

Changing filter parameters over time with keyframes

When you're setting your filter's parameters, you can change those settings over time by creating keyframes within the filter and giving each keyframe a different value. Before going forward, we recommend you read the section "Using Keyframes for More Audio Control," earlier in this chapter, for an overview on keyframes. Also, we cover more general keyframe tricks (like changing, moving, and deleting them) in the section "Changing the volume for part of a clip" (also earlier in this chapter), so make sure that you read that section to fill out your keyframe expertise. However, because setting keyframes is a bit different for filters, we're covering what's appropriate here as well:

1. **Open the clip you want to set keyframes for in the Viewer and click the Filters tab so that you can see whatever filter you've applied.**

2. **Play your audio clip from the Canvas or Timeline windows (not the Viewer).**

You can click the Play button in the Canvas window or use the familiar JKL keyboard commands to play back and forth or the spacebar for play/stop. As your movie plays, notice that the Filter tab window actually has a playhead of its own, and that playhead moves in synch with the playheads for the Timeline and Canvas windows (see Figure 12-14). Think of these playheads as one big happy family — but keep your eye on the Filter playhead from now on.

Insert/Delete Keyframe buttons Playhead

In point Out point

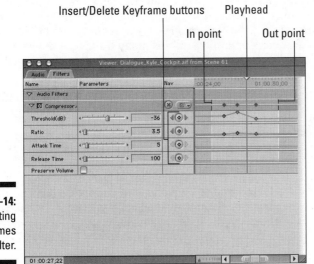

Figure 12-14:
Setting
keyframes
for a filter.

3. Stop the filter playhead where you want to place a keyframe by pressing the spacebar on your keyboard.

If you didn't stop at the perfect frame, you can position the playhead more precisely by using your ← and → keys.

4. Set your first keyframe by clicking the Insert/Delete Keyframe button for the filter parameter you want to set a keyframe for.

You see a keyframe symbol appear at the filter's playhead position (the symbol looks like a diamond, as shown in Figure 12-14). But make sure that you're pressing the Keyframe button associated with the parameter you want to change! If a filter has, say, six different parameters, you'll see six Keyframe buttons to click. Be sure to click the right one!

When you set this first keyframe, it uses the current value for the parameter you're setting it for.

5. Move the Filter's playhead to the next frame you want to set a keyframe for.

You can only set keyframes within the clip you've applied your filter to. Although you can move the filter's playhead to frames past that clip's outpoint, you won't be able to set keyframes there.

You need to set two total keyframes to change a parameter from one value to another over time.

6. **Change the parameter's value and Final Cut will automatically create a new keyframe set at that new value.**

   To change a parameter's value, just type in a new number or use whatever slider controls are available. When you change the parameter's value, Final Cut automatically sets a new keyframe at that point in time. Notice how the parameter's overlay line moves either up or down from your first keyframe to this new one; the line visually shows how the parameters values change from one keyframe to the next. The change is sudden or gradual, depending on how many frames lie between your two keyframes and how much the parameter's values are changing between them as well.

7. **Keep setting values and changing keyframes as much as you like.**

   You're free to set more keyframes so that you can change a parameter's value again and again and again over time, ad infinitum. Experiment to find the settings that achieve the effect you're looking for.

8. **When you're finished, render your keyframed audio clip.**

   Make sure it's selected on the Timeline, and choose Sequence⇨Render Selection. Now play it back on the Timeline. If you want to make more adjustments to the clip's audio filters, do so by using the Viewer's Filters tab again.

Disabling and deleting filters

If you want to turn off a filter temporarily — without losing any of its settings — you can toggle it off and back on again by clicking the little check box next to the filter's name (refer to Figure 12-14).

To delete a filter altogether (and lose whatever settings you've adjusted), just click its name to select it and press your Delete key.

Getting quick access to your favorite filters

If you take the time to tweak a filter's settings and you know that you want to apply those same custom settings to another audio clip, save that filter as a Favorite.

1. **Open Final Cut's Effects window by choosing Window⇨Effects or clicking the Effects tab in the Browser window.**

2. **Click and drag your customized filter from the Viewer's Filter tab to the Favorites bin in the Effects window.**

   That's it! But we recommend that you rename the transition now (as you would any clip in the Browser window), so you can recognize it later.

Now you can apply the filter to any clip on the Timeline by choosing Effects⇨Audio Filters⇨Favorites and picking the custom filter from the Favorites submenu.

Equalization filters

Equalization filters (that's *EQ filters* for short) let you raise or lower the volume *not* of your entire clip, but of individual sound frequencies within that clip. Having that capability is incredibly useful because sound is made up of a wide range of frequencies, where each frequency determines the sound's *pitch* (how high or low it sounds). For instance, the deepness of man's voice puts it on a different frequency than the higher quality of a woman's voice, while the low rumble of a car engine in the distance would be on a different frequency than the hiss of recording tape.

You may come across audio you want to use in your film but that's been marred by some unwanted element — for instance, the buzz of a room's old fluorescent lights or the hum of traffic. Fortunately, you can use an EQ filter to isolate a certain frequency within your audio and lower its volume so that it's less noticeable.

That's the good news about EQ filters. Now for some bad news: First, don't expect these filters to solve any *major* problems with your audio because they're geared toward making subtle shifts (not much help if your crew recorded a quiet, touching scene while a neighbor ran his leaf-blower all day long). Second, getting good results from these filters takes a lot of trial and error — if you're not careful, you can end up distorting the audio. Experience helps with this.

At any rate, Final Cut sports three equalization filters that specialize at working with different ranges of frequencies, and each offers different parameters you can tweak. If you want to explore each of these, we suggest that you search out a more comprehensive book, such as *Final Cut Pro 2 Bible* by Zed Saeed with Keith Underdahl (Hungry Minds, Inc.).

Echoes and reverberations

You can use Final Cut's Echo and Reverberation filters to better match sound to the physical setting of your movie. Reverb in particular is useful to match the acoustics you'd find in a wide variety of enclosed settings — for instance, a sprawling auditorium. Echo is a bit more extreme — use it to match sound for big outdoor settings like a huge canyon.

Both filters let you set the following parameters, so you can hone your effect to perfection:

✔ **The Effect Mix slider:** This sets how much of the original, unfiltered sound is mixed together with the effect the filter creates. The higher the number, the more affected your sound will be.

✔ **The Effect Level slider:** This one sets the volume of the affected sound in decibels (as opposed to the volume of the original, unaffected sound).

✔ **The Brightness slider:** This last one gives the effect more punch (without changing its volume). Experiment with this to get a feel for its effects.

If you're using Reverb, click the Type pop-up menu to set the style of reverb you want, depending on the kind of environment you're trying to acoustically match (a tunnel, a medium-sized room, a long hallway, and so on).

For the Echo filter, you can also use its Feedback slider to set how long each echo lasts; and use its Delay Time slider to set the time between each echo.

Compression and expansion filters

Sometimes, you want to expand or limit a clip's dynamic range. The *dynamic range* is the range between your clip's softest and loudest volume. (See the sidebar "The highs and lows of dynamic range," elsewhere in this chapter, for more information.)

For example, by choosing the Compressor/Limiter filter, you can compress (that is, shorten) the dynamic range of a clip by lowering the volume on only the clip's loudest points. You may want to use a filter like this when working with a dialogue track where a character goes from speaking softly to shouting in short order, and you want to drop the volume on her shouts. (You could always try adjusting the clip's volume by setting *keyframes* — as we cover earlier in this chapter — but a filter can do the same thing with a much more subtle touch.)

On the other hand, you could use the Expander/Noise Gate filter to increase a clip's dynamic range by raising the volume on only the parts that are too soft — for instance, if our actor goes from whispering to shouting, and you feel the shouts are at a perfect volume but the whispers aren't picking up.

When you use either of these filters, you have four different controls to fiddle with:

✔ **The Threshold slider:** This sets how low a clip's volume can go before the filter does its thing (in the case of the Expander) or how high the clip's volume can go before the filter does its thing (for the Compressor).

✔ **The Ratio slider:** This one sets the amount of compression or expansion you do to your clip after its high or low volume passes the threshold.

✔ **The Attack Time slider:** This slider sets how quickly the filters react to changes in your clip's volume.

✔ **The Release Time slider:** This last slider sets how slowly the filter eases out of its volume change.

Noise reduction filters

These three filters all help reduce unique kinds of noise you recorded accidentally, maybe thanks to a microphone not being tuned right or some electrical conflicts in your recording setup. Remember, too, that you can use an equalization filter to reduce other kinds of noise (like the dull hint of traffic outside or the hum of fluorescent lights on set and so on):

✔ **The Vocal De-Esser:** This one eases any heavy *S* sounds your microphone picked up as an actor speaks.

✔ **The Vocal De-Popper:** This cuts down the harsh pop of spoken *P* sounds picked up by an overly sensitive mike.

✔ **The Hum Remover:** This one is a little more obscure. (Well, actually, it's a lot more obscure.) Use it to cut down on the hum from electrical equipment in the background. (You can't hear these hums on set, but your recording equipment picks them up nonetheless.)

Chapter 13

Special Effects and Corrections with Video Filters

Seems like someone has taken the "special" out of special effects these days: What was once strange and wonderful on the screen has become commonplace. For example, switching from color to black and white in the middle of a film was once considered cutting edge. Now, you can do it in one frame — and from your desktop! What was just a dream for the editor of modest means is now at anyone's fingertips. Final Cut hands the film nut a bag of tricks that would make Houdini bug-eyed with envy.

In this chapter, we explain the filters and other tools available to help you create these effects. You can think of a *filter* as an effect that modifies the clip in some way, such as adding a color or blur to it. We explain how to use filters to control the look, color, and consistency of your project. And, we explain some methods for and limits to fixing those ugly but never-to-be-repeated clips you just have to have in your project.

The word *color* comes up a lot in this chapter. No doubt about it: Color *is* a deep subject, and some people spend their lives learning about it. One of the spectacular features of Final Cut (especially version 3) is that it offers tools for controlling color at many levels *without* requiring a Ph.D. on the subject. Yet, as easy as the tools are to use, these same controls and tools satisfy the expert as well. Try out the steps in this chapter on a clip or two and play with your new magic wands. Color has never been so easy or just plain fun to control.

You need to render the clips or sequence to view the results in real time; see Chapter 16.

Shooting Video with Effects in Mind

If you're shooting the video, plan ahead. Think about the look of the project before you ever get to the field. If you're doing an artsy short in *film noir* (that dark, shadowy look that Hitchcock and others made so popular in the '30s), high-contrast lighting and appropriate camera settings can do a lot more for your project than any filter in Final Cut. Or, if you want a high-contrast clip that emphasizes primary colors, say, for an instructional video for children, make sure that you shoot with lots and lots of light. Giving you a rundown of all the considerations for shooting your footage is outside the scope of this book, but you can check out more in *Digital Video For Dummies*, 2nd Edition, by Martin Doucette, published by Wiley.

Special effects video filters and controls in Final Cut can do some amazing things, but there are limits. Post-production isn't the place for turning lead into gold or a sow's ear into the proverbial silk purse. If the video is ugly to start with, chances are it will be ugly after you edit it.

Going Black and White

A great place to start with this whole color thing is getting rid of it. That's right, go black and white. Although many, if not most, of today's cameras offer the option to shoot in black and white, rarely does that actually happen. Why? The color shot simply contains so much information that you'd be silly not to take advantage of it, even if you plan to drop the color in your post-production.

So why go black and white? If it's a family video, your son's complexion is going to look a whole lot better in black and white, and so is Aunt Maude's gaudy living-room sofa. Seriously, removing color is a way to give punch to your video, resurrect *film noir*, create a background for a color object or text, or go retro.

Making a colored clip black and white

Going black and white is easy to do:

1. **In the Browser, find the clip you want to convert to black and white and drag it to the Viewer**

   You can also double-click the clip in the Browser to load it into the Viewer.

2. **In the Browser window, click the Effects tab and then click the little triangle next to the Video Filters bin.**

3. **In the Video Filters bin, click the little triangle next to the Image Control bin to open it.**

   In the Image Control bin, you can find the Desaturate filter, as shown in Figure 13-1.

4. **Click and drag the Desaturate filter from the Browser to anywhere in the Viewer window.**

   Your clip immediately becomes black and white because the Desaturate filter is applied at a 100% strength by default.

5. **Click the Filters tab in the Viewer window.**

6. **Use the Amount slider, shown in Figure 13-1, to control the level of desaturation to your liking.**

   Placing the slider in the middle creates a value of zero, or no change. Dragging the slider to the left creates negative values and super-saturates the color in the clip. If the value is all the way to the right (numerical value of 100), all the color is removed and only a black and white image remains.

7. **Drag the clip to the Canvas window and drop it on the Overwrite overlay, which appears over the Canvas window.**

   This sends the clip to the Timeline.

8. **Select your clip in the Timeline and choose Sequence⇨Render Selection.**

   After the clip has finished rendering, place the playhead just before the clip in the Timeline and press the spacebar to play the clip.

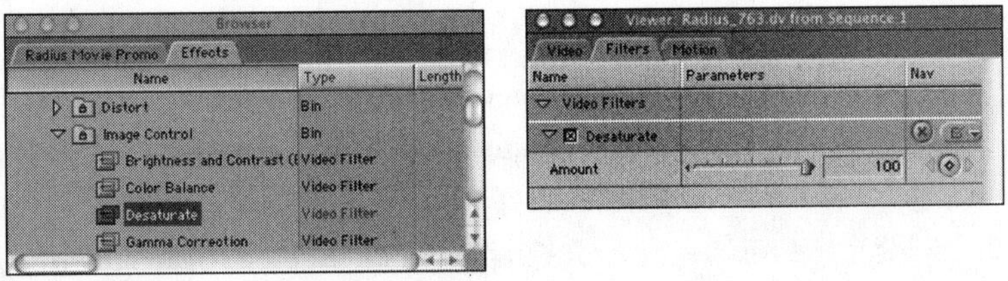

Figure 13-1:
The Desaturate filter is used to create a black and white clip or sequence.

Creating a gradual fade to black and white

What if you want to begin a clip in color but fade to black and white? This is similar to the previous sequence but with the introduction of *keyframes*. We detail keyframes in Chapters 12 and 14.

1. **Follow Steps 1 through 4 in the preceding section.**

2. **Drag the clip from the Viewer to the Canvas window.**

   This makes the clip appear in the Timeline.

   You can also drag the clip from the Viewer directly into the Timeline.

3. **In the Timeline, click and drag the playhead so that it's located at the point where you want the clip to start becoming black and white.**

   This location can be at the very start of the clip or a little bit into the clip.

4. **In the Viewer window, on the Filters tab, change the Desaturate filter's Amount slider to a value of 0.**

   At the 0 setting, the clip's color is unaffected.

5. **On the Filters tab, click the Add Keyframe button (it has a diamond shape and is shown in Figure 13-2) to create a keyframe at the playhead.**

   Final Cut places the keyframe at the playhead location automatically.

6. **Click and drag the playhead to the point in your clip where you want the fade to black and white to be completed.**

   If it is more convenient, move the playhead in the Timeline window, because the playhead in the Viewer and Timeline are synchronized.

   The location can be somewhere around halfway through your clip.

7. **On the Filters tab, change the Desaturate filter's Amount value to 100.**

   This step automatically creates a new second keyframe for you.

   At this stage, you have two keyframes: The first one is set to 0 Amount at the start of the clip, and the second one is set to 100 Amount about halfway through the clip. Final Cut automatically creates an animation between the two keyframes, changing the Amount value from 0 to 100 in the time that lapses between the two keyframes.

8. **Select your clip in the Timeline and choose Sequence⇨Render Selection.**

   After the rendering process has finished, place your playhead just before the clip in the Timeline and press the spacebar to play the clip. Your clip will now have an animated effect from full color to a complete black and white look.

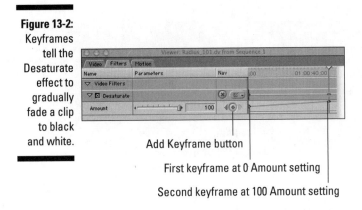

Figure 13-2:
Keyframes
tell the
Desaturate
effect to
gradually
fade a clip
to black
and white.

Add Keyframe button

First keyframe at 0 Amount setting

Second keyframe at 100 Amount setting

Getting That Old, Grainy Film Look

Attention is hard to get in a media-crowded world. Not everyone or every pro-ject needs to go high-tech with films that look like something from the 21st cen-tury. Some projects make more sense looking old or oddly out of fashion. We know an energetic senior citizen who wears spiked hair and knee-high boots. This lady gets noticed! And when you meet her, she actually has a story to tell. She gets to tell it — a lot. She's oddly out of fashion, but she gets your attention because she gets you to look. A film with a different look — if it fits the film and its message — can get the right kind of attention from the viewers.

Say you got this cool inspiration from a short film you viewed on the Sci-Fi channel. But how did the film get that gritty, grainy look? Probably a Noise generator in Final Cut. Here's how you can create the same effect:

1. **Drag a clip from the Browser to the Timeline into a video track.**

   See Chapter 6 if you need a refresher on how to put your clips in the Timeline.

2. **Click the Effects tab in the Browser window.**

3. **Click the triangle next to Video Generators to open it and then click the triangle next to Render to open it. In the Render bin, locate the Noise generator.**

4. **Drag the Noise generator (which works just like a clip) to the track above the clip in the Timeline.**

5. **Drag the ends of the Noise generator so that the clip stretches out to cover the entire clip or sequence on the tracks beneath it. (See Figure 13-3.)**

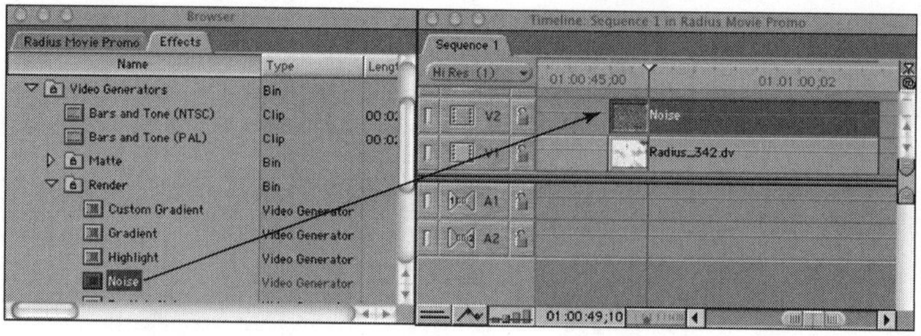

Figure 13-3:
Drag the
Noise
generator
from the
Effects tab
to the track
above your
clip in the
Timeline.

6. **In the Timeline, drag the playhead over the Noise clip in the Timeline.**

7. **Double-click the Noise generator clip in the Timeline so that it loads into the Viewer window.**

8. **In the Viewer window, click the Motion tab and click the little triangle next to the Opacity setting.**

9. **Move the Opacity slider as shown in Figure 13-4 to get the grainy look to your liking.**

   This effect is shown in the Canvas window as you move the Opacity slider. Keep moving the slider until the amount of grain you want is generated.

10. **Select the Noise generator clip in the Timeline and choose Sequence⇨Render Selection.**

   After the rendering process is complete, move the playhead just before the clip in the Timeline and press the spacebar to play the clip.

Figure 13-4:
The Noise
generator
clip's
Opacity can
be modified
under the
Motion tab
to create a
grainy look
for your
project.

Noise looks considerably different on your tiny little computer Canvas preview window than it does on a TV. You need to experiment with the final product to find the right opacity setting to get the effect you want in your project. Having a TV hooked up to your Final Cut workstation is a big help here — if you need help doing that, see Chapter 2. If you're generating a movie for the Web, skip the noise if you can. It doesn't compress well and tends to *pixilate* (develop a checkered pattern) if you reduce the dimensions.

Changing Colors

Changing colors of your clip is cool, and it's really easy. But first a caution: This section is *not* about color correction. You can find info on that topic later in this chapter. This section is about giving a colored look to a clip or a project and about shifting colors to match a particular look and feel. These tools are great and give you power to change the color of the sun. No, really. That golden hot-sun-autumn-washed-out look in *Oh, Brother, Where Art Thou?* isn't far from your reach. You can also make an ever-so-subtle change in a clip to warm it up or cool it down.

We discuss video generator mattes and the RGB Balance filters in this section. Later in the section "Creating a Polished-Looking Video," we discuss a third tool, Tint.

Using mattes

An easy way to create a color change effect is to simply add a *filter*, something like those tinted, plastic, color filters of old that you may have clamped over the lens of your 35mm camera. But this is much easier, and you have all the colors of the rainbow at your disposal! In Final Cut, a filter can be an effect that alters the clip in some way, such as adding a sepia tint or a glow to it. In Final Cut, this type of filter is called a *matte*. Specifically, if you want to have a glow or over a particular clip as if the subjects were in a kind of golden fog, here's how to do it:

1. **Drag a clip from the Browser to a video track on the Timeline.**

2. **Click the Effects tab in the Browser window.**

3. **Click the small triangle for the Video Generators bin to open it and then click the Matte triangle to open the Matte bin.**

4. **In the Matte bin, find the Color matte.**

5. **Drag the Color matte (which works just like a clip) to the track above the clip in the Timeline.**

6. **Drag the ends of the Color matte so that the matte clip stretches out to cover the entire clip on the track beneath it. (This is similar to Figure 13-3.)**

7. **In the Timeline, place the playhead anywhere on the Color matte so that you can preview the effect.**

   If you do this, you can later see changes you make to the Color matte in the Canvas window.

8. **Now double-click the Color matte in the Timeline and then click the Controls tab in the Viewer window.**

9. **In the Color parameters area of the Controls tab, click the triangle to reveal the color controls, as shown in Figure 13-5.**

   Here, you have a few ways to select a color. You can click the small square color swatch and select a yellowish color from the Color Picker selection box that pops up. (Refer to Figure 13-5.)

   Alternatively, you can click the Eyedropper tool. After your cursor turns into an eyedropper, you can click any color you like in your clip as displayed in the Canvas window. The Color matte then picks up the color that you selected with the eyedropper.

   As another alternative, you can use the sliders labeled H, S, and B to alter the Hue, Saturation, and Brightness settings of your color. You can preview any changes you make in the square color swatch and applied to the Color matte.

10. **Next, click the Motion tab in the Viewer window and click the little triangle next to Opacity.**

Click the color swatch to access the Color Picker

Eyedropper tool

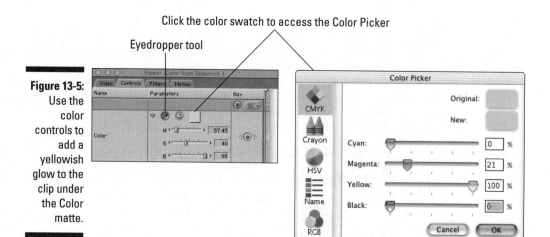

Figure 13-5:
Use the color controls to add a yellowish glow to the clip under the Color matte.

11. **Move the slider in the Opacity pane until the transparency of the Color matte is just right.**

    Note that, if your playhead is located over the clips in the Timeline, the Canvas window shows you an update of the final color effect.

12. **Select the Color matte clip in the Timeline and choose Sequence⇨Render Selection.**

    After the rendering process is complete, locate the playhead just before the clips in the Timeline and press the spacebar to play the clip.

Using the RGB Balance tool

Rather than using an overlay or a low-opacity matte, you can actually change the color of any given part of the spectrum in your video by using the RGB Balance tool. The controls are precise, and the numbers next to the sliders enable you to track and record your edits. Here's how to change color with RGB Balance filter:

1. **Drag a clip from the Browser to a video track in the Timeline.**

2. **In the Timeline, drag the playhead anywhere on the clip so that later you can see a good preview of the effect in the Canvas.**

3. **In the Timeline, select the clip that you want to color and double-click the clip.**

    This step loads the clip into the Viewer window.

4. **Click the Filters Tab in the Viewer window.**

5. **Click the Effects tab in the Browser window.**

6. **Click the Video Filters bin to open it, and then click the Color Correction bin.**

7. **Find the RGB Balance filter in the Color Correction bin and drag it onto the clip in the Timeline.**

8. **On the Filters tab in the Viewer, use the RGB Balance parameters to adjust the colors and thus achieve the look you want.**

    The video image is made up of three color channels: Red, Green, and Blue. The Red set of sliders, for example, works on changing the amount of red in the highlights (whites), midtones (grays), and blacks of the image. So you have individual control of the amount of R, G, or B in either the highlights (whites), midtones (grays), and blacks. To create a golden glow, you increase the highlights and mids for both Red and Green. Because R + G = Yellow and tweaking just the highlights makes the overall look lighter, this gives the clip a sunny, yellow feel.

Figure 13-6 generally points out areas of highlights, midtones, and blacks in a clip.

TIP

Those tiny sliders are a pain, but they have one redeeming feature: Those tiny, tiny arrows at the ends of each slider enable you to change the numeric color values one at a time. Use the numbers to keep track of where you were and where you are. If you mess up, the tiny Reset button (marked with a red X, as shown in Figure 13-6) at the top resets everything to default.

9. **Select your clip in the Timeline and choose Sequence⇨Render Selection.**

After the rendering process is complete, locate the playhead just before the clip in the Timeline and press the spacebar to play and view the clip.

Figure 13-6:
RGB Color
Balance
provides
controls to
change the
Red, Green,
and Blue
color
balance in
your blacks,
whites, and
midrange
(grays)
values.

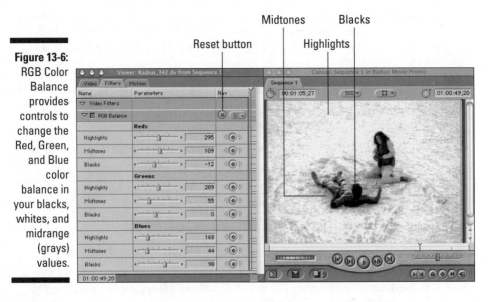

TIP

If you have used Adobe Photoshop, you'll feel right at home with the RGB Balance controls. The RGB Balance tool in Final Cut is in many ways identical to the Color Balance tool in Photoshop.

Those Amazing Color Correction Tools

With the arrival of version 3 and its color correction tools, Final Cut steps into a whole new realm of features that have the look and feel as well as the precision of high-end video editing hardware. The professionals love it, and even if you're new to editing, you'll find that the layout of the features is convenient and that everything is logically labeled and placed. In this section, you find out how to access these spectacular tools, what they are for, and how to get started using them.

You can use color correction to match shots that were filmed under different lighting conditions, match video filmed on different cameras, or fix color problems (for example, if the subject's face is green because someone forgot to white balance his or her video camera).

Before you start, note that it's best to view your output on an NTSC or PAL television or professional video monitor. (For the details on setting this up, see Chapter 2.) The computer's RGB monitor isn't the best monitor to base your final decisions on.

Now, you're ready to get started. To make the color correction tools visible and then fix the colors to your liking, follow these steps:

1. **Make sure you have placed the clips in your sequence in the Timeline.**

2. **In the Timeline, click and drag the playhead any place on the clip that will give you a good view of an area that needs correction.**

   You can preview your changes in the Canvas window.

3. **Select your clip in the Timeline and double-click it.**

4. **Click the Filters tab in the Viewer window.**

5. **Click the Effects tab in the Browser window.**

6. **Click the Video Filters bin to open it, find the Color Correction bin within it, and then click the Color Correction bin to open it.**

7. **In the Color Correction bin, find the Color Corrector 3-Way and then click and drag it onto the clip in the Timeline.**

8. **Double-click the clip in the Timeline so that it loads into the Viewer window.**

   You now have a Color Corrector 3-Way tab in the Viewer window.

9. **In the Viewer window, click the Color Correction 3-way tab.**

10. **Drag away the Color Corrector 3-Way tab so that it appears in a separate window side-by-side with the Video tab of the Viewer window.**

    This makes it easy for you to see the result of your adjustments.

    The Color Corrector 3-Way filter defaults to the Visual view. If you find yourself in the Numeric view (with just numbers and sliders), click the Visual button in the upper-left corner.

11. **Click the Auto-Contrast button. (See Figure 13-7.)**

    This step maximizes the range from black to white in the clip, which is the starting point for any color correction for your clip. Also, notice that the Blacks, Mids, and Whites sliders automatically move to achieve the best overall luminance distribution in the image.

Blacks Select Auto-Balance button   Whites Select Auto-Balance button

Blacks Balance color wheel   Whites Balance color wheel

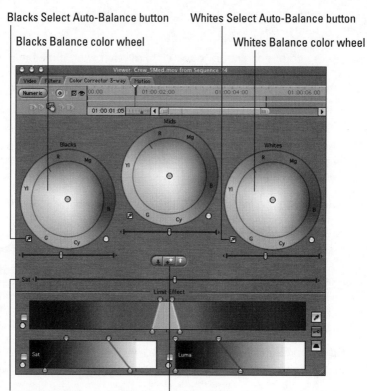

Figure 13-7:
Use the
visual
interface of
the Color
Corrector 3-
Way filter.

Saturation slider   Auto-Contrast button

12. **Click the Whites Select Auto-Balance color button.**

    This button looks like a tiny eyedropper under the Whites Balance color wheel.

    When this button is selected, your pointer turns into an eyedropper when placed over the Canvas or the Viewer window.

13. **With the eyedropper cursor, click an area of the picture that is supposed to be pure white in the Canvas or Viewer window.**

    Be very careful and don't select an overexposed area, such as a highlight or a white blown out light source. Select a well-exposed white surface in the right color temperature, such as a white bed sheet in the shot.

    When you click the white in an image, the Color Corrector filter analyzes the RGB mix of colors in the whites and adjusts the center knob of the Whites Balance to offset the mix of colors in your whites.

    In most cases, you immediately see a change in your whites. If they were green or bluish before, they'll be much closer to white after this step, even if they're not altogether pure white.

14. **Click the Blacks Select Auto-Balance color button.**

    This button looks like a little eyedropper under the Blacks Balance color wheel.

    When this button is selected, the pointer once again turns into an eyedropper when placed over the Canvas or the Viewer window.

15. **With the eyedropper cursor, click an area of the picture that is supposed to be pure black.**

    Don't select an underexposed area. Select a well-exposed black surface in the right color temperature, such as someone's black hair or an area of black paint.

16. **Adjust your saturation by using the Saturation slider in the Color Corrector.**

    Adjusting the Saturation slider is the final step in the color correction process.

You're probably wondering why, in the preceding steps, we never addressed the Mids controls (the color wheel in the center). To adjust Mids, you usually need a cinematographer's gray "chip chart," which is a piece of cardboard with a neutral gray on it. If you didn't use a chip chart during the shooting process, leave the Mids controls alone in the Color Corrector.

Fixing or Adjusting Exposures

Your sister is getting married, and you want the video of her wedding to be special. So you persuade two of your friends to bring their equipment, and the three of you film from every possible angle. When your sister's beau passes out at the altar, you know you have the material for a great family heirloom. But one of the cameras was a little off in its exposure. (*Exposure* refers to the range of bright to dark values in your image.) The footage from this camera doesn't match what was shot with the others. Your best scene is a bit bright; you need to adjust the exposure on the tumbling groom. Final Cut to the rescue! With one obvious tool and another that is somewhat obscure, you can do serious repair on your clip.

Be aware, however, that some exposure problems can't be fixed. Checking the results in the field is one of the best things you can do to make sure the final product is to your liking. For more on how to regulate exposure while shooting, see *Digital Video For Dummies*, 2nd Edition, by Martin Doucette, published by Wiley.

Two effects filters are your helpers in this correction process: Proc Amp and Brightness and Contrast. Proc Amp sounds like the opening band at a rock concert. (It actually stands for "Process Amplifier.") The Proc Amp filter enables you to adjust aspects of exposure during the editing process.

Here is a step-by-step guide to editing exposure levels in your project:

1. **Place your clip in the Timeline.**

2. **In the Timeline, click and drag the playhead anywhere on the to-be-adjusted clip so that you can see a good preview of the effect.**

   The effect is previewed in the Canvas window.

3. **Select your clip in the Timeline and double-click it.**

4. **Now click the Filters tab in the Viewer window.**

   This brings the Filters tab to the front.

5. **Click the Effects tab in the Browser window.**

6. **Click the Video Filters bin to open it. Within it, find the Image Control bin and click to open it.**

   Inside, locate Brightness and Contrast and Proc Amp.

7. **Drag each filter to the Filters tab in the Viewer window, also shown in Figure 13-8.**

8. **On the Filters tab, move the sliders or click the little arrows at the end of each slider until you get the desired results.**

   The Brightness and Contrast controls are pretty self-explanatory. The Proc Amp controls aren't as easy to figure out, so here's what these controls do:

   - **Setup:** Changes the black level in your clip. Your blacks should be deep and dark with no grays in them. Look for blacks in hair or dark areas of the shot.

   - **Video:** Affects the whites in your image. Adjust this slider until the whites start to bloom in the image and then back off.

   - **Chroma:** Affects the color level or saturation. Be sure to check on a NTSC or PAL video monitor for a final decision on the amount of color you want to add to your clip.

   - **Phase:** Gives you control over the hue in your clip. Whether you want to make the colors greener or redder, the Phase control can help.

   If you're a Photoshop user, you'll notice that Proc Amp is similar to the Adjust Hue/Saturation control.

   A handy reference to use is another shot in your project whose exposure and colors you like. Compare the two shots and make adjustments until you like what you see.

9. **Select your clip in the Timeline and choose Sequence⇨Render Selection.**

   After the rendering process is complete, locate the playhead just before the clip in the Timeline and press the spacebar to play and view the clip.

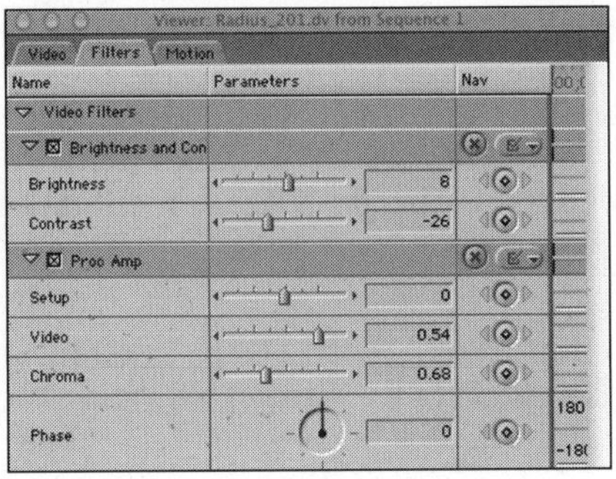

Figure 13-8:
The
Brightness
and
Contrast
filter and the
Proc Amp
filter help
you fix clips
with
exposure
problems.

Creating a Polished-Looking Video

Despite all the available tools, we still see video that looks like video, with generally flat colors, lack of depth, and limited color schemes. Maybe you've seen that infomercial for ab fitness equipment that looks like it was done by somebody's brother-in-law. It's flat and lifeless without sparkle or variety. No need for that. In this section, we discuss more cool filters and ideas that can help kill that video look and make your project look like it was done by a Hollywood crew. Just a dash of any of the following filter combinations can set your project apart:

- **Tint, Sepia, and Desaturate:** Using these three filters at once and experimenting can give your project a unique look. Double-click your selected clip, open the Filter pane by clicking the Filter tab, and drag each of these filers into the Filter pane. Kill some of the color with Desaturate. Try the Sepia controls and watch the results in the Canvas window. Then try Tint. You can turn off any one of the filters by clicking in the check box next to its name.

  The Sepia filter tints a clip with a sepia tone, the yellowish-brown color often seen in old photos. You can change the color of the tint by clicking a color picker or using two sliders (labeled Amount and Highlight) to control the amount and the brightness of the tint you apply. The Tint filter is less useful than the Sepia filter because you can only select the color and the amount. You may want to switch between the Tint and the Sepia and see which effect you find to be more pleasing.

  The Desaturate filter simply allows you to take out some color from your image. At the highest settings (100), the image becomes completely black and white.

- **Channel Blur, Channel Offset, Color Offset, and Invert:** Load these filters when working with a clip that is just plain dark and flat and turn it into something dramatic and fun. Blurring on a color channel (by adjusting just one of the RGB blur sliders in the Channel Blur effect) and leaving the rest alone can take a poorly focused shot and give it a deliberate and even soft focus in one or more parts of the color spectrum. Channel Offset shifts one color layer over to one side, creating a double-exposure look that can work as a transition (with keyframes) or a dream effect. The Color Offset effect alters the color values in the red, green, and blue channels with sliders. Invert looks like something out of an old science-fiction movie; it simply inverts all colors to their complimentary colors.

- ✔ **Sharpen and Edge Detection:** Found in the QuickTime bin, under the Video Filters bin in the Effects tab of the Browser window, these tools have a sharpening effect and can also be used to make a scene look more three-dimensional. A fuzzy and indistinct scene can be given clarity and drama. Instead of sliders, these filters are adjusted by selecting values from a drop-down menu. You need to experiment with the extremes in the numbers here to see the possibilities for these filters. Used together, they can produce dramatic, deliberately grainy results.

- ✔ **Emboss and Lens Flare:** Also in the QuickTime bin are several unusual tools for dramatically changing the look of a scene. Emboss mimics the Photoshop filter of the same name and turns the scene gray with hard edges (don't expect to use keyframes with this one). Lens Flare does just what it says: It gives you hundreds of possible lens flares like the rays and circles of light from the sun that sometimes appear on video or in photographs. You can select the size, shape, and color of the flare.

These are just a few of the many filters that can dramatically change a scene or a whole project.

Blurring the Action

"Hold still so I can take your picture!" Even in a video, you were just a streak across the screen. Your dad wasn't always patient with your desire to express yourself, especially in front of the camera. Now that you're in control, you can take advantage of the fact that blurring isn't a sign of a disorder but of action and motion. Blurring is good, in the right place of course. Final Cut's blurring filters enable you to bring your action into focus (pun intended).

Say that you have a scene with a flock of birds zipping by, but you were so good at following them with the camera that they don't seem to be moving at all. You want them to at least look like they're in flight. Here is how to use blurring filters to give the illusion of motion:

1. **Click and drag the playhead in the Timeline anywhere over the clip you want to affect, so that you can see a good preview of the effect in the Canvas window.**

2. **Select your clip in the Timeline and double-click it.**

3. **Now click the Filters Tab in the Viewer window.**

4. **Click the Effects tab in the Browser window.**

5. **Click the Video Filters bin to open it, and then click the Blur bin to open it.**

6. **Drag each of the blur filters (Gaussian, Radial, Wind, and Zoom) to Filters tab in the Viewer window.**

   The results in the Filter tab should look like Figure 13-9. (Okay, we don't have a flock of birds in video in our figure, but you get the idea.)

7. **Start by checking only the check box next to the Wind Blur filter. (Figure 13-9 shows the check boxes.)**

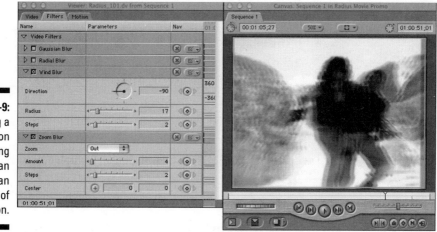

Figure 13-9: Using a combination of blurring filters can create an illusion of motion.

8. **Move the wind direction indicator and the sliders until you get the desired effect.**

   The Canvas window shows the results. You can move the playhead around in the Canvas window to see what the results look like in other parts of the clip.

9. **Try turning on the other blurring filters (by checking the boxes next to them) to exaggerate the blurring effect.**

   Consider using keyframes to turn on and off the blurring effect for one or more of the filters. This can further exaggerate the illusion of motion. (See Chapters 12 and 14 for more on keyframes.)

10. **Select the clip in the Timeline and choose Sequence⇨Render Selection.**

    After the rendering process is complete, press the spacebar to play and view the clip.

Speed Up, Slow Down, Reverse

Since the beginning of time, man has wanted to go back to where he started so that he could get it right the second time. We can't do that in real life, but we can in video and cinema, which makes the Reverse effect one of the oldest special effects in the history of filmmaking. You can also go faster, which is something most people *don't* want to do, but this effect can add to the look of your film, too. And of course, this section wouldn't be complete without slow motion. No matter the pace you want to set, the process is remarkably easy:

1. **Place your clip in the Timeline.**

2. **Now select your clip in the Timeline by double-clicking it.**

3. **From the menu bar, choose Modify⇨Speed.**

   Alternatively, you can select your clip and press ⌘+J.

   This step brings up the Speed dialog box, shown in Figure 13-10.

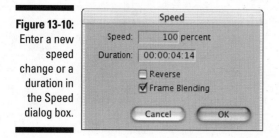

Figure 13-10: Enter a new speed change or a duration in the Speed dialog box.

4. **Leave the Frame Blending box checked or uncheck it, depending on how you're adjusting the motion.**

   The Frame Blending box is checked as the default. Frame Blending creates intermediate frames for speed changes. Under certain conditions (such as speed changes in whole numbers such as 12 percent, 25 percent, and so on) the Frame blending makes the image far superior than the one without Frame Blending. Your render times with Frame Blending are also a bit longer, but the wait is worth it.

   Perhaps the only argument for not using Frame Blending is when you're making drastic speed changes to short clips, such as taking a 15 frame clip and stretching it to make it 5 seconds long. In that case, Frame Blending creates too many intermediate frames for the effect to be smooth.

5. **If you want to change the speed (speed up or slow down), type the percentage of decrease or increase in the Speed text box.**

   By default, when the Speed dialog box comes up, the clip is playing at 100%, which is normal speed. Entering 200% in this box makes the clip play twice as fast, whereas entering 50% makes the clip play at half speed.

Alternatively, you can also enter a new duration for the shot, and Final Cut automatically calculates the speed change necessary to create the requested duration.

6. **To reverse a clip's playback, check the Reverse check box.**

7. **Click OK in the Speed dialog box.**

8. **Select the clip in the Timeline and choose Sequence⇨Render Selection.**

   After the rendering process is complete, press the spacebar to play and view the clip.

Chapter 14

Advanced Effects

• •

In This Chapter

▶ Understanding advanced effects tools

▶ The keys to keyframes

▶ Working with Wireframe mode

▶ Creating advanced effects by using the motion work space

▶ Zooming, panning, and going around in circles

• •

*F*inal Cut has powerful tools that let you do just about anything your imagination can come up with: No obstacle seems too big to overcome. The only real obstacle is wrapping your mind around all that is offered. Even with the Final Cut program's intuitive interface, you have to get a handle on a lot of little things. Give your brain a rest and walk through this chapter and its real-world examples. You can be a productive advanced effects editor in no time!

In this chapter, you work with motion effects, including taking stills and creating the illusion of panning, zooming, and so on. These advanced special effects let you spin visual straw into video gold. These techniques can be used in a lot of different ways and in combination with other elements, motion-related or not. After you see the options available and how to implement them, you will want to try them in your projects to enhance the story and the message.

Understanding Effects Motion Tools

Final Cut offers many different special effects that enhance the character and quality of your video. But sometimes those filters and tools alone, which we discuss in Chapter 13, aren't enough to perform the tasks you have in mind.

Professional editors in labs have tools available to them that let them vary and enhance effects in two import ways: over time and in space. We don't mean outer space, but three-dimensional space. The tools that control these two variables are called keyframes and Wireframes:

✔ **Keyframes** are marks on a Timeline that designate the frame where an action begins, changes, or ends. In Final Cut, they are diamond-shaped markers that can be used in the Viewer, Canvas, or the Timeline windows. Their relative position (up or down) on the Keyframe Timeline in these windows designates the degree of change. You learn how to place, use, and adjust these markers in this chapter. We also cover keyframes in Chapters 11, 12, and 13.

✔ **Wireframe** is a mode that lets you see the boundaries of your video or still. In this mode, the boundaries appear in the form of thin aqua lines that serve also as wire handles for the media. Turn on Wireframe mode, and you can manipulate the size, rotation, position, and shape of the selected video. You see how to use the Wireframe mode later in this chapter.

When you use these together, you can make all kinds of changes over the course of your project. One of the most frequent uses for the pairing of these effects is panning over the face of a still. This is the technique that Ken Burns used so effectively in his documentary series, *The Civil War*.

Before you can get down to serious motion editing, you must set up your workspace. Motion editing demands big windows. We recommend a 21-inch monitor. Another alternative is to get a second monitor. Drag your Audio Meters, Tool palette, and Browser window to this second monitor. When you realize that all those tabs in Final Cut windows can be their own separate window, you will crave more screen space. (See Chapter 2 for more on configuring a second monitor for your Final Cut system.)

Also, consider making good use of the docking feature in Mac OS X. OS X lets you drag items to the dock (at the bottom of your screen) and then retrieve them by clicking them inside the Dock. The orange button in the upper-left corner of a Final Cut window lets you send that window in the Mac OS X Dock, temporarily hiding it. Clicking the hidden window in the Dock brings your window right back.

Using Opacity Keyframes in the Timeline Window

One very useful option often underutilized by users of Final Cut is the overlay feature in the Timeline window. By using this feature in conjunction with keyframes, you can give the illusion of a cloud going by or create the shadow of a UFO appearing overhead.

In a few steps, you discover important keyframe concepts and how to make the overlay feature work for you. In the following, we change the Opacity of a clip dynamically, meaning that the Opacity fades up and down throughout the playing of the clip.

To work with the Overlay feature in the Timeline window, do the following:

1. **Place your clip on the Timeline by dragging it from the Browser.**

   To get a large view of the Timeline, click the Track Height button, as shown in Figure 14-1. This enlarged view is helpful during creation of keyframes in the Timeline.

2. **Click the Clip Overlays and Clip Keyframes buttons to see these elements within the Timeline.**

   The Clip Overlays button adds the display of filter (green) bars and motion (blue) bars within the Timeline, under the clips. These colored bars also indicate keyframe icons if keyframes have been applied to the filter or Motion effects on a clip.

Opacity Keyframes (black)

Smoothness handles (blue) | Opacity Level line graph

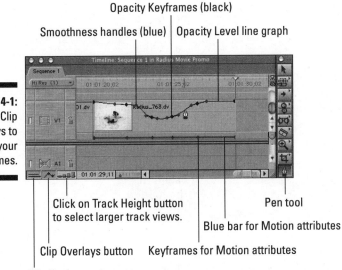

Figure 14-1:
Turn on Clip Overlays to view your keyframes.

Click on Track Height button to select larger track views.

Pen tool

Blue bar for Motion attributes

Clip Overlays button   Keyframes for Motion attributes

Clip Keyframes button

3. **Select the Pen tool from the Tools palette.**

   The cursor turns into a Pen point. The Pen tool lets you create keyframes in the Timeline window.

4. **Click on the thin black Opacity Level line graph (Figure 14-1) with the Pen point cursor to create a keyframe.**

5. **Repeat Step 4 until you have created a total of six keyframes on the Timeline.**

For any keyframe sequence to work, you need a start point, an end point, and points in between designating places where the pace of the change may be altered. In Figure 14-1, six keyframes define the changes we want to see in our overlay. Note that the keyframes have black diamond icons, whereas the handles to smooth those icons have blue diamond icons.

6. **To get these smoothness handles, Control+click the small back keyframe icons and select Smooth from the contextual menu.**

   Don't worry about getting the location just right with the first click. After you've created the keyframe, you can move it to where you want it.

7. **To make corrections or changes, hold down the Shift key and click and drag the keyframe.**

   Figure 14-2 illustrates the small yellow feedback box that comes up, providing numeric feedback on the new edit position in a timecode (+ or – and on the percentage of Opacity. (If you don't hold down the Shift key while dragging, you see only the timecode or the percentage of opacity, not both.)

Figure 14-2:
Shift+ dragging a keyframe lets you see the results of the move in a timecode and in a numeric value indicating the percentage of opacity.

Opacity keyframe being dragged   Feedback box

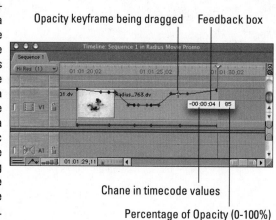

Chane in timecode values

Percentage of Opacity (0-100%)

8. **Select your clip in the Timeline and render the changes in Opacity by Sequence⇨Render Selection.**

9. **After the rendering process is complete, locate your playhead just before the clips in the Timeline and press the spacebar to play the clip.**

Using Keyframes in the Viewer Window

Most of the time when you use keyframes, you work in the Viewer window. The Viewer window provides hundreds of places to put keyframes and thousands of options for using them in combination. The following is a simple but fun keyframe for doing an imitation of a wipe from the early days of television: the thin horizontal line in the middle of the screen that showed up on old-time black-and-white TV sets just after you turned the set off:

1. **Place a video clip on the Timeline.**

2. **Drag and locate the playhead on the frame in the clip where you want to center the effect, and then double-click your clip to load it into the Viewer window.**

3. **In the Viewer window, select the Motion tab.**

4. **Click on the small triangle next to the Distort option to display Aspect Ratio (among other options).**

5. **Drag at the lower right edge of the Viewer window so that the Keyframe pane is made visible, as shown in Figure 14-3.**

   Note the thin green animation line in the middle of the Keyframe pane for Aspect Ratio. You set keyframes on this green line to change and animate the aspect ratio of your clip.

Click triangle to reveal details of the Distort attribute

Keyframe pane area

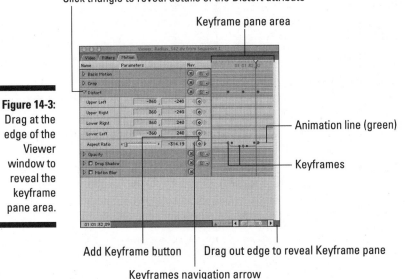

Figure 14-3: Drag at the edge of the Viewer window to reveal the keyframe pane area.

Animation line (green)

Keyframes

Add Keyframe button

Drag out edge to reveal Keyframe pane

Keyframes navigation arrow

6. **To set keyframes on the green Aspect Ratio animation line, click the Add Keyframe button at the left of the keyframe pane.**

   Final Cut automatically sets the keyframe at the current location of your playhead.

   Alternatively, you can create keyframes by clicking the Pen tool on the Tool palette and then clicking on the green animation line in the keyframe pane wherever you want to create a keyframe. The advantage to this method is that you can add a keyframe *anywhere* on the green animation line. (Using the Add Keyframe button adds a keyframe *only* at the current location of the playhead.)

7. **Repeat Step 6 until you've created three keyframes along the green animation line.**

   Don't set the keyframes more than 1.5 seconds apart. To be convincing, the transition we're creating should occur over a short span of time (1.5 seconds or less).

8. **Click and drag the center keyframe down to the bottom of the Keyframe pane.**

   This step lowers the value of the Aspect Ratio of your clip. Alternatively, you can just park the playhead on the center keyframe (using the keyframe navigation arrows) and drag the Aspect Slider all the way to the left so that the setting reads -10000.

9. **Control+Click on one keyframe and select the Smooth option from the pop-up menu that appears.**

   The Smooth option smoothes out the transition between keyframes, as opposed to the linear and abrupt changes that the keyframes create by default.

10. **Repeat Step 9 for each keyframe marker that you created in Step 7.**

    This step smoothes out the changes between all three keyframes. For most users, smoothing between keyframe values provides a more pleasing transition.

11. **Select the clip in the Timeline and Sequence⇨Render Selection to render it.**

12. **Place your playhead just before the clips in the Timeline and press the spacebar to play and view the clip, as shown in Figure 14-4.**

You should have a retro effect like that of an old TV turning off: The image squeezes down to a line before vanishing. Groovy!

Figure 14-4:
This special effects retro wipe uses the Distort property to create the illusion of a television being shut off.

Creating a Multiple Screen Effect

To get an idea of what a Wireframe does, think about a pair of eyeglasses. You can use your frames to twist, shift, adjust, or remove your glasses, all while keeping your fingers off the lenses. Wireframe mode in Final Cut does the same thing and more for your video clips: Turn on Wireframe, and you can distort, rotate, or move your clip off screen. You can even do some neat tricks like zoom and enlarge — all from the comfort of your Canvas or Viewer window.

Wireframe appears as an aqua-colored frame around your clip and creates an X inside the frame of the clip. The Wireframe mode gives you a center point to adjust location, corner points to adjust size or distort, and side *wires* for rotating. You won't use the Wireframe mode all the time, but when you do, it's a powerful and easy-to-use tool.

In the next steps, we're going to use Wireframes to do a fun effect: create a multiple screen segment in your sequence. This was cutting-edge stuff in the movies in the 1960s. In recent years, this technique has been used for everything from a retro look to cutting-edge advertising.

1. **Place two clips in your Timeline, one in track V1 and the other in track V2, one over the other, as shown in Figure 14-5.**

   It doesn't matter which clip is in which track, but keep in mind that the clip that you see in the Canvas window is the clip in track V2 (the top track) because it's the top clip. The clip in V1 is hidden behind it.

   If the Canvas window isn't visible, use the Command+2 shortcut to bring it up.

Figure 14-5:
The top clip
must be
selected,
and the
playhead
must be
over the
clips for the
Wireframe
to be seen
in the
Canvas
window.

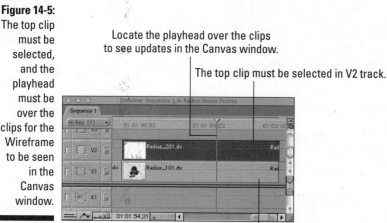

Locate the playhead over the clips
to see updates in the Canvas window.

The top clip must be selected in V2 track.

Place one clip in the V1 track of your Timeline.

2. **Place the playhead anywhere over your clips in the Timeline.**

   This step ensures that the Canvas window displays your clips and updates the effect you're about to create.

3. **Select the clip in V2 (the top track) by clicking it.**

   Step 3 is important because Wireframe handles show up only on currently selected clips and only if the playhead is somewhere in the selected clip in the Timeline. Many times, users go nuts trying to figure out why they're not seeing Wireframes — almost always, the problem is that they don't have the clip selected in the Timeline.

4. **From the View pop-up menu in the Canvas window (see Figure 14-6), select Image+Wireframe.**

   The Wireframe appears. The number 2 in the center of the frame lets you know that the clip in the V2 track is displayed.

5. **Click and drag any corner handle on the Wireframe toward the center of the frame so that the image is approximately 40 percent of its original size.**

   You need not be concerned about the precise 40% size: Just drag until the clip is approximately smaller than half its original size. Note that as the image of the top clip shrinks, the clip behind it (on the lower track) appears.

6. **Now click anywhere on the V2 (top) clip and drag it to the upper-right, as shown in Figure 14-7.**

Number 2 indicates clip lies in video track 2.

Select Image + Wireframe
to bring up wireframe view.

Wireframe handles

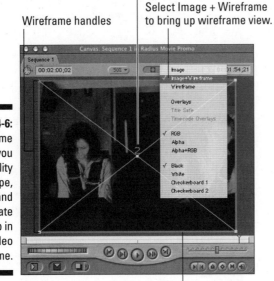

Figure 14-6:
Wireframe
gives you
the ability
to reshape,
resize, and
relocate
your clip in
the video
frame.

Wireframe has an aqua outline.

Drag the top clip to the
upper-right corner of the frame.

Figure 14-7:
Drag
anywhere
on the clip
you just
shrunk and
move it to
the upper-
right corner.

The bottom clip (in video track 1) is
visible once the top clip is shrunk down.

7. **In the Canvas window, select the video clip from the V1 track (the lower clip) and resize it by dragging one of its corners.**

   Without worrying about precision, make this clip about the same size as the first one you shrunk.

   When you click the background clip in the Canvas window, it automatically becomes selected in the Timeline as well. The Wireframe view is turned off from the first clip and is presented on the clip you just selected.

8. **Move the lower clip you just shrunk to the lower-left corner of the Canvas window by clicking anywhere on the image and dragging it (Figure 14-8).**

9. **To render, select the top clip and select Sequence⇨Render Selection.**

10. **After the rendering is complete, place your playhead just before the clips in the Timeline and press the spacebar to play your clip.**

The Sixties are back!

Note that you can continue to layer clips in the video tracks and size them as shown in the previous exercise. Final Cut allows you up to 99 video tracks.

Figure 14-8: Multiple screens, a swinging 1960s effect brought to life.

Using the Motion Tab to Create Advanced Effects

After you have a handle on keyframes and Wireframe, it's time to put them together. At this point, putting them together may sound like learning the equivalent of rubbing your tummy and patting your head at the same time, but that's not the case. We saved a practical tool collection until now: the rest of the features in the Motion tab in the Viewer window. The Motion tab has extraordinary controls for doing very precise motion adjustments through numerical controls and the various Keyframe panes provided. Used in combination with Wireframe, all manner of changes can be made. In the following sections of this chapter, you discover the steps for moving, panning, and other motion effects.

Here are the basic steps to create a zany distortion effect and animation with Wireframe:

1. **Place any clip in the Timeline and click it once to select it.**

   Make sure that the playhead is located on any frame in the clip so that you can preview your changes in the Canvas as you edit.

2. **In the Viewer, click the Motion tab and double-click the clip that you selected in Step 1.**

   This opens the clip in the Motion tab and activates the motion tools for your clip.

3. **Click and drag the lower right corners of both the Canvas and Viewer windows to enlarge them.**

   Enlarging the windows allows you to work better in the next few steps.

4. **Click on the little triangles next to the Basic Motion, Crop, and Distort panes in the Motion tab to open them (Figure 14-9).**

5. **Select the Distort tool from the Tool palette.**

   The Distort tool is located in the Tool Palette along the Crop tool level, as shown in Figure 14-9. Access the Tool palette by choosing Window⇨Tool.

6. **Select the clip in the Timeline by clicking it with your pointer cursor.**

   You can activate the pointer cursor by clicking the button with the arrow in it from the Tool palette.

7. **From the View pop-up menu in the Canvas window (refer to Figure 14-6), select Image+Wireframe.**

8. **With the Distort tool selected, drag the corners of the video clip in the Canvas window, as shown in Figure 14-10.**

9. **In the Crop pane (shown in Figure 14-9), enter the following values:**

    - **Left:** 0
    - **Right:** 9
    - **Top:** 13
    - **Bottom:** 6
    - **Edge Feather:** 0

    Amazing control, isn't it? With the numeric tools in the Motion tab, every important dimension, angle, and degree can be controlled precisely and then repeated anywhere.

To finish off this effect, you set crop lines for just a few seconds and then remove them by setting some keyframes. These next steps create an animation where you start with a cropped clip and then uncrop it:

Click open the Basic Motion, Crop, and Distort triangles.

Figure 14-9:
Click open
the Basic
Motion,
Crop, and
Distort
panes.

Wireframe handles

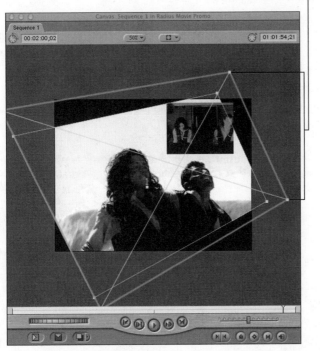

Figure 14-10:
Wireframe handles can be moved completely out of the frame.

1. **Open the Keyframe pane wide enough so that you can see the length of the clip in the pane by dragging at the lower-right corner of the Viewer window.**

   If you look carefully, you can see an area of light gray in the keyframe pane, shown in Figure 14-11. Note that only a very slight difference in gray distinguishes the clip and its end from the background, so set this up with care. Setting up keyframes of this sort is tough if you're viewing just a little sliver of the clip.

2. **Click and drag the playhead to move it to the point where you want to set the keyframes for the starting Crop values (as shown in Figure 14-11).**

   The starting crop values for all clips are always set to 0. You need to set the keyframes for these crop values for your clip. Ideally, this spot should be a few seconds into your clip.

3. **Set keyframes by clicking the Add Keyframe button on the values you want to change; in this case, the values for Right, Top, and Bottom in the Crop pane.**

   Click once on the Add Keyframe buttons for the Right, Top, and Bottom values. This set of keyframes start your animation. They should look like the starting set of keyframes shown in Figure 14-11.

4. **Click and drag the playhead to move it to the location where you want the values to start changing.**

   This location should be past the first set of keyframes you just set, but it can be just about anywhere after that point. The timing is up to your discretion.

5. **Set keyframes by using the sliders.**

   If you change the Crop values by using the sliders in this step, Final Cut automatically creates new keyframes. This set of keyframes creates the change from the first set of keyframes. The new keyframes should look like the middle set of keyframes shown in Figure 14-11.

   You should make sure that the Canvas window is open in this step so that you can see the Cropping changes you're creating. If the Canvas window isn't visible, use the Command+2 shortcut to bring it up.

Crop value sliders   Middle keyframe with altered crop values

Add Keyframe button

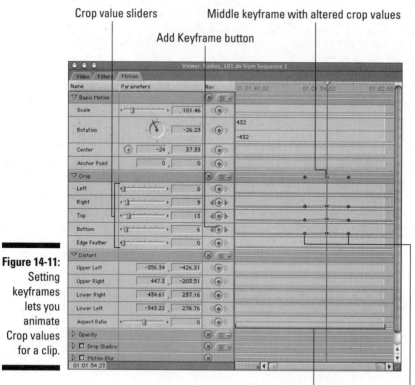

Figure 14-11: Setting keyframes lets you animate Crop values for a clip.

Light gray area indicates the duration of the clip

Start and end keyframes set to 0

6. **Move the playhead further into the clip and set keyframes with Crop values back to 0, as shown in Figure 14-11.**

   You should once again move your playhead forwards in the keyframe pane and set keyframes by dragging the Right, Top, and Bottom Crop sliders so that their value reads 0. Final Cut automatically creates the ending set of keyframes.

7. **Render by selecting the clip and Sequence⇨Render Selection.**

8. **After your clip has finished rendering, place your playhead just before the clips in the Timeline and press the spacebar to play it.**

   Your clip starts out with no cropping. Gradually, your clip is cropped and then returns to a clean, uncropped state.

Using these steps, you can create keyframes for any setting under the Motion tab and create complex animations.

Zooming, Panning, and Rotating

After you're comfortable with the location of the tools and their functions, you can start building some of those great effects you have been wanting to try. Zooming, panning, and rotating are features that you can use again and again, sometimes all at once. *Zooming* is the effect of going in closer to the picture. *Panning* is the process of moving across a picture, left to right or right to left. *Rotating* is simply the process of turning the picture to the left or the right, like a steering wheel.

In this next exercise, we show you how to zoom in, pan across, and rotate a still photograph that you've scanned into Final Cut. Dig out a photo from your archive and try this exercise yourself.

This task may look difficult, but rest assured, it isn't. In fact, doing this is so easy that you may do it again and again just for the fun of it!

Here's how to import a still image into Final Cut and create a series of motions on it:

1. **To import your image into Final Cut, select the Browser window and File⇨Import⇨Files.**

   You're presented with the Choose a File dialog box.

2. **Locate the still image on your drive, select it, and click the Import button in the Choose a File dialog box.**

The still image is imported into Final Cut and looks and works very much like a video clip.

3. **Click and drag your still image from the Browser window to your Timeline.**

4. **Click the clip to select it in the Timeline, making sure that the playhead is located on a frame in the still clip so that you can preview in the Canvas window as you edit.**

   The results should look something like Figure 14-12.

Figure 14-12:
Importing a still image and dropping it into the Timeline makes it look like a video clip in the Canvas window.

Some black areas appear around the edge of the image if the proportions of your image aren't exactly the same as the video frame. Don't worry: This is normal.

5. **Click the Motion tab in the Viewer window and double-click the still clip in the Timeline.**

   This step opens the clip in the Motion tab and activates the motion tools for your clip.

6. **Drag open the Canvas and Viewer windows wider for a better workspace.**

   Both the Canvas and the Viewer windows can be resized by dragging at their lower-right corners. Enlarging the windows allows you to have a better view of your work.

7. **In the Motion tab of the Viewer, click the triangle next to the Basic Motion pane to open it.**

   To create your starting set of keyframes, you need to view the Scale, Rotation, and Center properties by clicking the small triangle next to the Basic Motion setting.

8. **Drag the playhead in the Timeline to the beginning of your clip.**

   You can drag the playhead to the beginning of the clip either in the Timeline or in the Viewer window's Keyframe pane. The clip is indicated by the light gray area in the keyframe pane.

9. **Set keyframes for Scale, Rotation, and Center by clicking the Add Keyframe button for each of the properties.**

   This step creates the Scale, Rotation, and Center keyframes at default values.

10. **Drag your playhead further into the clip by a few seconds.**

    Exactly how far you drag it is up to you.

11. **Change the Scale, Rotation, and Center values to create new keyframes.**

    At this stage, if you use the sliders or the numeric fields for each of the Scale, Rotation and Center values, Final Cut automatically creates new keyframes for these values.

12. **Select the still clip in the Timeline by clicking it with your pointer cursor.**

13. **From the View pop-up menu in the Canvas window, select Image+ Wireframe (refer to Figure 14-6).**

    Having the Image + Wireframe mode enabled enables you to move the clip around in the Canvas window by dragging the Wireframe handles.

14. **Create the final set of keyframes for your animation.**

    You can further move your playhead a few seconds into the still clip and create a new set of keyframes by changing the values for the Scale, Rotation, and Center, either via the sliders or by entering values numerically.

    After you render, Final Cut automatically creates the animations between these keyframes. You should also keep an eye on the Canvas window to view the settings and changes that you're creating.

15. **To render your movements in the still image, select the still clip and Sequence⇨Render Selection.**

16. **After your clip has finished rendering, place your playhead just before the clip in the Timeline and press the spacebar to play it.**

    Figure 14-13 shows the animation that is possible by changing the Scale, Rotation, and Center settings. (The top image is how the image looked when it was first imported.)

Figure 14-13:
Animation is
created on a
still image
with
cropping,
panning,
and
zooming.

Chapter 15

Compositing

· ·

· ·

*C*ompositing is merging two or more different images into one. An example of compositing is the old trick of making an actor appear in front of a background they were never in. The actor is first filmed in front of a solid color background. Later, the background is removed and the actor placed in front of a beach, exploding building, or something else. Another miracle of compositing is the collage of images and text — all moving and fading in and out gracefully — that you typically see at the beginning of a news or sports program or a documentary.

In this chapter, we talk about how these popular examples of compositing are done. Some (but not all) of the concepts and tools used for compositing overlap somewhat with the effects, such as scaling and moving images, which we cover in Chapter 14.

Choosing a Composite Mode

Composite modes in effect allow you to set how the colors of one clip mix into the colors of the second clip. Final Cut has many composite modes that can be loosely grouped in two categories: practical and artistic.

The Multiply composite mode, which eliminates white pixels from an image, is an example of the practical kind. You might use it if, for example, you have a still image from which you want to drop a white background. Similarly, the Screen mode drops out black pixels.

Artistic composite modes are generally for creating a pretty, colorful picture based on the interaction of the colors in the two clips. For example, the Difference mode subtracts the color values of the bottom clip from the top clip. Figure 15-1 shows the results of two clips when combined with a Difference mode. As you can see, the Difference mode is best reserved for moments when you want to play the artist: It doesn't have much of a practical function.

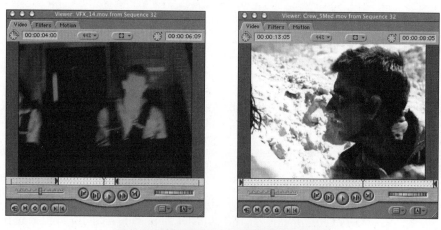

Figure 15-1:
The clip on the left was placed on top of the clip on the right, and the Difference Mode was applied to the top clip.

Final Cut offers 13 composite modes. We explain what effect each mode has on your image. If you can't grasp what these modes do by reading, don't worry about it too much. Even the most experienced composite mode users don't go by mathematical descriptions of pixel behavior when it comes to choosing composite modes. Most just try out a few until they like what they see. You should do the same.

Here, for the record, is a brief explanation of each composite mode's effect:

- **Normal:** This is the default mode for all clips that are edited into the Timeline. The Normal mode shows the clip without any modifications.

- **Add:** Combines the values of the color pixels of the top clip with the bottom clip and creates a final image that is brighter than the two combined.

- **Subtract:** This mode subtracts the values of the color pixels of the top clip from the bottom clip. The final image is darker than the two you started with.

- **Difference:** Difference mode subtracts the color values of the *bottom* clip from the top clip. This mode can give you some artistically interesting combinations depending on the colors of the two clips.

- **Multiply:** This mode compares the color values of the pixels of the top clip with the clip below it and then multiplies the two values together. If the image is dark, this mode has little effect. This mode darkens a light image. Multiply, commonly used to drop out white backgrounds from stills and other images, is one of the more useful modes. For example, if someone gave you a Photoshop still with a logo against a white background, you can use the Multiply mode to drop out the white and place the logo over the video layer of your choice.

- **Screen:** This mode is another one of those useful modes than can save the day in a pinch. This mode, in effect, drops out the black pixels of a clip. If you have a video clip, or a still, which has an element you want to save over black background, you can apply this mode to the clip to eliminate the black pixels. If you find it hard to live without the mathematical explanation of this mode, here it is: Screen mode compares the color values of the pixels in the top clip to the bottom clip and multiplies the inverse of each. Now you know, my friend.

- **Overlay:** Combines the color values between the two layers and maintains the highlights and the shadows. This mode is often used to combine images together as they appear to merge into one another.

- **Hard Light:** The Hard Light mode multiplies the colors, depending on the color values of the clip. This mode often creates a slightly dramatic colorful look to the final composite. Again, it depends on the colors you have in your layers and experimenting can produce quite a pleasing effect.

- **Soft Light:** This mode darkens or lightens the layers. The colors that result from this compositing mode depend on the original layer color.

- **Darken:** Compares the color values of the two layers and displays the darker of the two.

- **Lighten:** The opposite of Darken, this mode compares the color values of the two layers and displays the lighter of the two.

- **Travel Matte-Alpha:** Applies a matte to the top clip, using information from the bottom clip. Travel mattes are used to create halos or cutout borders that combine the two layered clips. The Alpha option of this mode ignores the RGB channels and only looks for the Alpha channel, if one is present. Alpha channels are channels that can be created in images when working in Adobe Photoshop and other such photo editing applications. Alpha channels describe the portions of the image that are transparent.

✔ **Travel Matte-Luma:** This mode works just like the preceding one, except that instead of the Alpha channel, luminance values (black and white values) are used to create the final matte. The advantage here is that no alpha is needed. Anything that is black in the image will be invisible (transparent), whereas anything that is white in the image will be visible (or opaque).

For readers who have worked in the Adobe Photoshop or After Effects applications, keep in mind that the 13 Final Cut composite modes behave exactly as they do in the Adobe applications.

Applying a Composite Mode

Composite modes are used on layered clips in the Timeline. To apply a composite mode, you must first add two clips to the Timeline, right on top of one another. (See Chapter 6 if you need a refresher on how to do so.) Figure 15-2 shows how these layered clips appear in the Timeline.

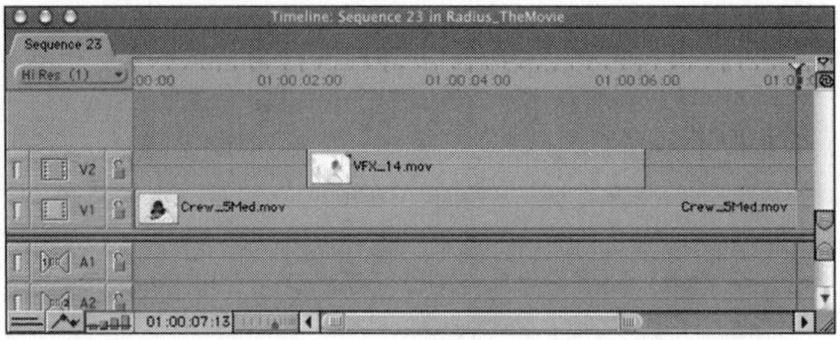

Figure 15-2: Composite Modes are applied to the topmost clip in a layered setting.

After you place the two clips, follow these steps:

1. **Select the top clip.**

2. **Choose Modify⇨Composite Mode and choose one of the Composite modes you see in the submenu, as shown in Figure 15-3.**

   The composite mode is applied to the topmost clip on the Timeline.

Note that composite modes create an effect between two layers, working *downwards*. In essence, the layer that has the composite mode needs another layer beneath it to show an effect. You *can* technically apply the composite mode to the bottom layer, but it will not show any changes because there is no layer beneath the bottom layer.

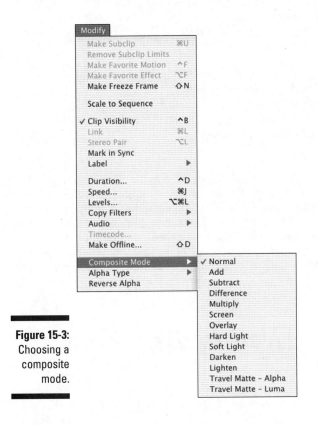

Figure 15-3:
Choosing a
composite
mode.

What Are Those Alpha Channels, Anyway?

Most video clips have three channels of color: red, green, and blue. (*Channels* are no more than layers that work together to create a final image.) These colors are combined to create all the other colors you see in the clip. However, some video and still images can be created with a fourth channel, the *alpha channel*. This alpha channel contains information that pertains to the transparency of the clip. Alpha channels tell Final Cut which parts of the image to make visible and which portions to make invisible. For example, in Adobe's After Effects application, you can create a QuickTime movie that has an image of an animated logo against an alpha channel background.

You can import this QuickTime movie into Final Cut and layer it above a video track. Final Cut recognizes the alpha channel and makes it transparent, while the logo remains visible and composites cleanly over your bottom video track. Alpha channels are important if you want to create a collage or use stills and video clips in your movie.

Alpha channels can be separated into different types, such as straight, black, or premultiplied. A detailed explanation is outside the scope of this book, but in general, these types have to do with where and how the transparency information is stored. The most common type is the straight Alpha: This is the mode many animators and Photoshop artists use to create their stills and movies.

In some situations, Final Cut may misinterpret the alpha. This may be obvious in some artifacts such as edge-fringing or halos around your final composited image. These artifacts make your final composite look grungy and rough at the edges. If you find yourself in this situation, select the clip in the Timeline and choose Modify⇨Alpha Type and choose a different type of alpha from the submenu. Experiment with different alpha types: The problem should disappear and the edges should appear smooth when you choose the correct one.

Mattes and Keys (Not the Door Kind)

Mattes and keys are common in applications devoted to compositing and creating special effects. Even though Final Cut is mainly a nifty editing application, it has many features and functions built into it that allow you to create some interesting composting effects.

Mattes are nothing more than still image files that are used to create various cutout effects. In fact, mattes can be thought of as cardboard cutouts. Think of the mattes that surround a professionally framed art print or photograph. That is the principle of creating mattes in Final Cut, too. Of course, mattes in the digital world are much more versatile than a piece of cardboard. In Final Cut, you can fill the inside and the outside of the matte with different video or stills and still maintain the shape of the matte. You see this in effect in the next section.

Keys, on the other hand, eliminate certain color or luminance values from an image to create transparency. Keys are used to create, among other things, the "weatherperson effect" on your local news: A meteorologist is photographed in front of a blue or green background and later the color is filled in with the image of a satellite weather map.

Creating a simple Travel matte

A Travel matte is a matte that uses three clips: the foreground is the top layer, the matte goes in the middle, and the background clip is placed at the bottom. To create a Travel matte, you ideally need three elements: the matte itself and two clips. The matte itself can be created in an application such as Adobe Photoshop.

In this section, we create a Travel matte by using an oval mask created in Photoshop as a matte and two clips from the sci-fi movie, *Radius*. These three elements are shown separately in Figure 15-4.

To begin, make sure that the matte has been created in Adobe Photoshop and imported into your Final Cut project via the File⇨Import⇨File menu command. (For more details on importing media into Final Cut, see Chapter 4.)

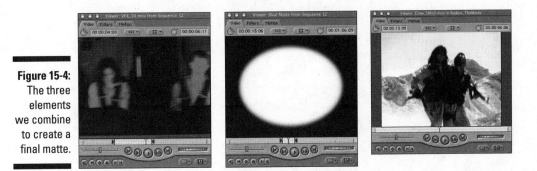

Figure 15-4:
The three elements we combine to create a final matte.

The following steps explain how to make a Travel matte with these three elements:

1. **Create a new sequence and drag the three elements from the Browser of your Final Cut project into the Timeline in the following order:**

   1. Place the clip you want to use as a background at the bottom (on the V1 layer in the Timeline).

   2. Place your matte or cutout on the V2, or middle, track.

   3. Place your foreground in the top track (in this case, V3).

   Figure 15-5 shows the final layering in the Timeline.

2. **Select the top clip (on track V3) and choose Modify⇨Composite Mode⇨ Travel Matte-Luma.**

   Your final travel matte appears in the Canvas window with the two composited clips and a feathered outline created from the matte itself, as shown in Figure 15-6.

Foreground   Matte

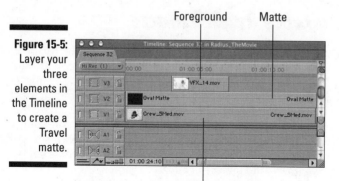

Figure 15-5:
Layer your
three
elements in
the Timeline
to create a
Travel
matte.

Background

Figure 15-6:
The final
Travel
matte.

Note that our matte was created in Adobe Photoshop and used a simple black and white image with a feathered outline. Because the values in the image are black and white (as opposed to an alpha channel), we used the Travel Matte-Luma option. If, however, our Photoshop matte had used alpha channels, we would have selected the Travel Matte-Alpha option. Whether a matte uses an alpha channel versus black and white values is up to whoever creates the image in Photoshop. In general, using alpha channels wherever possible is best because alphas provide the cleanest final composites.

Compositing with keys

Another way of creating composites is by using keys. A key is created using a clip in which the subject is filmed against a blue or green background. The colored background is later eliminated and replaced with a background element.

This process sounds simple, but creating a good clean key is quite a bit of work. Many companies, such as Ultimatte and others, specialize in creating high-end plug-ins and applications whose sole purpose is clean green screening. Final Cut's tools aren't nearly as sophisticated as some on the market, but they're not a bad place to start. We use Final Cut's keying tools to put a shot of our friend Toby the cat into the sci-fi shootout of our choice.

Shooting for green screen

If you're struggling to create a good green screen effect, remember this adage from the pros of keying: Most of the work for green screening is done by the time the video ends up in your hands. That means that the real trick to getting a good, clean key is to shoot it right in the first place.

Shooting for green screening is an art and a skill. Some of the best directors in Hollywood call upon companies and professionals who specialize in shooting for green screening.

Note that the choice between the color blue and green is often an artistic decision. The general rule is that if a lot of flesh tone is in the shots, use a green color. If however, your final composite may have bluish lights or other bluish tonal ranges, using blue may be easier.

Here are some rules to abide by when shooting for blue or green screening:

- **Use the right color:** The blue or green you may see in the green screening shots is not just any green or blue. These paints are a standard color and should be obtained from a photo supply or specialty paint store. Do your research before you start using the paint leftover from painting your den last year. Many photo supply shops also sell background cloth with the right shade of blue or green. This hanging cloth saves you the trouble of painting for hours.

- **Light and paint the background evenly:** Avoid variations in lighting. (This goes for the paint itself as well. The screen should be painted evenly, without any blemishes.) Uneven lighting or painting can create patches of varying color that are hard to key out separately.

- **Keep your distance:** Maintain a distance of at least 10 feet between your subject and the background. This avoids any green spills on the subjects, which will complicate your efforts to get a proper key later. (*Spills* are shades of the paint that fall on the foreground subjects as green or blue reflected light from the background.)

- **Shoot at best possible quality:** Many people argue that perhaps the DV format (because of its high 5:1 ratio of compression) isn't the ideal format for shooting green screen material. If your budget can accommodate it, shoot with high-end broadcast formats, such as Digital Betacam from Sony. Also, avoid single-chip CCD cameras, such as the ones used in the consumer DV camcorders. Whenever possible, use a three-chip camera.

To create a key, follow these steps:

1. **Drag your shots from the Browser to the Timeline.**

   Place your key (the subject shot against a green or blue background) on the top track, and place the background you want to insert on the bottom video track.

   For the example, our key is a cat filmed against a green screen, and the background is a scene from the sci-fi movie *Radius*. The two elements are shown in Figure 15-7.

Toby the cat | Gun-toting madman on planet Zoltan

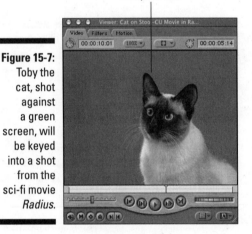 

Figure 15-7: Toby the cat, shot against a green screen, will be keyed into a shot from the sci-fi movie *Radius*.

2. **Select the green screen layer (in this case, Toby the cat) by clicking it and then choose Effects⇨Video Filters⇨Key.**

   The Blue and Green Screen filter is applied to your top clip.

3. **To adjust filter settings, double-click the green screen key layer to open it into the Viewer window.**

4. **Click the Filters tab, as shown in Figure 15-8.**

   The settings for the Blue and Green Screen filter appear.

5. **From the Key Mode drop-down list, choose Blue or Green, depending on the color of your video's background.**

6. **Keeping an eye on the image in the Canvas, click and drag the Color Level slider to a lower setting until the color or the blue or green screen disappears.**

   Drag the slider slowly so that you can see the green color in your video drop out bit by bit. You may have to tweak this to your satisfaction. The slider defaults to 100.

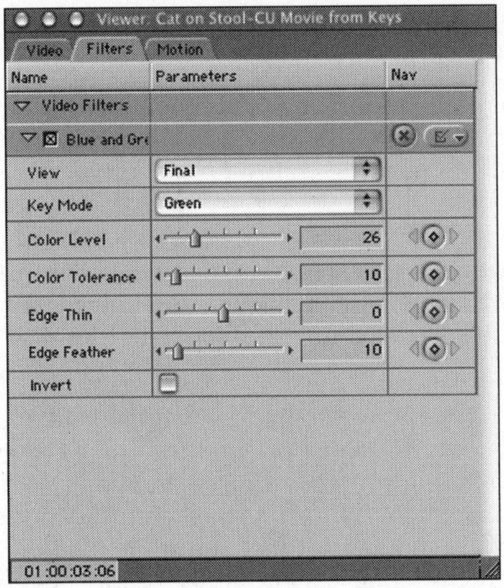

Figure 15-8:
The Blue and Green screen filter settings.

7. **Adjust Edge Thin and Edge Feather by clicking and dragging their sliders.**

The Edge Thin creates a choking in or out of the outer boundaries of your subject. The Edge Feather creates a slight feather to that edge. Tweak both these controls to your needs.

In this case, we also scaled the cat a bit and moved it to one side to better fit the scene, although a cat probably has no business being in a shootout on planet Zoltan anyway. The final results are shown below in Figure 15-9. George Lucas has nothing on this baby!

Figure 15-9:
No cats were harmed in the making of this *For Dummies* book.

Tips for getting clean keys

The basic key filters in Final Cut are just the first step in getting a clean key. You can use many other tools under Effects⇨Video Filters⇨Key that can help you clean up your key in Final Cut. Here's a brief rundown of a few of them:

- **Luma Key:** The Luma Key filter allows a key based on luminance values (such as black and white) as opposed to color values. For example, if you have shot an all white element against a solid black background, you may want to use this key to drop out the blacks and retain the white element.

- **Difference Matte:** This type of key compares two layers and eliminates what they have in common. You must prepare for this matte in the shooting phase. The Difference Matte requires that you shoot the shot twice, once with the subject in front of the background, and the second time with just the background and without the subject. Ideally, these shots should be exactly the same, except for the subject of course. Use a tripod to steady your camera when shooting for a Difference Matte and make sure that nothing varies between the shots except the subject that you want to key over. The final results compare the two layers and eliminate the background, while retaining the subject.

  The main advantage to the Difference Matte method is that your background doesn't have to be blue or green. It can be anything, as long as it doesn't change.

- **Spill Suppressors:** In many cases, when you finish shooting your green screen shots, you may notice that your subjects often have a slight color spill on them from the green or the blue background. A *spill* is a reflection of the background green or blue that happens to fall on your foreground subject and is often seen on your subject's shoulders and head. Final Cut has two spill suppressors, one for green and one for blue. These suppressors eliminate color spills, which are otherwise quite difficult to get rid of using a simple key. To apply a suppressor, click your clip in the Timeline to select it, and then choose Effects⇨Video Filters⇨ Key⇨Spill Suppressor - Green or Blue.

- **Use the matte tools:** You can find numerous matte tools that are useful for creating clean keys. For example:

  - **8-Point and 4-Point Garbage mattes:** Garbage mattes are rough mattes or masks that are used to eliminate parts of the image that won't be used in the final key. For example, in some keying work, you may see that the edges of the frame of your video continue to show up as a slight line at the edge. By using a Garbage Matte, you can quickly mask out the areas around your subject and simply get rid of the frame edges.

To apply the Garbage mattes, select them under Effect⇨Video Filters⇨Matte menu. After the 4-point or 8-point Garbage mattes are applied, your image displays four or eight points (clearly labeled). You can move these points by clicking the cross hairs under the Filter setting and clicking different portions of the image to create a new mask.

- **Matte Choker:** The Matte Choker is the ideal substitute for the Edge Thin slider found in some of the Final Cut key filters. *Edge thinning* is the process of removing the outer edges of your subject. The Edge Thin sliders in Final Cut key filters often produce a harsh edge. Use the Matte Choker instead to slightly *choke* (move the matte inward around the subject) your matte in to cut out some of the green or blue fringes that may appear around the edges. The Matte Choker is applied by choosing Effect⇨Video Filters⇨Matte⇨Matte Choker. Slider settings allow you to decide how much edge thinning you want to do and also to be able to "feather" or soften the edge.

A combination of a Screen filter, a Matte Choker, and a Spill Suppressor is often necessary to create a final clean composite, as shown in Figure 15-10.

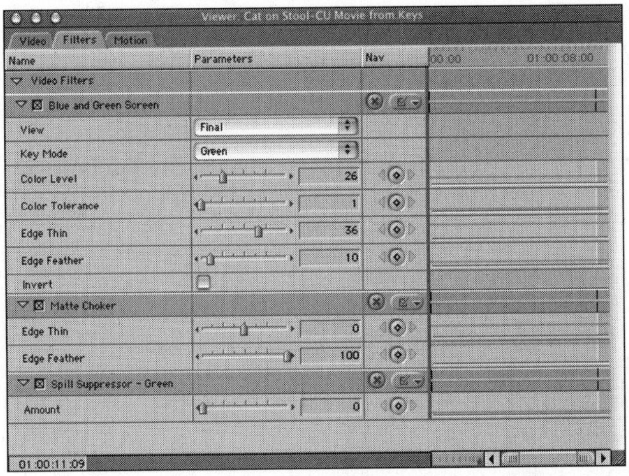

Figure 15-10: A Screen filter, a Matte Choker, and a Spill Suppressor have all been applied to create a final key.

Compositing an Image Collage

Image collages and short bumpers are a common sight on television, especially news show openers. In these collages, various video images and stills are combined with text to create a dramatic opening for the show.

Using Final Cut, you can create various collages of this type and combine them to create short opens for your shows and videos. In the next few sections, we cover the basics of creating collages: creating motion paths for your images, fading the images in and out, and animating effects on these video clips.

Creating a motion path

A common sight in a video collage is that of a video moving across the screen over another piece of video. This is a common, yet powerful effect to create multiple areas of visual interest for the audience.

Follow these steps to create a motion path for a clip:

1. **To make one clip move over another, create a layered sequence first.**

   Create a new sequence and add two clips, one into the V1 and another into the V2 track of your Timeline. The clip in V2 should be the one you intend to move above the clip in V1.

2. **Select the top clip in the Timeline and double-click it to open it in the Viewer window.**

3. **At the top of the Canvas window, choose Image+Wireframe from the View pop-up menu, shown in Figure 15-11, to see your video as well as the wireframe.**

   See Chapter 14 if you need the basics on wireframes.

   Remember to activate the Wireframe view in the Canvas window. Otherwise, you will not be able to move your clip.

Figure 15-11: Choose Image+Wire frame from the View menu.

4. **In the Viewer, click and drag the playhead to a point in the Timeline where you want to begin the clip's motion.**

   You can also move the playhead in the Canvas or the Timeline, if you feel more at ease there. All three playheads (in Viewer, Canvas, and Timeline) are locked together whenever you open a clip from the Timeline into the Viewer.

5. **If you want your clip (the one that you want to move) to appear small on the screen, scale your clip by clicking the Motion tab in the Viewer window and using the Scale slider to bring the value down to 50%.**

   This makes the clip 50% of its original size. Only after you scale the top clip down will the bottom clip be seen underneath.

6. **Click the Selection tool (arrow pointer) in the Tool palette to select it.**

7. **With the Selection tool, click and drag the center point of the clip in the wireframe and move it in the Canvas to where you want the movement to start, as shown in Figure 15-12.**

Figure 15-12:
Move your clip to the starting position.

8. **Add a keyframe by Control+clicking the Add Keyframe button at the bottom of the Canvas (or the Viewer) and choosing Center from the pop-up menu that appears, as shown in Figure 15-13.**

   Adding a keyframe locks the starting position of the clip to the place where you just moved it.

9. **Click and drag the playhead to the ending point for the motion of your clip.**

10. **Using the Selection (arrow pointer) tool, click and drag the center of the clip and move it to a new position.**

    Final Cut automatically adds a new keyframe for this position and creates a motion path for you.

11. **You can now render and play the clip to see this animation at work.**

    To render the clips, select the top clip and select Sequence⇨Render Selection. Then press the spacebar to play your clips in the timeline.

    You can create a motion path with many points by continuing to move the playhead further along in time and then moving the clip to another position.

You can also move the bottom clip (independently of the top clip) by performing Steps 2 through 11 again, but applied to the bottom clip this time around. You may or may not choose to scale down the bottom clip as well.

Figure 15-13:
Add a
Center
keyframe.

Fading images in and out

Another typical compositing effect is individual video clips fading in and out. Final Cut has many different ways of creating a fade in and a fade out. However, in the following steps, we outline the best method to use when you have layered a few clips in the Timeline and need to create fades for a clip in time to the other clips. This method involves animating the Opacity value of the clip to create a fade up and a fadeout by setting keyframes.

Follow these steps to create a fade-in and fade-out for a clip:

1. **Create a new sequence and add two clips, one into the V1 and another into the V2 track of your Timeline.**

2. **Double-click the top clip to open it into the Viewer.**

3. **Click the Motion tab in the Viewer window.**

   On the Motion tab (Figure 15-14), you can create animations for numerous attributes of a clip: Scale, Rotation, Center, Anchor Point Crop, Distort, Opacity, Drop Shadow, and Motion Blur. In this case, you are animating the Opacity of a layer to create a fade in and fade out.

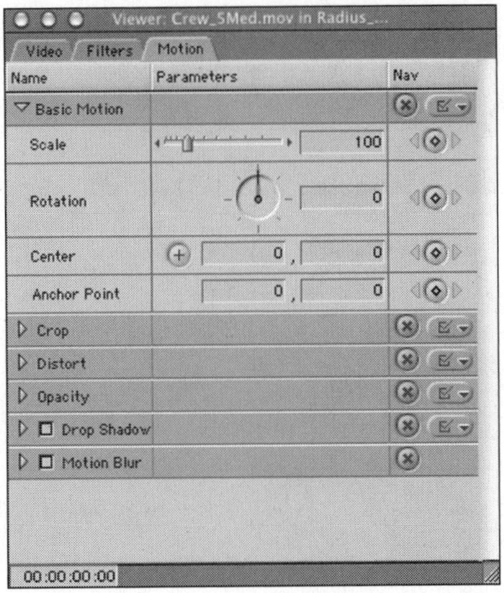

Figure 15-14:
Details of
the Motion
tab.

4. **Click the small Opacity triangle.**

   You see a slider and a few buttons for setting keyframes.

5. **Enlarge the Motion tab by clicking and dragging out the lower-right corner of the window.**

6. **Set an Opacity keyframe by dragging the Opacity slider down to 0 and checking the Set Keyframe button, as shown in Figure 15-15.**

   The Set Keyframe button is the small round button with a diamond-shaped icon inside it.

   You just created the first frame of your fade in at 0% Opacity.

7. **Move the playhead forward about one second.**

   Here you set another keyframe at 100%, creating a 1-second fade from 0% Opacity to 100% Opacity.

8. **Set another keyframe by simply dragging the Opacity slider so that it reads 100%.**

   Final Cut automatically sets another keyframe, as shown in Figure 15-16.

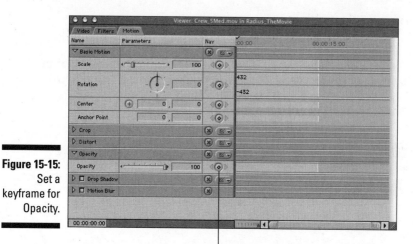

Figure 15-15:
Set a
keyframe for
Opacity.

Click to set an Opacity keyframe

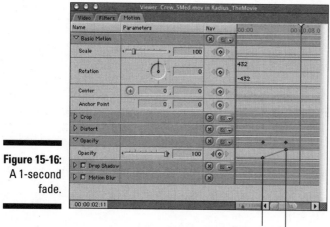

Figure 15-16:
A 1-second
fade.

First keyframe of fade-in

Second keyframe of fade-in

9. **Move the playhead to where you want the fade out of the clip to start.**

10. **Click the Set Keyframe button to set another keyframe.**

    The Opacity value of this keyframe is automatically 100%.

11. **Move the playhead to the spot where you want the very end of the fade out.**

12. **Set a keyframe at 0% Opacity by moving the Opacity slider down to 0%.**

    Final Cut automatically sets a keyframe for you.

At this stage in the exercise, you have a fade in and a fade out for your clip. Select your clip and choose Sequence⇨Render Selection to render it. Next play your fadeout by pressing the spacebar to play the clip in the timeline.

Figure 15-17 shows a fade in and a fade out set on a clip in the Motion tab.

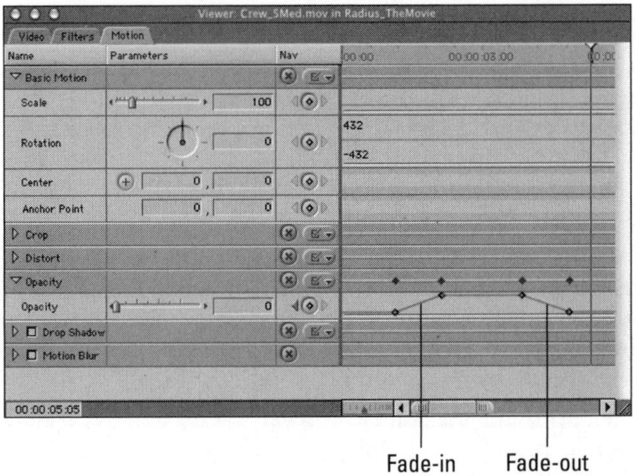

Figure 15-17: A fade in and a fade out on a clip.

Fade-in   Fade-out

Other Compositing Effects on the Motion Tab

If you've worked through the exercises in this chapter, you should have a fairly good idea of how to layer clips and create sophisticated compositing effects.

If you spend some time experimenting with the options on the Motion tab, you will see that other attributes, such as Scale, Drop Shadow, and others, can all be animated independently of one another. Now that you know how to animate a few of the Motion attributes, you can feel free to go into the Motion tab and animate any of the other attributes. The principles that you just learned in the last two exercises (creating a motion path and fading in or out) apply to all the other Motion attributes.

Final Cut allows for 99 video tracks. Each clip has these Motion attributes, which can be animated across time. This combination of 99 video tracks and unlimited animation on clips makes for a very powerful way of creating collages and layering clips. In fact, *restraint* may be the key word for best results.

Here's a short tour of the other animation attributes available on the Motion tab:

- ✔ **Scale:** Scale changes the size of the clip and maintains the proportions. For example, by using the slider, you can scale the clip to 25%. This causes the clip to be 25% of its original size.

  Similarly a 50% scale is 50% the size of the original.

  As with any other attributes in the Motion tab, you can move the slider or enter the number directly in the number field.

- ✔ **Rotation:** Rotates a clip around its center. The Rotation controls also include a small clock-like face. The black hand indicates the current rotation of the clip, and the small red hand indicates how many times the clip has been set to rotate. You can use a negative number (to move counter-clockwise) or a positive number, for a clockwise motion.

- ✔ **Center:** Sets the center point of the clip. Center is the attribute you should animate when you want to move the clip from one spot to another in the frame. Here you can also set the location of the clip by clicking the Center Point Control (the small circle with a + sign in it) and clicking with it anywhere in the Canvas.

- ✔ **Anchor Point:** Anchor Point of the clip allows you to set the center of rotation on a clip. For example, if the Anchor Point is set to the center of a rectangle, the rectangle, when rotated, rotates at the center. However, if the Anchor point is set to a corner, the same rectangle rotates from its corner. You can even set the anchor point outside of the clip itself.

- ✔ **Crop:** When you open the Crop attribute, you see sliders for Left, Right, Top, Bottom, and Edge Feather. These sliders allow you to crop the clip from all four sides and set a slight, soft feather for your crop.

- ✔ **Distort:** Distort also has five sliders: Upper Left, Upper Right, Lower Right, Lower Left, and Aspect Ratio. The first four sliders allow you to distort the appropriate corners of your clip. The Aspect Ratio slider allows you to create a squeeze effect vertically (if you drag the slider left) or horizontally (if you drag the slider right).

- ✔ **Opacity:** Allows you to reduce or increase the transparency of the clip. At 0%, the clip is transparent (or invisible). At 100% opacity, the clip is opaque (or fully visible).

- ✔ **Drop Shadow:** Allows you to put a drop shadow behind a clip. Drop shadows are shadows that fall at an angle behind the clip. You have to first check the small Drop Shadow check box. Then you can change the settings for the type of Drop Shadow that you want.

  You can change the following settings under the Drop Shadow effect, shown in Figure 15-18:

  - • **Offset:** Changes the distance between the clip and the drop shadow. A higher offset value creates the illusion of the clip being further away from its background.

- **Angle:** Controls the angle at which the drop shadow falls in relation to the clip.

- **Color:** Working on a late-night hair-replacement infomercial? Need some gawd-awful way to add tackiness to your text? Well, Final Cut has just the thing for you. Use this control to change the color of the drop shadows on your fonts!

- **Softness:** This control changes the softness of the drop shadow for a softer, gentler drop effect.

- **Opacity:** At 100% opacity, the drop shadow is completely solid. A lower setting produces a slightly transparent drop shadow.

✔ **Motion Blur:** Adds a slight and soft blur to the edge of moving items. This is often used to create realistic motion on items. Otherwise, moving objects tend to have sharp edges and look too computer-generated (which of course they are).

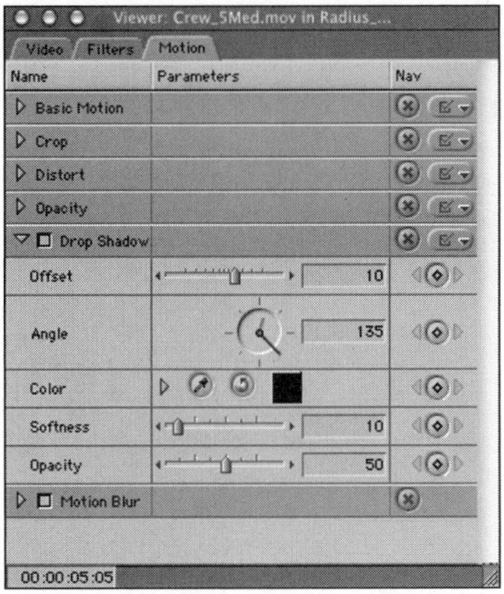

Figure 15-18:
The Drop Shadow effect on the Motion Tab of the Viewer window.

Adding More Effects to Your Repertoire

In this chapter, we limit our discussion of compositing to the effects found on the Motion tab of the Viewer window. However, Final Cut has a nearly endless array of effects you can apply to your clips.

To apply an effect to a clip, select it in the Timeline and then choose your effect from Final Cut's Effects menu. Alternatively, you can drag the effects from the Browser and drop them onto the clips in the Timeline. To change any attributes of the effects you just applied, double-click the clip to load it into the Viewer and click the Effects tab. Your effect will appear under this tab, ready to be animated. All the principles of animating motion attributes that we explain in this chapter apply to effects as well.

Working with effects controls

When working with effects, sliders, and other controls you encounter, knowing a few handy shortcuts can make your life easier. Here are just a few:

✔ When using the slider controls, hold down the ⌘ key to slow the slider's movement and work with finer increments.

✔ Sliders generally move in increments of whole numbers. For values precise to two decimal points, hold down the Shift key when moving the sliders.

✔ If you're using the Angle controls, hold down the Shift key to move the values to 45-degree increments.

✔ Hold down the ⌘ key to slow the movement of the Angle control for finer incremental control.

Chapter 16

Secrets of Rendering

. . . .

. . . .

*M*ost people in video believe that the Gods of Digital Video invented rendering to punish mortal editors for the sins of their past lives. Why? Well, *rendering* is when Final Cut calculates how to display a video clip or play an audio clip after you add a new effect or filter to it (one that wasn't there originally). The problem is that Final Cut sometimes has to take a moment (to put it charitably) to do this, and in the grand scheme of things, rendering can eat up your time.

You can bring raw video from your DV camera, and Final Cut plays it without any rendering. But if you want to superimpose a title over that video or apply a color filter, the video has to be rendered so that it includes that new effect. As an example, rendering a title over a 1-minute DV clip on Zed's G3 laptop took 1.25 minutes. To make matters worse, you have to re-do your renders every time you want to change a single element in them (to make red text green, for instance). What's more, those renders can take up valuable space on your hard drive, as Final Cut creates a separate video or audio file for each one and stores it on your drive. Even if you're not so sure about the existence of Digital Video gods, you'll probably find that rendering is an annoying-but-unavoidable fact of life in Final Cut.

The good news is that this chapter can help you better understand rendering, do it more efficiently, and better control your render files so that they take up less space and aren't misplaced accidentally.

What Is Rendering?

When a clip plays in a Final Cut sequence, or the Viewer, a media file is playing the clip for you. This file exists as a piece of digital video on your hard drive. If you add a few effects to the clip, Final Cut has to calculate the effect for each frame on the fly. To do so in real time with 30 frames every second exceeds the capacity of most Mac computers.

This is where rendering comes in.

During the rendering process, Final Cut combines the video (or audio) information of your clip with the effects or transitions applied to the clip and then generates a new media file, called a *render cache file*. After you render your clip, the render cache file is what plays when you view the clip with the effect in the sequence. Just as clips have media files that play from the disk, the render cache files are like media files for the effects or the transition positions of your edited sequences.

Understanding Rendering Status

You can see the rendering status of your clips in the Timeline window. As shown in Figure 16-1, the Timeline contains two rendering status bars, just over the timecode ruler. The upper status bar is for video and the lower one for audio. You have to look closely sometimes because the render status bars are thin and located quite close to one another. The colors on these bars indicate what clips on the Timeline require rendering.

Here's what each color means:

- ✔ **Red:** The clip needs to be rendered. Sorry, hang out and relax.

- ✔ **Dark gray:** No need to render. This color is for clips whose clip and sequence settings match and clips that don't have any effects.

- ✔ **Green:** This is for effects that don't need rendering and can be played in real time. You see this color if you're lucky enough to be using Final Cut in any real-time configuration available. (See the sidebar "Real time or not?")

- ✔ **Yellow:** Good news: Yellow indicates that Final Cut can show a real-time approximation of the final effect during playback. Bad news: To get the real final effect, you still need to render the material. That's life!

- ✔ **Light gray:** The clip has already been rendered! Don't worry about it, dude. Go party!

Video Render status bar

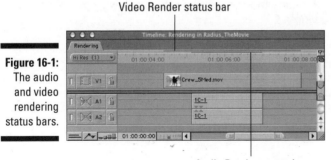

Figure 16-1:
The audio
and video
rendering
status bars.

Audio Render status bar

You may encounter two other indicators that mean you need to render. The first one is a big white `Unrendered` message over a blue background in the Viewer or the Canvas window. The message fills up these windows and is hard to miss. The second indicator is a steady beep you may hear. This beeping indicates that the audio material can't be played in real time and requires rendering.

Rendering a Clip or Sequence

When you encounter any kind of rendering indicator, it is best to stop and render before you proceed. Within Final Cut, you can render your material in many ways. Here are some of the ways to render your material:

- ✔ **Rendering a clip or an effect:** Select the clip or the transition and choose Sequence⇨Render Selection.

- ✔ **Rendering an entire sequence:** Open the sequence by double-clicking it in the Browser and then choose Sequence⇨Render All.

- ✔ **Rendering a portion of a sequence:** Select one or more clips or effects in the Timeline or use the I and O keys to set an in and an out point in the sequence. Then choose Sequence⇨Render Selection. Remember that you can set in and out points in the Viewer, Timeline, and the Canvas windows.

- ✔ **Batch rendering sequence:** Select the sequences you want to render in the Browser and choose Sequence⇨Render All.

A progress bar like the one shown in Figure 16-2 indicates the percentage of rendering that has been finished, along with an estimated time.

You may cancel rendering anytime by pressing the Esc key or pressing ⌘+. (that is, ⌘+the period key).

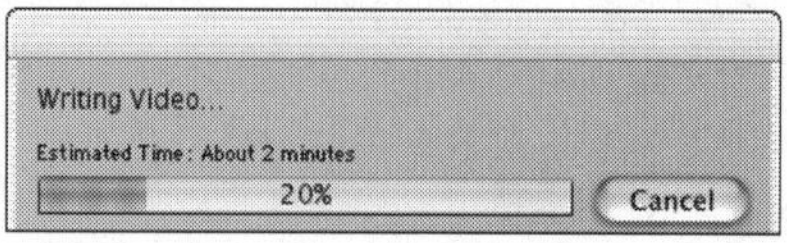

Figure 16-2:
The rendering progress bar.

> Writing Video...
>
> Estimated Time : About 2 minutes
>
> [========   20%   ] [Cancel]

There is a handy way to quickly get a rough preview of your effect before you begin rendering. In the Timeline or the Viewer, drag the playhead across the clip with the effect, and Final Cut attempts to update the effect as fast as your computer will allow. Drag it slow enough so that Final Cut can keep up, and you will get a fairly good idea of the look of your final rendered effect.

Real time or not?

Among the latest and greatest features in Final Cut Pro 3 are the real-time effects. No need to render! To take advantage of these software-based, real-time effects, you need a 500 MHz (or faster) Power Mac G4 or PowerBook G4 with 256MB of RAM. No extra hardware is needed.

Depending on your computer's speed, you may see a variety of transitions and effects in real time. If you click the Effects tab in the Browser and look in the Transitions and Effects folders, you can see certain items listed in bold text; these are the effects that can work in real time on your computer.

If you're using DV video, you can see the following in real time:

✔ **Cross Dissolve**

✔ **Iris transitions:** Diamond, Oval, Point, Rectangle, and Star

✔ **Wipe transitions:** Center, Clock, Edge, Inset, and V

✔ **Color Corrector 3-way filter**

✔ **Real-time motion effects:** Opacity, Scale, Center, Offset, Crop, and Aspect

If you're working with video other than DV, you can look up the Apple-approved, third-party video capture cards. Many of these cards, such as the Aurora Igniter, feature real-time effects when working with high-end video.

The real-time features are under constant development at Apple. So for the latest information, visit the Final Cut Pro site at www.apple.com/finalcutpro.

Understanding Render Quality Levels

Final Cut has four different render quality levels. You can select a level from the drop-down list in the upper-left corner of the Timeline window, as shown in Figure 16-3. The quality setting you choose is critical because it affects the time it takes to render. By using a lower quality level (Low Res or Draft) while you do rough edits and previews of your effect, you can save time. For a final output, you need to re-render everything at the highest quality level (Hi Res).

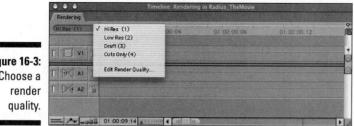

Figure 16-3:
Choose a
render
quality.

Final Cut generates a render cache file for each render level. For example, if you're working at Draft setting and render a dissolve, Final Cut creates a render cache file for that dissolve at Draft quality. If you then switch over to Hi Res setting, you need to re-render the dissolve at the Hi Res setting. However, if you switch back to Draft setting, the render cache file from the Draft render will become active, and you won't have to render again at Draft quality.

Choosing a render quality level

Final Cut has four different render quality levels that you can choose from. You use different levels for different purposes. In the following list, we explain how to use each level and what each level's default settings are:

- ✔ **Hi Res (1):** This is the level to use for your final renders, when you're preparing to lay off your material to tape. The Hi Res level creates a render cache file that has the same frame rate and resolution as your sequence settings. When using this level, the highest image and motion quality are created. All renders include proper field rendering, frame blending, and motion blur, and all filters are rendered as well.

- ✔ **Low Res (2):** Using the Low Res level creates a file that has the same frame rate but *half* the resolution of your sequence settings. Filters are enabled in this setting, but field rendering, frame blending, and motion blur are not rendered. Use this level for rough rendering for speed and a quick preview, but not for a final output.

✔ **Draft (3):** The Draft level creates a render cache file that has *half* the frame rate as well as *half* the resolution of your sequence settings. Filters are enabled under this setting, but field rendering, frame blending, and motion blur are not used. Use this level when you want to preview rough geometric moves, such as scaling and motion paths. This level is not for preparing the final output.

✔ **Cuts Only (4):** Clearly, as the name suggests, this is a Cuts Only level. When using this level, the base track plays (which is Video 1 or V1), but without any transitions or other effects. In short, this level works at high resolution but ignores any transitions and effects. So, for example, if you have created some dissolves and color effects in your Timeline, a playback in this mode simply plays the clips, and you can't see any of the color effects or dissolves.

Note that you can edit the default settings to your liking, which we explain in the next section.

Editing render quality levels

Each render quality level has specific settings that are employed when that render level is engaged in the Timeline window. For example, in the Draft level, the settings are chosen so that the frame rate and the resolution are half that of your original sequence. The power of render quality levels is that you can customize any level to your needs.

To edit your render quality levels, follow these steps:

1. **Choose Sequence⇨Render Quality⇨Edit Render Qualities (Shift+Y).**

   Alternately, you can also choose Edit Render Quality from the drop-down list located at the top left of the Timeline window.

   The Render Quality Editor appears, as shown in Figure 16-4.

2. **Click a render level tab and edit the settings on the tab to your liking.**

   The settings under the tabs are fairly simple and easy to edit. For example, you can rename the level if you like. You can also uncheck or check Field Rendering, Motion Blur, and Enable Frame Blending. These three options all contribute to smoother effects and speed changes for your clips, but for a rough render, they are unnecessary.

Here you can also choose to Play Base Layer Only. This option plays only the V1 track of your Timeline and ignores any effects or transitions. You can also choose the Draft Render option for faster, but rough quality renders.

The High Quality Playback option plays back your DV video at best quality at all times, but it can be slower to view, depending on the speed of your computer's processor. A computer with a G4 processor will display your video a lot faster and smoother than a G3 processor.

You can also adjust the Frame Rate and Resolutions settings. A lower percentage in the Frame Rate drop-down list creates faster renders but with slightly jerky playback. In the Resolution drop-down list, a higher setting results in slower renders, and a lower setting produces faster rendering times. Of course, before you layback your material to tape, you have to render at the 100% resolution and 100% frame rates.

3. **Click OK when you're done.**

   Your new choices and changes will now be in effect for the Render Levels you just edited. Alternately, you can also click Save As Default Set to use these newly edited presets as your default values at all times.

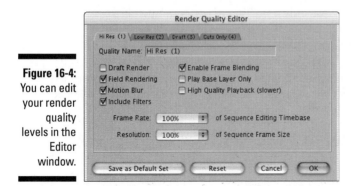

Figure 16-4: You can edit your render quality levels in the Editor window.

Planning Efficient Rendering

Rendering takes time, pure and simple. Each time you make a change to an effect or a transition, you'll probably have to re-render. The time that rendering sucks up can be significant, not to mention the simple aggravation factor, while a producer breathes down the back of your neck.

You can do a few things to minimize the time you need to give up to rendering. Here are some basic and simple rules you can follow to manage your rendering times:

- ✔ **Make your rough cut first and then add effects:** The rule here is to just plan ahead. If you can, work only with sequences with cuts. After you refine your rough cut to an acceptable look, then work on adding effects and transitions.

- ✔ **Disable updates to avoid unnecessary renders:** Another trick you can use is to disable any updates in the Viewer and Canvas windows by locking down the Caps Lock key. This way you can toggle the key on and off for when you want to just edit or lay out your effects and when you decide you're ready to render. Locking down the Caps Lock key avoids the time Final Cut must take to update effect changes. This delay can often slow down your work.

- ✔ **Start by using a low-quality setting:** You can start out by setting a lower quality Render Level, such as Low Res or Draft under the Render Level Quality drop-down list, located in the upper-left corner of every Timeline window. Only when you're satisfied with the final timing do you switch back the quality to High Res, again, under the Render Level Quality drop-down list, and render the final sequence for output.

- ✔ **Do test renders:** A trick that Zed uses is test rendering short sections of the Timeline. For example, if he adds a sepia tint to a clip that's 3 minutes long, he renders only a portion of the 3-minute clip, decides on the settings, and then moves on without waiting around to render the entire clip. Later, at the end of the day, he renders the entire 3-minute clip.

- ✔ **Take advantage of the batch rendering feature:** A third item to use is to do batch renders of sequences while you go off and do yoga in the hallway. The yoga won't make the renders go any faster, but it will make you feel a whole lot better.

If ever you drop a clip from the Browser into the Timeline and a red render line appears in the status bar (which we discuss earlier in this chapter), check to see whether there's a mismatch between the capture settings of the clip and the settings of the sequence preset. If a clip without an effect creates a red render line, this mismatch is the most likely culprit.

Managing Renders on Your Hard Drive

Whenever you render in Final Cut, a render cache file is generated. This render file is what Final Cut plays during the effect that was rendered. For example, imagine a dissolve between two clips. After the dissolve is rendered, the render file that's created from the two clips fading into one another plays when you play through the dissolve. While playing around the dissolve, however, the respective media files for the clips (not the render file) are used for playback.

Rendering can take time, and in certain projects, you may end up with hundreds, if not thousands of render cache files. It is therefore quite important to manage your render files efficiently, which we explain how to do in the following sections.

Setting storage for your render files

The first step in managing your render files is setting a proper location to store them. This is done on the Scratch Disks tab, which you can find out more about in Chapter 2. After you set the location, Final Cut organizes the files for you, which we explain in the next section. Note that if you don't set a location, Final Cut will default to storing your render files on you main system drive. Follow these steps to set a location for storing your render files:

1. **Choose Final Cut Pro⇨Preferences.**

2. **Click the Scratch Disks tab in the Preferences window (see Figure 16-5).**

3. **Make sure that Video Render and Audio Render boxes in the top row of buttons are checked.**

   The Video Capture button should also be checked if you are setting the scratch disk for your video captures as well.

4. **Click the Set button in the top row.**

   Note that Final Cut enables you to set numerous drives as your capture and render scratch disks. Here we're just using the top row of buttons to select just one drive. If you have more than one drive you'd like to assign as your capture or render scratch, click the relevant buttons in the next few rows.

   A dialog box appears showing your drives.

5. **In the dialog box, select a drive and then click Choose.**

6. **Click OK in the Scratch Disks dialog box when you are done.**

   Final Cut will now use the drive you selected to store your render files.

Locating your render files

So what happens after you specify a location to store your render files? Final Cut first creates a Final Cut Pro Documents folder under the Documents folder, which is located on your scratch disk. This Final Cut Pro Documents folder has folders for captured media, render files, and cache files for waveforms and thumbnails. In the Render Files folder, Final Cut creates a folder for each of your projects by name and stores all the render files for that project in the relevant folder. Figure 16-6 shows how Final Cut organizes the render files.

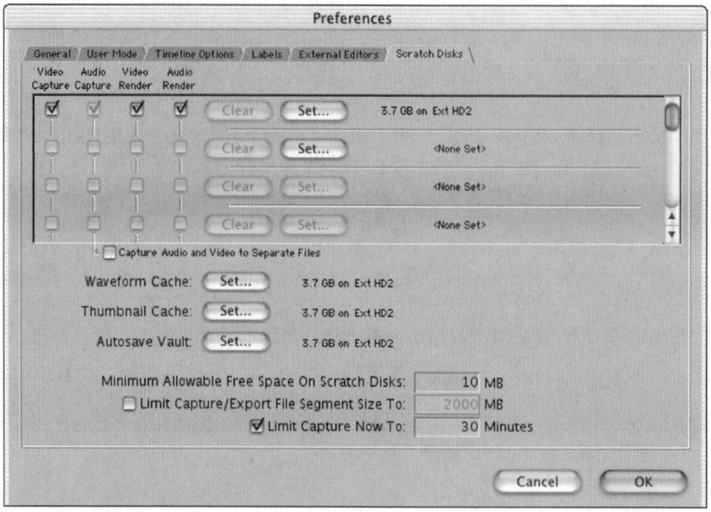

Figure 16-5:
Select a destination for your render files on the Scratch Disks tab.

The labels on these render files may at first seem confusing, but they are easy to decode. For example, take the render file `Final Sequenc-FIN-00000037`. The name tells you that this render file is from a sequence called Final Sequence and that this is the 37th render file from that sequence. The code FIN stands for the render quality that was used to create this render. Your render files may include any of the following four codes, depending on the quality you use:

Code	Setting Used to Render the Cache File
FIN	Hi Res (1)
WP1	Low Res (2)
WP2	Draft (3)
WP3	Cuts Only (4)

Dump those old renders?

What happens to renders when they grow old? No, they aren't put out to a peaceful pasture.

Each project has a separate folder under Render Files

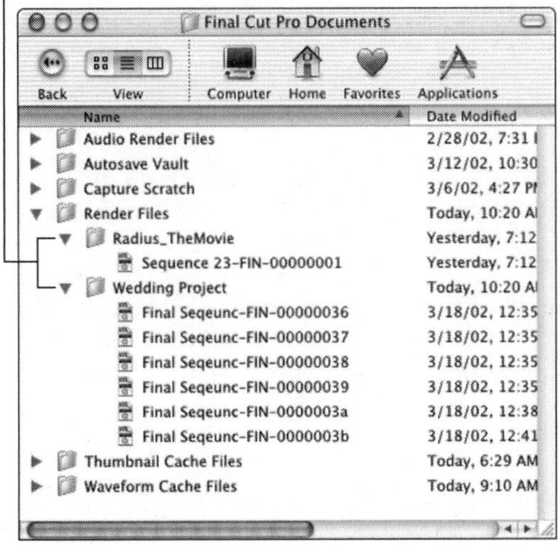

Figure 16-6:
Final Cut
organizes
render files.

Imagine this scenario: You render a 1-minute clip after you apply a blur and sepia tint effect to it. This creates a render cache file for the 1-minute clip. Because DV video takes up 3.6MB per second, this file takes up approximately 216MB.

Later, you decide that you need to lessen the blur effect on your clip. So you go ahead and make the change. Of course, you have to re-render your effect. This creates another render cache file, which is approximately 216MB as well. So now you have two large render cache files taking up space on your scratch disk, one of which is not being used at all. And of course, Final Cut has to save the first one for a while, in case you decide you liked the original render better and use the Undo command (⌘+Z) a few times to go back to your first render. Hmm . . . this all can get complicated.

Well, fear not. It is not as bad as it sounds. Final Cut holds onto an old - render cache file until it drops off the undo queue. So if you chose Final Cut Pro⇨Preferences and set your undo levels to 10 on the General tab, then you can go back 10 steps by using the Undo command (⌘+Z). This means that Final Cut holds onto your first render cache file until the second render is the 11th step in the undo queue. You can do at least 10 undoable actions after rendering the first file, but when the second render action becomes the 11th action, Final Cut automatically deletes the old render cache file.

So it sounds like you need not worry about running around to delete your old render cache files. However, in some cases, your projects may get quite large, and you may spread your render files out across so many disks and folders that you simply lose track of them. This can happen at times, despite the fact that Final Cut is very good at keeping your files organized. In addition, you may have created render files at various render qualities, and you now want to delete all but the ones done at the highest setting. In many cases, you may have rendered many times at the same render quality. This all can get pretty messy and disorganized.

In such a case, you have a few choices. One choice is to delete all render files and then re-render your entire sequence or sequences in the project. This may take time, but it does clean up the render cache file mess.

Apple engineers strongly recommend that you avoid manually deleting your old render cache files. In other words, don't just go through your render folders on the drives and toss all the render files into the trash. This may cause some issues later when you reopen the project. Final Cut may still look for the old render files and attempt to link to them.

The proper way to delete old render cache files is to use the Render Manager so keep reading.

Using the Render Manager

Apple engineers designed the Render Manager to help you do two key things: Delete render files from old or deleted projects, and delete files that are no longer needed, such as the ones done at a lower quality setting.

When you use the Render Manager, you see files from projects that are open as well as the ones that are not open. You can use the modification dates on these files to see what you want to save and what you want to delete.

To use the Render Manager, follow these steps:

1. **Choose Tools⇨Render Manager.**

   The Render Manager window (Figure 16-7) appears. In the Render Manager window, the files are sorted into folders by project and sequence name. The first main folder is the project folder, and the subfolders represent the sequences. Filenames are shown by quality level, such as Cuts Only (4), Draft (3), and so on.

2. **Click in the Remove column next to a file to add a check mark to the file you want to remove.**

3. **Click the OK button.**

   All checked off render files are removed. Bear in mind that files removed via the Render Manager cannot be restored. Even a ⌘+Z (to undo) won't work.

Sequence Name

Current Project Name

Other Projects

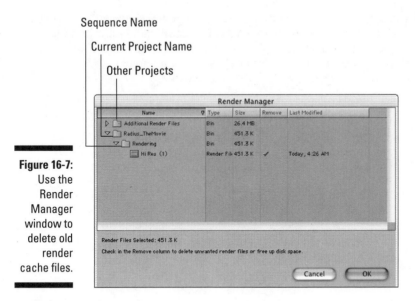

Render Manager

Name	Type	Size	Remove	Last Modified
▷ ☐ Additional Render Files	Bin	26.4 MB		
▽ ☐ Radius_TheMovie	Bin	451.3 K		
▽ ☐ Rendering	Bin	451.3 K		
☐ Hi Res (1)	Render File	451.3 K	✓	Today, 4:26 AM

Render Files Selected: 451.3 K

Check in the Remove column to delete unwanted render files or free up disk space.

Cancel   OK

Figure 16-7:
Use the Render Manager window to delete old render cache files.

WARNING!

Files removed via the Render Manager cannot be restored by pressing ⌘+Z to undo.

A Word on Audio Rendering

Final Cut can play back up to 8 audio tracks in real time. However, as you add audio effects and transitions, the track costs add up, and you won't be able to play as many in real time. The trick here again is to render audio often.

To render individual audio clips with effects applied to them, select the audio clip and choose Sequence➪Render Selection. You can also mark in and out points (using the I and O keys) in the Timeline and then choose Sequence➪Render Selection to just render the audio items between the in and out points.

An efficient method of rendering audio is to choose Sequence➪Mixdown Audio. If you invoke this command, Final Cut renders all audio tracks, including audio effects and audio transitions all into one render cache file. This feature is very handy when your audio tracks multiply along with audio effects or audio transitions. However, it has one major drawback: If you change any item on the audio tracks, such as a volume node or an effect setting, you have to Mixdown Audio again.

A key way to prevent dropped audio frames when you layback the audio to tape is to use the Sequence⇨Mixdown Audio feature and mix your audio down to one render cache file. This prevents the overhead that otherwise would be placed on the processor to calculate the audio in real time.

Part V
Outputting Your Masterpiece

The 5th Wave   By Rich Tennant

DAD ADDS MULTIMEDIA SOUND AND GRAPHICS TO THE TRADITIONAL CAMPFIRE GHOST STORY.

In this part . . .

When you're finished editing and adding any transitions, titles, effects, and so on, you're ready for Part V, which focuses on outputting your movie to its final destination. We show you how to record your finished masterpiece back to video tape (for tape duplication or broadcast), and how to save your finished movie to a QuickTime digital file, which you can later burn to a DVD or CD-ROM, or broadcast over the Internet.

Chapter 17

Recording to Tape

. . . .

. . . .

*O*ne of the last stages of working on a project in Final Cut is to record your edited project from a sequence back to tape. Recording your final edited project to tape is the most common method for delivering your project to a broadcast house or to a client.

As with anything else in Final Cut, you have numerous options and choices available to you at this stage. Make your final choice based on your equipment and the needs of your clients or whomever is awaiting the delivery of the final master tape.

Setting Up for Recording

Before you record your edited project to tape, you must first set up your equipment for recording back to tape. You must also check some equipment issues and verify settings in Final Cut before you proceed. Check the following before preparing to record your project to tape:

1. **Connect your equipment.**

   If you have a basic DV setup, which simply entails connecting a DV device, such as a camera, directly to your computer with a FireWire cable, your life is going to be rather simple. Because a FireWire cable handles both the in and the out of video and audio, you should just confirm that your FireWire port on the Mac is hooked up to your DV device using a FireWire cable.

If you're recording to a VHS or other format, flip ahead to the sections "Recording to VHS" and "Recording to other kinds of decks" for more information.

2. Set the proper mode.

Check to make sure that your DV deck or camera is in VCR mode. Sometimes the VCR mode is also labeled VTR (Video Tape Recorder). Final Cut will not record to your DV device if it is set to camera mode. If, by any chance, your DV device has multiple inputs (often labeled Video 1 or Video 2 or Line 1 or Line 2), be sure to check that you're on the right input. Video decks often have an Input button that switches the inputs to the deck or the camera. The indications for the Input selected appear either on the front panel of the deck or inside the viewfinder of the camera.

3. Check the Final Cut settings.

Choose Final Cut Pro⇨Easy Set Up. Under the Easy Setup window, check to make sure that under External Video For Playback, you have chosen Apple FireWire, as shown in Figure 17-1. The External Video For Recording should show the Same as Playback setting. This setting indicates that you're ready to output via FireWire.

Figure 17-1:
Check the
Easy Setup
box before
recording
to tape.

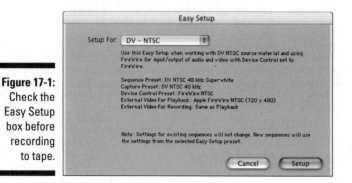

4. Prepare your sequence.

You may not need to render, depending on your project, but to be on the safe side, take the following steps to prepare your sequence for recording:

1. Render your sequence by double-clicking it to open it and choosing Sequence⇨Render All.

This step ensures that any and all items that need rendering will be properly rendered. Without rendering, some of the items, such as effects, may not play at all in your sequence.

2. Choose Sequence⇨Mixdown Audio.

This step renders all the audio in a sequence. If you don't follow this step, your sequence may drop frames during playback or have hiccups in the audio.

Look out for dropped frames!

Many other editing systems come with video cards that perform most of the processing tasks otherwise done by the computer, but not Final Cut. Final Cut relies almost entirely on the processing power of your computer. In some cases, if the requirements of the video overwhelm the processing power of your computer, Final Cut will *drop* some video frames, resulting in jittery playback and hiccups in your video. This is highly undesirable. *Dropped frames* are simply frames that Final Cut has missed in playback or capture because your computer's processor had too many things to think about all at once.

To be sure that you're notified if frames are dropped as you record to tape, choose Final Cut Pro⇨Preferences and, under the General tab, make sure that the Report Dropped Frames During Playback option is checked, as shown in Figure 17-2.

Check here to report dropped frames

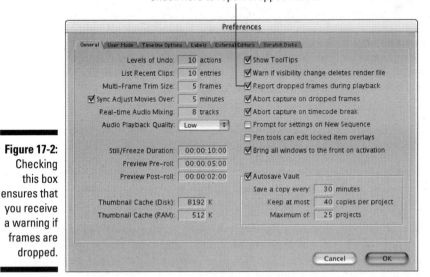

Figure 17-2:
Checking this box ensures that you receive a warning if frames are dropped.

Checking this option assures that Final Cut warns you about any dropped frames that may occur during recording to tape. If you do get this warning, you may take steps to prevent frames from being dropped, such as increasing the memory allocation for Final Cut, closing all other applications, and suspending any network tasks that may be taking place. Then restart your computer and attempt to record to tape again.

Recording to DV tape with a camera or deck

If you're recording to a DV device, such as a camera or a deck, you have much less to worry about as opposed to someone who is recording to a format such as Betacam SP or others. With a DV camera or deck, you only need a single FireWire cable to connect the device and the computer. Traveling over this FireWire cable is your video, audio, timecode, and even device control information. The *device control information* is what allows Final Cut to control the transport mechanism (play, rewind, fast-forward, and so on) of your deck or camera.

The one item you do need to check is to make sure that your DV device is switched to VCR (or VTR, depending on your deck or camera) as opposed to camera. A basic DV camera often has a setting to choose between a camera or a VCR function. Final Cut will not record back to a camera that is in camera mode.

You may also want to check the recording prevention tab on your DV tape to be sure that it isn't in Save setting. DV tapes have a small tab on one side that switches between Record (meaning you can erase over the tape) and Save, which means you cannot record over your tape.

Recording to VHS

VHS remains one of the most common video formats around. When you rent a movie on tape from your local video store, it is in VHS format. If you're recording back to a VHS tape deck, you need only use your FireWire device to convert your DV signal to analog for the VHS. Most DV cameras and decks have analog video and audio out connectors. These connectors look very much like the stereo RCA-type connections found on the back of your home stereo, as shown in Figure 17-3. Most VHS decks also have RCA-type video and audio inputs. All you need is a pair of RCA-type connectors (available from Radio Shack and other stores that sell stereos) to connect the video and audio outputs of your DV device to the video and audio inputs of your VHS deck. To connect your equipment, follow these steps:

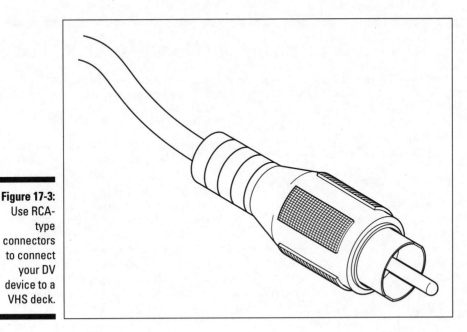

Figure 17-3:
Use RCA-
type
connectors
to connect
your DV
device to a
VHS deck.

1. **Run an RCA connector from the video output of your DV device to the video input of your VHS deck.**

2. **Run another RCA connector from the audio output of your DV device to the audio input of the VHS deck.**

3. **Be sure to hook up the output of your VHS deck to a television so that you can see if the recording is proceeding successfully.**

Don't just assume that recording is taking place. For example, some VHS decks have multiple inputs, sometimes labeled Line 1 and Line 2. You may need to switch these inputs on the remote control of your VHS deck to make sure that you're receiving the signal from your DV deck. Do a test recording and then play back from the VHS deck to make sure you have recorded to tape before proceeding for a final output.

Recording to other kinds of decks

If you're attempting to record to a format other than DV or VHS, you can look into purchasing an Apple-approved, third-party video card (listed at www.apple.com/finalcutpro). This card enables you to output your video from your Final Cut Timeline to your deck. Using a video card, you can output to professional formats, such as Betacam SP and others. Of course, you can use this same card to capture your footage as well.

A word on resolution and compression

If you captured DV video *into* your Final Cut workstation, it is best to *output* it as DV as well. You can certainly use your DV camera or a Sony Media Converter to convert the DV signal to analog and record back to a VHS deck. However, sending that analog signal to a Betacam SP or higher tape formats isn't going to *increase* the resolution of the DV signal.

DV video has a compression of 5:1. This means that DV compresses the video to 1/5th the size of its uncompressed state. This compression is efficient, and the video resolution looks quite good. But sometimes the DV format can show its limitations, such as during recompression with text and other effects. When used with some effects, especially after it's rendered a few times, DV can show blockiness and slight deterioration around the edges of text and objects. Certain broadcasters may not accept DV formats, although their numbers are growing smaller day by day.

If you want to avoid the limitations of DV and work with high-end formats like Digital Betacam or Betacam SP, you're best off purchasing an Apple-approved, third-party card that is meant for capturing high-end video and then outputting your video back to the deck of your choice by using the same card. This path can entail a fair amount of expense because you need to purchase the video card, a high-end tape deck, as well as perhaps faster drives to handle the high data rate. But depending on your needs, this may just be the ticket for you.

Another very common option chosen by Final Cut users is a Sony Media Converter. Sony, as well as numerous other companies, make small and affordable media converters that allow you to convert your FireWire signal to an analog signal. You simply connect the FireWire cable from your computer into your media converter and then connect the analog outputs (often consumer-style RCA connectors) to the tape deck of your choice.

Recording to Tape

When you're ready to record your show back to tape, you can use three main approaches. In the next few sections, we explain the pros and cons of each of these approaches. The three possible recording methods from Final Cut are

- ✔ Playing back from Timeline
- ✔ Printing to video
- ✔ Editing to tape

Each of these methods has some advantages as well as some disadvantages. But more than anything else, the path you take is dictated by the type of equipment you have and the ultimate destination of your tape.

Recording directly from the Timeline

This method may sound just too good to be true, but it is real, and it works like a charm. In this method of recording to tape, you just press the Record button on your deck or camera and play your Timeline in Final Cut. If the settings in Final Cut are correct and all your hardware is set up correctly (see the earlier section "Setting Up for Recording" to verify proper setup), your Timeline records back to tape.

- ✔ **Pros:** The most obvious pro is that this method is fast and easy. In our opinion, this is *the* Official Dummies recording method. You don't have to bother with any dialog boxes and struggle with incomprehensible settings. Your entire Timeline, whatever may be in it, is simply sent to tape. This method also frees you from worrying about timecode or control track on your tape. In some other methods of recording to tape, your tape needs to be *striped* or, in other words, needs to have a timecode or control track laid down on it. Not so when you record from the Timeline. (More on control tracks in the "Insert versus assemble edits" sidebar, elsewhere in this chapter.)

- ✔ **Cons:** The main disadvantage of this method is lack of control. You can't do much to specify if you want to simply edit one shot into a tape that already has a project on it, also known as "insert" editing. You also cannot specify any "leader" elements, such as color bars or slates, to go before your show. If you want bars and other elements in the beginning of your tape, see the print to video method that we describe later in this chapter.

To record directly from the Timeline, perform the following steps:

1. **Open your sequence and render all items by choosing Sequence⇨Render All or by pressing the ⌘+R shortcut.**

   Before you record to tape, you must make sure that all items have been properly rendered. This step ensures that all effects and other items have been rendered and are now ready to go to tape. Without rendering, some effects may not play.

2. **Choose Sequence⇨Mixdown Audio to mix your sequence's audio.**

   This step is critical to avoid dropping frames during your recording process. Processing demands created on the computer by audio tracks in your sequence can often cause frames to be dropped. Mixing down your audio mixes the audio tracks, creates a single file that Final Cut plays during the playback, and avoids any on-the-fly recalculations for audio sampling rates.

3. **Locate your playhead to the start point.**

   Note that you should place your playhead on a blank area of the Timeline just before your project starts. Whatever is under the playhead will be recorded to your tape, so placing the playhead just before your movie starts helps to avoid an abrupt beginning.

4. **Press Record on your deck or camera.**

   Wait a few seconds after you press Record. Some decks take a few seconds to get up to speed, and you don't want your project to start the moment your tape plays. After a few seconds, you're ready to play your Timeline.

5. **Press the spacebar to play your Timeline.**

6. **Press the spacebar to stop playback.**

   When you're done, press the spacebar again to stop playback. You can also press the Stop button on your deck to stop recording.

 If you like, instead of pressing the spacebar for playback, you can choose other playback options from the Mark⇨Play submenu. You have choices such as In to Out, which plays only from any in to out points you may have marked in your sequence, and Reverse, which plays backwards from the current position.

Printing to video

Another option you have to record your Timeline to tape is the Edit⇨Print to Video option. This option lets you add industry standard color bars, countdowns, and slates to the beginning of the tape. In essence, this differs from playing your Timeline in the sense that it allows you to add some elements before and after your sequence:

- ✔ **Pros:** A simple dialog box allows you to add bars, a slate, and other options to your edited movie without adding them into the Timeline. You can also loop your sequence, which may be important in some situations for you. (Venues such as video kiosks and convention booths often require videos to be looped for playback throughout the shows.)

- ✔ **Cons:** The cons in this method are a lack of precise controls, such as *insert editing,* a type of editing that allows you to insert shots with frame accuracy into a tape that already has some material on it.

To print to video, follow these steps:

1. **Render all the items on your Timeline by double-clicking the sequence to open it and choosing Sequence⇨Render All.**

2. **Choose File⇨Print to Video.**

   The Print to Video dialog box appears, as shown in Figure 17-4.

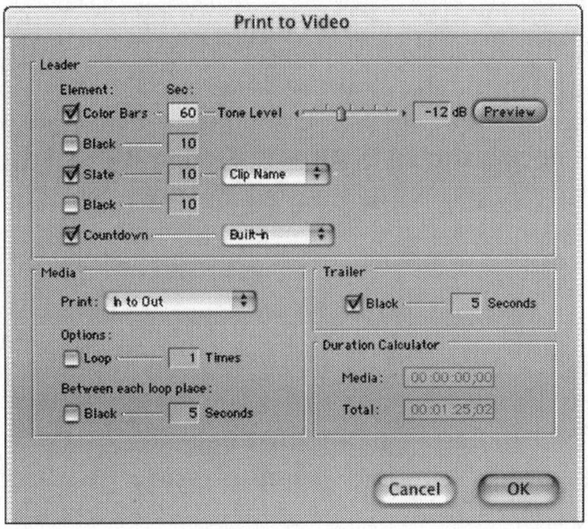

Figure 17-4:
The Print
to Video
dialog box.

3. **Select your options in the Print to Video dialog box.**

   The Print to Video dialog box is divided into Leader, Media, Trailer, and Duration Calculator sections:

   • Leader choices are elements that appear before your movie, whereas the Trailer choices follow your movie. For example, under the Leader area, you can check the Color Bars option and then specify how many seconds of color bars you want. (For more on working with color bars, see Chapter 3.) You can also use these sections to add a few seconds of black at the end or beginning of your tape to avoid an abrupt start or stop of your movie. (We recommend that you use this feature.)

   • The Duration Calculator shows you the final length of the media you have selected when printing to tape. The Media box shows the total length of all your media clips; the Total box displays the Media length plus the length of all extra elements you may have added, such as color bars or black.

   • The choices under the Media section allow you to loop a sequence and the media you want printed to tape: For example, you can print the sequence from the in point to the out point, or loop it 10 times.

4. **Click OK when you're done with your selections.**

5. **When Final Cut displays a message that it is OK to start recording, press Record on your deck.**

   Depending on your choices in the Print to Video dialog box, Final Cut may take some time to render some of these elements. After you get a message to start recording, press Record on your deck. Wait a few seconds and then click OK in the dialog box that gives you the message to start recording. Final Cut begins playing back the leader, and then your show, and finally the trailer choices you made.

In some cases, you may want Final Cut to start recording on your deck and stop recording automatically. If you want to use this feature, choose Final Cut Pro⇨Audio/Video Settings. Under the Device Control tab, edit your Device Control preset by clicking the Edit button. Under the Device Control Preset Editor, turn on the Auto Record and PTV After option and enter a time you prefer in the time field. After Final Cut has edited the video to tape, it stops after the time you specified.

Editing to tape

The third option, called Edit to Tape (under the File menu), lets you do sophisticated, frame-accurate inserts and assemble edits, provided you have the right kind of deck. (See the sidebar later in this chapter entitled, "Insert versus assemble edits.") This option is best reserved for high-end decks, such as the ones that use Betacam SP or Digital Betacam tapes. These decks tend to be quite sophisticated (with a price to match) and are common sight in production companies and broadcast environments.

- ✔ **Pros:** The Edit to Tape method allows for the most sophisticated control of any of the recording options. You can choose to just insert a shot into the middle of a project that exists on tape. You can even select, if you prefer, to edit just the Video or the audio portion of that shot as well. Another advantage to this type of editing is that you can specify exactly in which frame of the tape you want the edit to occur and using what timecode. For any production environment and broadcast situation, this type of control is critical.

- ✔ **Cons:** If there are any disadvantages to Edit to Tape operation, it is that on DV tapes, you cannot perform an insert edit. Also the frame accuracy of the insert edit depends on the frame accuracy of the deck you're using. Often, the decks may have a slight offset and may be a frame or two off from being frame accurate. For the general user, however, the most significant drawback is the high cost of the required equipment.

Performing an Edit to Tape operation

To perform an Edit to Tape operation, follow these steps:

1. **Choose File⇨Edit to Tape.**

   The Edit to Tape window appears. This window looks very much like Final Cut's Canvas window, except for some critical differences. Figure 17-5 shows the Edit to Tape window.

2. **Choose Editing from the drop-down list at the top of the Edit to Tape window to do an Insert Edit. For an Assemble edit, choose Mastering.**

   If you're unsure of the difference between Editing and Mastering, see the sidebar "Insert versus assemble edits," later in this chapter.

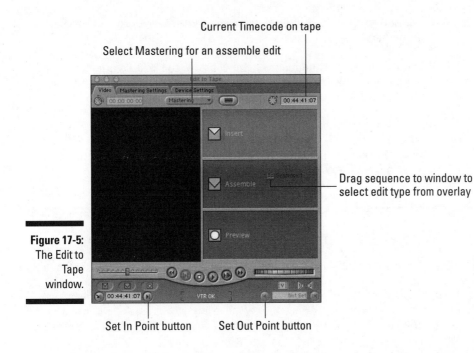

Current Timecode on tape

Select Mastering for an assemble edit

Drag sequence to window to
select edit type from overlay

Figure 17-5:
The Edit to
Tape
window.

Set In Point button   Set Out Point button

3. **Double-click the sequence you want to edit to tape to open it.**

   If you prefer, you can set an in and an out point in your sequence (by
   using the I and the O keys). When you perform the Edit to Tape operation, only the video between the in and out points is edited to tape. In
   the absence of an in or an out point, the entire sequence is edited to
   tape.

4. **Set your in and out points on the tape.**

   By using the Shuttle or the Jog sliders, you can move around on your
   tape and set an in and an out point. (Note that if you're in Mastering
   mode, you can only set an in point. If you're in Editing mode, you can set
   both in and out points.) To set in or out points, cue the tape to the
   desired spot and click the Mark In or Mark Out buttons as appropriate.
   You can also manually set in and out points by entering timecodes in the
   In and Out Timecode fields. If you're about to perform an insert edit, getting these in and out points correctly selected is critical. For a more
   detailed explanation of setting in and out points, see Chapter 6.

5. **If you're in Mastering mode (for an Assemble edit), click the Mastering
   Settings tab at the top of the Edit to Tape window.**

   Under the Mastering Settings tab, you can choose your leader and other
   options for recording. Add leader and trailer elements, such as color
   bars and black, as you desire.

6. **Click and drag your sequence from the Browser window to the Edit to Tape window.**

As you drag your sequence over the window, the Edit Overlay appears. The choices shown in the Edit Overlay are Insert, Assemble, and Preview. Drop your sequence on the appropriate choice.

The Edit to Tape operation begins automatically. You can press the Esc key to cancel an Edit to Tape operation at any time. If any rendering is required before the edit to tape operation, a dialog box appears to step you through the process of rendering.

Insert versus assemble edits

If you are a DV user and work exclusively with DV cameras and decks, you can skip this sidebar and not miss a thing. If, on the other hand, you are working in a broadcast environment and are staring at a Betacam SP or Digital Betacam deck, you should read this sidebar before you attempt to record your video from Final Cut Pro to tape.

You can perform two types of edits when recording your video to tape using the Edit to Tape option in Final Cut: insert and assemble.

During an insert edit, you can select between audio and video tracks (or make edits to both audio and video). An insert edit does *not* record control or timecode tracks. During an assemble edit to tape, on the other hand, *all* tracks are recorded (audio, video, control, and timecode).

But why should you care which tracks are recorded? All videotapes have video and audio tracks on them. Videotapes also have a *control track* and a *timecode* track. A control track is a simple track of tick markers that is used by the deck for maintaining the proper speed. If you use the Print to Video command to record to a

videotape, this control track is also recorded on the tape on its own track. Breaks usually occur in the control track when you stop recording. You want to avoid these breaks on your master tapes at all costs. Broadcast engineers don't like tapes with broken control tracks because they can cause glitches and rolls when played through equipment.

To avoid breaks during an assemble edit, you first need to make sure that you have at least six seconds of tape before the in point of your video. At the end of an assemble edit, you should let the edit run a few seconds longer to avoid any breaks in the tracks.

Here's where it gets tricky: Although an insert edit does *not* record control or timecode tracks on a tape, these tracks must be present on the tape for the insert edit to be successful. For this reason, editors often use *black and coded tapes*. These are tapes that have had black and timecode previously recorded on them. Note that insert edits cannot be performed on DV tapes. For DV tapes, only assemble edits are possible.

Performing insert edits with frame accuracy

Another feature of insert edits in the Edit to Tape window is that they are *frame accurate*. That means that, under proper conditions, you can replace just one shot on your tape that lies in the middle of a recorded project. This feature allows for a greater degree of control — many editors use it to fix issues with their projects. For example, you may have edited down an entire hour-long show to your tape and then, after the fact, decided that you want to replace the video of just one shot in the show, which you've already put on tape. Using the Insert Edit overlay in the Edit to Tape window, you can replace just the video of a single shot on your tape.

However, before you take such a severe step of insert editing onto your master tape, you need to be sure that your Final Cut setup is frame accurate. Video decks can occasionally end up with a slight offset on frame accuracy, and this offset can cause a glitch when you perform an insert edit.

In order to confirm the frame accuracy of your system, you need to create a sequence that consists of a series of single frames. These single frames can be colored slugs or color bars and other clearly identifiable frames. The important item is that each one of these shots needs to have a duration of just one frame.

1. **Line up five of these frames in a sequence, such as a white frame, a frame of color bars, a black frame, a red frame, and a yellow frame.**

2. **Use the Edit to Tape function to perform an insert edit to a specific timecode (such as 1:00:10:00) on a test videotape.**

3. **Slowly jog back on your tape and see which frame has actually edited to the starting point on tape.**

   If a frame is earlier than what you wanted edited to tape, your system has a *drift* of -1 frame. If a frame is later than what you wanted edited to 1:00:10:00, your system has an *offset* of +1.

4. **Next, choose Final Cut Pro⇨Audio/Video settings and then click on the Device Control Presets window.**

5. **Select your preset and click the Edit button.**

6. **In the Device Control Preset editor window, edit the Playback Offset setting to account for the frame offset.**

   Figure 17-6 shows this setting in the lower left of the dialog box. For example, if the offset was -1, enter 1 into the Playback Offset setting. On the other hand if the offset was +1, then enter -1 into the Playback Offset field.

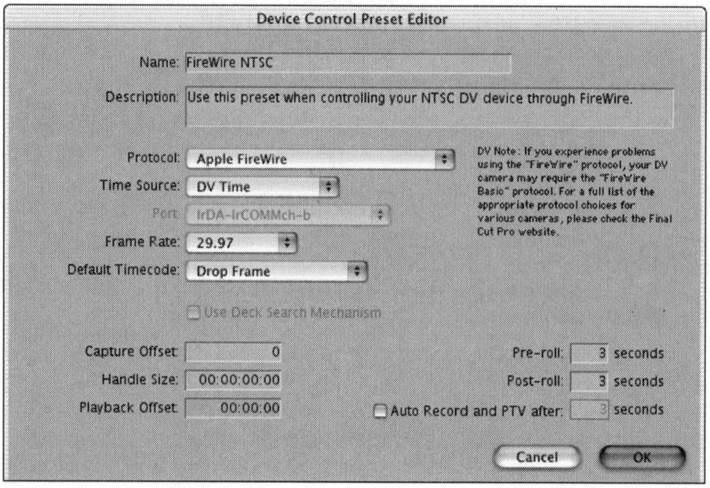

Figure 17-6:
The Device
Control
Preset
Editor.

Now you, too, can be a slick and sophisticated editor doing insert edits with frame accuracy.

Online versus Offline

When working with Final Cut and editing in general, you may come across the terms *offline* and *online.* These terms may impact you because producers may often ask you to work offline in Final Cut. In this section, we explain what all this means.

The terms *offline* and *online* originated a few years back when nonlinear editing (NLE) systems, such as Final Cut, had not achieved data rates high enough for broadcast resolution. In other words, you could capture and edit at a low resolution, using the earlier manifestations of NLEs, but these systems weren't capable of working at resolutions high enough to go directly to broadcast. These may sound like the dark days of video technology, but that was life for many of us.

In those days, the rough, low-resolution edit was considered an *offline* edit. After an offline rough draft was done, the entire show was re-created in an *online* setup. The Online Room could be a very expensive tape-to-tape edit room or just a more expensive NLE that could handle the high data rates for broadcast.

In many ways, these terms perhaps no longer apply because you can do both your offline and online on Final Cut Pro. However, in some cases, the term *online* may still indicate an expensive and very sophisticated Edit Room where super-high-tech features, such as real-time color correction or audio sweetening facilities, may be available.

In some cases, an offline edit may be simply creating a rough cut, which you later want to refine and finalize in an online edit room. This online room may consist of a much higher-end Final Cut Pro system, which uses third-party video cards and allows for higher-quality video. Or, the online room may be a tape-to-tape edit room.

With Final Cut 3, Apple has introduced a new feature called OfflineRT, which stands for Offline Real Time. Using this feature, you can capture video into Final Cut at extremely low resolution, which allows for large quantities of media on small drives, and then edit your project. The effects work in real time when using this feature, hence the term RT. Later, you can recapture just your edited show at a higher resolution. For more on the OfflineRT feature, see Chapter 9.

Another common method for moving from an offline to an online process is the export of Edit Decision Lists. *Edit Decision Lists* (EDLs) are a data record of your edits. EDLs enable you to do your rough cut at home on a basic Final Cut system, but then export the EDL and enter an expensive and high-end editing environment for the refining of your project. With an EDL and your original media, you can re-create your rough edit on a high-end system, adding all the bells, whistles, and polish that a high-end system offers. For more on working with EDLs, see Chapter 3.

Chapter 18

Exporting Your Movie to a Digital File

• •

In This Chapter

▶ Using QuickTime to play your videos

▶ Understanding codecs

▶ Choosing the right data rate

▶ Exporting videos one at a time or by the batch

▶ Compressing video with add-on software

• •

*I*n this multimedia world, many Final Cut projects never wind up on videotape. Instead, they are exported to a digital file so that they can be broadcast on the Internet or played back on DVDs and CD-ROMs. DVDs have become a popular format for watching movies at home, and a DVD is a good way to show someone a high-quality version of your edited video.

The process of preparing material for Web or DVD or CD-ROM is full of confusion and myths. So in this chapter, we tackle some underlying concepts about digital video that many people never grasp.

For instance, a lot of people think that if you export a project into a QuickTime file, it's ready for the Internet. Right? Wrong. Why not? Because raw digital video files are *way* too big to send over the Internet, unless you expect your audience to spend about a week downloading them! That raw video still has to be compressed into a smaller file size, which can also be done in QuickTime, where a lot of the video data is tossed out. The result of this compression is a video file that's not full screen, and not 100 percent sharp, but the compressed video is small enough to be conveniently transmitted via a modem or DSL line.

Later in this chapter, we also show you how to export video from Final Cut Pro for use in add-on software that allows for better compression and data rates.

Working with QuickTime Video

QuickTime has been described as the Swiss Army knife of multimedia. That is quite true, but we think that description sells QuickTime way too short. Most people think that QuickTime is the little QuickTime Player that allows you to play movies on your computer (Figure 18-1). In fact, QuickTime is an entire multimedia architecture. This versatile and vast architecture allows for media creation, delivery, and translation of all kinds. QuickTime consists of over 200 separate components. QuickTime is at the same time a file format and a set of applications, plug-ins, and whatnot that enables users to seamlessly work between multimedia of many types.

Figure 18-1:
The
QuickTime
Player
represents
only the
tip of the
QuickTime
iceberg.

What does all this have to do with Final Cut, and why should you know about QuickTime? Well, first Final Cut is based entirely on the QuickTime architecture. If you are working with Final Cut, you have access to all the components of QuickTime. Don't worry; you won't have to launch any special applications or learn a new interface. QuickTime works seamlessly and transparently, which means that it works behind the scenes and you never know it. And no additional purchase is necessary: If you bought and installed Final Cut, the QuickTime components were installed as well.

In the next few sections, we show you how to use this multimedia Swiss Army knife to pry open just about anything . . . er, to take the movies that you edited in Final Cut and prepare them for all kinds of other formats, such as Web streaming, CD-ROM or DVD-ROM playback, and any other multimedia use you can think up for your video.

Getting to Know Codecs

If you are going to be preparing your video for the Web or CD-ROM, the word *codec* will fast become part of your vocabulary. Video files, as they exist when you edit them in Final Cut, are simply too large to stream over the Web or even to download in a reasonable amount of time. (*Streaming* means to send video as a continuous stream that is played back on the fly as it's being transmitted, as opposed to a *download*, where the viewer's computer waits to begin playback until the entire movie has been transmitted to the viewer's hard drive.) Hence, compression is used to reduce the size of the video files and, at the same time, to preserve as much of the quality as possible. You use QuickTime for compressing and selecting your codec as well.

The components that compress the video are called codecs. The word *codec* is short for compression/decompression. There are codecs for audio and video. Also, there are many kinds of codecs: Some are meant for streaming, whereas others are intended strictly for capturing and playing back video. Some codecs are hardware-based, but those are outside the scope of this book. We focus on software-based codecs in this chapter. Which codec you choose and how you use it has impact on the final outcome of your compression, and throughout this chapter, we tell you some of the considerations you need to think about before you decide which codec you want to use.

For better video compression, keep the backgrounds of your shots simple and use a tripod. If you're interested in why this helps, see the sidebar "Shooting with compression in mind."

Because so many codecs are available, we briefly cover a few basic ones that you'll need to choose from when preparing your material. Bear in mind that this tour of the codecs is done in the context of preparing your video for Web streaming or CD-ROM playback. We say that because many video codecs are designed for video capture and playback but are not suitable for streaming or low-data rate playback, such as the type needed for CD-ROMs. Data rates are important because you can use very high data rates for video that plays in your computer. But CD-ROMs or DVDs as well as the Internet require low data rates. We discuss data rates later in this chapter.

If you're working on a Mac and you're using Final Cut and QuickTime, many video and audio codecs are automatically loaded onto your computer. Later in this chapter, we show you where in the export process you select the proper codec. Many companies make and sell codecs that you can purchase and install on your Mac. After installing (which is simply dragging the codecs to your System folder) these codecs, they're then available through the usual QuickTime export methods, which we outline later in this chapter.

Looking at the Video Codecs

The goal of a video codec is to compress your video down to a data rate so that it can be played on the Web or on a CD-ROM or DVD. The trick for the codec is to maintain as much of the quality as possible. When creating movies for the Web, be aware of the difference between streaming and downloading a movie. Streaming occurs as an instant start and playback of video over the Web. Downloading requires the users to download the file to their computers first. QuickTime also has a third option called "Fast Start." Fast Start is something that lies in between streaming and downloading. Fast Start movies begin playing as they download to your drive.

Here are some of the most common codecs used for compressing video:

- **Sorenson Video:** Sorenson is the codec of choice for Apple Computer and for good reason. By far one of the best codecs, Sorenson Video delivers extremely good quality and very small data rates. *Data rate* is simply defined as the amount of data that the compressed video passes every second through the computer or the modem that is being used. When we first used Sorenson Video, we were surprised how small a data rate we could use, while still managing to get a decent image of our compressed movies.

  Sorenson comes in two flavors: the basic and the Developer Edition. The basic version is free, and if you have installed Final Cut successfully on your computer, you already have the basic version. The Developer Edition costs around $299 and has what's called Variable Data Rate (VBR), which is slower when it comes to compressing video because it takes one pass to analyze the video and another to compress it, but the image quality is simply wonderful. If you are serious about compressing for the Web or CD-ROM or DVD playback, be sure to get the Developer Edition. It is well worth the money.

- **Cinepak:** Cinepak used to be the default codec for Apple Computers. This is now an aging codec that still performs quite well. This codec is ideal for playback on slower computers. Another nice feature of Cinepak is that it plays on the Windows platform without much trouble.

- **H.263:** Because this codec was created for video conferencing, it's an extremely efficient and smart codec that can deliver quality. Under certain conditions, such as video with high motion, we've tested Sorenson and H.263, and we've noticed that H.263 comes out looking a whole lot better. Definitely a codec to consider.

- **MPEG-1:** MPEG stands for Motion Pictures Experts Group, and it represents a new type of codec. This codec has good quality, but it is generally not a preferred choice for Web streaming. (The reasons have to do with how MPEG creates intermediate frames that do not work well over the low bandwidth available through modems.) It is, however, a good choice if you want the audience to download the video and then play it off their computer drives.

✔ **MPEG-2:** MPEG-2 is becoming popular because it is used for compressing movies for DVD playback. Although this codec isn't well suited for Web streaming, it does provide high quality at DVD playback rates. MPEG type compressions are ill suited for Web streaming because the type of compression it uses creates intermediate frames that require other full frames to be present.

Looking at the Audio Codecs

Your Mac already has numerous audio codecs installed in it. These codecs, like others, are accessible via the QuickTime dialog box, which we guide you through later. Many companies also sell advanced versions of their audio codecs that are useful for professional work. You can purchase and install these codecs, which you can then access via the QuickTime dialog box.

Here are some of the more common codecs for compressing audio:

✔ **QDesign music codec:** This is the codec of choice if you have instrumental music to compress. This codec can produce extremely high-quality files and still maintain a data rate so small that you can stream it over a very slow (14.4 Kbps) modem. Using music with vocals in it is also fine with this codec, but avoid it if you have just voice to compress.

✔ **Qualcomm PureVoice:** If you have voices in your file that you want to compress, use the Qualcomm PureVoice codec. It works to create very small and streamable files at very low data rates. This codec is best reserved for the human voice; it doesn't work well with music.

✔ **MP3:** MP3 is short for MPEG Layer 3 audio. MP3 music files have become the big thing on the Web in the last few years. This is a great codec for compressing music files to a small size, but it is not an ideal codec for streaming on the Web. Streaming MP3s causes chokes and skips. However, for downloading over the Web, MP3s work very well.

✔ **IMA:** A decent audio codec that works easily on both the Mac and Windows machines, IMA is good for older machines, but it creates slightly larger files because of its low compression.

Shooting with compression in mind

Compression is a sophisticated and complex science, and codecs perform very tricky computations at blinding speeds. Knowing how video codecs work can actually help you shoot material for better compression. Video codecs perform *spatial* and *temporal* compression. Spatial compression means that a codec takes large areas of similar color and compresses them down to tiny numbers. Codecs love large areas of solid colors. If you are preparing to shoot a video that will later be compressed for the Web, make sure that the subject of your video is not sitting in front of a complex or patterned background. Keeping the background simple helps the codec to work more efficiently and to create smaller video files of high quality.

Video codecs also do temporal encoding; that is, they only save a complete frame every so often. They mostly save the areas of the image that are changing between those complete frames. If a shot stays the same with just a person's head moving in the frame, that shot is going to compress well. If, however, you use a handheld camera and the framing of the shot keeps changing every second, then that shot is going to make the codec work a whole lot harder and create low-quality files that may also be quite large. In short, for best results, keep your background simple and use a tripod to minimize change from frame to frame.

Knowing Your Data Rates

Before we plunge into the act of exporting movies from Final Cut, you need to know about one more critical item — data rates. Imagine that each modem hooked up to the Internet is a pipeline. Think of slow modems (14.4K for example) as thin pipelines and fast modems (cable and DSL) as fat pipelines. Each of these pipelines can handle a certain data rate. If your compressed movie goes above the data rate, proper playback of the movie is doubtful. The movie may choke and stutter during playback or even stop playing altogether.

Knowing the limits of your data rates is key to creating movies that play efficiently and well. In addition to a maximum data rate, each pipeline (modem on the Internet) also has a preferred frame size for compressed movies. When you export your movie from Final Cut into QuickTime, you can select a data rate for it. You need to stick with the proper data rate and the frame size for the modem type you expect your audience to use if you want your streaming movie to play correctly. To be on the safe side, cater to the slowest modem rate you expect your viewers to have. That way, you cover any faster connections as well.

Table 18-1 shows the rates and frame sizes for various types of Internet connections. When exporting a QuickTime movie from Final Cut, you can control the frame size of your final output.

Table 18-1	Data Rates for Common Internet Connections		
Connection Type	Data Rate in Kilobits per Second	Data Rate in Kilobytes per Second	Frame Size
28.8 Kbps	20 Kbps	2.5 KBps	160 x 120 pixels
56.6 Kbps	40 Kbps	5 KBps	160 x 120 pixels
ISDN	96 Kbps	12 KBps	192 x 144 pixels
DSL	140 Kbps	17 KBps	240 x 180 pixels
T1	160 Kbps	20 KBps	240 x 180 pixels
Cable Modems	1000 Kbps	125 KBps	320 X 240 pixels

If you are referring to other literature or learning about streaming video on the Web, be aware that data rates are often listed in both Kbps (kilo*bits* per second) and KBps (Kilo*bytes* per second). The difference between bits and bytes is critical: *A byte is 8 times larger than a bit.* If you see rates listed in KBps, multiply the number by 8 to get Kbps. If however you see data rates reported as Kbps, divide the number by 8 to get KBps.

The rates for modems are actually lower than advertised. For example, rarely does your 56K modem even approach the 56 Kbps setting. This has to do with the analog phone lines that modems use and the overhead placed by both your computer's software and the server software.

Export Away!

Final Cut enables you to export from the sequence video files that are compressed for various kinds of deliveries. You can also select and export files from the Browser. For example, after editing and finishing your DV-based video, you can then compress it for playback on a CD-ROM or on the Web.

Follow these steps to export a video for CD-ROM or the Web from Final Cut Pro:

1. **In Final Cut, select a clip or a sequence in the Browser by clicking it.**

2. **Choose File⇨Export⇨QuickTime.**

   The Save dialog box appears, as shown in Figure 18-2.

3. **In the Where drop-down list, indicate where you want to save the exported file and then type a name for your movie in the Save As box.**

   If you are going to be embedding this movie into an html document for the Web, be sure to give your movie a .mov extension. It is generally a good idea to add the .mov extension at all times when exporting for the Web or the CD-ROM.

4. **From the Format drop-down list, choose QuickTime Movie.**

5. **Select a setting from the Use drop-down list.**

   The settings under the Use menu are divided into Streaming and CD-ROM categories. The CD-ROM settings are fairly easy to understand. You can choose a 1X or a 2X CD-ROM and choose a Sorenson or Cinepak codec. The 1X or 2X indicates the speed of your intended audience's CD-ROM drive. (CD-ROM drives are rated for single speed (1X), double speed (2X), and so on.) For more about the two codecs, see the earlier section "Looking at the Video Codecs."

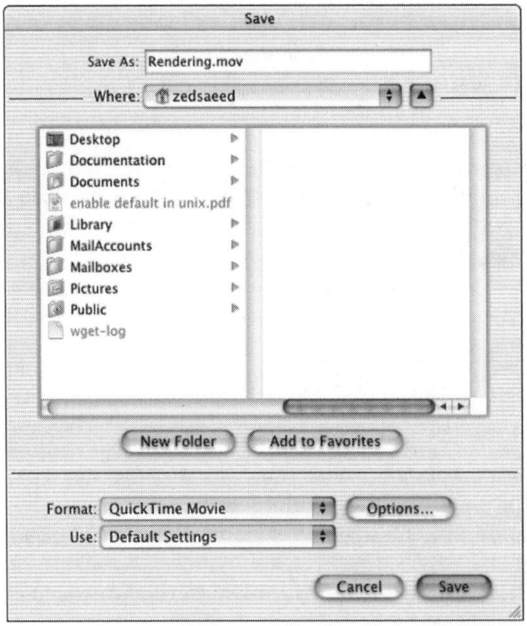

Figure 18-2:
The Save
dialog box.

For the streaming settings, you first have to decide on a data rate (refer to Table 18-1). Next you should think about whether your video has music or voice and about the type of motion present in your video.

Final Cut helps you by suggesting the best settings for various types of movies in the streaming settings pop-up box shown in Figure 18-3. For example, say you are exporting a music video with lots of quick shots and motion in the frame, with only music (as opposed to vocals) in the soundtrack. Your likely audience uses a 56 Kbps modem. In this situation, you select the Streaming 40kbps-Music-High Motion setting. If your video contains voice and music, select one of the music choices.

6. Click the Options button to access the codec and size options.

The Movie Settings dialog box appears, as shown in Figure 18-4.

Note that if you have selected a setting in the Use menu in the previous step, then Step 6 is not necessary. Only resort to Step 6 if you have a better understanding of your requirements and want to skip the presets offered in the Use menu.

Final Cut helps you select the right settings for your movie

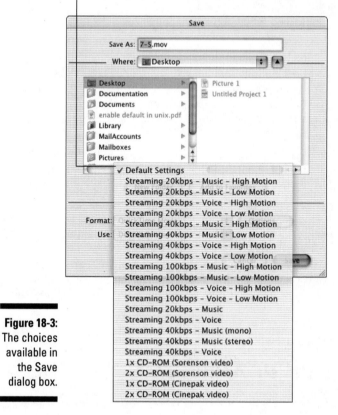

Figure 18-3:
The choices available in the Save dialog box.

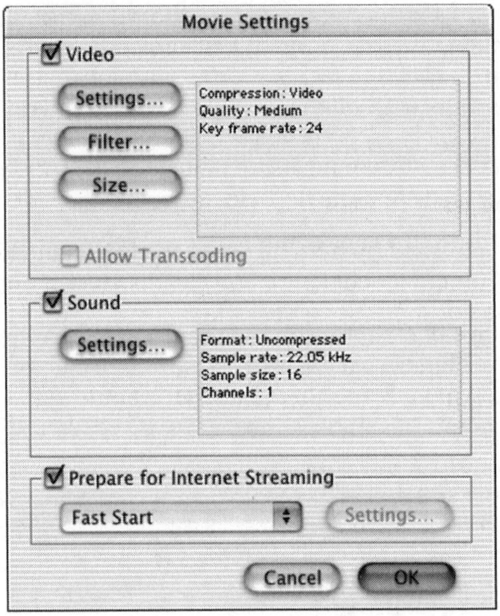

Figure 18-4:
The Movie
Settings
dialog box.

The Movie Settings dialog box enables you to custom select video and audio settings. For example, click the Settings button inside the Movie Settings dialog box, and you get the Compression Settings choices. Here, under the Compressor menu, you can select the codec of your liking, such as Sorenson and others.

In the Movie Settings dialog box, you can click the Size button and then select the Use Custom Size option. This option enables you to set the width and height of your movie.

After selecting the desired settings, click OK in the Movie Settings dialog box.

7. **When you are ready to export the movie, click Save.**

The progress of your export appears in a status bar. You can cancel this export anytime by pressing the Esc key. To play your movie, double-click the movie on your desktop after it has been exported and view it in the QuickTime player.

Exporting a Batch of Movies

Instead of exporting one movie at a time, you can export a batch of movies. This can help you set up a queue, which can export your movies while you do something else, like shopping for a director's chair. Exporting by the batch is a good idea if you have a lot of movies to export because exporting several movies one at a time can be time-consuming.

To batch export, follow these steps:

1. **Select the items you want to export in the Browser.**

   You can select multiple clips by holding down the Command key and clicking each clip (Command+clicking). You can also select clips or sequences within one or more open projects.

2. **Choose File⇨Batch Export.**

   The Export Queue window appears displaying your selected items, as shown in Figure 18-5. A new bin is automatically created for each batch of your selections. Settings in the Export Queue are applied on a bin-by-bin basis, so the same settings apply to all the clips in a particular bin. If the default bin structure is not to your liking, you can create new bins by choosing File⇨New⇨Bin and move items between them.

The status of your export is shown here

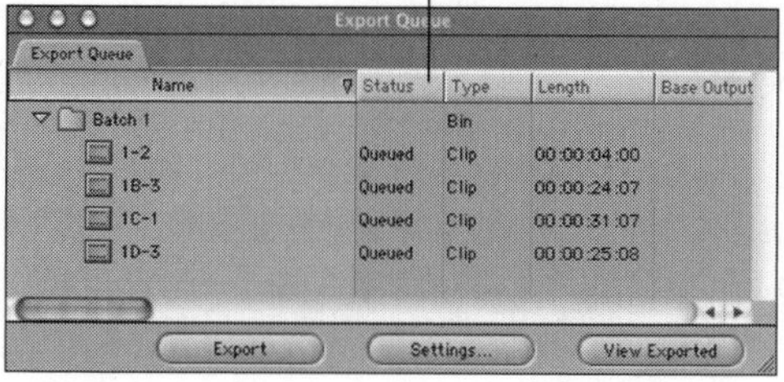

Figure 18-5:
The Export
Queue
window.

3. **Select a bin in the Queue and click the Settings button at the bottom of the Export Queue window.**

   The Batch settings window appears, as shown in Figure 18-6.

4. **Click the Set Destination button in the Settings window and select a location to save the exported files.**

5. **Select QuickTime from the Format drop-down menu in the Batch settings window.**

6. **Use the Settings drop-down menu in the Batch settings window to select the settings for your final compressed movie.**

   The choices under the Settings menu are divided into Streaming and CD-ROM categories. For the CD-ROM settings, you can choose a 1X or a 2X CD-ROM and choose a Sorenson or Cinepak codec.

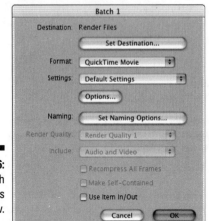

Figure 18-6:
The Batch
settings
window.

For the streaming settings, you need to decide on a data rate, and then choose whether your video has music or voice and the type of motion present in your video. For example, say your movie basically shows someone talking (with very little motion occurring in the frame) and only voice is in the soundtrack. If you want to stream it over a 28.8 Kbps modem, you select the Streaming 20kbps-Voice-Low Motion setting.

If you need to select a codec, other than Sorensen or Cinepak, use the Options button in the Settings window. Clicking the Options button takes you to the Movie Settings window where you can select a codec (under Settings button) and choose a size (by using the Size button).

7. **In the Batch settings window, you can click the Set Naming Options button and choose how you want to name your final exports.**

   For example, you can check the Add Custom Extension and type **.mov** if you are embedding your movie in an HTML document on the Web.

8. **Check the Use Item In/Out box in the Batch settings window if you want to export the portions of a clip or sequence that you have previously marked with in or out points.**

   You have the choice of marking in and out points in your clip or the sequence, pressing the I and O keys. In absence of in and out points, the entire clip or the sequence is exported. Note that marking the in and out points is a process that needs to take place before you take this series of steps to Batch Export.

9. **Click OK to close the dialog box.**

10. **To begin a Batch Export, select the bin or bins you want to export in the Export Queue dialog box by clicking them and then clicking the Export button.**

You can also select individual items within bins in the Export Queue window and then press the Export button.

The progress of your exports is displayed in a dialog box that appears. You can click Cancel or press the Esc key to end your export at any time. When an item is exported, the status of the item changes to Done in the Status column of the Export Queue window.

Improving Your Exports with Add-On Software

Final Cut seems to have it all: You can capture, add titles and effects of all kinds, record back to tape, and even export to the Web or to a CD-ROM or DVD. But can one piece of software do it all in the best manner possible? The answer is, well, not quite. Many other software developers out there saw the need for efficient and fast applications that enable you to export movies for the Web, and have answered the need with solutions of their own.

If you plan to do a few exports here and there, you may want to stay with Final Cut. If, however, you're setting up a Web or a CD-ROM operation and you will be exporting and compressing all day long, we suggest looking at other options.

In the next few sections, we briefly cover one such product, Cleaner 5 EZ, an application that has become very popular for exporting material for the Web and CD-ROM playback. We also talk about how to properly export your video to work with third-party products.

Exporting video for add-on software

Before you can start working with third-party software to compress video, you first need to export your video from Final Cut to these applications.

In this section, we show you how to export from Final Cut in preparation for working with add-on software that you can purchase.

After you have exported a movie from Final Cut, this movie can then be brought into one of the many applications available for Web and CD-ROM compression and prepared properly.

To export from Final Cut, follow these steps:

1. **Select your clip or sequence in the Browser and then choose File⇨Export⇨Final Cut Pro Movie.**

   The Save dialog box appears, as shown in Figure 18-7.

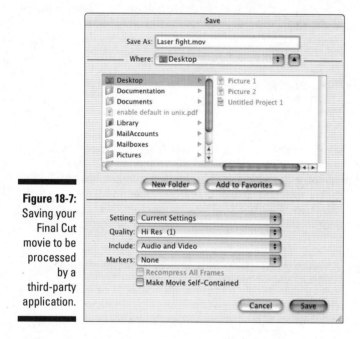

Figure 18-7:
Saving your
Final Cut
movie to be
processed
by a
third-party
application.

2. **Select Current Settings in the Setting drop-down list.**

3. **Choose Hi Res (1) in the Quality drop-down list.**

4. **Choose which tracks you want to export in the Include drop-down list.**

   Here you can elect to export just Video Only or Audio Only, or Audio and Video.

5. **Be sure to leave the Make Movie Self-Contained option unchecked.**

   Leaving the Make Movie Self-Contained setting unchecked creates a reference movie file. A *reference* movie is a movie that remains linked to the original media that created it, as opposed to a *self-contained* movie, which is just that, self-contained. Reference movies export much faster and have a smaller file size than self-contained movies. You can drag reference files directly into a third-party Web compression application (such as Cleaner 5 EZ) like any other movie file. Note, however, that if you move this reference file to another workstation, the reference file needs the media files that it's dependent on in order to play correctly.

So, be careful not to delete or move any media files that this reference file may link to.

Self-contained movies, on the other hand, are much larger in size but have the advantage of not being dependent on the original media files. Self-contained movies can be moved to a different workstation without any playback problems.

6. **Name your exported file in the Save As box, select a location in the Where box, and click the Save button.**

   After the export process is complete, you can move the exported movie file from the Mac desktop into any add-on application.

To see how one such application, Cleaner 5 EZ, works, read on.

Looking at Cleaner 5 EZ

Media Cleaner Pro (now called Cleaner 5) has long been the standard third-party application for compressing movies for the Web. Over the last several years, it has been reinvented many times. The full version is known as Cleaner 5, an expensive and sophisticated application. A basic and easy-to-use version is known as Cleaner 5 EZ. The EZ version is a bit clunky (it has no MPEG support, it is slow, and has no batch features) but is a good one to get started with for your basic needs. In the next few steps, we explain just how easy the EZ version really is when you want to prepare your movies for the Web:

1. **Follow the manufacturer's instructions for installing Cleaner 5 EZ.**

   An application icon for Cleaner 5 EZ is automatically placed on your desktop as part of installation.

2. **Start Cleaner 5 EZ by double-clicking its application icon.**

   The project window for the Cleaner 5 EZ appears.

3. **Drag and drop the exported Final Cut Pro movie from your desktop (or wherever you saved it after export) to the Cleaner 5 EZ project window.**

   The first frame of the movie appears in the small window, as shown in Figure 18-8.

4. **From the Setting drop-down menu in the project window, choose Settings Wizard.**

   The first panel in the Settings Wizard appears. This is the Delivery Medium panel.

Figure 18-8:
The main
project
window for
Cleaner EZ.

5. **Click in the radio button that corresponds to the option you want.**

   Each choice is well explained in the accompanying text. (This is after all the EZ version!) For this example, we choose WWW because we want to prepare this movie to stream for the Web.

6. **Click the Continue button in the lower right when you're done.**

   The Format panel appears.

7. **Select from the three main format choices: QuickTime, Real, or Windows Media.**

   Features for each format are described in detail. For this example, we selected QuickTime. This panel explains the merits of each format choice.

8. **Click the Continue button in the lower right after you make your choice.**

   The Delivery Style panel is displayed, as shown in Figure 18-9.

9. **Choose a delivery style from your three choices: real-time streaming or two flavors of progressive streaming.**

   For this example, we chose the *Progressive Streaming (high quality)* setting based on the descriptions in this box because the clip is fairly short.

   Real-time streaming is, of course, just that. Your movies stream in real time. In progressive streaming, the movie plays as it downloads.

10. **Click the Continue button in the lower right when you're done.**

    The Alternates panel appears next.

11. **Choose the type of Internet connection you expect your audience to have.**

We picked the 56 Kbps modem for this example because most Web users have this type of connection. Of course, the 56 Kbps works for anyone who has a slower or a faster modem. Viewers with slow modems will experience a slight delay, whereas users with 56K or higher speed modems will experience no delay at all.

12. **Click the Continue button in the lower right when you are done.**

    The Soundtrack panel, which appears next, has two sections.

13. **In the top panel of the Soundtrack window, choose whether the audio or the video portion of your movie gets priority.**

    The top section helps decide the trade-off between image and sound quality. To have better sound, you have to sacrifice some video quality and vice versa.

14. **In the lower panel, choose what type of soundtrack you have in your movie.**

    The lower section allows you to choose the type of audio codec that will be used to compress your final movie. The choices here are Soundtrack Is Mostly Speech, Soundtrack Is Mostly Music, and Soundtrack Contains Range of Material.

    Note that, as you make these choices, the Cleaner EZ Wizard is automatically selecting the ideal codec and streaming settings for you.

15. **Click the Continue button in the lower right when you're done.**

    This brings up the Optimize panel.

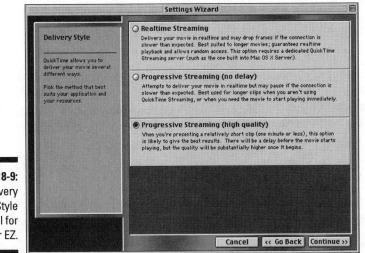

Figure 18-9:
The Delivery Style panel for Cleaner EZ.

16. **Select a motion rate from the list of choices.**

    The choices in the Optimize panel include High-Quality Image, Smooth Motion, Large Image, and Slide Show.

    Your choices in the Optimize panel help balance the image quality against the frame rate that you get. In this panel, we chose Smooth Motion because, as the summary explains, we place the need for smooth motion over image quality.

17. **Click the Continue button to bring up the Options panel.**

    The Options panel, shown in Figure 18-10, is next, where you can select numerous options for your final movie.

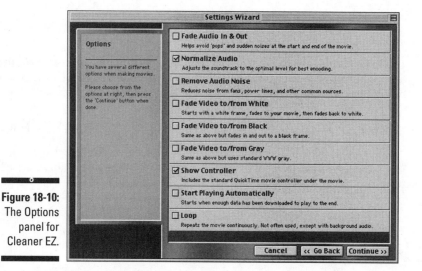

Figure 18-10:
The Options panel for Cleaner EZ.

For example, you can choose to have a video or an audio track fade up and fade out. Other options include the choice to see the QuickTime Movie controller in the playback window, and whether you want to loop your movie to play over and over again.

18. **Click the Continue button in the lower right.**

    The last panel, That's It!, appears. The EZ Wizard summarizes your choices in this panel.

    Here, you can also change any of these settings you see by simply using the pull-down menus or entering new numbers in fields such as Dimensions and Frame Rate.

19. **When you are satisfied with the settings, click the Finish button.**

    This step brings you back at the main window of the Cleaner 5 EZ project window.

20. **Click Start to begin compressing your movie.**

    The Save dialog box appears.

21. **Select a name and destination for your final movie and click the Save button.**

    Sit back and relax as Cleaner EZ begins the compression for your movie in the Output window.

    Cleaner 5 EZ beeps when the movie is done.

    Play your final movie in the Output window by clicking the small right-pointing arrow (also known as the Play button).

Part VI
Part of Tens

The 5th Wave   By Rich Tennant

THE NEW HOLLYWOOD

CUT! PASTE!

In this part . . .

Here, we offer some ten-odd tips for how to manage long projects in Final Cut: everything from establishing a logical bin structure to naming clips intelligently. We also serve up ten simple things you can do to become a more capable Final Cut editor, from honing your creative and technical know-how to upgrading your current Mac setup.

Chapter 19

Almost Ten Tips for Managing Big Projects

● ●

In This Chapter

▶ Keeping media organized on your hard drive

▶ Creating bins like they're going outta style

▶ Naming clips

▶ Documenting clips

▶ Finding clips fast

▶ Keeping your bearings with markers

▶ Nesting sequences into bigger ones

▶ Saving on hard drive space

● ●

*O*ne of the nice things about Final Cut is that it's really good at cutting projects as short as a 30-second TV commercial or as long as a feature film. But if you're working on longer-form projects (features and documentaries especially come to mind), you see that some particular challenges arise: For example, getting overwhelmed by all the media you'll keep at your disposal (possibly *thousands* of separate video and audio clips!) is easy, and running low on hard drive space trying to keep all that media online is easy, too. So here are a few tips to keep those big projects under control. We cover each of these topics in detail elsewhere, but it makes sense to point them out again, in one place, with big projects in mind.

Keep Your Media Organized

After you import your media into the Browser, Final Cut remembers where on your hard drives each clip of media really is — that is, you only have to find a clip in the Browser to work with it, rather than fishing through lots of folders on your hard drive for the right file. That's a nice feature, but it doesn't mean you should get lazy or careless about where you store the original media clips on your hard drive — that is, they shouldn't be strewn in all sorts of random folders on your drive (or on multiple drives) because at some point, you'll probably need to work with those media files outside of Final Cut. For instance, maybe you need to clear off some space on your hard drive without affecting your movie's media — if the media is stored in a variety of folders and mixed in with unrelated media or files, figuring out what files can stay or go is a lot harder (and accidentally deleting some media is a lot easier). Here are a couple of tips for organizing the media files on your drive:

- **Keep media files for different projects in different folders or on different hard drives:** Don't capture media for Film A into Film B's folder. (You can target these media folders when you capture — see Chapter 3.)

- **Keep a project's media files in a single folder:** Nesting related folders within a master folder — for instance, in your Film A folder, you may have subfolders for Video, Sound, Music, and Dialogue — is fine, but keeping all related files and folders in a master folder is a good idea.

- **Divide media logically between multiple drives:** Keeping your media on a single hard drive is always nice, but if you have too much media, try to organize the drives in a logical way — for instance, maybe keep Scenes 1–50 on Drive A, 51–100 on Drive B, and so on.

- **Keep your source tapes on hand and organized:** Just because you've captured video and audio from your original tapes doesn't mean that you should let those tapes out of your sight. You may need them to do your online edit, or you may need them in case some of your captured media is lost. (Occasionally, QuickTime files get corrupted, or your entire hard drive could crash.) To make life easier on yourself, keep your source tapes clearly labeled, and store them in a safe secure place that you can easily get to.

Use Bins, Lotsa Bins!

When you're importing media clips, don't let them clutter up the Browser window — the more clips you have there, the harder it gets to find any particular one (check out Figure 19-1). Instead, create bins (folders) for each of your project's scenes (for instance, Scene 1, Scene 2, Scene 3, and so on) and store your video and audio clips in their scene's bin. (If your film doesn't have traditional scenes, figure out some other themes you can use to organize clips by.) If you're dealing with lots of clips per scene, you might even create sub-bins within your Scene bins — say, for video, music, dialogue, and sound effects.

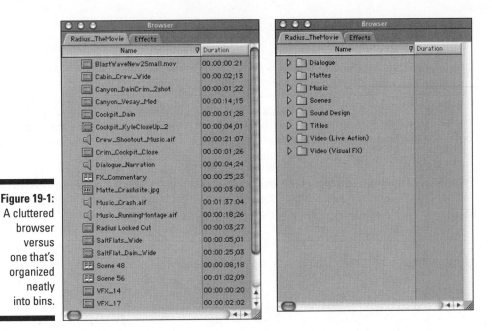

Figure 19-1:
A cluttered browser versus one that's organized neatly into bins.

You can import a clip directly into the bin of your choice, rather than importing straight to the Browser and *then* dragging the clip into a bin. Just open a bin in its own window by double-clicking it; then choose File⇨Import to send a clip right into that window.

You can drag files and folders directly from your Mac's desktop to the bin of your choice in the Browser.

Keep Your Clip Names Informative

Remember: When importing or capturing media, try to name your clips in a way that says as much as possible about them in a consistent, systematic way. If you're disciplined about doing this, you make it a lot easier to find a given clip because a quick look at its name can tell you a lot about it. For instance, don't just name one clip "Dan's Close-up at the Dinner Table," and then name another clip "Everyone at the Dinner Table," and name a third clip "Medium shot of Pam." Instead, try "DinnerTable_Dan_Closeup," "DinnerTable_Pam_Medium," and "DinnerTable_Group_Wideshot." Naming your clips with this kind of systematic approach (you're free to use your own systems, of course) makes spotting media, either in the Browser or after it's on the Timeline, easy.

Document Your Clips

Besides naming clips, Final Cut lets you thoroughly document each clip with an FBI-like dossier — for example, you can detail a clip's scene and its take, describe its contents, add several additional comment lines, apply labels to it (for "best take," "alternate shot" and so on), and more. To do so, just select the clip in the Browser, choose Edit⇨Item Properties, and click the Logging Info tab (as shown in Figure 19-2).

Of course, we're the first to admit that documenting your clips to this extent is a bit of a pain (you're an editor, not a librarian!), and we wouldn't blame you if you didn't go *all out*. But the fact is that doing a little advance legwork here can save you a lot of time when you're sifting through hundreds of clips for just the right one: For instance, you can quickly organize the Browser to show clips by their labels or find clips (using Final Cut's Find feature) by looking for keywords in your description or comments. See Chapter 5 for more about labeling and documenting clips.

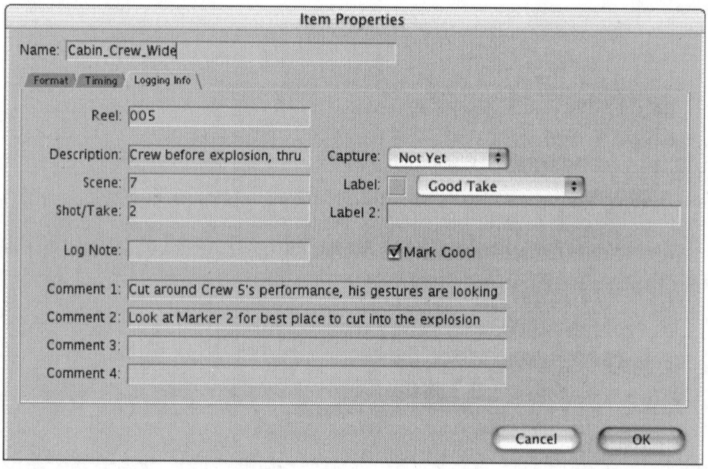

Figure 19-2:
Use the Item
Properties
box to
document
important
clips.

Name:	Cabin_Crew_Wide

Format Timing Logging Info

Reel: 005
Description: Crew before explosion, thru   Capture: Not Yet
Scene: 7   Label: Good Take
Shot/Take: 2   Label 2:
Log Note: ☑ Mark Good
Comment 1: Cut around Crew 5's performance, his gestures are looking
Comment 2: Look at Marker 2 for best place to cut into the explosion
Comment 3:
Comment 4:

Cancel   OK

Use the Find Feature

Final Cut's Find feature is incredibly powerful and can pull the proverbial needle out of a haystack when you're looking for a particular clip, or group of clips, without sifting through a sea of endless bins and unrelated clips (something any editor who works on long projects can definitely appreciate).

To search for media, just make sure the Browser window is active and then choose Edit➪Find. The Find dialog box, shown in Figure 19-3, lets you specify tons of different search criteria — you can search for keywords in a media clip's name, description, or comments (another reason why you should carefully name and document your clips!), or by labels you've applied, or by the clip's scene, log tape, or any number of other criteria (even the compression codec the clip uses or its frame size). You can also combine different search results — for example, finding only the clips in scenes 48 and 56 that you labeled as best or good takes and that feature the actress called Pam.

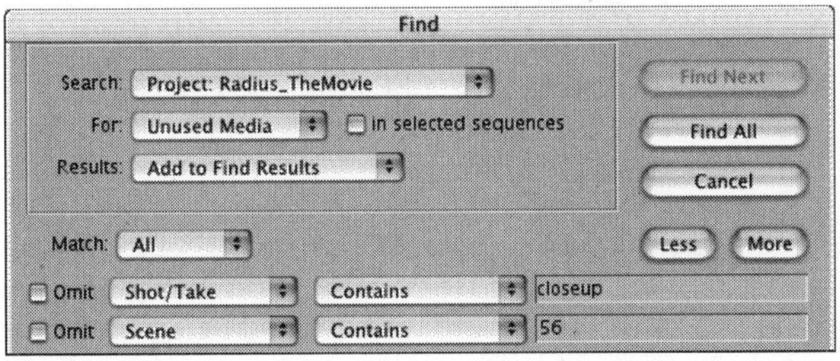

Figure 19-3:
Final
Cut's Find
dialog box.

Stay Oriented with Markers

You can place markers to highlight important moments in your movie or clips, which makes finding them in a hurry easier for you.

You can set two kinds of markers. The first variety is a Timeline marker, which you place in your Timeline sequence (maybe at the beginning of a new scene on the Timeline or at some notable event within a scene), as shown in Figure 19-4. The second variety is a clip marker, which you set within a single clip. Clip markers are especially handy for breaking up long clips into more manageable morsels — for instance, when you set markers within a clip, each marker becomes a subclip of the master clip, and you can open a subclip individually by clicking it in the Browser (as shown in Figure 19-5) or move it exclusively to the Timeline.

Figure 19-4:
Sequence
markers on
the Timeline.

Markers in the Browser

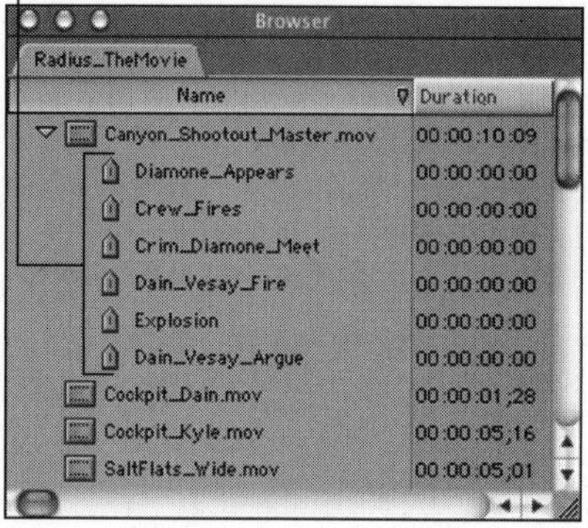

Figure 19-5:
A clip's
markers are
recognized
in the
Browser.

You set Timeline markers in the Timeline window and clip markers while looking at a clip in the Viewer window. Just position either window's playhead at a frame you'd like to mark and then press M on your keyboard. (You see a marker symbol appear at that point, as shown in Figure 19-4.) To give the marker a name, choose Mark➪Markers➪Edit. To search for Timeline markers, hold down the Control key, click the Timecode box (refer to Figure 19-4), and choose the marker you want to jump to from the pop-up menu that appears. To search for clip markers, you can use Final Cut's Find feature. Make the Timeline window active and choose Edit➪Find to search for markers in clips already on the Timeline, or make the Browser window active and choose Edit➪Find to search through all your project clips.

So much for your crash course in markers. To learn more about these handy little tools, check out Chapter 8.

Break Scenes into Sequences and Nest 'em Together

If you're working on a long project — anything more than 30 minutes, really — don't edit it all together in a single Timeline sequence. You'll find yourself getting disoriented easily when you're staring at an endless string of clips on the Timeline; also, the longer your sequence is, the more scrolling and zooming in and out you'll do.

Instead, break down a big film into smaller scenes (or acts, or some other kind of division) and build each of those smaller morsels in its own Timeline sequence. Then, when you want to watch your whole film, you can easily assemble it together by creating yet another sequence (this will be your master sequence) and then by nesting all your scene sequences into the new one — check out Figure 19-6. In other words, just drag your scene sequences from the Browser window into the master sequence (as if they were individual media clips) and arrange them on the Timeline in the order you'd like them to play. See Chapter 8 for more details.

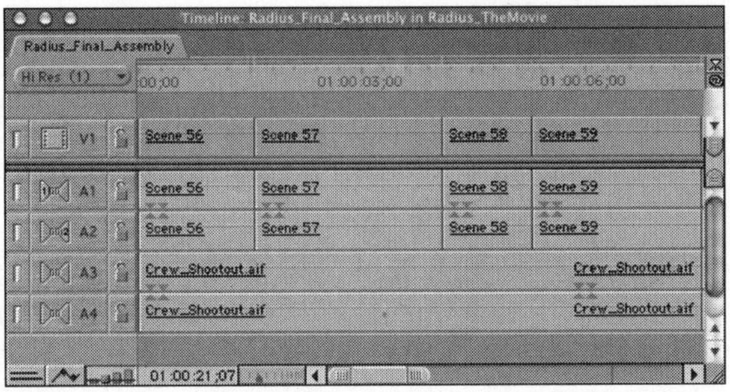

Figure 19-6: Nested sequences, with a clip of background music running beneath.

Save on Hard Drive Space

Long projects tend to eat up a lot of disk space, which is fine if you have endless hard drive storage. (*Remember:* You need roughly 13GB to store an hour of DV footage.) But storage can become quite a problem when you don't. If you find yourself running out of space, here are a couple of strategies we recommend to ease the shortage:

- ✔ **Save space with the OfflineRT codec:** Final Cut lets you capture video by using a special codec called OfflineRT, which takes about ten times less hard drive space as video captured with the popular DV codec (which you would normally use to capture video, unless your system sports a fancy add-on capture card from companies like Aurora or Pinnacle).

  So what's the catch? (There's always a catch, isn't there?) Well, OfflineRT's picture quality isn't nearly as good as DV — its video is sized at only 320 x 240 pixels (instead of DV's 720 x 480 pixels), which means that you can watch it only on your Mac's screen, not on an attached TV. You also notice more compression artifacts in your images than DV delivers.

  But here's the good news: OfflineRT's lower quality is often a moot point because you're not expected to record your final movie by using video in the OfflineRT format anyway. Instead, you use the format to capture preliminary versions of all your source footage (saving a lot of disk space in the process) and then edit your movie to perfection. Then, when you're done, you can quickly recapture only the video you ended up using in your final cut — but this time by using a much higher quality codec, such as DV. See Chapter 9 for more about capturing video in OfflineRT.

✔ **Sweep out old rendered files:** When you render video in your project — for instance, special effects, video transitions, color corrections, or super-imposed titles — Final Cut creates a new version of the clip, called a *rendered file*. Over time, these rendered files can pile up on your hard drive and hog a lot of disk space (especially if Final Cut is set to render clips at a high resolution). Of course, you'll want to keep some of these renders because you're using them in your final movie, but there may be others that you no longer need, just taking up valuable space. Fortunately, you can use Final Cut's Render Manager to skim through and delete all unused rendered files for your projects — see Chapter 16 for more.

✔ **Use Media Manager to trim projects:** When you finish editing a sequence and know that it's absolutely done, you can use Final Cut's Media Manager to toss out all the excess video and audio you imported, but ultimately never used (as shown in Figure 19-7). This file removal frees up some disk space for your next sequence. See Chapter 9 for more about the Media Manager.

Edited footage   Source files

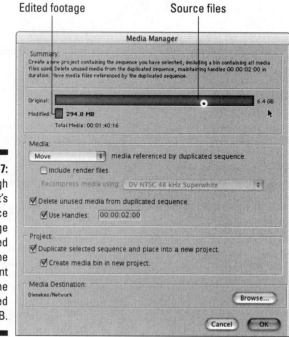

Figure 19-7: Although the project's source footage required 6.4GB, the content used in the film needed only 294MB.

✔ **Use Edit to Tape:** If you're *really* running low on hard drive space, you can finish a sequence (or a set of them) and then use Final Cut's Edit to Tape feature to record that sequence to videotape — perhaps a DV tape or maybe a higher-end format, such as Betacam SP or Digital Betacam. After the sequence is on tape, you're free to wipe your drive of all the media it used and then start a new sequence. When that one is done, you'll repeat the same steps, adding the new sequence to the same videotape, right after the last sequence you recorded.

This is a pretty extreme solution to the hard drive space problem, and it can cramp your editing style. Given how cheap hard drives are these days, you may just want to bite the bullet and buy a new one. If not, see Chapter 17 for more about the Edit to Tape feature.

Chapter 20

Ten Tips for Becoming a Better Editor

*A*fter you've gotten your feet wet with Final Cut, you can do plenty of things to nurture your abilities as an editor. Here are a few tips that cover everything from getting a better grip on how the Final Cut program's features work together to honing your creative instincts to improving your technical knowledge of the editing and post-production process and to upgrading your hardware and tools.

Try Out the Final Cut Tutorials

Final Cut includes a nice set of tutorials that take you through the basics of editing and effects compositing work, using video, audio, and still clips included on your software CDs. (You'll probably have to dig up the Tutorials CD in your Final Cut Pro 3 box because these tutorials aren't installed automatically with the main application.) Tutorials aren't great tools when you want to pick up a particular skill in a hurry, but they can help you soak in a broad topic involving many steps or options and save you time spent trying to dig up the right kind of media to practice a certain skill. This is especially true in the case of the Final Cut Effects tutorial, which is probably the best way to get acquainted with the program's big, broad feature set in this area.

Study (Don't Just Watch) Movies and Commercials

A great way to improve your picture-editing instincts is to carefully study all the professional editing work around us on television and in movies. Record a bunch of films, commercials, and music videos and watch them carefully — in fact, a good tactic is to watch with the volume turned off, so you can focus solely on how the shots move from one to another. You'll see that there is an infinite number of editing styles (fast and slow or super-stylized and subtly inconspicuous) and develop your own tastes. Finally, when you start to see the conscious design behind a sequence of shots — that is, how the editor uses shots in a particular order to communicate information and set a mood — you also start seeing a payoff in your own work.

Practice on Someone Else's Real-World Footage

The best way to improve your editing skills is to edit as much as possible, and we heartily recommend that you come up with practice projects to cut together in order to keep honing your skills. That being said, we know that constantly coming up with new footage to work on is hard. We used to record our own practice scenes on a video camera, but we eventually ran out of fresh ideas for new footage and grew frustrated with our video's raw (that is, *ugly*) look because it was too time-consuming to shoot it with a lot of polish. We eventually discovered a great alternative: borrowing real-world, professional footage from working editors. For instance, we found an editing company that loaned us the source footage for real-world commercials they had edited. It was a perfect solution for us: We could work with footage that looked great and offered lots of angles and perspectives to choose from. We could even compare our edit against the final version the editing company produced and learn from the differences.

So if you're looking for good practice material, try approaching established editors and see if they'll let you work on some of the projects they're finished with. Chances are, you can find someone willing to lend an editor-in-training a hand.

Go Online and Find a Community

We recommend two great Web sites for expanding your technical grasp of
Final Cut as well as your general editorial knowledge:

✔ **2-Pop.com** (www.2-pop.com) is a world-class site dedicated to all things
Final Cut. Here you can find reviews of the latest Final Cut updates, how-
to tutorials on particular features, and most importantly, a variety of
message forums where fellow users can answer just about any Final Cut
question you can imagine. (2-Pop has a couple of forums dedicated to
other digital media topics as well.)

✔ **EditorsNet** (www.editorsnet.com) is a great site for daily news about
the editing business and new products, but it really shines for its interviews with feature film editors and other pro editors talking about their
latest projects. These interviews and other articles give you a great perspective on both the art and the craft of real-world editing.

Join a Final Cut User Group

You can join (or just drop in on) a growing handful of user groups just for
Final Cut editors. Their members typically meet monthly for product demos
and helpful Q&A sessions. Some of the most active groups can be found in

✔ Boston (www.bosfcpug.org)

✔ Los Angeles (www.lafcpug.org)

✔ San Francisco (www.sfcutters.org)

To see if a Final Cut user group is near you (or a general Mac user group
that might have some active Final Cut users), go to the Apple site at
www.apple.com/usergroups/contact.html

Upgrade Your Hardware

Even if your hardware can technically handle Final Cut, you can add a few
items to really enhance your editing experience. A couple of suggestions, in
no particular order:

✔ A nice pair of speakers or headphones so that you can pick up the subtler details in your audio.

✔ A television monitor (any decent TV will do) so that you don't have to watch media clips in the Final Cut program's smallish Viewer or Canvas windows.

✔ If your Mac has 256 or 384MB of RAM, boosting it to 512 or 640MB makes Final Cut run a little faster overall. You won't see major speed gains, but you *will* see OS X's spinning cursor less.

✔ A programmable mouse or trackball — these sport extra buttons, which you can program to invoke Final Cut features that you use a lot.

Upgrade Your Software

Several software packages can be used along with Final Cut, depending on what type of video you're working with and what you do with the final product. After you become more experienced with Final Cut and more sure of what you want to do with your projects, you may want to buy additional software. The following software packages are ones you may want to consider:

✔ **Sorenson 3 Professional Edition:** If you save a lot of projects as QuickTime movies (for CD-ROM or the Internet), you probably do so by using the Sorenson 3 compression codec, which squeezes video into small file sizes while still delivering pretty good image quality. But you can get much better results (better looking images at even smaller file sizes) if you buy the Professional Edition of the Sorenson 3 codec. At $399 at the time of this writing, this product is expensive but gives your projects a polish that sets them apart. (Most movie trailers online are compressed with Sorenson's professional edition.) Check out www.sorenson.com for more.

✔ **Cleaner 5:** If you save a lot of projects as QuickTime movies (for DVD, CD-ROM, or the Internet), Cleaner gives you much better control over that process than Final Cut ever can. For starters, Cleaner lets you encode movies by the batch, automatically creating several compressed versions of the same movie. (For instance, you can make low-, medium-, and high-bandwidth versions of a movie trailer, each using settings that you customize ahead of time.) Cleaner saves time by letting you preview how encoded video will look after it's compressed and also lets you adjust image settings for your encodes (such as brightness and contrast). Finally, if you want to save your Final Cut movies in other video architectures, such as RealVideo or Windows Media (both popular on the PC), Cleaner can handle that, too. (See Chapter 18 for more on Cleaner 5.) Check out www.discreet.com for more.

✔ **Cinema Tools:** Apple's Cinema Tools lets you use Final Cut to edit movies that were originally shot on film and that will ultimately be projected in movie theaters (as opposed to digital or television playback, which doesn't require Cinema Tools). Working hand-in-hand with Final Cut (and in the hands of an experienced editor — this ain't kid stuff!), Cinema Tools converts your edits into instructions that an old-fashioned negative cutter uses to assemble the negative for your film (which, in turn, is converted to a positive film *print,* which can play on a film projector in a theater). See `www.apple.com/cinematools` for more.

Curl Up with a Good Book

Here are a couple of good books that can help bring your editing skills and general post-production knowledge to the next level:

✔ *In the Blink of an Eye: A Perspective on Film Editing,* by Walter Murch: If you read just one book on editing theory, make it this one. It's short and informal, and there's hardly any technical stuff in here. Instead, Murch focuses on editing from a creative standpoint, with an emphasis on telling a story and setting emotion through editing. The book also has a nice section on digital editing and its effect on the aesthetics of editing. Murch knows a thing or two about editing, by the way, with editing credits on such films as *American Graffiti; Apocalypse Now; The Godfather, Parts 2 and 3; Ghost; The English Patient;* and *The Talented Mr. Ripley.*

✔ *When the Shooting Stops, the Cutting Begins: A Film Editor's Story,* by Ralph Rosenblum and Robert Karen: Another little gem about the aesthetics of editing and the flow of the editing process as a film goes from raw dailies to rough to final cut. Rosenblum did most of his cutting in the '60s and '70s and goes in depth on his experiences working on classic films like *The Pawnbroker* and *Annie Hall.* (We recommend renting these at a video store to get the most out of the book.)

✔ *Understanding Comics,* by Scott McCloud: Okay, it's not about editing per se, but it's still surprisingly helpful for filmmakers (directors, storyboard artists, and especially editors). Written in comic book form, *Understanding Comics* explains how comics are composed, read, and understood. As you read it (it's a quick read), you realize that the principles behind comic design actually apply to visual language in general — and what is film if not a visual language? Give it a try; you won't regret it.

✔ *The Film Editing Room Handbook: How to Manage the Near Chaos of the Cutting Room,* by Norman Hollyn: If you're using Final Cut as a one-stop, all-in-one filmmaking machine (that is, not only editing but also outputting your final projects with it), this book won't be so useful. But if you're working in a more conventional post-production atmosphere where different parts of your film are handled outside Final Cut (for instance, your film's negative may be assembled for theatrical projection, or its sound, music, and dialog will be mixed elsewhere), this book is a great primer for all you need to know to navigate this sometimes-minefield.

✔ *Practical Art of Motion Picture Sound,* by David Lewis Yewdall: If you find yourself editing and affecting audio quite a bit, check out this volume. It's a great introduction to post-production audio topics from both a technical and artistic standpoint. Topics include planning an audio strategy for production and post-production, tips for recording better production audio (something a lot of all-in-one-filmmakers using Final Cut can appreciate), making preliminary versions of your score, recording sound effects, and dialog editing.

Index

• L •